In the Matter of

J. Robert Oppenheimer

J. Robert Oppenheimer. Reproduced from the Collections of the Library of Congress.

IN THE MATTER OF

J. Robert Oppenheimer

THE SECURITY CLEARANCE HEARING

Edited by **Richard Polenberg**

Cornell University Press   Ithaca and London

First published 2002 by Cornell University Press
First printing, Cornell Paperbacks, 2002

Printed in the United States of America

LIBRARY OF CONGRESS CATALOGING-IN-PUBLICATION DATA

In the matter of J. Robert Oppenheimer : the security clearance hearing / edited by Richard Polenberg.
    p. cm.
    Includes bibliographical references and index.
    ISBN 0-8014-3783-0 (cloth) — ISBN 0-8014-8661-0 (pbk.)
    1. Oppenheimer, J. Robert, 1904–1967—Trials, litigation, etc. 2. Hydrogen bomb—History. 3. Internal security—United States. 4. United States—Politics and government—1953–1961. 5. Physicists—United States—Biography. I. Polenberg, Richard.
    QC16.O62 I5 2002
530'.092—dc21   2001047165

Cornell University Press strives to use environmentally responsible suppliers and materials to the fullest extent possible in the publishing of its books. Such materials include vegetable-based, low-VOC inks and acid-free papers that are recycled, totally chlorine-free, or partly composed of nonwood fibers. Books that bear the logo of the FSC (Forest Stewardship Council) use paper taken from forests that have been inspected and certified as meeting the highest standards for environmental and social responsibility. For further information, visit our website at www.cornellpress.cornell.edu.

Cloth printing   10 9 8 7 6 5 4 3 2 1

Paperback printing   10 9 8 7 6 5 4 3 2 1

CONTENTS

ILLUSTRATIONS

PREFACE

On June 15, 1954, the Government Printing Office (GPO) published *In the Matter of J. Robert Oppenheimer,* a transcript of the famous physicist's hearing before the Atomic Energy Commission's Personnel Security Board. More than thirty witnesses testified at the hearing, which was held over a four-week period in April and May. The text came to 992 densely printed pages. Shortly thereafter, the GPO published the reports of the board and the commission, along with pertinent correspondence, comprising an additional 55 pages. The transcript contained a number of typesetting errors, although surprisingly few considering the haste with which publication was arranged. All discussions of classified matters were deleted, and the deletions—of words, phrases, and sometimes entire pages—were indicated by asterisks.

The demand from libraries, scholars, and other interested parties soon exhausted the supply of the GPO's edition. In 1970, the MIT Press reprinted the transcript and the accompanying reports with a foreword by Philip M. Stern, the author of an exceptionally fine book on the subject, *The Oppenheimer Case: Security on Trial* (1969), and with a highly useful index. But the MIT edition, too, has long been out of print.

The version presented here consists of about one-fourth of the original transcript. I include much of the testimony of the centrally important figures—Oppenheimer, Hans A. Bethe, Edward Teller, Leslie R. Groves, Isidor I. Rabi, Enrico Fermi, and George F. Kennan—but provide briefer excerpts from testimony that was less significant. To convey the underlying rancor, I include some of the angry exchanges between the opposing lawyers, and between Oppenheimer's attorneys and members of the board. I omit, however, lengthy discussions of such matters as whether a transcript of a 1943 interview between Oppenheimer and an army security officer accurately reflected the language on the tape recording. I leave out much that pertains to the past radical affiliations of Oppenheimer's friends and students in order to include most of the testimony that focuses on broad questions concerning ethics, morality, politics, loyalty, security, and international diplomacy.

My interest in J. Robert Oppenheimer goes back to the late 1970s, when I first read the four microfilm reels of the FBI file on the case. I have lectured on "The Ethical Responsibilities of the Scientist: The Case of J. Robert Oppenheimer" at Fermilab, the University of Illinois, the University of Notre Dame, Haifa University, the Weizmann Institute, Tel Aviv University, and at the Cornell University Department of Physics and Peace Studies Program, and have received many valuable suggestions from those in attendance. Hans A. Bethe and Dale R. Corson generously shared with me their recollections of Oppenheimer. I am indebted to Peter Agree who first encouraged me to undertake this project. I am particularly grateful for the sound advice I received from Sheryl A. Englund and Ange Romeo-Hall at Cornell University Press. I have had the good fortune to have had the index prepared by Jane Marsh Dieckmann. I also wish to thank my research assistants, Lauren Eisenstein and Charlotte Landers, who provided indispensable help.

I hope that this abridged version will do justice to the original, for no document better explains the America of the cold war—its fears and resentments, its anxieties and dilemmas—than *In the Matter of J. Robert Oppenheimer*. The Oppenheimer hearing also serves as a reminder of the fragility of individual rights and of how easily they may be lost.

RICHARD POLENBERG

September 2001

INTRODUCTION: "ALL THE EVIL OF THE TIMES"

1.

On May 6, 1954, weary and disheartened after a grueling month-long hearing to assess his "loyalty" and, therefore, his eligibility for security clearance, Dr. J. Robert Oppenheimer left Washington, D.C., and returned home to Princeton, New Jersey. Although Oppenheimer had headed the program to build an atomic bomb during World War II, and had chaired the Atomic Energy Commission's (AEC) General Advisory Committee from 1947 to 1952, neither his past service nor his eminence had shielded him from suspicion or from the snooping that so often accompanied it. While his case was before the AEC's Personnel Security Board, his telephone had been tapped, his mail tracked, and his whereabouts noted by the Federal Bureau of Investigation (FBI). The surveillance, which had begun before the hearing started, remained in place even after it ended, which accounts for the report filed on May 7 describing his reaction to the ordeal. Oppenheimer was overheard to say that it would take many weeks for the board to reach a decision and for the AEC to render final judgment, "but he believes he will never be through with the situation. He does not believe the case will come to a quiet end as all the evil of the times is wrapped in this situation."[1]

If we construe his phrase—"all the evil of the times"—to refer to the manifold ways in which, in the 1950s, a virulent strain of cold war anti-communism undermined ideals of decency, justice, and fair play, then Oppenheimer was surely right. Taken in combination, the various aspects of the case—Pres-

---

1. "Dr. J. Robert Oppenheimer: Summary for May 7, 1954." FBI Security File: J. Robert Oppenheimer (Scholarly Resources Microfilm), hereafter cited as FBI File.

ident Dwight D. Eisenhower's initial decision to suspend his clearance, the tactical maneuvering that preceded the hearing, the manner in which the inquiry was conducted, the process by which ostensibly secret testimony was made public, and the justifications offered by the board and the AEC for voting to deny clearance—provide a classic illustration of what is meant by "McCarthyism."

Use of the term is appropriate even though Senator Joseph McCarthy played virtually no personal role in the outcome. In the spring of 1954, the junior senator from Wisconsin was preoccupied with a different set of hearings: the Senate's permanent Subcommittee on Investigations was investigating his allegations that the United States Army had been engaged in "promoting, covering up, and honorably discharging known Communists."[2] The Army-McCarthy hearings began on April 22 and ended on June 17, thus coinciding almost exactly with the AEC deliberations in the Oppenheimer case. But where the Army-McCarthy contest took place in a gaudy atmosphere, replete with reporters, microphones, flash bulbs, and television cameras, the Oppenheimer hearing was conducted behind closed doors, with a civility that barely cloaked its contentiousness. Although newspapers printed the AEC's charges against Oppenheimer and his reply, and told their readers that an inquiry was under way, not a word of actual testimony was made public until mid-June, after the hearing had concluded.

If McCarthy's eventual downfall may be traced to his crude and offensive behavior during the Senate hearing, his continued influence was never more apparent than in the AEC's handling of the Oppenheimer case. Yet Oppenheimer was not merely a casualty of McCarthyism. He was, to a considerable degree, also the victim of his own stubborn pride. He insisted that the hearing go forward because he feared that if he acquiesced in the loss of his consultant's contract he would be conceding that he was "unworthy." He wanted to believe that the many contributions he had made to making the United States a nuclear power would outweigh his earlier radical associations; that his lofty standing in the scientific community would protect him from retaliation by a government anxious not to alienate members of that community; and that his personal friendship with many trusted leaders of the foreign policy, business, and educational establishments would compensate for the doubts he had expressed about developing the hydrogen bomb.

2.

The origins of the Oppenheimer hearing are usually traced to the letter that William L. Borden (formerly the chief of staff of the Joint Committee on Atomic Energy) wrote to FBI director J. Edgar Hoover on November 7, 1953, in

2. Cited in Robert Griffith, *The Politics of Fear: Joseph R. McCarthy and the Senate* (New York, 1970), 249.

which he asserted that the physicist was "more probably than not . . . an agent of the Soviet Union."[3] Hoover forwarded the letter to the AEC and to the White House, and on December 3 President Eisenhower secretly erected a "blank wall" between Oppenheimer and national security information. It was not until December 21, however, a week after Oppenheimer's return from a trip to Europe, that AEC chairman Lewis L. Strauss and general manager Kenneth D. Nichols met with him to explain that his clearance had been suspended. They also handed him a draft of the charges on which the suspension was based. Shaken and distraught, Oppenheimer, who had been given no inkling of what was in store for him, was informed that he could either contest the suspension or quietly terminate his consultant's contract and thereby avoid a hearing. Given only a day to decide, Oppenheimer, on the morning of December 23, informed Strauss that he wanted the opportunity to clear his name.

At this stage the Eisenhower administration was motivated less by a belief that Oppenheimer's continued clearance imperiled national security than by a fear that failure to act would expose it to attack from Senator McCarthy. As early as May 19, 1953, McCarthy and his aide Roy Cohn had visited FBI director J. Edgar Hoover to ask how he would react to an investigation of Oppenheimer. Hoover tried to dissuade McCarthy from proceeding, not because he wished to protect Oppenheimer, whom he distrusted, but because he thought the senator could bungle the investigation and antagonize scientists throughout the nation. In June, it was Lewis L. Strauss's turn to warn the Senate's Republican leadership that an investigation by McCarthy of Oppenheimer would be "a most ill-advised and impolitic move."[4] But by December, with Borden's letter circulating within the executive branch and likely to fall into McCarthy's hands, the Eisenhower administration thought it had to do something. The strategy succeeded: in April 1954, when McCarthy finally got around to denouncing Oppenheimer for having delayed work on the hydrogen bomb, he said he had decided against an investigation because of assurances "from top Administration officials that this matter would be gone into in detail."[5]

At the time, those who sympathized with Oppenheimer regarded a hearing by the AEC's Personnel Security Board as infinitely preferable to an inquiry by Senator McCarthy. A mudslinger if there ever was one, McCarthy was known for browbeating witnesses, scandal-mongering, and making wild allegations. By contrast, the *New York Herald Tribune* editorialized, the AEC hearing, which "should be in good hands and under sound procedures," would be "conducted with complete fairness." The board would be able to assess the scientist's life and work in their broad context, the argument went; "If

3. See 305.
4. Cited in Barton J. Bernstein, "In the Matter of J. Robert Oppenheimer," *Historical Studies in the Physical Sciences* 12 (1982): 207.
5. *The Washington Post*, April 14, 1954.

the case had been taken up by Senator McCarthy, such perspective and judgment would have been impossible."[6]

The proceedings before the Personnel Security Board had all the outward trappings of just such an impartial hearing. Oppenheimer was represented by a team of eminent attorneys headed by Lloyd K. Garrison. He was permitted to answer the charges against him in whatever way and at whatever length he wished. His lawyers were allowed to call as many witnesses as they wanted in his behalf, and the board made efforts to accommodate their schedules. His lawyers were allowed to cross-examine all the hostile witnesses to the extent they thought desirable. The discourse in the hearing room was ordinarily quite polite, punctuated only infrequently by harsh comments or bitter rejoinders. Oppenheimer's attorney complimented the members of the board for their courteousness, and they in turn thanked him for his cooperation. Without fail, the board members and the AEC attorney addressed Oppenheimer deferentially, either as "Dr. Oppenheimer" or, more simply, as "Doctor."

Yet if the "odious courtesies," as Kafka would have called them, were fully observed, the hearing in truth lacked fundamental elements of due process, the most egregious example being the surveillance of Oppenheimer by the FBI, which began on January 1, 1954. At the urging of Lewis L. Strauss, FBI agents observed Oppenheimer's home and office, listened in on his telephone conversations, and had him tailed wherever he went. The telephone taps were particularly useful in providing information about his travel plans, thus making it easier for informants to follow him. As the historians of the AEC report, "The only privacy accorded Oppenheimer by the FBI were conversations within his own home."[7]

What made this surveillance particularly sinister was that it inevitably picked up information concerning Oppenheimer's discussions with his attorneys, information that was passed on to Strauss who then passed it on to Roger Robb, the attorney retained by the AEC to present the case against Oppenheimer. So patently unethical was this aspect of the surveillance that it troubled the FBI agent in Newark who was in charge. He questioned the propriety of the coverage "in view of the fact that it might disclose attorney-client relations." He was told that the "rather full spot surveillances and the technical surveillance" were "of great assistance." Not only was the surveillance justified on the grounds that "there is no criminal action pending against Oppenheimer," but the FBI also wished to guard against the danger that he might defect: "Our chief concern is to know immediately of any indication that Oppenheimer might flee."[8]

A preposterous fear, indeed, and a telling reflection of the times, it nevertheless helped rationalize continued surveillance. The bugs and wiretaps

6. Editorial, *New York Herald-Tribune*, April 14, 1954.

7. Richard G. Hewlett and Jack M. Holl, *Atoms for Peace and War, 1953–1961: Eisenhower and the Atomic Energy Commission* (Berkeley, 1989), 80.

8. Cited ibid., 81.

were kept in place, and it is also possible that the FBI "had successfully secured an informant among Oppenheimer's inner circle of friends and associates."[9] Consequently, Strauss received reports, almost daily, regarding Oppenheimer's efforts to obtain legal counsel, to develop a defense strategy, and to line up witnesses in his behalf. The FBI even forwarded information about the meetings of partners in the law firm Oppenheimer retained—Paul, Weiss, Rifkind, Wharton & Garrison—at which they discussed the conditions under which they would handle the case, and the degree to which various members of the firm would participate in it.

Any acquaintance of Oppenheimer's, no matter how prominent or respectable, could be caught in the spidery web of surveillance. Here, for example, is what the FBI discovered as it followed Oppenheimer during one twenty-four-hour period. On the afternoon of January 10, 1954, Oppenheimer flew from New York City to Boston to attend a meeting of the Harvard College Board of Overseers, which was scheduled for the following morning, and he returned to New York City later that afternoon. The FBI obtained reports on his doings from four confidential sources "of known reliability." These informants observed Oppenheimer as he arrived at the airport terminal in Boston at 6:15 P.M., overheard the arrangements he made to share a taxicab, followed him to a 7:00 P.M. dinner party in Cambridge, waited outside until midnight when he left, trailed him as he was driven to the Harvard faculty club, noted that he attended the Board of Overseers meeting at 11 A.M. the next morning, reported that his return flight was canceled because of a snowstorm but that Oppenheimer boarded a 3 P.M. train to New York City after telephoning his wife to let her know that he would arrive at Pennsylvania Station at 7:20 P.M. The FBI report noted that the dinner party was hosted by U.S. District Court judge Charles E. Wyzanski, that one of the guests, Robert Fiske Bradford, was a former Republican governor of Massachusetts, and that another guest, McGeorge Bundy, was dean of the faculty of arts and sciences at Harvard.[10]

On April 7, as the date of the hearing approached, the FBI agent in Newark again inquired as to whether the surveillance at Princeton ought to be terminated. He noted that the telephone tap had periodically furnished Strauss with information "mainly bearing on the relationship between Oppenheimer, his attorneys, and potential witnesses for Oppenheimer at the forthcoming AEC hearing. Absolutely no information of security interest has been obtained from the technical." All the charges against Oppenheimer, the agent continued, related to his activities in the period before 1943 and to his alleged opposition to the hydrogen bomb. "We have no substantial information of a pro-communist nature concerning Oppenheimer subsequent to 1943." Since Oppenheimer would be in Washington once the hearing began, "there appears

9. Ibid., 85.
10. Special Agent, Boston, Report, January 13, 1954, FBI File.

to be no logical reason for continuing the technical surveillance." But a note at the bottom of the agent's wire reads: "Strauss requested tech be continued for about 2 weeks till after hearing."[11] And on April 13, a day after the hearing began, Strauss agreed that while physical surveillance of Oppenheimer in Washington was unnecessary, the telephone tap in Princeton ought to be continued "as it has been most helpful."[12]

Although Oppenheimer had reason to suspect his telephone was tapped, he did not know how extensive the surveillance was or how fatally it undermined the principle of attorney-client confidentiality. He and his lawyers were all too aware, however, of another objectionable aspect of the proceedings. For a week before the hearing began, the members of the Personnel Security Board—Gordon Gray, Thomas A. Morgan, and Ward V. Evans—immersed themselves in the secret files that the FBI and other agencies had compiled on Oppenheimer over the years. Worse still, the board members examined the files in the presence of Roger Robb, the AEC attorney who would soon present the case against Oppenheimer. Far from facing a panel that had no preformed opinion, Oppenheimer would appear before men whose minds, to some extent, had already been made up by the reading of dossiers that contained (as secret dossiers always do) derogatory information, much of it unsubstantiated. Meanwhile, Robb had an opportunity to put a negative spin on the files, an opportunity, it must be assumed, he did not let pass. At the very least, as a result of a week's socializing with the board members, Robb "became their close associate, not an attorney presenting material before an impartial panel."[13]

Oppenheimer's attorney, Lloyd K. Garrison, could not contain the damage because the AEC rejected his requests either to see the secret files or to meet with the board in advance to respond, even in general terms, to concerns raised by information contained in them. Garrison remembered having "a kind of sinking feeling" when he realized that the board had "a week's immersion in FBI files which we would never have the privilege of seeing, and of coming to the hearings with that intense background of study of the derogatory information." As a result of the board's "preliminary immersion in the secret files," Garrison realized, "a cloud of suspicion hung over Robert Oppenheimer."[14]

That cloud would not have been dispelled even if Garrison had succeeded in obtaining security clearance since he still would not have been granted access to secret FBI files. But, in fact, he never obtained clearance and his failure to do so placed Oppenheimer at a serious disadvantage. On January 18, 1954, the AEC informed Garrison that it was willing to expedite his application for a "Q" clearance, but he insisted that two of his colleagues, Herbert Marks and

11. W. A. Branigan to A. H. Belmont, April 7, 1954, ibid.
12. J. E. Hoover to the Attorney General, April 13, 1954, ibid.
13. Bernstein, "In the Matter," 218.
14. Philip M. Stern, *The Oppenheimer Case: Security on Trial* (New York, 1969), 527–28.

Samuel Silverman, also be cleared. When the AEC balked, Garrison decided to withdraw his own request, explaining, "We felt that unless all three of us were given clearance, none of us should be. . . . [W]e would be working constantly together, and it would be impractical for one of us to be privy to documents and testimony whose nature he would have to conceal from the others." Not until March 26, two weeks before the hearing opened, did Garrison reconsider and request clearance as "a precautionary measure to ensure that at all times there would at least be one person who could be at Robert's side."[15] By then it was too late. At four different times during the course of the hearing Oppenheimer's attorneys were asked to leave the room, and at no time were they permitted to see any material in Oppenheimer's dossier that remained classified.

3.

The surveillance, suspicion, and secrecy all rendered Oppenheimer particularly vulnerable, and Roger Robb was quick to exploit his advantage. As Robb understood, he did not have to prove beyond a reasonable doubt that Oppenheimer was a security risk; rather, Oppenheimer had to persuade the board that he was not one. To do this, Oppenheimer thought, required that he be cooperative, even to the extent of answering questions about the political affiliations of friends and former students. In effect, he played the role of an informer, however distasteful he found it. At one point, after listing a number of names, Oppenheimer was asked, "would you break them down? Would you tell us who the Communists were and who the fellow travelers were?" Oppenheimer finally exclaimed, "Is the list long enough?"[16] His embarrassment at having named the names of men and women who trusted him was made all the more acute in mid-June when the AEC suddenly decided to publish the transcript of the hearings, which, it had been assumed, would remain secret.

There was, however, one person about whom Oppenheimer refused to express doubts: his younger brother, Frank. One of the more insidious aspects of Robb's questioning was his attempt to use Robert's loyalty to Frank to undermine his credibility. By 1954, Frank Oppenheimer's past membership in the Communist Party was a matter of record, and he had paid a high price for it. Frank joined the Party (along with his wife, Jacquenette) in 1937 when he was a graduate student in physics at the California Institute of Technology; he left the Party in 1941, shortly before being employed at the Radiation Laboratory at Berkeley. After the war he joined the physics department at the University of Minnesota. In 1947, when a newspaper report asserted he had been a Communist, he issued a denial. But in 1949, subpoenaed to testify under oath before the House Committee on Un-American Activities, Frank admitted his

15. Ibid., 509–14.
16. See 75.

past membership; he agreed to talk about his own involvement although not to implicate anyone else. He submitted his resignation to the University, not anticipating it would be accepted, but in fact it quickly was. Frank moved to Colorado, where he became a sheep rancher, and that is what he was doing at the time of his older brother's security hearing.

Even after all these years, it remains excruciatingly painful to observe Robb's effort to turn brother against brother. Having gotten Robert to admit that even in the 1940s he believed that membership in the Communist Party "was inconsistent with work on a secret war project," Robb then asked whether the same was true for former members of the Party, such as Frank. When Oppenheimer replied that it all depended "on the character and the totality of the disengagement and what kind of a man he is, whether he is an honest man," Robb asked what test he applied in the 1940s to "satisfy yourself that a former member of the party is no longer dangerous?" "In the case of a brother, you don't make tests," he answered. His brother, Oppenheimer said, had told him he left the Party in 1941. "You were satisfied at that time that your brother was not a member of the party any more?" "Yes." "How did you reach that conclusion?" "He told me." "That was enough for you?" "Sure." Had Oppenheimer informed security officers at Berkeley about Frank's past membership? "Did you tell [them] he had been a member of the Communist Party?" "I don't think so." Finally, having gotten Oppenheimer to agree that the fact that a person says he is no longer a Party member "does not show that he is no longer dangerous as a security risk," Robb asked, "Do you think your brother today would be a good security risk?" "I rather think so."[17]

Oppenheimer's desire to protect his brother may well explain his unwillingness, during and after the war, to tell the whole truth about the "Chevalier incident," which played a central role at the hearing. In February or March 1943, just before leaving California for Los Alamos, Oppenheimer had a conversation with Haakon Chevalier, a left-wing friend and a professor of French at Berkeley. Chevalier reported that a mutual acquaintance, George Eltenton, a British engineer, had said there might be a way to get information about atomic research at the Radiation Laboratory to the Russians. That would be terribly wrong, Oppenheimer said, and the matter was quickly dropped, but he neglected to report it to security officers at Los Alamos, and when he finally did he invented a partly fictitious story. Indeed, at first he refused even to provide Chevalier's name. The FBI believed it had credible evidence—and so informed the AEC—that Oppenheimer failed to divulge all the details because to do so would have implicated his brother, Frank.

Whether Chevalier had approached each brother separately, or had spoken to Frank who then spoke to Robert, remains unclear. What is certain is that Robert had informed General Leslie R. Groves, the head of the Manhattan Project, that Frank was involved, but only after extracting a promise from Groves not to tell anyone. According to the historians of the Atomic En-

17. See 56–58.

ergy Commission, "Oppenheimer secured Groves's pledge not to report his brother's name to the FBI, thereby incredibly implicating the head of the Manhattan Project in his story."[18] A man of his word, Groves did not mention Frank's name in any report he made during the war. At the 1954 hearing, however, Groves said of Oppenheimer: "It was always my impression that he wanted to protect his brother, and that his brother might be involved in having been in this chain, and that his brother didn't behave quite as he should have, or if he did, he didn't even want to have the finger of suspicion pointed at his brother, because he always felt a natural loyalty to him, and had a protective attitude toward him."[19] There were no follow-up questions from Robb about Groves's covering up of Oppenheimer's "cock-and-bull" story during the war.

But Robb pursued Oppenheimer relentlessly for having concocted the story. Relying on the transcripts of Oppenheimer's conversations with an army counterintelligence officer, Lt. Col. Boris T. Pash, Robb made it appear that Oppenheimer was a habitual, inveterate liar. Robb's first question: "Did you tell Pash the truth about this thing?" "No," Oppenheimer said. Robb's second question: "You lied to him?" "Yes," Oppenheimer replied. Robb's third question: "What did you tell Pash that was not true?" Oppenheimer answered truthfully: "That Eltenton had attempted to approach members of the project—three members of the project—through intermediaries." Robb's fourth question: "What else did you tell him that wasn't true?" When Oppenheimer said, "That is all I really remember," Robb, referring to the transcript, asked a fifth question: "That is all? Did you tell Pash . . . ," and then implied that Oppenheimer's failure to remember everything he had said in a decade-old interview amounted to purposeful deception. When Oppenheimer again admitted making up the story, Robb asked, "Why did you do that, Doctor?" One would have thought Oppenheimer's reply—"Because I was an idiot"—would have sufficed. But Robb was not done: "Is that your only explanation, Doctor?"[20]

Not only did Robb pillory Oppenheimer for having lied about the Chevalier incident; he also exploited the "fabrication and tissue of lies"—an inaccurate description, perhaps, but one that Robb at one point induced Oppenheimer to accept—to shake the credibility of witnesses testifying in Oppenheimer's behalf. When, for example, friendly witnesses maintained that Oppenheimer's lack of truthfulness in the Chevalier incident was insignificant in view of his overall record and, in any case, had no sinister connotations, Robb asked whether they would have reported a suspicious overture under similar circumstances, a question that naturally allowed only one answer. When James B. Conant (who was formerly president of Harvard University and was then serving as United States High Commissioner to Germany) appeared, it was board member Ward V. Evans who asked: "Wouldn't you have reported it just

18. Hewlett and Holl, *Atoms for Peace and War*, 96.
19. See 78.
20. See 67–68.

as quickly as you could?" "I think I would have, yes. I hope I would have; let us put it that way." At this point, Robb injected: "When you did report it, Doctor, you would have told the whole truth about it?" "I hope so." "I am sure you would."[21]

Robb also raised another subject designed to humiliate Oppenheimer—his overnight visit to his former fiancée, Jean Tatlock, in Berkeley, in June 1943. Although Oppenheimer had admitted seeing her, his statement had not mentioned staying at her apartment. Now he said that Tatlock had wanted to see him "because she was still in love with me." Robb's questions were pitiless: "You have no reason to believe she wasn't a communist, do you? . . . You spent the night with her, didn't you? . . . That is when you were working on a secret war project? . . . Did you think that consistent with good security? . . . You didn't think that spending a night with a dedicated Communist . . . ?" Robb's questions were presumably designed to show that Oppenheimer was careless about security; but by reiterating the suggestive phrase "spending the night," he was characterizing Oppenheimer as an adulterer.[22]

Yet Robb wanted more from Oppenheimer than an admission that he had once lied to security officials or had behaved indiscreetly. One of the AEC's chief allegations was that Oppenheimer had opposed a crash program to develop the hydrogen bomb in 1949, and had slowed progress toward the weapon by letting other physicists know his position. Robb therefore wanted Oppenheimer to confess that, having worked on the atomic bomb, his opposition to the hydrogen bomb could not have been based on moral scruples. The implication was clear: if Oppenheimer's reservations about the hydrogen bomb were not ethically derived, they must have been motivated by pro-Russian sentiment.

Partly to avoid the trap Robb was setting, Oppenheimer, when asked whether he had "moral scruples" about the use of the atomic bombs against Japanese cities, replied, "terrible ones," although as Robb well knew, and Oppenheimer had earlier admitted, he had voiced no such doubts before the bombing of Hiroshima and Nagasaki. This colloquy then followed: "But you supported the dropping of the atom bomb on Japan, didn't you?" "What do you mean support?" "You helped pick the target, didn't you?" "I did my job which was the job I was supposed to do. I was not in a policymaking position at Los Alamos. I would have done anything that I was asked to do, including making the bombs in a different shape, if I had thought it was technically feasible."[23]

4.

In view of the many disadvantages Oppenheimer faced during Robb's hostile cross-examination, and the admissions he made, the outcome was never

21. See 152–53.
22. See 74.
23. See 97.

in doubt. Just a week into the proceeding, well before most of Oppenheimer's witnesses had even appeared, Lewis L. Strauss told an FBI agent "that he was most happy with the way the Oppenheimer hearing was going and said he had been in conference each day with Rolander and Robb who are handling the matter before the board and was convinced that in view of the testimony to date the board could take no other action but to recommend the revoking of Oppenheimer's clearance."[24] The hearing concluded on May 6 and three weeks later, on May 27, the board issued just such a report. Filled with sanctimonious self-praise—"the Board has allowed sympathetic consideration for the individual to go hand in hand with an understanding of the necessities for a clear, realistic, and rugged attitude toward subversion, possible subversion, or indeed broader implications of security"—the majority report, signed by Gordon Gray and Thomas A. Morgan, concluded that Oppenheimer was "a loyal citizen" but that his "continuing conduct and associations" reflected a disregard for security requirements, and that his views regarding the hydrogen bomb program were "sufficiently disturbing as to raise a doubt as to whether his future participation . . . would be clearly consistent with the best interests of security."[25]

Now Oppenheimer and his attorneys faced a truly Kafka-esque situation. The board's report went to the AEC's general manager, Kenneth D. Nichols, for his use in formulating a recommendation to the full commission, which would make the final determination. By this point, however, none of Oppenheimer's judges were saying what they really believed. Gray and Morgan did not believe Oppenheimer was a loyal citizen, but only that the evidence did not prove conclusively that he was not loyal. Ward V. Evans submitted a minority report that he did not write: his draft was so embarrassingly inadequate that Roger Robb—of all people!—rewrote it, which may explain why it was long on rhetoric and short on facts. Oppenheimer's lawyers labored over a response defending him against the board's charge that he had delayed production of the hydrogen bomb, even as Nichols was drafting a letter of "transmittal" to the AEC—again, with the assistance of Roger Robb—that reformulated the charges, eliminating any criticism of Oppenheimer for the advice he had given on the hydrogen bomb. Neither Nichols nor Robb, however, really thought that Oppenheimer was blameless on this count; they merely feared alienating the scientific community if he were to be condemned for having given his honestly considered opinion on a technical matter.

If ever a person charged with impartially weighing evidence and making an evenhanded ruling ought to have recused himself, it was AEC chairman Lewis L. Strauss. From the outset, he had masterminded the crusade against Oppenheimer. He had been instrumental in arranging for the intrusive FBI surveillance. He had offered Robb advice on how to cross-examine witnesses. He had put pressure on witnesses reluctant to appear if he thought their testimony

24. A. H. Belmont to L. V. Boardman, April 17, 1954, FBI File.
25. See 355, 360.

would work to Oppenheimer's disadvantage. He had resolved to vote against restoring Oppenheimer's security clearance long before he read the transcript of the hearing, the Personnel Security Board's report, Garrison's brief filed in Oppenheimer's behalf, or Kenneth D. Nichols's letter of transmittal. According to the historian Barton Bernstein, Strauss's opinion, which was joined by commissioners Eugene Zuckert and Joseph Campbell, "was simply a way of expressing Strauss's suspicion and hostility without moving so far beyond the evidence to invite full-scale attacks on Strauss himself, the AEC, the loyalty-security system, and the Eisenhower administration."[26]

Roger Robb, who had a hand in drafting the Personnel Security Board's majority and minority reports, and Nichols's letter of transmittal, also helped Strauss write the AEC's final opinion. Returning to the theme of Oppenheimer's "fundamental defects in character," Strauss and Robb cited several examples that they thought had been adequately documented in the hearing, but then went on to suggest, without offering any proof, that the work of military intelligence, the FBI, and the AEC "all at one time or another have felt the effect of his falsehoods, evasions, and misrepresentations."[27] At the end as in the beginning there was the implication that secret information, stored in sensitive files, available only to those with the highest-level security clearance, supported a conclusion that, to those not having access to the information, may well have seemed unreasonable.

On learning of the AEC's four-to-one vote against Oppenheimer, President Eisenhower, his press secretary noted, "personally called Strauss to congratulate him on the fine job he had done in handling a most difficult situation. The president expressed hope that handling of the Oppenheimer case would be such a contrast to McCarthy's tactics that the American people would immediately see the difference."[28] Notwithstanding the president's belief that the procedures followed in the Oppenheimer hearing contrasted sharply with McCarthy's inquisitorial tactics, those procedures were marred by personal bias, political partisanship, and procedural irregularities. Lewis L. Strauss, Kenneth D. Nichols, Roger Robb, and J. Edgar Hoover had an instinct for the jugular no less sure than Joe McCarthy's.

They also had an instinct for public relations that would have done McCarthy proud. Given Oppenheimer's eminence, Borden's letter, the president's "blank wall," and the rather complicated logistics of the Personnel Security Board hearing, it was only a matter of time before the story broke. From the outset, therefore, both sides realized it would be advantageous to place its version before the public in the most favorable light possible. In this contest, however, Oppenheimer was overmatched, hampered by a fear of

26. Bernstein, "In the Matter," 242–43.
27. See 383.
28. James Hagerty Diary, June 29, 1954, cited in Bernstein, "In the Matter," 241.

alienating those who sat in judgment on him, while Strauss, of course, had no such concerns.

In January 1954, *New York Times* reporter James Reston found himself, by chance, in a seat next to Oppenheimer on a flight from Washington to New York City. Reston described him as "thin and slightly stooped, with short gray hair and startling blue eyes," but more importantly, sensed that Oppenheimer seemed "unaccountably nervous in my presence and obviously under some strain." So Reston, on his return to the Capital, began "snooping around and asking 'What's wrong with Oppenheimer these days?' "[29] The trail soon led to Lloyd K. Garrison who eventually turned over the AEC's letter suspending the physicist's clearance but got Reston to agree not to publish anything, at least until Oppenheimer had prepared his reply. At about the same time, Joseph and Stewart Alsop of the *New York Herald Tribune*, ardent admirers of Oppenheimer, also discovered what had been going on. Strauss knew about Reston's contact with Garrison (from an FBI report) and of the *Times*'s arrangement to withhold publication (from its publisher).

On April 9, three days before the hearing was to begin, both sides became alarmed at the prospect that Joe McCarthy—who made a statement darkly alluding to an eighteen-month delay in producing the hydrogen bomb—was going to break the news of the charges against Oppenheimer and the suspension of his clearance. Both Oppenheimer and Strauss, for different reasons, preferred that the first public account be a responsible one, that is, Reston's in the *Times*, although neither wanted the onus of having breeched the agreed-upon confidentiality. At a White House meeting on April 9, Eisenhower's press secretary James Hagerty and Strauss devised a strategy they hoped would induce the *Times* to publish the story. Strauss had pledged to let the newspaper know if the story was going to break elsewhere; he now retracted that pledge; that led the *Times* to tell Garrison the story was about to break, and he, in turn, authorized the *Times* to release the text of the documents and Reston's article. When the story appeared on the morning of April 13, Gordon Gray, knowing nothing of the intrigue, sharply rebuked Garrison and Oppenheimer for going public.

This was only the first of several attempts to use the press for the purposes of influencing public opinion. On June 1, Oppenheimer's camp released the text of the Personnel Security Board report and Lloyd K. Garrison's rebuttal, thereby infuriating Eisenhower, who remarked: "This fellow Oppenheimer is sure acting like a Communist. He is using all the rules that they use to try to get public sentiment in their corner on some case where they want to make an individual a martyr."[30] Then, on June 15, the AEC decided to release the full transcript of the hearings. That decision, which violated assurances of confidentiality given to all the witnesses, was made after Strauss received two FBI

29. James Reston, *Deadline: A Memoir* (New York, 1991), 221–26.
30. James Hagerty Diary, June 1, 1954, cited in Bernstein, "In the Matter," 240.

surveillance reports, one claiming that Oppenheimer was considering releasing only those parts of the transcript favorable to himself, the other that Oppenheimer's attorneys had been overheard saying that publication of the entire transcript "would have a devastating effect on Oppenheimer's image."[31] The accidental, if temporary, loss of a classified document by one of the AEC commissioners permitted Strauss to obtain approval for publication.

Publication of the transcript did not have a devastating effect on Oppenheimer but it certainly embarrassed him. There, for all to see, were his confessions of wrongdoing, his willingness to inform on his former students and colleagues, his discomfort when asked about the night with Jean Tatlock, and, above all, his seemingly inexplicable timidity in the face of Robb's bull-dog-like cross-examination. To make doubly certain that releasing the transcript would have the desired effect, the AEC provided the press with a memorandum drawing attention to the passages in the 992-page document in which Oppenheimer admitted that the original story he told security officers about the Chevalier incident in 1943 was "a tissue of lies."

"Had we anticipated the way in which the Commission was to present the transcript to the public," Lloyd K. Garrison recalled, "we might have published it first ourselves, through Mr. Reston." Garrison explained that Oppenheimer had decided against releasing the document partly because of the assurances of secrecy given to witnesses, and partly because the case was still pending before the AEC. There was still a chance, however remote, that the commission would find in his favor, Garrison explained, but "if we were to publish the transcript in advance of the decision, we might disturb the Commission and perhaps prejudice the outcome."[32]

The immediate response to the publication of the transcript focused on the merits of the AEC's decision. A few who had sympathized with Oppenheimer were now persuaded that the evidence justified the action, while others, like Joseph and Stewart Alsop, thought the testimony demonstrated a miscarriage of justice as notorious as that in the infamous Dreyfus case.[33] Unfortunately, not nearly as much attention was paid at the time to the broader significance of the transcript, which provided an invaluable source of information about the history of nuclear development during the war, the debate among scientists over the hydrogen bomb, the conflict between the foreign policy and military establishments over national defense, the controversy over the proper standards to apply in assessing an individual's loyalty, and the ethical and moral dilemmas involved in combating the perceived menace of communism. Like a latter-day Greek tragedy, the transcript also offered insight into such timeless traits of human character as honor, fortitude, and humility, and, sadly enough, their less admirable counterparts: treachery, timidity, and pride.

31. Ibid., 241.
32. Stern, *Oppenheimer Case*, 522.
33. Joseph and Stewart Alsop, *We Accuse! The Story of the Miscarriage of American Justice in the Case of J. Robert Oppenheimer* (New York, 1954).

THE SETTING AND
THE PARTICIPANTS

In March 1947, the Atomic Energy Commission moved its headquarters to a building located at Nineteenth Street and Constitution Avenue N.W., which had been used during World War II by the Joint Chiefs of Staff. But the AEC retained space in Building T-3, a "temporary" structure, located three blocks away, at Sixteenth and Constitution, not far from the Washington Monument, and that is where the Personnel Security Board held its month-long hearing in the case of J. Robert Oppenheimer.

Room 2022, in which the testimony was taken, was rectangular-shaped. It was "a sort of long dark room," participants recalled, "all very bare." Three tables in the center were arranged in the form of a "T," with the head table parallel to the right side of the room as one entered it. The members of the board were seated at that table: Gordon Gray in the middle, flanked by Ward V. Evans to his left and Thomas A. Morgan to his right. The recorder, Albert J. Gasdor, was positioned in front of them. Two long, narrow tables, perpendicular to the head table, were reserved for the attorneys. To the board members' right, their backs to the windows, were the AEC's lawyers: Roger Robb and Carl Arthur Rolander Jr., and a classification officer. Opposite them, facing the windows, were Oppenheimer's attorneys: Lloyd K. Garrison, Herbert S. Marks, Samuel J. Silverman, and Allan B. Ecker. Witnesses were seated when they testified in a chair, located at the base of the "T," facing the members of the board.

Behind the chair was a leather sofa on which Oppenheimer sat when he was not testifying. Witnesses therefore would see him as they entered the room, but would have their backs to him as they testified.

In selecting the Personnel Security Board, Lewis L. Strauss, the Atomic Energy Commission chairman, and William Mitchell, the general counsel, had certain considerations in mind. For obvious reasons, they wanted one of the members to be a lawyer and another to be a scientist. They sought individuals whose stature was such that their decision would carry weight. They preferred that one and possibly two of the board members be Democrats to avoid the risk that a ruling might appear to be politically motivated. In fact, however, they wanted individuals who were likely to rule against Oppenheimer, although there was no way to guarantee that outcome. According to an FBI memorandum, Strauss told Mitchell that "if this case is lost the atomic energy program and all research and development connected thereto will fall into the hands of 'left-wingers.' . . . [I]f Oppenheimer is cleared, then 'anyone' can be cleared regardless of the information against them."

Gordon Gray, forty-five years of age, president of the University of North Carolina since 1950, had exactly the right credentials, Strauss and Mitchell believed, to serve as the board chairman. Born to a wealthy Winston Salem, North Carolina, family—his father was head of R.J. Reynolds Tobacco Company—Gray went to a private preparatory school in Virginia, attended the University of North Carolina, and then entered Yale Law School, receiving his degree in 1933. Elected a state senator in 1939 and 1941, he enlisted in the army as a private during World War II, rose to the rank of captain, later served as Assistant Secretary of the Army, and wound up, in 1949, as President Harry S. Truman's Secretary of the Army. He was a Democrat, although a conservative one who had refused to support Adlai Stevenson in 1952 because he considered the nominee soft on communism.

Joining Gray on the board was Thomas A. Morgan, who had recently retired as president and chairman of the board of the Sperry Corporation. Like Gray, he hailed from North Carolina, but the two men's backgrounds could not have been more dissimilar. The son of an impoverished tobacco farmer, Morgan had to walk three miles every day to get to public school, earned money while attending high school by working as a carpenter and traveling salesman, and in 1908, at the age of nineteen, enlisted in the navy. While serving as an apprentice electrician on a battleship, he met Elmer Sperry, the inventor of the gyrocompass, and made such a favorable impression that when he was discharged from the service in 1912 Sperry invited him to join his company. By the late 1920s Morgan had become its president. He retired in 1952, but continued, among other things, to chair the United Negro College Fund drive in New York City. He was described as "a baldish man with gray eyes who bore a rose tattoo on his left arm."

Both Gray and Morgan were Democrats, but the third member of the board, Dr. Ward V. Evans, was a rock-ribbed conservative Republican who was quoted as saying, "The closest I ever came to being a Communist was voting for Franklin Roosevelt in 1932." Born in Pennsylvania in 1883, he attended Franklin and Marshall College, taught for a few years at a private school near Poughkeepsie, New York, and eventually decided to study for a doctorate in chemistry, which he received from Columbia University in 1916. He served in the army during World War I, and afterward he taught chemistry and served as department chairman at Northwestern University. After his retirement, he moved to Loyola University of Chicago, where he taught from 1947 to 1951. He had previously served on AEC hearing boards in Chicago.

In security clearance hearings, typically, the Atomic Energy Commission utilized its own lawyers who tried to present all the evidence, pro and con, to the members of the board. But the highly unusual circumstances of the Oppenheimer hearing led the agency to depart from this practice. Reaching outside the counsel's office, Strauss selected an attorney who would, in truth, act as a prosecutor. Roger Robb's name was suggested to Strauss by Deputy Attorney General William P. Rogers. The forty-seven-year-old Robb was a Yale graduate who had gone on to receive a law degree at Yale in 1931, and then spent seven years as an Assistant United States Attorney in Washington, D.C. Since 1938 he had engaged in private practice, handling a number of high-profile cases and earning a reputation as a skilled, combative trial lawyer.

Assisting Robb in preparing the case, although he did not question any of the witnesses, was Carl Arthur Rolander Jr. Born in Kansas in 1920, Rolander did not attend college; instead, at the age of twenty, he went to work for the Federal Bureau of Investigation. He remained with the FBI until 1944, when he entered the army, and in 1947 he joined the staff of the Atomic Energy Commission. Meanwhile, he attended Catholic University, working toward a law degree, which he received in 1949. Given his background, it was only logical for him to become the AEC's deputy director of security, and at the hearing he would sometimes decide whether or not certain documents could be declassified.

One of the reasons why Strauss turned to Roger Robb was his fear that the AEC's own staff lacked the courtroom experience to deal with the high-powered legal team Oppenheimer was assembling. To handle his defense, the physicist selected Lloyd K. Garrison, whom he had met in April 1953, when Garrison became a member of the board of trustees of the Institute for Advanced Study. A great-grandson of the abolitionist William Lloyd Garrison, and scion of a wealthy New York City family known for its contributions to literature as well as the law, Garrison, born in 1897, served in the navy during World War I, attended Harvard College, class of 1919, and went on to Harvard Law School, receiving his degree in 1922. He signed on with a prominent Wall Street law firm, but left after a few years to branch out on his own. In 1932 he became dean of the University of Wisconsin Law School, where he remained until 1945, taking leaves as necessary to serve the federal government in the area of labor-management relations: he was chairman of the National Labor Relations Board in 1934, and later general counsel, executive director, and eventually chairman of the National War Labor Board from 1942 to 1945. When the war was over, he became a partner in the New York City firm of Paul, Weiss, Rifkind, Wharton & Garrison, but he still found time for social causes, serving, for example, as president and director of the National Urban League.

Oppenheimer's friend and trusted adviser, Herbert S. Marks, also participated in his defense. Marks at first resisted any formal involvement because of his prior association with the Atomic Energy Commission, but as the hearing progressed he assumed an ever larger role. Forty-seven years of age, Marks was a graduate of the University of Pennsylvania and Harvard Law School, class of 1932. Like many other Harvard Law graduates of his generation, he went to Washington to participate in the New Deal. He served as attorney and also general counsel for the Tennessee Valley Authority from 1934 to 1939, and the Bonneville Power Administration from 1939 to 1940. When the United States entered World War II, Marks became counsel to the War Production Board from 1941 to 1945. In 1946 he advised Under Secretary of State Dean Acheson on problems relating to atomic energy, and in 1947 he served as the AEC's general counsel. Since then he had been a partner in Marks and Trowbridge.

Two members of Garrison's law firm also aided in the defense. Samuel J. Silverman, whose parents had emigrated to the United States from Russia in 1913 when he was five years old, was a graduate of Columbia Law School. Like both Garrison and Marks, he served in various federal agencies, working as an attorney for the United States Railroad Retirement Board in 1936 and 1937, and for the Foreign Economic Administration in 1944. After the war he joined Paul, Weiss, Rifkind, Wharton & Garrison, where he acquired extensive trial experience. The final member of the defense team, Allan B. Ecker, a recent graduate of Harvard Law School, was present throughout the hearing, although he did not examine any of the witnesses.

The members of the Personnel Security Board, the attorneys representing the Atomic Energy Commission, and those defending Oppenheimer were, for the most part, accustomed to spending their working days in comfortable, well-appointed offices or boardrooms. But for four weeks in the spring of 1954 they appeared, each morning, in a small room in a shabby two-story building in downtown Washington, D.C., where J. Robert Oppenheimer's fate was to be decided.

THE HEARING

Monday, April 12

[As the proceedings begin, Gordon Gray reads into the record the AEC's letter to Oppenheimer written by General Manager Kenneth D. Nichols, which raised questions about his continued security clearance.]

DR. GRAY. The hearing will come to order.

This board, appointed by Mr. K. D. Nichols, General Manager of the Atomic Energy Commission, at the request of Dr. J. Robert Oppenheimer, is composed of the following members: Gordon Gray, chairman, Ward V. Evans and Thomas A. Morgan. All members of the board are present, and board counsels Roger Robb and C. A. Rolander. Dr. and Mrs. Oppenheimer are present. Present also are Mr. Lloyd K. Garrison, counsel for Dr. Oppenheimer. Would you identify your associates?

MR. GARRISON. Samuel J. Silverman, my partner, and Allen B. Ecker, associate of my firm.

DR. GRAY. An investigation of Dr. J. Robert Oppenheimer conducted under the provisions of section 10 (b) (5) (B) (i–iii) of the Atomic Energy Act of 1946 has revealed certain information which casts doubt upon the eligibility of Dr. Oppenheimer for clearance for access to restricted data as provided by the Atomic Energy Act of 1946. This information is as follows:

This is a letter addressed to Dr. J. R. Oppenheimer, the Institute for Advanced Study, Princeton, N.J., dated December 23, 1953, reading as follows:

Dear Dr. Oppenheimer:

Section 10 of the Atomic Energy Act of 1946 places upon the Atomic Energy Commission the responsibility for assuring that individuals are employed by the Commission only when such employment will not endanger the common defense and security. In addition, Executive Order 10450 of April 27, 1953, requires the suspension of employment of any individual

Gordon Gray, chairman of the Personnel Security Board. North Carolina Collection, University of North Carolina Library at Chapel Hill.

where there exists information indicating that his employment may not be clearly consistent with the interests of the national security.

As a result of additional investigation as to your character, associations, and loyalty, and review of your personnel security file in the light of the requirements of the Atomic Energy Act and the requirements of Executive Order 10450, there has developed considerable question whether your continued employment on Atomic Energy Commission work will endanger the common defense and security and whether such continued employment is clearly consistent with the interests of the national security. This letter is to advise you of the steps which you may take to assist in the resolution of this question.

The substance of the information which raises the question concerning your eligibility for employment on Atomic Energy Commission work is as follows:

Let the record show at this point that Mr. Garrison asked to be excused for a few minutes.

It was reported that in 1940 you were listed as a sponsor of the Friends of the Chinese People, an organization which was characterized in 1944 by the

House Committee on Un-American Activities as a Communist-front organization. It was further reported that in 1940 your name was included on a letterhead of the American Committee for Democratic and Intellectual Freedom as a member of its national executive committee. The American Committee for Democracy and Intellectual Freedom was characterized in 1942 by the House Committee on Un-American Activities as a Communist front which defended Communist teachers, and in 1943 it was characterized as subversive and un-American by a special subcommittee of the House Committee on Appropriations. It was further reported that in 1938 you were a member of the Western Council of the Consumers Union. The Consumers Union was cited in 1944 by the House Committee on Un-American Activities as a Communist front headed by the Communist Arthur Kallet. It was further reported that you stated in 1943 that you were not a Communist, but had probably belonged to every Communist-front organization on the west coast and had signed many petitions in which Communists were interested.

It was reported that in 1943 and previously you were intimately associated with Dr. Jean Tatlock, a member of the Communist Party in San Francisco, and that Dr. Tatlock was partially responsible for your association with Communist-front groups.

It was reported that your wife, Katherine Puening Oppenheimer, was formerly the wife of Joseph Dallet, a member of the Communist Party, who was killed in Spain in 1937 fighting for the Spanish Republican Army. It was further reported that during the period of her association with Joseph Dallet, your wife became a member of the Communist Party. The Communist Party has been designated by the Attorney General as a subversive organization which seeks to alter the form of Government of the United States by unconstitutional means, within the purview of Executive Order 9835 and Executive Order 10450.

It was reported that your brother, Frank Friedman Oppenheimer, became a member of the Communist Party in 1936 and has served as a party organizer and as educational director of the professional section of the Communist Party in Los Angeles County. It was further reported that your brother's wife, Jackie Oppenheimer, was a member of the Communist Party in 1938; and that in August 1944, Jackie Oppenheimer assisted in the organization of the East Bay branch of the California Labor School. It was further reported that in 1945 Frank and Jackie Oppenheimer were invited to an informal reception at the Russian consulate, that this invitation was extended by the American-Russian Institute of San Francisco and was for the purpose of introducing famous American scientists to Russian scientists who were delegates to the United Nations Conference on International Organization being held at San Francisco at that time, and that Frank Oppenheimer accepted this invitation. It was further reported that Frank Oppenheimer agreed to give a 6-weeks course on The Social Implications of Modern Scientific Development at the California Labor School, beginning May 9, 1946. The American-Russian Institute of San Francisco and the California Labor School have been cited by the Attorney General as Communist organizations within the purview of Executive Order 9835 and Executive Order 10450.

It was reported that you have associated with members and officials of the Communist Party including Isaac Folkoff, Steve Nelson, Rudy Lambert, Kenneth May, Jack Manley, and Thomas Addis.

It was reported that you were a subscriber to the Daily People's World, a west coast Communist newspaper, in 1941 and 1942.

It was reported in 1950 that you stated to an agent of the Federal Bureau of Investigation that you had in the past made contributions to Communist-front organizations, although at the time you did not know of Communist Party control or extent of infiltration of these groups. You further stated to an agent of the Federal Bureau of Investigation that some of these contributions were made through Isaac Folkoff, whom you knew to be a leading Communist Party functionary, because you had been told that this was the most effective and direct way of helping these groups.

It was reported that you attended a housewarming party at the home of Kenneth and Ruth May on September 20, 1941, for which there was an admission charge for the benefit of The People's World, and that at this party you were in the company of Joseph W. Weinberg and Clarence Hiskey, who were alleged to be members of the Communist Party and to have engaged in espionage on behalf of the Soviet Union. It was further reported that you informed officials of the United States Department of Justice in 1952 that you had no recollection that you had attended such a party, but that since it would have been in character for you to have attended such a party, you would not deny that you were there.

It was reported that you attended a closed meeting of the professional section of the Communist Party of Alameda County, Calif., which was held in the latter part of July or early August 1941, at your residence, 10 Kenilworth Court, Berkeley, Calif., for the purpose of hearing an explanation of a change in Communist Party policy. It was reported that you denied that you attended such a meeting and that such a meeting was held in your home.

It was reported that you stated to an agent of the Federal Bureau of Investigation in 1950, that you attended a meeting in 1940 or 1941, which may have taken place at the home of Haakon Chevalier, which was addressed by William Schneiderman, whom you knew to be a leading functionary of the Communist Party. In testimony in 1950 before the California State Senate Committee on Un-American Activities, Haakon Chevalier was identified as a member of the Communist Party in the San Francisco area in the early 1940's.

Let the record show that Mr. Garrison has returned to the hearing room.

It was reported that you have consistently denied that you have ever been a member of the Communist Party. It was further reported that you stated to a representative of the Federal Bureau of Investigation in 1946 that you had a change of mind regarding the policies and politics of the Soviet Union about the time of the signing of the Soviet-German Pact in 1939. It was further reported that during 1950 you stated to a representative of the Federal Bureau of Investigation that you had never attended a closed meeting of the

Communist Party; and that at the time of the Russo-Finnish War and the subsequent break between Germany and Russia in 1941, you realized the Communist Party infiltration tactics into the alleged anti-Fascist groups and became fed up with the whole thing and lost what little interest you had. It was further reported, however, that:

(a) Prior to April 1942, you had contributed $150 per month to the Communist Party in the San Francisco area, and that the last such payment was apparently made in April 1942, immediately before your entry into the atomic-bomb project.

(b) During the period 1942–45 various officials of the Communist Party, including Dr. Hannah Peters, organizer of the professional section of the Communist Party, Alameda County, Calif., Bernadette Doyle, secretary of the Alameda County Communist Party, Steve Nelson, David Adelson, Paul Pinsky, Jack Manley, and Katrina Sandov are reported to have made statements indicating that you were then a member of the Communist Party; that you could not be active in the party at that time; that your name should be removed from the party mailing list and not mentioned in any way; that you had talked the atomic-bomb question over with party members during this period; and that several years prior to 1945 you had told Steve Nelson that the Army was working on an atomic bomb.

(c) You stated in August of 1943 that you did not want anybody working for you on the project who was a member of the Communist Party, since 'one always had a question of divided loyalty' and the discipline of the Communist Party was very severe and not compatible with complete loyalty to the project. You further stated at that time that you were referring only to present membership in the Communist Party and not to people who had been members of the party. You stated further that you knew several individuals then at Los Alamos who had been members of the Communist Party. You did not, however, identify such former members of the Communist Party to the appropriate authorities. It was also reported that during the period 1942–45 you were responsible for the employment on the atom-bomb project of individuals who were members of the Communist Party or closely associated with activities of the Communist Party, including Giovanni Rossi Lomanitz, Joseph W. Weinberg, David Bohm, Max Bernard Friedman, and David Hawkins. In the case of Giovanni Rossi Lomanitz, you urged him to work on the project, although you stated that you knew he had been very much of a Red when he first came to the University of California and that you emphasized to him that he must forego all political activity if he came to the project. In August 1943, you protested against the termination of his deferment and requested that he be returned to the project after his entry into the military service.

It was reported that you stated to representatives of the Federal Bureau of Investigation on September 5, 1946, that you had attended a meeting in the East Bay and a meeting in San Francisco at which there were present persons definitely identified with the Communist Party. When asked the purpose of the East Bay meeting and the identity of those in attendance, you declined to answer on the ground that this had no bearing on the matter of interest being discussed.

It was reported that you attended a meeting at the home of Frank Oppenheimer on January 1, 1946, with David Adelson and Paul Pinsky, both of whom were members of the Communist Party. It was further reported that you analyzed some material which Pinsky hoped to take up with the legislative convention in Sacramento, Calif.

It was reported in 1946 that you were listed as vice chairman on the letterhead of the Independent Citizens Committee of the Arts, Sciences, and Professions, Inc., which has been cited as a Communist front by the House Committee on Un-American Activities.

It was reported that prior to March 1, 1943, possibly 3 months prior, Peter Ivanov, secretary of the Soviet consulate, San Francisco, approached George Charles Eltenton for the purpose of obtaining information regarding work being done at the Radiation Laboratory for the use of Soviet scientists; that George Charles Eltenton subsequently requested Haakon Chevalier to approach you concerning this matter; that Haakon Chevalier thereupon approached you, either directly or through your brother, Frank Friedman Oppenheimer, in connection with this matter; and that Haakon Chevalier finally advised George Charles Eltenton that there was no chance whatsoever of obtaining the information. It was further reported that you did not report this episode to the appropriate authorities until several months after its occurrence; that when you initially discussed this matter with the appropriate authorities on August 26, 1943, you did not identify yourself as the person who had been approached, and you refused to identify Haakon Chevalier as the individual who made the approach on behalf of George Charles Eltenton; and that it was not until several months later, when you were ordered by a superior to do so, that you so identified Haakon Chevalier. It was further reported that upon your return to Berkeley following your separation from the Los Alamos project, you were visited by the Chevaliers on several occasions; and that your wife was in contact with Haakon and Barbara Chevalier in 1946 and 1947.

It was reported that in 1945 you expressed the view that 'there is a reasonable possibility that it (the hydrogen bomb) can be made,' but that the feasibility of the hydrogen bomb did not appear, on theoretical grounds, as certain as the fission bomb appeared certain, on theoretical grounds, when the Los Alamos Laboratory was started; and that in the autumn of 1949 the General Advisory Committee expressed the view that 'an imaginative and concerted attack on the problem has a better than even chance of producing the weapon within 5 years.' It was further reported that in the autumn of 1949, and subsequently, you strongly opposed the development of the hydrogen bomb: (1) on moral grounds, (2) by claiming that it was not feasible, (3) by claiming that there were insufficient facilities and scientific personnel to carry on the development, and (4) that it was not politically desirable. It was further reported that even after it was determined, as a matter of national policy, to proceed with development of a hydrogen bomb, you continued to oppose the project and declined to cooperate fully in the project. It was further reported that you departed from your proper role as an adviser to the Commission by causing the distribution separately and in private, to top personnel at Los Alamos of the majority and minority reports of the General Advisory Committee on development of the hydrogen bomb for the purpose of trying to turn such top personnel against the development of the hydrogen bomb. It was further reported that you were instrumental in persuading other outstanding scientists not to work on the hydrogen-bomb project, and that the opposition to the hydrogen bomb, of which you are the most experienced, most powerful, and most effective member, has definitely slowed down its development.

In view of your access to highly sensitive classified information, and in view of these allegations which, until disproved, raise questions as to your veracity, conduct and even your loyalty, the Commission has no other recourse, in discharge of its obligations to protect the common defense and security, but to suspend your clearance until the matter has been resolved. Accordingly, your employment on Atomic Energy Commission work and your eligibility for access to restricted data are hereby suspended, effective immediately, pending final determination of this matter.

To assist in the resolution of this matter, you have the privilege of appearing before an Atomic Energy Commission personnel security board. To avail yourself of the privileges afforded you under the Atomic Energy Commission hearing procedures, you must, within 30 days following receipt of this letter, submit to me, in writing, your reply to the information outlined above and request the opportunity of appearing before the personnel security board. Should you signify your desire to appear before the board, you will be notified of the composition of the board and may challenge any member of it for cause. Such challenge should be submitted within 72 hours of the receipt of notice of composition of the board.

If no challenge is raised as to the members of the board, you will be notified of the date and place of hearing at least 48 hours in advance of the date set for hearing. You may be present for the duration of the hearing, may be represented by counsel of your own choosing, and present evidence in your own behalf through witnesses, or by documents, or by both.

Should you elect to have a hearing of your case by the personnel security board, the findings of the board, together with its recommendations regarding your eligibility for employment on Atomic Energy Commission work, in the light of Criteria for Determining Eligibility for Atomic Energy Commission Security Clearance and the requirements of Executive Order 10450, will be submitted to me.

In the event of an adverse decision in your case by the personnel security board, you will have an opportunity to review the record made during your appearance before the board and to request a review of your case by the Commission's personnel security review board.

If a written response is not received from you within 30 days it will be assumed that you do not wish to submit any explanation for further consideration. In that event, or should you not advise me in writing of your desire to appear before the personnel security board, a determination in your case will be made by me on the basis of the existing record.

I am enclosing herewith, for your information and guidance, copies of the Criteria and Procedures for Determining Eligibility for Atomic Energy Commission Security Clearance and Executive Order 10450.

This letter has been marked 'Confidential' to maintain the privacy of this matter between you and the Atomic Energy Commission. You are not precluded from making use of this letter as you may consider appropriate.

I have instructed Mr. William Mitchell, whose address is 1901 Constitution Avenue NW., Washington, D.C., and whose telephone number is Sterling 3-8000, Extension 277, to give you whatever further detailed information you may desire with respect to the procedures to be followed in this matter.

Very truly yours,

K. D. Nichols, *General Manager.*

J. ROBERT OPPENHEIMER: "The items of so-called derogatory information . . . cannot be fairly understood except in the context of my life and my work"

[Gray then reads Oppenheimer's reply, a document on which the physicist had labored over for a period of two months. Although Garrison collaborated in the writing, he recalled that "the language of the answer in its final form was Robert's, as befitted a document so intensely personal."]

[DR. GRAY, *cont.*] I think at this time, then, it would be appropriate for the record to reflect Dr. Oppenheimer's reply of March 4, 1954. I shall now read Dr. Oppenheimer's reply.

This is a letter addressed to Maj. Gen. K. D. Nichols, General Manager, United States Atomic Energy Commission, Washington 25, D.C.

Dear General Nichols:

This is in answer to your letter of December 23, 1953, in which the question is raised whether my continued employment as a consultant on Atomic Energy Commission work 'will endanger the common defense and security and whether such continued employment is clearly consistent with the interests of the national security.'

Though of course I would have no desire to retain an advisory position if my advice were not needed, I cannot ignore the question you have raised, nor accept the suggestion that I am unfit for public service.

The items of so-called derogatory information set forth in your letter cannot be fairly understood except in the context of my life and my work. This answer is in the form of a summary account of relevant aspects of my life in more or less chronological order, in the course of which I shall comment on the specific items in your letter. Through this answer, and through the hearings before the personnel security board, which I hereby request, I hope to provide a fair basis upon which the questions posed by your letter may be resolved.

THE PREWAR PERIOD

I was born in New York in 1904. My father had come to this country at the age of 17 from Germany. He was a successful businessman and quite active in community affairs. My mother was born in Baltimore and before her marriage was an artist and teacher of art. I attended Ethical Culture School and Harvard College, which I entered in 1922. I completed the work for my degree in the spring of 1925. I then left Harvard to study at Cambridge University and in Goettingen, where in the spring of 1927 I took my doctor's degree. The following year I was national research fellow at Harvard and at the California Institute of Technology. In the following year I was fellow of the international education board at the University of Leiden and at the Technical High School in Zurich.

In the spring of 1929, I returned to the United States. I was homesick for this country, and in fact I did not leave it again for 19 years. I had learned a great deal in my student days about the new physics; I wanted to pursue this myself, to explain it and to foster its cultivation. I had had many invitations to university positions, 1 or 2 in Europe, and perhaps 10 in the United States. I accepted concurrent appointments as assistant professor at the California Institute of Technology in Pasadena and at the University of California in Berkeley. For the coming 12 years, I was to devote my time to these 2 faculties.

Starting with a single graduate student in my first year in Berkeley, we gradually began to build up what was to become the largest school in the country of graduate and postdoctoral study in theoretical physics, so that as time went on, we came to have between a dozen and 20 people learning and adding to quantum theory, nuclear physics, relativity and other modern physics. As the number of students increased, so in general did their quality; the men who worked with me during those years hold chairs in many of the great centers of physics in this country; they have made important contributions to science, and in many cases to the atomic-energy project. Many of my students would accompany me to Pasadena in the spring after the Berkeley term was over, so that we might continue to work together.

My friends, both in Pasadena and in Berkeley, were mostly faculty people, scientists, classicists, and artists. I studied and read Sanskrit with Arthur Ryder. I read very widely, just mostly classics, novels, plays, and poetry; and I read something of other parts of science. I was not interested in and did not read about economics or politics. I was almost wholly divorced from the contemporary scene in this country. I never read a newspaper or a current magazine like Time or Harper's; I had no radio, no telephone; I learned of the stock-market crack in the fall of 1929 only long after the event; the first time I ever voted was in the presidential election of 1936. To many of my friends, my indifference to contemporary affairs seemed bizarre, and they often chided me with being too much of a highbrow. I was interested in man and his experience; I was deeply interested in my science; but I had no understanding of the relations of man to his society.

I spent some weeks each summer with my brother Frank at our ranch in New Mexico. There was a strong bond of affection between us. After my mother's death, my father came often, mostly in Berkeley, to visit me; and we had an intimate and close association until his death.

Beginning in late 1936, my interests began to change. These changes did not alter my earlier friendships, my relations to my students, or my devotion to physics; but they added something new. I can discern in retrospect more than one reason for these changes. I had had a continuing, smoldering fury about the treatment of Jews in Germany. I had relatives there, and was later to help in extricating them and bringing them to this country. I saw what the depression was doing to my students. Often they could get no jobs, or jobs which were wholly inadequate. And through them, I began to understand how deeply political and economic events could affect men's lives. I began to feel the need to participate more fully in the life of the community. But I had no framework of political conviction or experience to give me perspective in these matters.

In the spring of 1936, I had been introduced by friends to Jean Tatlock, the daughter of a noted professor of English at the university; and in the autumn, I began to court her, and we grew close to each other. We were at least twice close enough to marriage to think of ourselves as engaged. Between 1939 and her death in 1944 I saw her very rarely. She told me about her Communist Party memberships; they were on again, off again affairs, and never seemed to provide for her what she was seeking. I do not believe that her interests were really political. She loved this country and its people and its life. She was, as it turned out, a friend of many fellow travelers and Communists, with a number of whom I was later to become acquainted.

I should not give the impression that it was wholly because of Jean Tatlock that I made left-wing friends, or felt sympathy for causes which hitherto would have seemed so remote from me, like the Loyalist cause in Spain, and the organization of migratory workers. I have mentioned some of the other contributing causes. I liked the new sense of companionship, and at the time felt that I was coming to be part of the life of my time and country.

In 1937, my father died; a little later, when I came into an inheritance, I made a will leaving this to the University of California for fellowships to graduate students.

This was the era of what the Communists then called the United Front, in which they joined with many non-Communist groups in support of humanitarian objectives. Many of these objectives engaged my interest. I contributed to the strike fund of one of the major strikes of Bridges' union; I subscribed to the People's World; I contributed to the various committees and organizations which were intended to help the Spanish Loyalist cause. I was invited to help establish the teacher's union, which included faculty and teaching assistants at the university, and school teachers of the East Bay. I was elected recording secretary. My connection with the teacher's union continued until some time in 1941, when we disbanded our chapter.

During these same years, I also began to take part in the management of the physics department, the selection of courses, and the awarding of fellowships, and in the general affairs of the graduate school of the university, mostly through the graduate council, of which I was a member for some years.

I also became involved in other organizations. For perhaps a year, I was a member of the western council of the Consumer's Union which was concerned with evaluating information on products of interest on the west coast. I do not recall Arthur Kallet, the national head of the Consumer's Union; at most I could have met him if he made a visit to the west coast. I joined the American Committee for Democracy and Intellectual Freedom. I think it then stood as a protest against what had happened to intellectuals and professionals in Germany. I listed, in the personal security questionnaire that I filled out in 1942 for employment with the Manhattan District, the very few political organizations of which I had ever been a member. I say on that questionnaire that I did not include sponsorships. I have no recollection of the Friends of the Chinese People, or of what, if any, my connection with this organization was.

The statement is attributed to me that, while I was not a Communist, I 'had probably belonged to every Communist-front organization on the west coast and had signed many petitions in which Communists were interested.' I do not recall this statement, nor to whom I might have made it, nor the circumstances. The quotation is not true. It seems clear to me that if I said anything along the lines quoted, it was a half-jocular overstatement.

The matter which most engaged my sympathies and interests was the war in Spain. This was not a matter of understanding and informed convictions. I had never been to Spain; I knew a little of its literature; I knew nothing of its history or politics or contemporary problems. But like a great many other Americans I was emotionally committed to the Loyalist cause. I contributed to various organizations for Spanish relief. I went to, and helped with, many parties, bazaars, and the like. Even when the war in Spain was manifestly lost, these activities continued. The end of the war and the defeat of the Loyalists caused me great sorrow.

It was probably through Spanish relief efforts that I met Dr. Thomas Addis, and Rudy Lambert. As to the latter, our association never became close. As to the former, he was a distinguished medical scientist who became a friend. Addis asked me, perhaps in the winter of 1937–38, to contribute through him to the Spanish cause. He made it clear that this money, unlike that which went to the relief organizations, would go straight to the fighting effort, and that it would go through Communist channels. I did so contribute; usually when he communicated with me, explaining the nature of the need, I gave him sums in cash, probably never much less than a hundred dollars, and occasionally perhaps somewhat more than that, several times during the winter. I made no such contributions during the spring terms when I was in Pasadena or during the summers in New Mexico. Later—but I do not remember the date—Addis introduced me to Isaac Folkoff, who was, as Addis indicated, in some way connected with the Communist Party, and told me that Folkoff would from then on get in touch with me when there was need for money. This he did, in much the same way that Addis had done before. As before, these contributions were for specific purposes, principally the Spanish War and Spanish relief. Sometimes I was asked for money for other purposes, the organization of migratory labor in the California valleys, for instance. I doubt that it occurred to me that the contributions might be directed to other purposes than those I had intended, or that such other purposes might be evil. I did not then regard Communists as dangerous; and some of their declared objectives seemed to me desirable.

In time these contributions came to an end. I went to a big Spanish relief party the night before Pearl Harbor; and the next day, as we heard the news of the outbreak of war, I decided that I had had about enough of the Spanish cause, and that there were other and more pressing crises in the world. My contributions would not have continued much longer.

My brother Frank married in 1936. Our relations thereafter were inevitably less intimate than before. He told me at the time—probably in 1937—that he and his wife Jackie had joined the Communist Party. Over the years we saw one another as occasions arose. We still spent summer holidays together. In 1939 or 1940 Frank and Jackie moved to Stanford; in the autumn of 1941 they came to Berkeley, and Frank worked for the Radiation Laboratory. At that time he made it clear to me that he was no longer a member of the Communist Party.

As to the alleged activities of Jackie and Frank in 1944, 1945, and 1946: I was not in Berkeley in 1944 and 1945; I was away most of the first half of 1946; I do not know whether these activities occurred or not, and if I had any knowledge of them at the time it would have been very sketchy. After Christmas of 1945 my family and I visited my brother's family for a few days during the holidays, and I remember that we were there New Year's Eve and New Year's Day in 1946. On New Year's Day people were constantly dropping in. Pinsky and Adelson, who were at most casual acquaintances of mine, may have been among them, but I cannot remember their being there, nor indeed do I remember any of the others who dropped in that day or what was discussed.

It was in the summer of 1939 in Pasadena that I first met my wife. She was married to Dr. Harrison, who was a friend and associate of the Tolmans, Lauritsens, and others of the California Institute of Technology faculty. I learned of her earlier marriage to Joe Dallet, and of his death fighting in Spain. He had been a Communist Party official, and for a year or two during their brief marriage my wife was a Communist Party member. When I met her I found in her a deep loyalty to her former husband, a complete disengagement from any political activity, and a certain disappointment and contempt that the Communist Party was not in fact what she had once thought it was.

My own views were also evolving. Although Sidney and Beatrice Webb's book on Russia, which I had read in 1936, and the talk that I heard at that time had predisposed me to make much of the economic progress and general level of welfare in Russia, and little of its political tyranny, my views on this were to change. I read about the purge trials, though not in full detail, and could never find a view of them which was not damning to the Soviet system. In 1938 I met three physicists who had actually lived in Russia in the thirties. All were eminent scientists, Placzek, Weisskopf, and Schein; and the first two have become close friends. What they reported seemed to me so solid, so unfanatical, so true, that it made a great impression; and it presented Russia, even when seen from their limited experience, as a land of purge and terror, of ludicrously bad management and of a long-suffering people. I need to make clear that this changing opinion of Russia, which was to be reinforced by the Nazi-Soviet Pact, and the behavior of the Soviet Union in Poland and in Finland, did not mean a sharp break for me with those who held to different views. At that time I did not fully understand—as in time I came to understand—how completely the Communist Party in this country was under the control of Russia. During and after the battle of France, however, and during the battle of England the next autumn, I found myself increasingly out of sympathy with the policy of disengagement and neutrality that the Communist press advocated.

After our marriage in 1940, my wife and I for about 2 years had much the same circle of friends as I had had before—mostly physicists and university people. Among them the Chevaliers, in particular, showed us many acts of kindness. We were occasionally invited to more or less obviously leftwing affairs, Spanish relief parties that still continued; and on two occasions, once in San Francisco and once in Berkeley, we attended social gatherings of apparently well-to-do people, at which Schneiderman, an official of the Communist Party in California, attempted, not with success as far as we were concerned, to explain what the Communist line was all about. I was asked about the Berkeley meeting in an interview in 1946 with agents of the FBI. I did not then recall this meeting, and in particular did not in any way connect it with Chevalier, about whom the agents were questioning me; hence it seemed wholly irrelevant to the matter under discussion. Later my wife reminded me that the Berkeley meeting had occurred at the house of the Chevaliers; and when I was asked about it by the FBI in 1950, I told them so.

We saw a little of Kenneth May; we both liked him. It would have been not unnatural for us to go to a housewarming for May and his wife; neither my wife nor I remember such a party. Weinberg was known to me as a graduate student; Hiskey I did not know. Steve Nelson came a few times with his family to visit; he had befriended my wife in Paris, at the time of her husband's death in Spain in 1937. Neither of us has seen him since 1941 or 1942.

Because of these associations that I have described, and the contributions mentioned earlier, I might well have appeared at the time as quite close to the Communist Party—perhaps even to some people as belonging to it. As I have said, some of its declared objectives seemed to me desirable. But I never was a member of the Communist Party. I never accepted Communist dogma or theory; in fact, it never made sense to me. I had no clearly formulated political views. I hated tyranny and repression and every form of dictatorial control of thought. In most cases I did not in those days know who was and who was not a member of the Communist Party. No one ever asked me to join the Communist Party.

Your letter sets forth statements made in 1942–45 by persons said to be Communist Party officials to the effect that I was a concealed member of the Communist Party. I have no knowledge as to what these people might have said. What I do know is that I was never a member of the party, concealed or open. Even the names of some of the people mentioned are strange to me, such as Jack Manley and Katrina Sandow. I doubt that I met Bernadette Doyle, although I recognize her name. Pinsky and Adelson I met at most casually, as previously mentioned.

By the time that we moved to Los Alamos in early 1943, both as a result of my changed views and of the great pressure of war work, my participation in leftwing organizations and my associations with leftwing circles had ceased and were never to be reestablished.

In August 1941, I bought Eagle Hill at Berkeley for my wife, which was the first home we had of our own. We settled down to live in it with our new baby. We had a good many friends, but little leisure. My wife was working in biology at the university. Many of the men I had known went off to work on radar and other aspects of military research. I was not without envy of them; but it was not until my first connection with the rudimentary atomic-energy enterprise that I began to see any way in which I could be of direct use.

Let the record show that Mr. Oppenheimer has asked to be excused briefly.

THE WAR YEARS

Ever since the discovery of nuclear fission, the possibility of powerful explosives based on it had been very much in my mind, as it had in that of many other physicists. We had some understanding of what this might do for us in the war, and how much it might change the course of history. In the autumn of 1941, a special committee was set up by the National Academy of Sciences under the chairmanship of Arthur Compton to review the prospects and feasibility of the different uses of atomic energy for military purposes. I attended a meeting of this committee; this was my first official connection with the atomic-energy program.

After the academy meeting, I spent some time in preliminary calculations about the construction and performance of atomic bombs, and became increasingly excited at the prospects. At the same time I still had a quite heavy burden of academic work with courses and graduate students. I also began to consult, more or less regularly, with the staff of the Radiation Laboratory in Berkeley on their program for the electromagnetic separation of uranium isotopes. I was never a member or employee of the laboratory; but I attended many of its staff and policy meetings. With the help of two of my graduate students, I developed an invention which was embodied in the production plants at Oak Ridge. I attended the conference in Chicago at which the Metallurgical Laboratory (to produce plutonium) was established and its initial program projected.

In the spring of 1942, Compton called me to Chicago to discuss the state of work on the bomb itself. During this meeting Compton asked me to take the responsibility for this work, which at that time consisted of numerous scattered experimental projects. Although I had no administrative experience and was not an experimental physicist, I felt sufficiently informed and challenged by the problem to be glad to accept. At this time I became an employee of the Metallurgical Laboratory.

After this conference I called together a theoretical study group in Berkeley, in which Bethe, Konopinski, Serber, Teller, Van Fleck, and I participated. We had an adventurous time. We spent much of the summer of 1942 in Berkeley in a joint study that for the first time really came to grips with the physical problems of atomic bombs, atomic explosions, and the possibility of using fission explosions to initiate thermonuclear reactions. I called this possibility to the attention of Dr. Bush during the late summer; the technical views on this subject were to develop and change from them until the present day.

After these studies there was little doubt that a potentially world-shattering undertaking lay ahead. We began to see the great explosion at Alamogordo and the greater explosions at Eniwetok with a surer foreknowledge. We also began to see how rough, difficult, challenging, and unpredictable this job might turn out to be.

When I entered the employ of the Metallurgical Laboratory I filled out my first personnel security questionnaire.

Let the record show that Dr. Oppenheimer has returned to the hearing room.

Later in the summer, I had word from Compton that there was a question of my clearance on the ground that I had belonged to left-wing groups; but it was indicated that this would not prove a bar to my further work on the program.

In later summer, after a review of the experimental work, I became convinced, as did others, that a major change was called for in the work on the bomb itself. We needed a central laboratory devoted wholly to this purpose, where people could talk freely with each other, where theoretical ideas and experimental findings could affect each other, where the waste and frustration and error of the many compartmentalized experimental studies could be eliminated, where we could begin to come to grips with chemical, metallurgical, engineering, and ordnance problems that had so far received no consideration. We therefore sought to establish this laboratory for a direct attack on all the problems inherent in the most rapid possible development and production of atomic bombs.

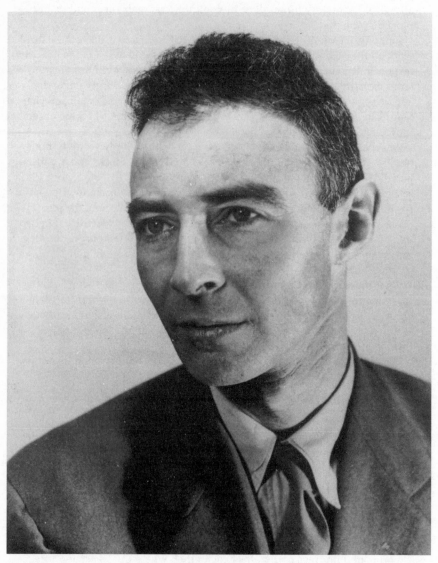

J. Robert Oppenheimer, 1945. Los Alamos Scientific Laboratory, courtesy AIP Emilio Segrè Visual Archives.

In the autumn of 1942 General Groves assumed charge of the Manhattan Engineer District. I discussed with him the need for an atomic-bomb laboratory. There had been some thought of making this laboratory a part of Oak Ridge. For a time there was support for making it a Military Establishment in which key personnel would be commissioned as officers; and in preparation for this course I once went to the Presidio to take the initial steps toward obtaining a commission. After a good deal of discussion with the personnel who would be needed at Los Alamos and with General Groves and his advisers, it was decided that the laboratory should, at least initially, be a civilian establishment in a military post. While this consideration was going on, I had showed General Groves Los Alamos; and he almost immediately took steps to acquire the site.

In early 1943, I received a letter signed by General Groves and Dr. Conant, appointing me director of the laboratory, and outlining their conception of how it was to be organized and administered. The necessary construction and assembling of the needed facilities were begun. All of us worked in close collaboration with the engineers of the Manhattan District.

The site of Los Alamos was selected, in part at least, because it enabled those responsible to balance the obvious need for security with the equally important need of free communication among those engaged in the work. Security, it was hoped, would be achieved by removing the laboratory to a remote area, fenced and patrolled, where communication with the outside was extremely limited. Telephone calls were monitored, mail was censored, and personnel who left the area—something permitted only for the clearest of causes—knew that their movements might be under surveillance. On the other hand, for those within the community, fullest exposition and discussion among those competent to use the information was encouraged.

The last months of 1942 and early 1943 had hardly hours enough to get Los Alamos established. The real problem had to do with getting to Los Alamos the men who would make a success of the undertaking. For this we needed to understand as clearly as we then could what our technical program would be, what men we would need, what facilities, what organization, what plan.

The program of recruitment was massive. Even though we then underestimated the ultimate size of the laboratory, which was to have almost 4,000 members by the spring of 1945, and even though we did not at that time see clearly some of the difficulties which were to bedevil and threaten the enterprise, we knew that it was a big, complex and diverse job. Even the initial plan of the laboratory called for a start with more than 100 highly qualified and trained scientists, to say nothing of the technicians, staff, and mechanics who would be required for their support, and of the equipment that we would have to beg and borrow since there would be no time to build it from scratch. We had to recruit at a time when the country was fully engaged in war and almost every competent scientist was already involved in the military effort.

The primary burden of this fell on me. To recruit staff I traveled all over the country talking with people who had been working on one or another aspect of the atomic-energy enterprise, and people in radar work, for example, and underwater sound, telling them about the job, the place that we were going to, and enlisting their enthusiasm.

In order to bring responsible scientists to Los Alamos, I had to rely on their sense of the interest, urgency, and feasibility of the Los Alamos mission. I had to tell them enough of what the job was, and give strong enough assurance that it might be successfully accomplished in time to affect the outcome of the war, to make it clear that they were justified in their leaving other work to come to this job.

The prospect of coming to Los Alamos aroused great misgivings. It was to be a military post; men were asked to sign up more or less for the duration; restrictions on travel and on the freedom of families to move about to be severe; and no one could be sure of the extent to which the necessary technical freedom of action could actually be maintained by the laboratory. The notion of disappearing into the New Mexico desert for an indeterminate period and under quasi military auspices disturbed a good many scientists, and the families of many more. But there was another side to it. Almost everyone realized that this was a great undertaking. Almost everyone knew that if it were completed successfully and rapidly enough, it might determine the outcome of the war. Almost everyone knew that it was an unparalleled opportunity to bring to bear the basic knowledge and art of science for the benefit of his country. Almost everyone knew that this job, if it were achieved, would be a part of history. This sense of excitement, of devotion and of patriotism in the end prevailed. Most of those with whom I talked came to Los Alamos. Once they came, confidence in the enterprise grew as men learned more of the technical status of the work; and though the laboratory was to double and redouble its size many times before the end, once it had started it was on the road to success.

We had information in those days of German activity in the field of nuclear fission. We were aware of what it might mean if they beat us to the draw in the development of atomic bombs. The consensus of all our opinions, and every directive that I had, stressed the extreme urgency of our work, as well as the need for guarding all knowledge of it from our enemies. Past Communist connections or sympathies did not necessarily disqualify a man from employment, if we had confidence in his integrity and dependability as a man.

There are two items of derogatory information on which I need to comment at this point. The first is that it was reported that I had talked the atomic-bomb question over with Communist Party members during this period (1942–45). The second is that I was responsible for the employment on the atomic-bomb project of individuals who were members of the Communist Party or closely associated with activities of the Communist Party.

As to the first, my only discussions of matters connected with the atomic bomb were for official work or for recruiting the staff of the enterprise. So far as I knew none of these discussions were with Communist Party members. I never discussed anything of my secret work or anything about the atomic bomb with Steve Nelson.

As to the statement that I secured the employment of doubtful persons on the project: Of those mentioned, Lomanitz, Friedman, and Weinberg were never employed at Los Alamos. I believe that I had nothing to do with the employment of Friedman and Weinberg by the Radiation Laboratory; I had no responsibility for the hiring of anyone there. During the time that I continued to serve as a consultant with the Radiation Laboratory and to advise and direct the work of some of the graduate students, I assigned David Bohm and Chaim Richman to a problem of basic science which might prove useful in analyzing experiments in connection with fast neutrons. That work has long been published. Another graduate student was Rossi Lomanitz. I remember vaguely a conversation with him in which he expressed reluctance to take part in defense research, and I encouraged him to do what other scientists were doing for their country. Thereafter he did work at the Radiation Laboratory. I remember no details of our talk. If I asked him to work on the project, I would have assumed that he would be checked by the security officers as a matter of course. Later, in 1943, when Lomanitz was inducted into the Army, he wrote me asking me to help his return to the project. I forwarded a copy of this letter to the Manhattan District security officers, and let the matter rest there. Still later, at Lomanitz' request, I wrote to his commanding officer that he was qualified for advanced technical work in the Army.

I asked for the transfer of David Bohm to Los Alamos; but this request, like all others, was subject to the assumption that the usual security requirements would apply; and when I was told that there was objection on security grounds to this transfer, I was much surprised, but of course agreed. David Hawkins was known to the personnel director at the laboratory, and I had met and liked him and found him intelligent; I supported the suggestion of the personnel director that he come to Los Alamos. I understand that he had had left-wing associations; but it was not until in March of 1951, at the time of his testimony, that I knew about his membership in the Communist Party.

In 1943 when I was alleged to have stated that 'I knew several individuals then at Los Alamos who had been members of the Communist Party,' I knew of only one; she was my wife, of whose disassociation from the party, and of whose integrity and loyalty to the United States I had no question. Later, in 1944 or 1945, my brother Frank, who had been cleared for work in Berkeley and at Oak Ridge, came to Los Alamos from Oak Ridge with official approval.

I knew of no attempt to obtain secret information at Los Alamos. Prior to my going there my friend Haakon Chevalier with his wife visited us on Eagle Hill, probably in early 1943. During the visit, he came into the kitchen and told me that George Eltenton had spoken to him of the possibility of transmitting technical information to Soviet scientists. I made some strong remark to the effect that this sounded terribly wrong to me. The discussion ended there. Nothing in our long standing friendship would have led me to believe that Chevalier was actually seeking information; and I was certain that he had no idea of the work on which I was engaged.

It has long been clear to me that I should have reported the incident at once. The events that led me to report it—which I doubt ever would have become known without my report—were unconnected with it. During the summer of 1943, Colonel Lansdale, the intelligence officer of the Manhattan District, came to Los Alamos and told me that he was worried about the security situation in Berkeley because of the activities of the Federation of Architects, Engineers, Chemists, and Technicians. This recalled to my mind that Eltenton was a member and probably a promoter of the FAECT. Shortly thereafter, I was in Berkeley and I told the security officer that Eltenton would bear watching. When asked why, I said that Eltenton had attempted, through intermediaries, to approach people on the project, though I mentioned neither myself nor Chevalier. Later, when General Groves urged me to give the details, I told him of my conversation with Chevalier. I still think of Chevalier as a friend.

The story of Los Alamos is long and complex. Part of it is public history. For me it was a time so filled with work, with the need for decision and action and consultation, that there was room for little else. I lived with my family in the community which was Los Alamos. It was a remarkable community, inspired by a high sense of mission, of duty and of destiny, coherent, dedicated, and remarkably selfless. There was plenty in the life of Los Alamos to cause irritation; the security restrictions, many of my own devising, the inadequacies and inevitable fumblings of a military post unlike any that had ever existed before, shortages, inequities, and in the laboratory itself the shifting emphasis on different aspects of the technical work as the program moved forward; but I have never known a group more understanding and more devoted to a common purpose, more willing to lay aside personal convenience and prestige, more understanding of the role that they were playing in their country's history. Time and again we had in the technical work almost paralyzing crises. Time and again the laboratory drew itself together and faced the new problems and got on with the work. We worked by night and by day; and in the end the many jobs were done.

These years of hard and loyal work of the scientists culminated in the test on July 16, 1945. It was a success. I believe that in the eyes of the War Department, and other knowledgeable people, it was as early a success as they had thought possible, given all the circumstances, and rather a greater one. There were many indications from the Secretary of War and General Groves, and many others, that official opinion was one of satisfaction with what had been accomplished. At the time, it was hard for us in Los Alamos not to share that satisfaction, and hard for me not to accept the conclusion that I had managed the enterprise well and played a key part in its success. But it needs to be stated that many others contributed the decisive ideas and carried out the work which led to this success and that my role was that of understanding, encouraging, suggesting and deciding. It was the very opposite of a one-man show.

Even before the July 16 test and the use of the bombs in Japan, the members of the laboratory began to have a new sense of the possible import of what was going on. In the early days, when success was less certain and timing unsure, and the war with Germany and Japan in a desperate phase, it was enough for us to think that we had a job to do. Now, with Germany defeated, the war in the Pacific approaching a crisis, and the success of our undertaking almost assured, there was a sense both of hope and of anxiety as to what this spectacular development might portend for the future. This came to us a little earlier than to the public generally because we saw the technical development at close range and in secret; but its quality was very much the same as the public response after Hiroshima and Nagasaki.

Thus it was natural that in the spring of 1945 I welcomed the opportunity when I was asked by Secretary Stimson to serve, along with Compton, Lawrence, and Fermi, on an advisory panel to his Interim Committee on Atomic Energy. We met with that committee on the 1st of June 1945; and even during the week when Hiroshima and Nagasaki were being bombed, we met at Los Alamos to sketch out a prospectus of what the technical future in atomic energy might look like: atomic war heads for guided missiles, improvements in bomb designs, the thermonuclear program, power, propulsion, and the new tools available from atomic technology for research in science, medicine, and technology. This work absorbed much of my time, during September and October; and in connection with it I was asked to consult with the War and State Departments on atomic-energy legislation, and in a preliminary way on the international control of atomic energy.

I resigned as director of Los Alamos on October 16, 1945, after having secured the consent of Commander Bradbury and General Groves that Bradbury should act as my successor.

There were then on the books at the laboratory, embodied in memoranda and reports and summarized by me in letters to General Groves, developments in atomic weapons, which could well have occupied years for their fulfillment, and which have in fact provided some, though by no means all, of the themes for Los Alamos work since that time. It was not entirely clear whether the future of atomic weapons work in this country should be continued at or confined to Los Alamos or started elsewhere at a more accessible and more practical site, or indeed what effect international agreements might have on the program. But in the meantime Los Alamos had to be kept going until there was created an authority competent to decide the question of its future. This was to take almost a year.

THE POSTWAR PERIOD

In November 1945, I resumed my teaching at the California Institute of Technology, with an intention and hope, never realized, that this should be a full-time undertaking. The consultation about postwar matter which had already begun continued, and I was asked over and over both by the Executive and the Congress for advice on atomic energy. I had a feeling of deep responsibility, interest, and concern for many of the problems with which the development of atomic energy confronted our country.

This development was to be a major factor in the history of the evolving and mounting conflict between the free world and the Soviet Union. When I and other scientists were called on for advice, our principal duty was to make our technical experience and judgment available. We were called to do this in a context and against a background of the official views of the Government on the military and political situation of our country. Immediately after the war, I was deeply involved in the effort to devise effective means for the international control of atomic weapons, means which might, in the words of those days, tend toward the elimination of war itself. As the prospects of success receded, and as evidence of Soviet hostility and growing military power accumulated, we had more and more to devote ourselves to finding ways of adapting our atomic potential to offset the Soviet threat. In the period marked by the first Soviet atomic explosion, the war in Korea and the Chinese Communist intervention there, we were principally preoccupied, though we never forgot long-term problems, with immediate measures which could rapidly build up the strength of the United States under the threat of an imminent general war. As our own atomic potential increased and developed, we were aware of the dangers inherent in comparable developments by the enemy; and preventive and defensive measures were very much on our minds. Throughout this time the role of atomic weapons was to be central. . . .

A quite different and I believe unique occurrence is cited as an item of derogatory information—that in 1946 I was 'listed as vice chairman on the letterhead of the Independent Citizens Committee of the Arts, Sciences, and Professions, Inc. * * * cited as a Communist front by the House Committee on Un-American Activities.' The fact is that in 1946, when I was at work on the international control of atomic energy, I was notified that I had been nominated and then elected as vice chairman of this organization. When I began to see that its literature included slogans such as 'Withdraw United States troops from China' and that it was endorsing the criticism enunciated by the then Secretary Wallace of the United States policy on atomic energy, I advised the organization in a letter of October 11, 1946, that I was not in accord with its policy, that I regarded the recommendations of Mr. Wallace as not likely to advance the cause of finding a satisfactory solution for the control of atomic energy, and that I wished to resign. When an effort was made to dissuade me from this course I again wrote on December 2, 1946, insisting upon resignation. . . .

I need to turn now to an account of some of the measures which, as Chairman of the General Advisory Committee, and in other capacities, I advocated in the years since the war to increase the power of the United States and its allies to resist and defeat aggression. . . .

In these years from early 1947 to mid-1952 the Committee met some 30 times and transmitted perhaps as many reports to the Commission. Formulation of policy and the management of the vast atomic-energy enterprises were responsibilities vested in the Commission itself. The General Advisory Committee had the role, which was fixed for it by statute, to advise the Commission. In that capacity we gave the Commission our views on questions which the Commission put before us, brought to the Commission's attention on our initiative technical matters of importance, and encouraged and supported the work of the several major installations of the Commission.

At one of our first meetings in 1947 we settled down to the job of forming our own views of the priorities. And while we agreed that the development of atomic power and the support and maintenance of a strong basic scientific activity in the fields relevant to it were important, we assigned top priority to the problem of atomic weapons. At that time we advised the Commission that one of its first jobs would be to convert Los Alamos into an active center for the development and improvement of atomic weapons. In 1945–46 during the period immediately following the war, the purposes of Los Alamos were multiple. It was the only laboratory in the United States that worked on atomic weapons. Los Alamos also had wide interests in scientific matters only indirectly related to the weapons program. We suggested that the Commission recognize as the laboratory's central and primary program the improvement and diversification of atomic weapons, and that this undertaking have a priority second to none. We suggested further that the Commission adopt administrative measures to make work at Los Alamos attractive, to assist the laboratory in recruiting, to help build up a strong theoretical division for guidance in atomic-weapons design, and to take advantage of the availability of the talented and brilliant consultants who had been members of the laboratory during the war. In close consultation with the director of the Los Alamos Laboratory, we encouraged and supported courses of development which would markedly increase the value of our stockpile in terms of the destructive power of our weapons, which would make the best use of existing stockpiles and those anticipated, which would provide weapons suitable for modern combat conditions and for varied forms of delivery and which in their cumulative effect would provide us with the great arsenal we now have. . . .

In view of the controversies that have developed I have left the subject of the super and thermonuclear weapons for separate discussion—although our committee regarded this as a phase of the entire problem of weapons.

The super itself had a long history of consideration, beginning, as I have said, with our initial studies in 1942 before Los Alamos was established. It continued to be the subject of study and research at Los Alamos throughout the war. After the war, Los Alamos itself was inevitably handicapped pending the enactment of necessary legislation for the atomic energy enterprise. With the McMahon Act, the appointment of the Atomic Energy Commission and the General Advisory Committee, we in the committee had occasion at our early meetings in 1947 as well as in 1948 to discuss the subject. In that period the General Advisory Committee pointed out the still extremely unclear status of the problem from the technical standpoint, and urged encouragement of Los Alamos' efforts which were then directed toward modest exploration of the super and of thermonuclear systems. No serious controversy arose about the super until the Soviet explosion of an atomic bomb in the autumn of 1949.

Shortly after that event, in October 1949, the Atomic Energy Commission called a special session of the General Advisory Committee and asked us to consider and advise on two related questions: First, whether in view of the Soviet success the Commission's program was adequate, and if not, in what way it should be altered or increased; second, whether a crash program for

J. Robert Oppenheimer at home in Princeton, with his children, Peter and Toni, and his dog, Buddy, 1948. Mrs. J. Robert Oppenheimer, courtesy AIP Emilio Segrè Visual Archives.

the development of the super should be a part of any new program. The committee considered both questions, consulting various officials from the civil and military branches of the executive departments who would have been concerned, and reached conclusions which were communicated in a report to the Atomic Energy Commission in October 1949.

This report, in response to the first question that had been put to us, recommended a great number of measures that the Commission should take the increase in many ways our overall potential in weapons.

As to the super itself, the General Advisory Committee stated its unanimous opposition to the initiation by the United States of a crash program of the kind we had been asked to advise on. The report of that meeting, and the Secretary's notes, reflect the reasons which moved us to this conclusion. The annexes, in particular, which dealt more with political and policy considerations—the report proper was essentially technical in character—indicated differences in the views of members of the committee. There were two annexes, one signed by Rabi and Fermi, the other by Conant, DuBridge, Smith, Rowe, Buckley and myself. (The ninth member of the committee, Seaborg, was abroad at the time.)

It would have been surprising if eight men considering a problem of extreme difficulty had each had precisely the same reasons for the conclusion in which we joined. But I think I am correct in asserting that the unanimous opposition we expressed to the crash program was based on the conviction, to which technical considerations as well as others contributed, that because of our overall situation at that time such a program might weaken rather than strengthen the position of the United States.

After the report was submitted to the Commission, it fell to me as chairman of the committee to explain our position on several occasions, once at a meeting of the Joint Congressional Committee on Atomic Energy. All this, however, took place prior to the decision by the President to proceed with the thermonuclear program.

This is the full story of my 'opposition to the hydrogen bomb.' It can be read in the records of the general transcript of my testimony before the joint congressional committee. It is a story which ended once and for all when in January 1950 the President announced his decision to proceed with the program. I never urged anyone not to work on the hydrogren bomb project. I never made or caused any distribution of the GAC reports except to the Commission itself. As always, it was the Commission's responsibility to determine further distribution.

In summary, in October 1949, I and the other members of the General Advisory Committee were asked questions by the Commission to which we had a duty to respond, and to which we did respond with our best judgment in the light of evidence then available to us.

When the President's decision was announced in January 1950, our committee was again in session and we immediately turned to the technical problems facing the Commission in carrying out the President's directive. We sought to give our advice then and in ensuing meetings as to the most promising means of solving these problems. We never again raised the question of the wisdom of the policy which had now been settled, but concerned ourselves rather with trying to implement it. During this period our recommendations for increasing production facilities included one for a dual-purpose plant which could be adapted to make materials either for fission bombs or materials useful in a thermonuclear program. In its performance characteristics, the Savannah River project, subsequently adopted by the Commission, was foreshadowed by this recommendation.

While the history of the GAC opposition to a crash program for the super ended with the announcement of the President's decision, the need for evaluation and advice continued. There were immense technical complications both before and after the President's decision. It was of course a primary duty of the committee, as well as other review committees on which I served, to report new developments which we judged promising, and to report when a given weapon or family of weapons appeared impractical, unfeasible or impossible. It would have been my duty so to report had I been alone in my views. As a matter of fact, our views on such matters were almost always unanimous. It was furthermore a proper function for me to speak my best judgment in discussion with those responsibly engaged in the undertaking.

Throughout the whole development of thermonuclear weapons, many occasions occurred where it was necessary for us to form and to express judgments of feasibility. This was true before the President's decision, and it was true after the President's decision. In our report of October 1949, we expressed the view, as your letter states, that 'an imaginative and concerted attack on the problem has a better than even chance of producing the weapon within 5 years.' Later calculations and measurements made at Los Alamos led us to a far more pessimistic view. Still later brilliant inventions led to the possibility of lines of development of very great promise. At each stage the General Advisory Committee, and I as its Chairman and as a member of other bodies, reported as faithfully as we could our evaluation of what was likely to fail and what was likely to work.

In the spring of 1951 work had reached a stage at which far-reaching decisions were called for with regard to the Commission's whole thermonuclear program. In consultation with the Commission, I called a meeting in Princeton in the late spring of that year, which was attended by all members of the Commission and several members of its staff, by members of the General Advisory Committee, by Dr. Bradbury and staff of the Los Alamos Laboratory, by Bethe, Teller, Bacher, Fermi, von Neumann, Wheeler, and others responsibly connected with the program. The outcome of the meeting, which lasted for 2 or 3 days, was an agreed program and a fixing of priorities and effort both for Los Alamos and for other aspects of the Commission's work. This program has been an outstanding success.

In addition to my continuing work on the General Advisory Committee there were other assignments that I was asked to undertake. Late in 1950 or early in 1951 the President appointed me to the Science Advisory Committee to advise the Office of Defense Mobilization and the President; in 1952 the Secretary of State appointed me to a panel to advise on armaments and their regulation; and I served as consultant on continental defense, civil defense, and the use of atomic weapons in support of ground combat. Many of these duties led to reports in the drafting of which I participated, or for which I took responsibility. These supplement the record of the General Advisory Committee as an account of the counsel that I have given our government during the last eight years.

In this letter, I have written only of those limited parts of my history which appear relevant to the issue now before the Atomic Energy Commission. In order to preserve as much as possible the perspective of the story, I have dealt very briefly with many matters. I have had to deal briefly or not at all with instances in which my actions or views were adverse to Soviet or Communist interest, and of actions that testify to my devotion to freedom, or that have contributed to the vitality, influence and power of the United States.

In preparing this letter, I have reviewed two decades of my life. I have recalled instances where I acted unwisely. What I have hoped was, not that I could wholly avoid error, but that I might learn from it. What I have learned has, I think, made me more fit to serve my country.

Very truly yours,

J. Robert Oppenheimer.

Princeton, N.J., March 4, 1954.

GORDON GRAY: "An inquiry and not . . . a trial"

[Having completed the reading of the two documents, Gray lays down the ground rules for the hearing.]

DR. GRAY. This board is convened to enable Dr. Oppenheimer to present any information he considers appropriate having a bearing on the documents just read and the information contained in them, this information being, of course, the same as that disclosed to Dr. Oppenheimer in Mr. K. D. Nichols's letter of December 23, 1953 to Dr. Oppenheimer and Dr. Oppenheimer's reply of March 4, 1954, and to provide a record as a basis for a recommendation to the General Manager of the Atomic Energy Commission as to Dr. Oppenheimer's eligibility for access to restricted data.

At this point, I should like to remind everyone concerned that this proceeding is an inquiry and not in the nature of a trial. We shall approach our duties in that atmosphere and in that spirit.

Dr. Oppenheimer, have you been given an opportunity to exercise the right to challenge any or all of the members of this Board?

DR. OPPENHEIMER. I have, indeed.

DR. GRAY. I should point out to you, sir, that if at any time during the course of this hearing it appears that grounds for challenge for cause arise, you will exercise your right to challenge for cause and the validity of the challenge will be determined in closed session by the members of the Board.

The proceedings and stenographic record of this board are regarded as strictly confidential between Atomic Energy Commission officials participating in this matter and Dr. Oppenheimer, his representatives and witnesses. The Atomic Energy Commission will not take the initiative in public release of any information relating to the proceeding before this board.

Now, at this time, Dr. Oppenheimer, you will be given the opportunity to present any material relevant to the issues before the board. At this point I think we shall find it necessary to exclude all witnesses except the one whose testimony is being given to the board under the provisions of the procedures which we must follow in this inquiry. . . .

I should like to ask Dr. Oppenheimer whether he wishes to testify under oath in this proceeding?

DR. OPPENHEIMER. Surely.

DR. GRAY. You are not required to do so.

DR. OPPENHEIMER. I think it best.

DR. GRAY. I should remind you, then, of the provisions of section 1621 of title 18 of the United States Code, known as the perjury statute, which makes it a crime punishable by a fine of up to $2,000 and/or imprisonment of up to 5 years for any person stating under oath any material matter which he does not believe to be true.

It is also an offense under section 1001 of title 18 of the United States Code, punishable by a fine of not more than $10,000 or imprisonment for not more than 5 years, or both, for any person to make any false, fictitious, or fraudulent statement or representation in any matter within the jurisdiction of any agency of the United States.

I think that before you proceed, Mr. Garrison, that it would be well to administer the oath to Dr. Oppenheimer.

J. Robert Oppenheimer, do you swear that the testimony you are to give the board shall be the truth, the whole truth and nothing but the truth, so help you God?

DR. OPPENHEIMER. I do.

DR. GRAY. May I also point out that in the event that it is necessary for anyone to disclose restricted data during his statements before this board shall advise the Chairman before such disclosure in order that persons unauthorized to have access to restricted data may be excused from the hearing.

Now, Dr. Oppenheimer, you may proceed, and I gather from what Mr. Garrison said, that he will at this point make a statement to the Board.

J. ROBERT OPPENHEIMER: "Exploding one of these things as a firecracker over a desert"

[Oppenheimer's attorney, Lloyd K. Garrison, makes an opening statement and then gives Oppenheimer an opportunity to describe more fully his work at Los Alamos and his views concerning atomic energy in the postwar years.]

MR. GARRISON. Mr. Chairman, members of the board, I would like to say at the outset that far from having thought of challenging any member of the board, we appreciate very much the willingness of men of your standing and responsibilities to accept this exacting and onerous job in the interests of the country. I express my appreciation to you.

We cannot help but be conscious of the fact that for the past week the members of the board have been examining a file containing various items about Dr. Oppenheimer to which we have had, and to which we shall have no access at all. I have been told that this is a large file, and I suppose a great deal of time has been spent on it. I am sure that it goes without saying that we are confident that the minds of the members of the board are open to receive the testimony that we shall submit.

If, as a result of going through the file, there are troublesome questions which have arisen, any items of derogatory information not mentioned in the Commission's letter of December 23, I know we can count on you to bring those to our attention so that we may have an adequate opportunity to reply to them. . . .

DR. GRAY. I think you need have no concern on that score, Mr. Garrison.

MR. GARRISON. I am sure not. I would like at this point to read into the record a letter from Dr. Oppenheimer to Chairman Strauss of the Atomic Energy Commission, dated December 22, 1953. I would be glad to give copies to the members of the board.

I shall explain the purpose in a moment of reading this letter to you.

This letter is addressed to Adm. Lewis L. Strauss, Chairman of the Atomic Energy Commission, Washington, D.C., and is dated December 22, 1953, and reads as follows:

Dear Lewis:

Yesterday, when you asked to see me, you told me for the first time that my clearance by the Atomic Energy Commission was about to be suspended. You put to me as a possibly desirable alternative that I request termination of my contract as a consultant to the Commission, and thereby avoid an explicit consideration of the charges on which the Commission's action would otherwise be based. I was told that if I did not do this within a day, I would receive a letter notifying me of the suspension of my clearance and of the charges against me, and I was shown a draft of that letter.

I have thought most earnestly of the alternative suggested. Under the circumstances this course of action would mean that I accept and concur in the view that I am not fit to serve this Government, that I have now served for some 12 years. This I cannot do. If I were thus unworthy I could hardly have served our country as I have tried, or been the Director of our Institute in Princeton, or have spoken, as on more than one occasion I have found myself speaking, in the name of our science and our country.

Since our meeting yesterday, you and General Nichols told me that the charges in the letter were familiar charges, and since the time was short, I paged through the letter quite briefly. I shall now read it in detail and make appropriate response.

Faithfully yours,

                                        Robert Oppenheimer.

I have presented that, Mr. Chairman, simply to show that there has been no disposition on Mr. Oppenheimer's part to hold onto a job for the sake of a job. It goes without saying that if the Commission did not wish to use his services as a consultant that was all right with him. The point of this letter is that he felt that he could not in honor and integrity of his person simply resign and leave these questions unadjudicated. Fully realizing the terrible burden of going forward with this matter, and the natural risks in any proceeding of this character, including what may go on outside of these walls, nevertheless went forward. . . .

Far from being to his discredit, far from casting doubt on his desire to serve his country as best he sees how to do it, I think our witnesses will persuade you beyond any doubt that his conduct in the hydrogen bomb matter was beyond any reproach; that it was an exercise of the most honest judgment done in the best interests of the country, and that his whole record since the war is rather astonishingly filled with a continuous series of efforts to strengthen the defenses of the United States in a world threatened by totalitarian aggression.

I was surprised to find that about half of his working time since 1945 has been devoted to service on Government boards and committees, from 1945 on, as a volunteer citizen, placing his talents at the service of the country. The richness and the variety of the services that he rendered in those capacities will be vividly brought out in the testimony.

I would like to say that everything he has done since the war, the hydrogen bomb and all the rest, has been done in a blaze of light. There has been not one thing that has not been done in the full daylight of the work of the Government and subjected to the most searching criticism of the ablest men in science and government, all doing each in their own way what they could do to serve the country.

I believe this record will be one which will persuade this board that to exclude Dr. Oppenheimer from the capacity that he continue to serve the Government as he has in the past would be contrary to the best interests of all of us. . . .

Whereupon J. Robert Oppenheimer was called as a witness and, having been previously sworn, was examined and testified as follows:

DIRECT EXAMINATION

By Mr. Garrison: . . .

Q. I would like to begin, Dr. Oppenheimer, with the war years . . .

THE WITNESS. Now, there are a few points I might make about this period. After the test but before the use of the bombs in Japan, I had a meeting with General Groves in Chicago to get some last minute arrangements fixed for the combat use of the weapon. I asked him at that time, how do you feel about this super—the super was our code name for what we then thought of the hydrogen bomb, and we don't know any more than we did when he came up, there was a little work but very inconclusive. As a matter of fact, the decisive measurements on the behavior of tritium were on my desk when I got home—

DR. EVANS. What, sir?

THE WITNESS. The decisive measurements on the tritium—these are declassified now, as you know—were on my desk when I got back from Trinity, General Groves was unclear whether his mandate and therefore mine extended to fiddling with this next project. I so reported to the people in the laboratory, who were thinking about it.

The second point I would not think to mention except that Mr. Garrison has asked me and that is whether there was any change in tempo after the war against Germany ended. There was, but it was upward. It was upward simply because we were still more frantic to have the job done and wanted to have it done so that if needed, it would be available.

In any case, we wanted to have it done before the war was over, and nothing much could be done. I don't think there was any time where we worked harder at the speedup than in the period after the German surrender and the actual combat use of the bomb.

The third thing is that I did suggest to General Groves some changes in bomb design which would make more efficient use of the material; and they have long since been done, of course. He turned them down as jeopardizing the promptness of the availability of bombs. He and I may not entirely agree about how long a delay would have been involved, but the very fact that any delay was involved was unacceptable.

Finally, there was, of course, a great deal of discussion—and I will return to the formal aspects of that—about the desirability of using the bombs in Japan. I think the hotbed of this discussion was in Chicago rather than in Los Alamos. At Los Alamos I heard very little talk about it. We always assumed, if they were needed, they would be used. But there were places where people said for the future of the world it would be better not to use them.

This problem was referred to me in a capacity different than director of Los Alamos. We did everything we could to get them out there and as fast and smooth as possible.

There was, however, at Los Alamos a change in the feel of people. I am talking vaguely because this is a community now of seven or eight thousand people, of whom maybe 1,000 or more are scientists and very close to each other, talking all the time. This was partly a war measure, but it was also something that was here to stay. There was a great sense of uncertainty and anxiety about what should be done about it.

The generation of that kind of public—of a concern very similar to the public concern—that followed Hiroshima and one natural outgrowth of which was our abortive effort to establish quite a new relation among nations in the control of atomic energy; that was not something that had its roots very far back; it started toward the end when the war was about over.

Hiroshima was, of course, very successful, partly for reasons unanticipated by us. We had been over the targets with a committee that was sent out to consult us and to consider them, and the targets that were bombed were among the list that seemed right to us.

The Secretary of War deleted one target, and I have always been glad he did. That was the unbombed and culture capital of Japan, Kyoto. He struck that off. The two that were hit were among the targets selected. We sent a mission on out from Los Alamos to assemble, test the bombs on Tinian, and to fly with the B–29's that went out over the targets, and also to go in as soon as they could get clearance from General MacArthur. . . . to see what mess we made of those two towns.

. . . In May I was asked to serve on the interim committee which Mr. Stimson set up.

Q. This prevented your leaving.

A. Yes; this was before I left Los Alamos. Lawrence, Fermi, and Arthur Compton were the other members of this panel. We met with the interim committee I think on the 1st of June—I am not certain—of 1945 for a very prolonged discussion which was attended by all members of the committee, all members of the panel, and for most of the time General Marshall.

Apart from trying to make as vivid as we could the novelty, the variety, and the dynamic quality of this field, which we thought very important to get across, that this was not a finished job and there was a heck of a lot we didn't know, much of the discussion resolved around the question raised by Secretary Stimson as to whether there was any hope at all of using this development to get less barbarous relations with the Russians.

The other two assignments which the panel had—one was quite slight. We were asked to comment on whether the bomb should be used. I think the reason we were asked for that comment was because a petition had been sent in from a very distinguished and thoughtful group of scientists: "No, it should not be used." It would be better for everything that they should not. We didn't know beans about the military situation in Japan. We didn't know whether they could be caused to surrender by other means or whether the invasion was really inevitable. But in back of our minds was the notion that the invasion was inevitable because we had been told that. I have not been able to review this document, but what it said I think is characteristic of how technical people should answer questions.

We said that we didn't think that being scientists especially qualified us as to how to answer this question of how the bombs should be used or not; opinion was divided among us as it would be among other people if they knew about it. We thought the two overriding considerations were the saving of lives in the war and the effect of our actions on the stability, on our strength and the stability of the postwar world. We did say that we did not think exploding one of these things as a firecracker over a desert was likely to be very impressive. This was before we had actually done that. The destruction on the desert is zero, as I think Mr. Gray may be able to remember. He had seen all these tests.

[After citing lavish testimonials to Oppenheimer's wartime contribution from President Franklin D. Roosevelt and General Leslie R. Groves, Garrison provides excerpts from various public statements of Oppenheimer's regarding the control of nuclear energy. Then the hearing is adjourned for the day.]

Tuesday, April 13

GORDON GRAY: "Strictly confidential"

[When the hearing opens, Gordon Gray expresses his anger that the AEC's letter to Oppenheimer and his reply have been leaked to the press. Garrison and Oppenheimer explain the circumstances under which James Reston of the *New York Times* and Joseph and Stewart Alsop of the *New York Herald Tribune* obtained the material.]

MR. GRAY. I would like to call the proceeding to order.

The chairman of the board has a few observations to make, and I have a few questions to ask on behalf of the board.

I should like to read again for the record a statement which I made yesterday, that the proceedings and stenographic record of this board are regarded as strictly confidential between Atomic Energy Commission officials participating in this matter, and Dr. Oppenheimer, his representatives, and witnesses. The Atomic Energy Commission will not take the initiative in public release of any information relating to proceedings before this board.

The board views with very deep concern stories in the press which have been brought to the attention of members of the board. I personally have not had time to read the New York Times article, but I am told that both the Nichols letter to Dr. Oppenheimer, of December 23, and his reply of March 4, are reprinted in full. Without having any information whatsoever, I have to assume that this was given to the New York Times.

DR. OPPENHEIMER. It says so in the paper.

MR. GRAY. I do not suggest that represents a violation of security. I have a serious question about the spirit in keeping with the statement we made for the record yesterday about these proceedings being a matter of confidential relationship between the Commission and the board representing the Commission, and Dr. Oppenheimer and his representatives and witnesses.

We were told yesterday before this hearing began that you were doing all you could to keep this out of the press. You said you were late yesterday because you had "fingers in the dike," I believe was your expression, which I found somewhat confusing against subsequent events in the day when you say that you gave everything that you had to the press. We agreed yesterday that it would be very unfortunate to have this proceeding conducted in the press. There was no dissent from that view which was expressed, I believe, by all of us.

I think that it should be perfectly apparent, particularly to the attorneys involved, that this board faces real difficulties if each day matters about this proceeding appear, not on the basis of rumors or gossip, but on the basis of information handed directly to the press. I think it only fair to say for the record that the board is very much concerned.

I should like to ask some questions for the record about the authorized spokesman for Dr. Oppenheimer. I assume in addition to Dr. Oppenheimer that Mr. Garrison, Mr. Silverman, and Mr. Ecker are actively and officially associated in this proceeding.

I should like to ask who else is working on this who may be talking to the press?

Mr. GARRISON. Mr. Chairman, perhaps you could let me answer that question by a little history. The letter from the Commission was given on December 23. I came into the case early in January. Almost immediately, or perhaps the middle of January, it became quite apparent from inquiries that Mr. Reston addressed both to the Atomic Energy Commission and to Dr. Oppenheimer, that he already had information that clearance had been suspended, and that proceedings were going forward against Dr. Oppenheimer. He was most anxious to obtain background information from us.

We explained to him the nature of the proceedings and our earnest desire that this not be the subject—

Dr. OPPENHEIMER. May I correct that. Was this your conversation with Reston, because I believe the initial conversations were with me. He called and he was very persistent in calling. I tried to evade it. I knew what it would be about. After about 5 or 6 days of persistent telephoning, he talked to my wife, and said that he had this story and he wished I would talk to him.

I talked to him on the phone. I said I thought it contrary to the national interest that the story should be published, that I did not propose to discuss it with him, but if the time came when it was a public story, I would be glad to discuss it with him.

That was mid-January. I don't remember the date. I am depending on counsel's memory. I believe that was the substance of our talk. He told me two things. First, that my clearance had been revoked. That was the story he had heard. That this had been cabled, telegraphed, and broadcast to submarine commanders throughout the fleet and Army posts throughout the world, and second, that Senator McCarthy was fully aware of this and thought I ought to know that. That was the end of that discussion.

I was given to understand by proffers of kindness but not other sign that the Alsops knew the situation. Later this was confirmed by one of the prospective witnesses.

Mr. GRAY. You did not talk with either one of the Alsops?

Dr. OPPENHEIMER. I have not talked to either one of the Alsops until very recently, and I will describe those conversations. This was long ago, and it was my affair, and I thought my memory would be more vivid than yours.

MR. GARRISON. Why don't you tell of your conversation with the Alsops?

DR. OPPENHEIMER. That is not until very recently. Stewart Alsop called co-counsel, that is Herbert Marks, whose name should be in these proceedings—when would that have been, Saturday, Friday—quite recently, saying that they had the story and were frantic to publish, and that I should call Joe Alsop, who is up in Connecticut at a rest home.

MR. GARRISON. In Garrison, N.Y.

DR. OPPENHEIMER. I did call him there. I put on my spiel, the thing that I have said to everyone, that I thought this story coming out before the matter was resolved could do the country no good. Either I was a traitor and very, very important secrets had been in jeopardy over the last 12 years, or the Government was acting in a most peculiar way to take proceedings against me at this moment. This is the impression that I feared would be made. Neither impression could be good. Having both of them could be only doubly bad.

Therefore, not as far as I was concerned, but as far as what I thought was right, I urged Joe Alsop to hold his story, not to publish it. We did not discuss any substantive things except that Alsop told me how apprehensive he was that Senator McCarthy would come out with it. I believe that was all I said to Joe Alsop. He said he thought I was making a great mistake, but I said it was my mistake.

I recognized of course that he could publish any moment that he wanted to.

MR. GRAY. May I ask, as of this time or 10 o'clock yesterday morning, had you given the New York Times these documents?

DR. OPPENHEIMER. These documents were given to Reston by my counsel Friday night, I believe, without any instruction as to what he was to do with them, as background material.

MR. GRAY. So that you knew when you made the statement here yesterday morning that you were keeping the finger in the dike that these documents, dated December 23, and March 4, were already in the possession of the New York Times.

DR. OPPENHEIMER. Indeed we did.

MR. GARRISON. Mr. Chairman, they were given to Mr. Reston with instructions not to be used unless it became essential for the Times to release the story because others were going to do likewise. We hoped even as of yesterday—the last word we had with Mr. Reston was after lunch—we hoped even as of yesterday that this could be held off, although I told you at the start that it might be only a matter of hours.

MR. GRAY. You didn't indicate to me in any way—if you attempted to do so, it is a matter of my misinterpretation—that you had given documents which relate to these confidential proceedings and are part of these proceedings.

You mentioned Mr. Marks. Who else is authorized to speak for you, Dr. Oppenheimer?

MR. GARRISON. No one else. Mr. Marks is not counsel of record in this proceeding. He has been associated with us from the start because of his knowledge of past history. I am still seeking his guidance and help.

MR. GRAY. He is assisting, I take it, in preparing these documents which you present?

MR. GARRISON. No; we did all that work ourselves.

MR. GRAY. May I ask specifically for the record who prepared the excerpts about which I asked the question yesterday?

MR. GARRISON. We did in our own office. I did. Mr. Ecker worked on them.

MR. GRAY. I should like to know, Mr. Garrison, why it was yesterday that not one of the three of you could answer the question as to whether these paragraphs were consecutive or came from consecutive pages. It is apparent that someone else had prepared them.

MR. GARRISON. No, Mr. Chairman.

MR. GRAY. I have drawn a conclusion. If I am wrong—

MR. GARRISON. I am very sorry that such thoughts should even occur to you. What happened was that some weeks ago I went through Dr. Oppenheimer's writings and I marked particular sections and passages from a lot of them that seemed to me to be worthy of presentation to the board, and I asked that they be extracted and copied out. I have not been over them for some time. To be frank with you, I have had so much else to do.

MR. GRAY. My point in raising all this is that if there are a good number of people who are not appearing here who are going to be talking to the press, I would like to know what control or lack of control there may be in this situation. That is why I am raising this thing.

MR. GARRISON. Yes.

MR. GRAY. I think these stories are very prejudicial to the spirit of inquiry that I tried to establish as an atmosphere for this hearing as we started yesterday. I would very much regret that what would appear to be to the board possible lack of cooperation in conducting these proceedings in the press if that were prejudicial to what are the basic fundamental issues involved.

GORDON GRAY: "Those who are not cleared . . . will necessarily be excused"

[Dr. Mervin J. Kelly, a physicist who serves as president of the Bell Telephone Laboratory in New York City, now testifies, explaining that he first met Oppenheimer in 1946, and later served on a research and development board panel that Oppenheimer chaired. When his testimony deals with classified information, Oppenheimer's attorneys, who lack security clearance, must leave the room.]

DIRECT EXAMINATION

By Mr. Garrison: . . .

Q. What would you say as to Dr. Oppenheimer's reputation for straightforwardness, directness, veracity?

A. Among his peers, he is, first, known and recognized for his accuracy of
thought and cleanness of expression. His words are considered generally
well weighed and meaningful because of their accuracy and temperate. I
would know of no one that knew him as well as I that would feel that he
overstated his position.

As to his veracity and dedication, I know of no one in the program, with
the high clearances that he has had, and that I have, Q and top secret, everything he has done and said gives a full appearance to a great dedication, as
full an appearance as any of us that are in and still cleared.

Q. Would you say that as chairman of this panel he made a contribution to
the national welfare?

A. I am sure that he did. In the form that he writes all of his things, getting the
views of the full committee that he shared, as to what the forward looking
program should be, getting it clean, orderly, and well placed was a great
contribution, as anyone working in the atmosphere of the Pentagon knows
the great need for, that is, of getting direction and aim and purpose well
spelled out. It was in this report of the panel which was his fine, clean writing, but which was the views of all of us which he shared.

Q. What have you to say as to his reputation for integrity and patriotism and
your own personal feeling about that?

A. Among his peers, those who know him and know his work, I would say
his reputation is the highest. As to my own personal belief, I know of no one
in the program that I would have any more confidence in their integrity and
dedication than I would of Dr. Oppenheimer. . . .

By Mr. Robb: . . .

Q. Did you make any comment in your report on the matter of thermonuclear
warheads or fusion weapons?

A. I have not seen the report since it was issued. I would feel confident it was
not there because it was not a matter of discussion. If it was, that is 4 years
ago. I can't remember. It is three and a quarter years ago.

Mr. Robb. Mr. Chairman, I would like to read the witness something from the
report, which is classified.

The Witness. I have Q clearance; I can look at it.

Mr. Gray. In that event, those who are not cleared in this hearing room will
necessarily be excused.

Dr. Oppenheimer. Since this is a report I wrote, is this one I may listen to?

Mr. Robb. Absolutely, Doctor.

J. Robert Oppenheimer walking with his lawyer Lloyd K. Garrison, April 1954. Ralph Morse/TimePix.

MR. GARRISON. Mr. Chairman, we hoped that this might not arise, but if it is the feeling of the board that it is important to its own understanding of the case to put this kind of question, of course it is entirely acceptable to us, and we shall withdraw.

MR. GRAY. I believe that would be best, Mr. Garrison.

(Counsel for Dr. Oppenheimer withdrew.)

(Classified transcript deleted.)

MR. GRAY. Would you excuse me—

MR. ROBB. I think counsel can come back now.

MR. GRAY. That is what I was thinking. I don't want them excluded any more than necessary.

(Counsel for Dr. Oppenheimer returned to the hearing room.) . . .

J. ROBERT OPPENHEIMER: "When you see something that is technically sweet, you go ahead and do it"

[When Oppenheimer resumes testifying, Garrison asks him to discuss his work as chairman of the AEC's General Advisory Committee (GAC) from 1947 to 1952. Oppenheimer explains the nature of the reservations he expressed in 1949 when the GAC considered a crash program to develop the hydrogen bomb, and denies that he later tried to dissuade physicists from working on the weapon.]

Whereupon, J. Robert Oppenheimer resumed the stand as a witness, and having been previously sworn, was examined and testified further as follows:

DIRECT EXAMINATION (continued)

THE WITNESS. I had a communication. I can't find it as a letter, and I don't know whether it was a letter or phone call. It was from Dr. Conant. He said that this would be a very great mistake.

By Mr. Garrison:

Q. What would be a great mistake?

A. To go all out with the super. Presumably he also will testify to this. He did not go into detail, but said if it ever came before the General Advisory Committee, he would certainly oppose it as folly.

The General Advisory Committee was called to meet in Washington, and met on two questions which were obviously related. The first was, was the Commission doing what it ought to be doing. Were there other things which it should now be undertaking in the light of the Soviet explosion.

The second was the special case of this; was it crash development, the most rapid possible development and construction of a super among the things that the Commission ought to be doing.

Now I have reviewed for you in other connections some of the earlier hydrogen-bomb tale. The work on it in the summer of 1942, when we were quite enthusiastic about the possibility, my report on this work to Bush, the wartime work in which there were 2 discoveries, 1 was very much casting doubt on the feasibility, and 1 which had a more encouraging quality with regard to the feasibility. Of the talks with General Groves in which he had indicated that this was not something to rush into after the war. Of the early postwar work, prior to the establishment of the Commission. Of our encouragement to the Commission and thus to Los Alamos and also directly to Los Alamos to study the problem and get on with it in 1947 and 1948.

The GAC record shows I think that there were some thermonuclear devices that we felt were feasible and sensible and encouraged. I believe this was in 1948. But that we made a technically disparaging remark about the super in 1948. This was the judgment we then had. I remember that before 1949 and the bomb, Dr. Teller had discussed with me the desirability of his going to Los Alamos and devoting himself to this problem. I encouraged him to do this. In fact, he later reminded me of that, that I encouraged him in strong terms to do it.

Now, the meetings on—

By Mr. Garrison:

Q. The meeting of October 19?
A. The meeting of October 19, 1949. Have we the date right?
Mr. ROBB. October 29.
THE WITNESS. October 29. I think what we did was the following. We had a first meeting with the Commission at which they explained to us the double problem: What should they do and should they do this? We then consulted a number of people. * * *

We had consultations not with the Secretary of State, but with the head of the policy planning staff, who represented him, George Kennan, as to what he thought the Russians might be up to, and where our principal problems lay from the point of view of assessment of Russian behavior and Russian motives. We had consultations with the Military Establishment, . . .

Prior to this meeting there had been no great expression of interest on the part of the military in more powerful weapons. The atomic bomb had of course been stepped up some, but we had not been pressed to push that development as fast as possible. There had been no suggestion that very large weapons would be very useful. The pressure was all the other way; get as many as you can.

We discussed General Bradley's analysis of the effects of the Russian explosion, and what problems he faced and with the staff, of course.

Then we went into executive session. I believe I opened the session by asking Fermi to give an account of the technical state of affairs. He has always been interested in this possibility. I think it occurred to him very early that the high temperatures of a fission bomb might be usable in igniting lighter materials. He has also an extremely critical and clear head. I asked others to add to this. Then we went around the table and everybody said what he thought the issues were that were involved. There was a surprising unanimity—to me very surprising—that the United States ought not to take the initiative at that time in an all out program for the development of thermonuclear weapons.

Different people spoke in different ways. I don't know how available to you the actual record of this conversation is or even whether it fully exists. But there was not any difference of opinion in the final finding. I don't know whether this is the first thing we considered or whether we considered the Commission's other question first. I imagine we went back and forth between the two of them.

To the Commission's other question, were they doing enough, we answered no. Have you read this report, because if you have, my testimony about it will add nothing. . . .

By Mr. Garrison:

Q. I think you better say what you recollect of it.

A. I recollect of it that the first part of the report contained a series of affirmative recommendations about what the Commission should do. I believe all of them were directed toward weapons expansion, weapons improvement and weapons diversification. Some of them involved the building of new types of plant which would give a freedom of choice with regard to weapons. Some of them involved just a stepping up of the amount. I don't think that this expressed satisfaction with the current level of the Commission effort.

On the super program itself, I attempted to give a description of what this weapon was, of what would have to go into it, and what we thought the design would be. I explained that the uncertainties in this game were very great, that one would not know whether one had it or not unless one had built it and tested it, and that realistically one would have to expect not one test, but perhaps more than one test. That this would have to be a program of design and testing.

We had in mind, but I don't think we had clearly enough in mind, that we were talking about a single design which was in its essence frozen, and that the possibility did not occur to us very strongly that there might be quite other ways of going about it. Our report had a single structure in mind—or almost a single structure—whose characteristics in terms of blast, of damage, of explosive force, of course, and certainly we tried in the report to describe as faithfully as we knew how. I think in the report itself we were unanimous in hoping that the United States would not have to take the initiative in the development of this weapon. . . .

I find that the report has a letter of transmittal, that it has a section on affirmative actions to be taken, that it has a section on super bombs and that it has these two annexes of which you have heard.

As far as length is concerned, the section on affirmative actions and the section on super bombs are about equal, and I guess I can't tell you what is in the one on affirmative actions except in the very general terms I used before.

The first page of the page-and-a-half of the report on the super bomb is an account of what it is supposed to be, what has to be done in order to bring it about, and some semiquantitative notions of what it would take, what kind of damage it would do, and what kind of a program would be required. The essential point there is that as we then saw it, it was a weapon that you could not be sure of until you tried it out, and it is a problem of calculation and study, and then you went out in the proper place in the Pacific and found out whether it went bang and found out to what extent your ideas had been right and to what extent they had been wrong.

It is on the second page that we start talking about the extent of damage and the first paragraph is just a factual account of the kind of damage, the kind of carrier, and I believe I should not give it—I believe it is classified, even if it is not possibly entirely accurate.

I would like to state one conclusion which is that for anything but very large targets, this was not economical in terms of damage per dollar, and then even for large targets it was uncertain whether it would be economical in terms of damage per dollar. I am not claiming that this was good foresight, but I am just telling you what it says in here.

I am going to read two sentences:

"We all hope that by one means or another, the development of these weapons can be avoided. We are all reluctant to see the United States take the initiative in precipitating this development. We are all agreed that it would be wrong at the present moment to commit ourselves to an all-out effort towards its development."

This is the crux of it and it is a strong negative statement. We added to this some comments as to what might be declassified and what ought not to be declassified and held secret if any sort of a public statement were contemplated. If the President were going to say anything about it, there were some things we thought obvious and there would be no harm in mentioning them. Actually, the secret ones were out in the press before very long.

The phrase that you heard this morning, "We believe that the imaginative and concerted attack on the problem has a better than even chance of producing the weapon * * * "—I find that in this report, and in this report there is, therefore, no statement that it is unfeasible. There is a statement of uncertainty which I believed at the time was a good assessment. You would have found people who would have said this was too conservative, it could be done faster and more certainly, and you would find other people who would say that it could not be done at all; but the statement as read here, no member of the General Advisory Committee objected to, and I have heard very little objection to that as an assessment of the feasibility at that time.

This is the report itself, and there are parts of it which I think you should read but, for the record, there are parts that I cannot get into here.

MR. ROBB. Mr. Chairman, I think it might be well for the record to show at this point that the board has read the entire report. . . .

THE WITNESS. One important point to make is that lack of feasibility is not the ground on which we made our recommendations.

Another point I ought to make is that lack of economy, although alleged is not the primary or only ground, the competition with fission weapons is obviously in our minds. The real reason, the weight, behind the report is, in my opinion, a failing of the existence of these weapons would be a disadvantageous thing. It says this over and over again.

I may read, which I am sure has no security value, from the so-called minority report, Fermi and Rabi.

"The fact that no limits exist to the destructiveness of this weapon makes its very existence and the knowledge of its construction a danger to humanity as a whole. It is necessarily an evil thing considered in any light. For these reasons, we believe it important for the President of the United States to tell the American public and the world that we think it is wrong on fundamental ethical principles to initiate the development of such a weapon."

In the report which got to be known as the majority report, which Conant wrote, DuBridge, Buckley and I signed, things are not quite so ethical and fundamental, but it says in the final paragraph: "In determining not to proceed to develop the super bomb, we see a unique opportunity of providing by example some limitations on the totality of war and thus of eliminating the fear and arousing the hope of mankind."

I think it is very clear that the objection was that we did not like the weapon, not that it couldn't be made.

Now, it is a matter of speculation whether, if we had before us at that time, if we had had the technical knowledge and inventiveness which we did have somewhat later, we would have taken a view of this kind. These are total views where you try to take into account how good the thing is, what the enemy is likely to do, what you can do with it, what the competition is, and the extent to which this is an inevitable step anyway.

My feeling about the delay in the hydrogen bomb, and I imagine you want to question me about it, is that if we had had good ideas in 1945, and had we wanted to, this object might have been in existence in 1947 or 1948, perhaps 1948. If we had had all of the good ideas in 1949, I suppose some little time might have been shaved off the development as it actually occurred. If we had not had good ideas in 1951, I do not think we would have it today. In other words, the question of delay is keyed in this case to the question of invention, and I think the record should show—it is known to you—that the principal inventor in all of this business was Teller, with many important contributions * * * other people, * * * It has not been quite a one-man show, but he has had some very, very good ideas, and they have kept coming. It is probably true that an idea of mine is embodied in all of these things. It is not very ingenious but it turned out to be very useful, and it was not enough to establish feasibility or have a decisive bearing on their feasibility.

The notion that the thermonuclear arms race was something that was in the interests of this country to avoid if it could was very clear to us in 1949. We may have been wrong. We thought it was something to avoid even if we could jump the gun by a couple of years, or even if we could outproduce the enemy, because we were infinitely more vulnerable and infinitely less likely to initiate the use of these weapons, and because the world in which great destruction has been done in all civilized parts of the world is a harder world for America to live with than it is for the Communists to live with. This is an idea which I believe is still right, but I think what was not clear to us then and what is clearer to me now is that it probably lay wholly beyond our power to prevent the Russians somehow from getting ahead with it. I think if we could have taken any action at that time which would have precluded their development of this weapon, it would have been a very good bet to take that, I am sure. I do not know enough about contemporary intelligence to say whether or not our actions have had any effect on theirs but you have ways of finding out about that.

I believe that their atomic effort was quite imitative and that made it quite natural for us to think that their thermonuclear work would be quite imitative and that we should not set the pace in this development. I am trying to explain what I thought and what I believe my friends thought. I am not arguing that this is right, but I am clear about one thing: if this affair could have been averted on the part of the Russians, I am quite clear that we would be in a safer world today by far.

MR. GRAY. Would you repeat that last sentence. I didn't quite get it.

THE WITNESS. If the development by the enemy as well as by us of thermonuclear weapons could have been averted, I think we would be in a somewhat safer world today than we are. God knows, not entirely safe because atomic bombs are not jolly either.

I remember a few comments at that meeting that I believe it best that people who are coming here to testify speak for themselves about; I am not sure my memory is right—comments of Fermi, of Conant, of Rabi, and of DuBridge as to how they felt about it. . . .

I think we have to keep strictly away from the technical questions. I do not think we want to argue technical questions here, and I do not think it is very meaningful for me to speculate as to how we would have responded had the technical picture at that time been more as it was later.

However, it is my judgment in these things that when you see something that is technically sweet, you go ahead and do it and you argue about what to do about it only after you have had your technical success. That is the way it was with the atomic bomb. I do not think anybody opposed making it; there were some debates about what to do with it after it was made. I cannot very well imagine if we had known in late 1949 what we got to know by early 1951 that the tone of our report would have been the same. You may ask other people how they feel about that. I am not at all sure they will concur: some will and some will not. . . .

I believe that in every subsequent GAC report where we gave advice on the thermonuclear program, on the super part of it or the other parts of it, that the problem before us was what to do and how to get on with it, what made sense and what did not make sense, and that the moral and ethical and political issues which are touched on in these two annexes were never again mentioned, and that we never again questioned the basic decisions under which we were operating.

We tried, I think, throughout to point out where the really critical questions were. There was a tendency in this job, as in many others, to try to solve the easy problems and try to leave the really tough ones unworried about, and I think we kept rubbing on the toughest one, that this had to be looked into. That was done not completely; perhaps it is not absolutely done completely today, but the situation developed in a most odd way because, by the spring and summer of 1951, things were not stuck in the sense that there was nothing to do, but they were stuck in the sense that there was no program of which you could see the end.

Now, different people responded differently to that. Teller also pointed out quite rightly that there were other possibilities that might turn up and other people took a very categorical view that the whole business was nonsense.

MR. GARRISON. Scientifically nonsense.

THE WITNESS. Scientifically nonsense. I believe my own record was one that it looked sour but we have had lots of surprises and let's keep open-minded. . . .

It is also alleged that I kept people from working on the hydrogen bomb. If by that it is meant that a knowledge of our views which got to be rather widespread had an effect, I cannot deny it because I don't know, but I think I can deny that I ever talked anybody out of working on the hydrogen bomb or desired to talk anybody out of working on the hydrogen bomb. You will have some testimony on this, but since I don't know who the people are who are referred to in the General Manager's letter, what I say might not be entirely responsive. . . .

In the late summer and autumn of 1950, I had an obvious personal worry. I had made as chairman, and had participated in, the recommendation against the development of the super. The super was a big item on the program. It wasn't going very well, and I wondered whether another man might not make a better chairman for the General Advisory Committee. I discussed it with several physicists. I remember discussing it with Teller and

Bacher. Teller says that he does not remember discussing it with me. The general advice was: Let's all stick together as well as we can and don't resign and don't change your position.

MR. ROBB. What was that date?

THE WITNESS. In the summer of 1950.

When I got back in the autumn of 1950, the first meeting, I went to see Mr. Dean, who was Chairman of the Commission, and Commissioner Smyth and told them about my problem, and they said that obviously the chairman should be someone who would be comfortable with them—what would be their suggestions? They protested in very forceful terms that I should not quit as chairman, and that they would be very unhappy if I did, that I ought to carry on.

I also took the thing up with our committee, but our committee was not a very responsive group when it came to electing other chairmen, and I got no place. I did not feel that I ought to resign as chairman or refuse to serve. I thought I ought to do what was comfortable for the Commission and the committee, and I tried to ascertain what that was. . . .

I would like to summarize a little bit this long story I think you will hear from people who believed at the time, and believe now that the advice we gave in 1949 was wrong. You will hear from people who believed at the time and who even believe now that the advice we gave in 1949 was right. I myself would not take either of these extreme views.

I think we were right in believing that any method available consistent with honor and security for keeping these objects out of the arsenals of the enemy would have been a good course to follow. I don't believe we were very clear and I don't believe we were ever very agreed as to what such course might be, or whether such a course existed. I think that if we had had at that time the technical insight that I now have, we would have concluded that it was almost hopeless to keep this resource out of the enemy hands and maybe we would have given up even suggesting that it be tried. I think if we had had that technical knowledge, then we should have recommended that we go ahead full steam, and then or in 1948 or 1946 or 1945.

I don't want to conceal from you, and I have said it in public speeches so it would not make much sense to conceal from you the dual nature of the hopes which we entertained about the development of bigger and bigger weapons, first the atomic bomb, and then its amplified version, and then these new things.

On the one hand, as we said at the time, and as I now firmly believe, this stuff is going to put an end to major total wars. I don't know whether it will do so in our lifetime. On the other hand, the notion that this will have to come about by the employment of these weapons on a massive scale against civilizations and cities has always bothered me. I suppose that bother is part of the freight I took into the General Advisory Committee, and into the meetings that discussed the hydrogen bomb. No other person may share that view, but I do.

[Garrison presents an affidavit from Dr. John H. Manley, chair of the physics department at the University of Washington, who served as secretary of the General Advisory Committee from 1946 to 1951, stating that Oppenheimer "is in no sense whatever a security risk." Garrison then introduces further testimonials to Oppenheimer's varied contributions from former president Harry S. Truman and former AEC chairman, Gordon Dean, after which the hearing adjourns.]

Wednesday, April 14

J. Robert Oppenheimer: "Both an older brother and in some ways perhaps . . . a father"

[Garrison concludes his direct examination by asking Oppenheimer to describe his relationship with his brother, Frank, who has admitted that he was once a member of the Communist Party.]

DIRECT EXAMINATION (continued)

By Mr. Garrison:

Q. Dr. Oppenheimer, will you tell the board something about your brother Frank, your relations with him?

A. He was 8 years my junior.

Q. It was just you and Frank in the family?

A. We were the only children. I think I was both an older brother and in some ways perhaps part of a father to him because of that age difference. We were close during our childhood, although the age gap made our interests different. We sailed together. We bicycled together. In 1929 we rented a little ranch up in the high mountains in New Mexico which we have had ever since, and we used to spend as much time there as we could in the summer. For my part that was partly for reasons of health, but it was also a very nice place.

My brother had learned to be a very expert flutist. I think he could have been a professional. He decided to study physics. Since I was a physicist this produced a kind of rivalry. He went abroad to study. He studied at Cambridge and at Florence. He went to college before that at Johns Hopkins.

When he came back to this country; he did take his doctor's degree at the California Institute of Technology.

We were quite close, very fond of one another. He was not a very disciplined young man. I guess I was not either. He loved painting. He loved music. He was an expert horseman. We spent most of our time during the summer fiddling around with horses and fixing up the ranch.

In the very first year he had two young friends with him who were about his age, and I was the old man of the party. He read quite widely, but I am afraid very much as I did, belles lettres, poetry.

DR. EVANS. Was your father there at that time?

THE WITNESS. My father was alive. He did occasionally visit at the ranch. His heart was not very good. This is almost 10,000 feet high, so he did not spend much time there. We could not put him up. It was a very primitive sort of establishment. There was of course the tension which a very intimate family relation of this kind always involves, but there was great affection between us.

He worked fairly well at physics but he was slow. It took him a long time to get his doctor's degree. He was very much distracted by his other interests.

In 1936, I guess it was, he met his present wife and married. I am not completely sure of the date, but I could check it. After that, a good deal of the warmth of our relations remained, but they were less intimate and occasionally perhaps somewhat more strained. His wife had, I think, some friends and connections with the radical circles in Berkeley. She was a student there. She had a very different background than Frank. She certainly interested him for the first time in politics and left-wing things. It was a great bond between them.

As I wrote in my answer, not very long after their marriage they both joined the Communist Party. This was in Pasadena. I don't know how long thereafter, but not very long thereafter, Frank came to Berkeley and told me of this. We continued to be close as brothers are, but not as it had been before his marriage.

He once asked me and another fellow to come visit one of the meetings that he had in his house, which was a Communist Party meeting. It is, I think, the only thing recognizeable to me as a Communist Party meeting that I have ever attended. . . .

DR. EVANS. This was not a closed meeting of the Communist Party?

THE WITNESS. It was not closed because it had visitors. I understood the rest of the people were Communists. This was on the occasion of one of my visits to Berkeley and Pasadena. The meeting made no detailed impression on me, but I do remember there was a lot of fuss about getting the literature distributed, and I do remember that the principal item under discussion was segregation in the municipal pool in Pasadena. This unit was concerned about that and they talked about it. It made a rather pathetic impression on me. It was a mixed unit of some colored people and some who were not colored.

I remember vividly walking away from the meeting with Bridges and his saying, "What a sad spectacle" or "What a pathetic sight," or something like that.

MR. GRAY. Did you give the approximate date of this, Doctor?

THE WITNESS. I can give it roughly.

MR. GRAY. I mean within a year.

THE WITNESS. It would have been not before 1937 or after 1939. I think I ought to stress that although my brother was a party member, he did a lot of other things. As I say, he was passionately fond of music. He had many wholly non-Communist friends, some of them the same as my friends on the faculty at Caltech. He was working for a doctor's degree.

He spent summers at the ranch. He couldn't have been a very hard working Communist during those years.

I am very foggy as to what I knew about the situation at Stanford but my recollection is that I did not then know my brother was still in the party. He has testified that he was, and that he withdrew in the spring of 1941. He lost his job at Stanford. I never clearly understood the reasons for that, but I thought it might be connected with his communism.

We spent part of the summer of 1941 together at the ranch, about a month. That was after my marriage. He and his wife stayed on a while. Then they were out of a job. Ernest Lawrence asked him to come to Berkeley in the fall, I don't remember the date, but I think it is of record, and work in the radiation laboratory. That was certainly at the time not for secret work. He and I saw very little of each other that year.

My brother felt that he wanted to establish an independent existence in Berkeley where I had lived a long time, and didn't want in any sense to be my satellite. He did become involved in secret work, I suppose, shortly after Pearl Harbor. I don't know the precise date.

He continued with it and worked terribly hard during the war. I have heard a great many people tell me what a vigorous and helpful guy he was, how many hours he spent at work, how he got everybody to put their best to the job that was his. He worked in Berkeley. He worked in Oak Ridge. He came for a relatively brief time to New Mexico, where his job was as an assistant to Bainbridge in making the preparations for the test of July 16.

This was a job that combined practical experience, technical experience, a feeling for the country, and I think he did very well. He left very early— left long before I did—and went back to Berkeley. We did not see him again until the New Year's holidays in 1945 and 1946. After that, when we came back to Berkeley, we saw something of them, quite a little of them, until they moved to Minnesota.

As you probably know, he resigned from the University of Minnesota— his assistant professorship there—in the spring of 1949 at the time he was testifying before the House committee that he had been a member of the Communist Party. The university accepted his resignation. He has not been able to get a job since, or at least not one that made sense.

He had in the summer of 1948, maybe, or the winter of 1948–49, acquired a piece of property in southwest Colorado. It is also fairly high. It is in the Blanco Basin. I think he got it because it was very beautiful, and thought it would be nice to spend summers there. In any case, he and his wife and children moved up there, and have been trying to build it up as a cattle ranch ever since. They have been there, I think, with no important exceptions, from 1949 until today. This life is not what he was cut out for and I don't know how it will go.

I try to see him when I can. It does not come out to being much more than once a year. I think the last time I saw him was in late September or October of last year. Usually he would come down to Santa Fe, and we would have an evening together or something like that. I had the feeling the last time that I saw him that he was thoroughly and wholly and absolutely away from this nightmare which has been going on for many, many years.

These are at least some of the things that I wanted to say. I would like to say one more thing.

In the Commission's letter—

By Mr. Garrison:

Q. Perhaps I could ask you about that.

On page 6 of the Commission's letter, which talks about Haakon Chevalier, there is a statement, I am quoting, "that Haakon Chevalier thereupon approached you either directly or through your brother, Frank Friedman Oppenheimer, in connection with this matter."

Was your brother connected with this approach by Chevalier to you?

A. I am very clear on this. I have a vivid and I think certainly not fallible memory. He had nothing whatever to do with it. It would not have made any sense, I may say, since Chevalier was my friend. I don't mean that my brother did not know him, but this would have been a peculiarly roundabout and unnatural thing.

Q. You spoke about attending at your brother's invitation that little Communist Party meeting in Pasadena somewhere in the late thirties, and that reminds me to ask you about another portion of the Commission's letter.

On page 3, I will just read a paragraph:

"It was reported that you attended a closed meeting of the professional section of the Communist Party of Alameda County, Calif., which was held in the latter part of July or early August, 1941, at your residence, 10 Kenilworth Court, Berkeley, Calif., for the purpose of hearing an explanation of the change in Communist party policy. It was further reported that you denied that you attended such a meeting and that such a meeting was held in your home."

Dr. Oppenheimer, did you attend a closed meeting of the professional section of the Communist Party of Alameda County which is said to have been held in your house in the latter part of July or early August, 1941?

A. No.

Q. Did you ever attend at any time or place a closed meeting of the professional section of the Communist Party of Alameda County?

A. No.

Q. Were you ever asked to lend your house for such a meeting?

A. No.

Q. Did you ever belong to the professional section of the Communist Party of Alameda County?

A. I did not. I would be fairly certain that I never knew of its existence.

Q. Did you ever belong to any other section or unit of the Communist Party or to the Communist Party?

A. No.

Q. Apart from the meeting in Pasadena, to which we have just referred, have you ever attended a meeting which you understood to be open only to Communist Party members, other than yourself?

A. No.

Q. Have you ever had in your house at any time any meeting at which a lecture about the Communist Party has been given?

A. No.

Q. Do you recall any meeting in your house at any time at which a lecture about political affairs of any sort was given?

A. No. . . .

J. Robert Oppenheimer: "In the case of a brother you don't make tests"

[Roger Robb begins his cross-examination of Oppenheimer and quickly moves to the issue of Robert's left-wing affiliations and Frank's membership in the Communist Party. He then questions Oppenheimer about several former students whom he knew to hold radical views yet recommended for positions at Los Alamos.]

CROSS-EXAMINATION

By Mr. Robb: . . .

Q. Doctor, in your opinion, is association with the Communist movement compatible with a job on a secret war project?

A. Are we talking of the present; the past?

Q. Let us talk about the present and then we will go to the past.

A. Obviously not.

Q. Has that always been your opinion?

A. No. I was associated with the Communist movement, as I have spelled out in my letter, and I did not regard it as inappropriate to take the job at Los Alamos.

Q. When did that become your opinion?

A. As the nature of the enemy and the nature of the conflict and the nature of the party all became clearer. I would say after the war and probably by 1947.

Q. Was it your opinion in 1943?

A. No.

Q. You are sure about that?

A. That association—

Q. With the Communist movement.

A. The current association?

Q. Yes.

A. I always thought current association—

Q. You always thought that?

A. That is right.

Q. There had never been any question in your mind that a man who is closely associated with the Communist movement or is a member of the Communist Party has no business on a secret war project; is that right?

A. That is right.

Q. Why did you have that opinion? What was your reason for it?

A. It just made no sense to me.

Q. Why not.

A. That a man who is working on secret things should have any kind of loyalty to another outfit.

Q. Why did you think that the two loyalties were inconsistent?

A. They might be.

Q. Why?

A. Because the Communist Party had its own affairs, and its own program which obviously I now know were inconsistent with the best interests of the United States, but which could at any time have diverged from those of the United States.

Q. You would not think that loyalty to a church would be inconsistent with work on a secret war project, would you?

A. No.

Q. And of course that was not your view in 1943, was it?

A. No.

Q. Doctor, what I am trying to get at is, What specifically was your reason for thinking that membership or close association with the Communist Party and the loyalties necessarily involved were inconsistent with work on a secret war project?

A. The connection of the Communist Party with a foreign power.

Q. To wit, Russia.

A. Sure.

Q. Would you say that connection with a foreign power, to wit, England, would necessarily be inconsistent?

A. Commitment would be.

Q. No; I said connection.

A. Not necessarily. You could be a member of the English speaking union.

Q. What I am getting at, Doctor, is what particular feature of the Communist Party did you feel was inconsistent with work on a secret war project?

A. After the Chevalier incident I could not be unaware of the danger of espionage. After the conversations with the Manhattan District security officers,
I could not be but acutely aware of it.

Q. But you have told me, Doctor, that you always felt that membership or
close association in the Communist Party was inconsistent with work on a
secret war project. What I am asking you, sir, is why you felt that. Surely
you had a reason for feeling that, didn't you?

A. I am not sure. I think it was an obviously correct judgment.

Q. Yes, sir. But what I am asking you is to explain to me why it was obvious
to you.

A. Because to some extent, an extent which I did not fully realize, the Communist Party was connected with the Soviet Union, the Soviet Union was a
potentially hostile power, it was at that time an ally, and because I had been
told that when you were a member of the party, you assumed some fairly
solemn oath or obligation to do what the party told you.

Q. Espionage, if necessary, isn't that right?

A. I was never told that.

Q. Who told you, Doctor?

A. My wife.

Q. When?

A. I don't remember.

Q. Prior to 1943?

A. Oh, yes.

Q. Doctor, let me ask you a blunt question. Don't you know and didn't you
know certainly by 1943 that the Communist Party was an instrument or a
vehicle of espionage in this country?

A. I was not clear about it.

Q. Didn't you suspect it?

A. No.

Q. Wasn't that the reason why you felt that membership in the party was inconsistent with the work on a secret war project?

A. I think I have stated the reason about right.

Q. I am asking you now if your fear of espionage wasn't one of the reasons
why you felt that association with the Communist Party was inconsistent
with work on a secret war project?

A. Yes.

Q. Your answer is that it was?

A. Yes.

Q. What about former members of the party; do you think that where a man
has formerly been a member of the party he is an appropriate person to
work on a secret war project?

A. Are we talking about now or about then?

Q. Let us ask you now, and then we will go back to then.

A. I think that depends on the character and the totality of the disengagement
and what kind of a man he is, whether he is an honest man.

Q. Was that your view in 1941, 1942, and 1943?

A. Essentially.

Q. What test do you apply and did you apply in 1941, 1942, and 1943 to satisfy yourself that a former member of the party is no longer dangerous?

A. As I said, I knew very little about who was a former member of the party. In my wife's case, it was completely clear that she was no longer dangerous. In my brother's case, I had confidence in his decency and straightforwardness and in his loyalty to me.

Q. Let us take your brother as an example. Tell us the test that you applied to acquire the confidence that you have spoken of?

A. In the case of a brother you don't make tests, at least I didn't.

Q. Well—

A. I knew my brother.

Q. When did you decide that your brother was no longer a member of the party and no longer dangerous?

A. I never regarded my brother as dangerous. I never regarded him—the fact that a member of the Communist Party might commit espionage did not mean to me that every member of the Communist Party would commit espionage.

Q. I see. In other words, you felt that your brother was an exception to the doctrine which you have just announced?

A. No; I felt that though there was danger of espionage that this was not a general danger.

Q. In other words, you felt—I am talking now about 1943—that members of the Communist Party might work on a secret war project without danger to this country; is that right?

A. Yes. What I have said was that there was danger that a member of the Communist Party would not be a good security risk. This does not mean that every member would be, but that it would be good policy to make that rule.

Q. Do you still feel that way?

A. Today I feel it is absolute.

Q. You feel that no member of the Communist Party should work on a secret war project in this country, without exception?

A. With no exception.

Q. When did you reach that conclusion?

A. I would think the same timing that I spoke of before as the obvious war between Russia and the United States began to shape up.

Q. Could you give us the dates on that?

A. Sure. I would have thought that it was completely clear to me by 1948, maybe 1947.

Q. 1946?

A. I am not sure.

Q. Doctor, let me return a bit to the test that you might apply to determine whether a member of the Communist Party in 1943 was dangerous. What test would you apply, or would you have applied in 1943?

A. Only the knowledge of the man and his character.

Q. Just what you yourself knew about him?

A. I didn't regard myself as the man to settle these questions. I am stating opinions.

Q. That is what I am getting at. You have testified that your brother, to your knowledge, became a member of the Communist Party about 1936; is that right?

A. Yes, 1937, I don't know.

Q. When is it your testimony that your brother left the party?

A. His testimony, which I believe, is that he left the party in the spring of 1941.

Q. When did you first hear that he left the party?

A. I think in the autumn of 1941.

Q. In the autumn?

A. Yes.

Q. Is that when he went to Berkeley to work in the Radiation Laboratory?

A. Yes, on unclassified work.

Q. But he shortly began to work on classified work, is that right?

A. The time interval, I think, was longer.

Q. Shortly after that. Shortly after Pearl Harbor?

A. I am not clear about that. It was within a year certainly, probably about 6 months.

Frank Oppenheimer after testifying before the House Committee on Un-American Activities, 1949. Popperfoto/ Archive Photos.

Q. You were satisfied at that time that your brother was not a member of the party any more?

A. Yes.

Q. How did you reach that conclusion?

A. He told me.

Q. That was enough for you?

A. Sure.

Q. Did you know that your brother at that time and for quite a while after that denied both publicly and officially that he had ever been a member of the Communist Party?

A. I remember one such denial in 1947.

Q. Did you know that your brother's personnel security questionnaire, which he executed when he went to work at Berkeley, failed to disclose his membership in the Communist Party?

A. No, I knew nothing about that.

Q. Did you ask him about that?

A. No.

Q. You knew, didn't you, sir, that it was a matter of great interest and importance to the security officers to determine whether or not anyone working on the project had been a member of the Communist Party?

A. I found that out somewhat later.

Q. Didn't you know it at that time?

A. It would have made sense.

Q. In 1941?

A. It would have made sense.

Q. Yes. Did you tell anybody, any security officer or anybody else, that your brother had been a member of the Communist Party? Did you tell them that in 1941?

A. I told Lawrence that my brother—I don't know the terms I used—but I certainly indicated that his trouble at Stanford came from his Red connections.

Q. Doctor, I didn't ask you quite that question. Did you tell Lawrence or anybody else that your brother, Frank, had actually been a member of the Communist Party?

A. I doubt it.

Q. Why not?

A. I thought this was the sort of thing that would be found out by normal security check.

Q. You were not helping the security check, were you, sir?

A. I would had if I had been asked.

Q. Otherwise not?

A. I didn't volunteer this information.

Q. You think your brother today would be a good security risk?

A. I rather think so.

Q. Beg pardon?

A. I think so.

Q. Doctor, will you agree with me that when a man has been a member of the

Communist Party, the mere fact that he says that he is no longer a member, and that he apparently has no present interest or connections in the party, does not show that he is no longer dangerous as a security risk?

A. I agree with that.

Q. Beg pardon?

A. I agree with that.

Q. You agree with that.

A. I would add the fact that he was in the party in 1942 or 1938, did not prove that he was dangerous. It merely created a presumption of danger. This is my view, and I am not advocating it.

Q. In other words, what you are saying is that a man's denial that he is a member and his apparent lack of interest or connections is not conclusive by any means; is it?

A. No.

Q. Did you feel that way in 1943?

A. I would think so.

Q. Or 1942?

A. I would think so. I need to state that I didn't think very much about the questions you are putting and very little in the terms in which you are putting them. Therefore, my attempt to tell you what I thought is an attempt at reconstruction.

Q. Yes, but you couldn't conceive that you would have had a different opinion in 1943 on a question such as that, would you, Doctor?

A. No.

Q. Have you ever been told, Doctor, that it was the policy of the Communist Party, certainly as early as 1943, or say certainly as early as 1941, that when a man entered confidential war work, he was not supposed to remain a member of the party?

A. No.

Q. No one has ever told you that?

A. No.

Q. Can you be sure about that, sir? Does that statement come as a surprise to you?

A. I never heard any statement about the policy of the party.

Q. Doctor, I notice in your answer on page 5 you use the expression "fellow travelers." What is your definition of a fellow traveler, sir?

A. It is a repugnant word which I used about myself once in an interview with the FBI. I understood it to mean someone who accepted part of the public program of the Communist Party, who was willing to work with and associate with Communists, but who was not a member of the party.

Q. Do you think though a fellow traveler should be employed on a secret war project?

A. Today?

Q. Yes, sir.

A. No.

Q. Did you feel that way in 1942 and 1943?

A. My feeling then and my feeling about most of these things is that the judgment is an integral judgment of what kind of a man you are dealing with. Today I think association with the Communist Party or fellow traveling with the Communist Party manifestly means sympathy for the enemy. In the period of the war, I would have thought that it was a question of what the man was like, what he would and wouldn't do. Certainly fellow traveling and party membership raised a question and a serious question.

Q. Were you ever a fellow traveler?

A. I was a fellow traveler. . . .

Q. Doctor, do you think that social contacts between a person employed in secret war work and Communists or Communist adherents is dangerous?

A. Are we talking about today?

Q. Yes.

A. Certainly not necessarily so. They could conceivably be.

Q. Was that your view in 1943 and during the war years?

A. Yes; I think it would have been. My awareness of the danger would be greater today.

Q. But it is fair to say that during the war years you felt that social contacts between a person employed in secret war work and Communists or Communist adherents were potentially dangerous; is that correct?

A. Were conceivably dangerous. I visited Jean Tatlock in the spring of 1943. I almost had to. She was not much of a Communist, but she was certainly a member of the party. There was nothing dangerous about that. There was nothing potentially dangerous about that.

Q. But you would have felt then, I assume, that a rather continued or constant association between a person employed on the atomic-bomb project and Communists or Communist adherents was dangerous?

A. Potentially dangerous; conceivably dangerous. Look, I have had a lot of secrets in my head a long time. It does not matter who I associate with. I don't talk about those secrets. Only a very skillful guy might pick up a trace of information as to where I had been or what I was up to. Passing the time of day with a Communist—I don't think it is wise, but I don't see that it is necessarily dangerous if the man is discreet and knows what he is up to.

Q. Why did you think that social contacts during the war years between persons on the project—by the project, I mean the atomic-bomb project—and Communists or Communist adherents involved a possibility of danger?

A. We were really fantastic in what we were trying to keep secret there. The people who were there, the life, all of us were supposed to be secret. Even a normal account of a man's friends was something that we didn't want to get out. "I saw the Fermis last night"—that was not the kind of thing to say.

This was a rather unusual kind of blanket of secrecy. I don't think, if a Communist knows that I am going to Washington to visit the AEC, that is going to give him any information. But it was desired that there be no knowledge of who was at Los Alamos, or at least no massive knowledge of it.

Q. Did you have any talk with your brother, Frank, about his social contacts at the time he come on the project?

A. When he came to work for Ernest Lawrence, before there was any classified work, before I knew about it and before he was involved in it, I warned
him that Ernest would fire him if he was not a good boy. That is about all I
remember.

Q. You didn't discuss with him his social contacts?

A. No.

Q. Either at that time or subsequently?

A. If you mean did he ever tell me that he had seen So-and-So, I don't know.

Q. No.

A. I don't believe we had a systematic discussion.

Q. Did you ever urge him to give up any social contacts who might have been
Communists or Communist adherents?

A. I don't know the answer to that. It doesn't ring a bell.

Q. If you did, it made no impression on you?

A. Not enough to last these years. . . .

J. ROBERT OPPENHEIMER: "Then I invented a cock-and-bull story"

[Robb now directs his questions to Oppenheimer's failure to notify the security forces at Los Alamos in 1943 after his friend Haakon Chevalier mentioned that a mutual acquaintance, George Eltenton, had suggested it might
be possible to obtain secret information for the Soviet Union.]

Q. . . . Doctor, on page 22 of your letter of March 4, 1954, you speak of what
for convenience I will call the Eltenton-Chevalier incident.

A. That is right.

Q. You describe the occasion when Chevalier spoke to you about this matter. Would you please, sir, tell the board as accurately as you can and in
as much detail as you can exactly what Chevalier said to you, and you
said to Chevalier, on the occasion that you mention on page 22 of your
answer?

A. This is one of those things that I had so many occasions to think about that
I am not going to remember the actual words. I am going to remember the
nature of the conversation.

Q. Where possible I wish you would give us the actual words.

A. I am not going to give them to you.

Q. Very well.

A. Chevalier said he had seen George Eltenton recently.

MR. GRAY. May I interrupt just a moment? I believe it would be useful for Dr.
Oppenheimer to describe the circumstances which led to the conversation,
whether he called you or whether this was a casual meeting.

MR. ROBB. Yes, sir.

THE WITNESS. He and his wife—

By Mr. Robb:

Q. May I interpose, Doctor? Would you begin at the beginning and tell us exactly what happened?

A. Yes. One day, and I believe you have the time fixed better than I do in the winter of 1942–43, Haakon Chevalier came to our home. It was, I believe, for dinner, but possibly for a drink. When I went out into the pantry, Chevalier followed me or came with me to help me. He said, "I saw George Eltenton recently." Maybe he asked me if I remembered him. That Eltenton had told him that he had a method, he had means of getting technical information to Soviet scientists. He didn't describe the means. I thought I said "But that is treason," but I am not sure. I said anyway something, "This is a terrible thing to do." Chevalier said or expressed complete agreement. That was the end of it. It was a very brief conversation.

Q. That is all that was said?

A. Maybe we talked about the drinks or something like that.

Q. I mean about this matter, Doctor, had Chevalier telephoned you or communicated with you prior to that occasion to ask if he might see you?

A. I don't think so. I don't remember. We saw each other from time to time. If we were having dinner together it would not have gone just this way. Maybe he called up and said he would like to come.

Q. It could have been that he called you and you said come over for dinner; is that correct?

A. Any of these things could have been.

Q. You said in the beginning of your recital of this matter that you have described that occasion on many, many occasions; is that right?

A. Yes.

Q. Am I to conclude from that that it has become pretty well fixed in your mind?

A. I am afraid so.

Q. Yes, sir. It is a twice told tale for you.

A. It certainly is.

Q. It is not something that happened and you forget it and then thought about it next, 10 years later, is that correct?

A. That is right.

Q. Did Chevalier in that conversation say anything to you about the use of microfilm as a means of transmitting this information?

A. No.

Q. You are sure of that?

A. Sure.

Q. Did he say anything about the possibility that the information would be transmitted through a man at the Soviet consulate?

A. No; he did not.

Q. You are sure about that?

A. I am sure about that.

Q. Did he tell you or indicate to you in any way that he had talked to anyone but you about this matter?

A. No.

Q. You are sure about that?

A. Yes.

Q. Did you learn from anybody else or hear that Chevalier had approached anybody but you about this matter?

A. No.

Q. You are sure about that?

A. That is right.

Q. You had no indication or no information suggesting to you that Chevalier had made any other approach than the one to you?

A. No.

Q. You state in your description of this incident in your answer that you made some strong remarks to Chevalier. Was that your remark, that this is treasonous?

A. It was a remark that either said—this is a path that has been walked over too often, and I don't remember what terms I said this is terrible.

Q. Didn't you use the word "treason"?

A. I can tell you the story of the word "treason."

Q. Would you answer that and then explain?

A. I don't know.

Q. You don't know now?

A. No, I don't know.

Q. Did you think it was treasonous?

A. I thought it was terrible.

Q. Did you think it was treasonous?

A. To take information from the United States and ship it abroad illicitly, sure.

Q. In other words, you thought that the course of action suggested to Eltenton was treasonous.

A. Yes.

Q. Since Eltenton was not a citizen, if it was not treasonous, it was criminal; is that correct?

A. Of course.

Q. In other words, you thought that the course of conduct suggested to Eltenton was an attempt at espionage; didn't you?

A. Sure.

Q. There is no question about it. Let me ask you, sir: Did you know this man Eltenton?

A. Yes; not well.

Q. How had you come to know him?

A. Perhaps "know" is the wrong word. I had met him a couple of times.

Q. How?

A. I remember one occasion which was not when I met him, but when I remember seeing him. I don't remember the occasion of my meeting him. Do you want me to describe the occasion I saw him?

Q. Yes, sir.

A. I am virtually certain of this. Some time after we moved to Eagle Hill, possibly in the autumn of 1941, a group of people came to my house one afternoon to discuss whether or not it would be a good idea to set up a branch of the Association of Scientific Workers. We concluded negatively, and I know my own views were negative. I think Eltenton was present at that meeting.

DR. EVANS. What was that?

THE WITNESS. I think Eltenton was present at that time. That is not the first time I met him, but it is one of the few times I can put my finger on.

By Mr. Robb: . . .

Q. What did you know about Eltenton's background in 1943 when this Eltenton-Chevalier episode occurred?

A. Two things, three things, four things: That he was an Englishman, that he was a chemical engineer, that he had spent some time in the Soviet Union, that he was a member of the Federation of Architects, Engineers, Chemists, and Technicians—five things—that he was employed, I think, at Shell Development Co.

Q. How did you know all those things?

A. Well, about the Shell Development Co. and the Federation of Architects, Engineers, Chemists, and Technicians, I suppose he told me or someone else employed there told me. As for the background in Russia, I don't remember. Maybe he told me; maybe a friend told me. That he was an Englishman was obvious.

Q. Why?

A. His accent.

Q. You were fairly well acquainted with him, were you not?

A. No. I think we probably saw each other no more than 4 or 5 times.

Q. Did you see Eltenton after this episode occurred?

A. No.

Q. Have you ever seen him since?

A. No.

Q. Could that have been on purpose on your part? Have you avoided him?

A. I have not had to, but I think I would have.

Q. You have mentioned your conversation with Colonel Lansdale which I believe you said took place at Los Alamos?

A. Yes.

Q. In which he told you he was worried about the security situation at Berkeley. I believe we agreed that worry would naturally include a fear of espionage?

A. That is right.

Q. Did he mention any names in connection with that worry?

A. Lomanitz was obviously in the picture, and I believe that is the only one.

Q. Weinberg?

A. I don't think he did.

Q. But Lomanitz obviously?

A. Lomanitz.

Q. When did you first mention your conversation with Chevalier to any security officer?

A. I didn't do it that way. I first mentioned Eltenton.

Q. Yes.

A. On a visit to Berkeley almost immediately after Lansdale's visit to Los Alamos.

Q. Was that to Lieutenant Johnson; do you remember?

A. I don't remember, but it was to a security officer there.

Q. At Berkeley?

A. That is right.

Q. If the record shows that it was to Lieutenant Johnson on August 25, 1943, you would accept that?

A. I would accept that.

Q. You mentioned the Eltenton incident in connection with Lomanitz, didn't you?

A. The context was this. I think Johnson told me that the source of the trouble was the unionization of the radiation laboratory by the Federation of Architects, Engineers, Chemists, and Technicians. Possibly I had heard that from Lansdale. The connection that I made was between Eltenton and this organization.

Q. In your answer at page 22 you say, referring to the Eltenton episode: "It has long been clear to me that I should have reported the incident at once."

A. It is.

Q. "The events that lead me to report it, which I doubt ever would have become known without my report, were unconnected with it."

You have told us that your discussion with Colonel Lansdale encompassed the subject of espionage. Of course, you have told us also that the Eltenton matter involved espionage; is that correct?

A. Let us be careful. The word "espionage" was not mentioned.

Q. No?

A. The word "indiscretion" was mentioned. That is all that Lansdale said. Indiscretion was talking to unauthorized people who in turn would talk to other people. This is all I was told. I got worried when I learned that this union was connected with their troubles.

Q. But, Doctor, you told us this morning, did you not, that you knew that Lansdale was worried about espionage at Berkeley; is that correct?

A. I knew he was worried about the leakage of information.

Q. Isn't that a polite name for espionage?

A. Not necessarily.

Q. I will ask you now, didn't you know that Lansdale was concerned about the possibility of espionage at Berkeley?

A. About the possibility; yes.

Q. Yes.

A. That is right.

Q. So, Doctor, it is not quite correct to say that the Eltenton incident was not connected with your talk with Lansdale, is it?

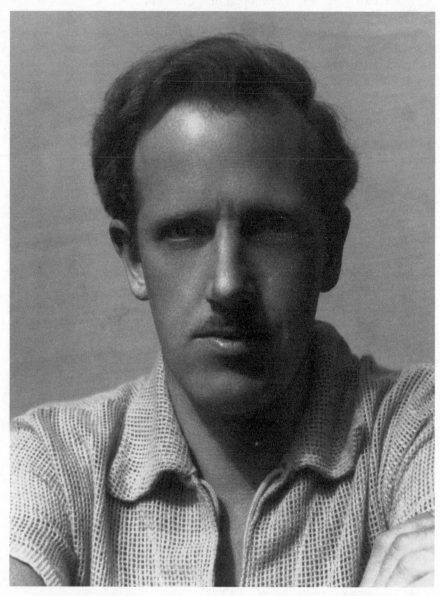

Haakon Chevalier, 1930s. Courtesy of the Bancroft Library, University of California, Berkeley.

A. I didn't mean it in that sense. I meant that it had nothing to do with Chevalier or Eltenton with respect to the events that aroused this.

Q. But your talk with Lansdale did have to do with the subject which included Chevalier and Eltenton, didn't it?

A. I have described it as well as I can. Chevalier's name was not mentioned; Eltenton's name was not mentioned; and espionage was not mentioned.

Q. I didn't say that. But it had to do with the subject which involved Chevalier or at least Eltenton?

A. Sure; that is why I brought it up.

Q. What did you tell Lieutenant Johnson about this when you first mentioned Eltenton to him?

A. I had two interviews, and therefore I am not clear as to which was which.

Q. May I help you?

A. Please.

Q. I think your first interview with Johnson was quite brief, was it not?

A. That is right. I think I said little more than that Eltenton was somebody to worry about.

Q. Yes.

A. Then I was asked why did I say this. Then I invented a cock-and-bull story.

Q. Then you were interviewed the next day by Colonel Pash, were you not?

A. That is right.

Q. Who was he?

A. He was another security officer.

Q. That was quite a lengthy interview, was it not?

A. I didn't think it was that long.

Q. For your information, that was August 26, 1943.

A. Right.

Q. Then there came a time when you were interviewed by Colonel Lansdale.

A. I remember that very well.

Q. That was in Washington, wasn't it?

A. That is right.

Q. That was September 12, 1943.

A. Right.

Q. Would you accept that?

A. Surely.

Q. Then you were interviewed again by the FBI in 1946; is that right?

A. In between I think came Groves.

Q. Pardon?

A. In between came Groves.

Q. Yes. But you were interviewed in 1946; is that right?

A. That is right.

Q. Now let us go back to your interview with Colonel Pash. Did you tell Pash the truth about this thing?

A. No.

Q. You lied to him?

A. Yes.

Q. What did you tell Pash that was not true?

A. That Eltenton had attempted to approach members of the project—three members of the project—through intermediaries.

Q. What else did you tell him that wasn't true?

A. That is all I really remember.

Q. That is all? Did you tell Pash that Eltenton had attempted to approach three members of the project—

A. Through intermediaries.

Q. Intermediaries?

A. Through an intermediary.

Q. So that we may be clear, did you discuss with or disclose to Pash the identity of Chevalier?

A. No.

Q. Let us refer, then, for the time being, to Chevalier as X.

A. All right.

Q. Did you tell Pash that X had approached three persons on the project?

A. I am not clear whether I said there were 3 X's or that X approached 3 people.

Q. Didn't you say that X had approached 3 people?

A. Probably.

Q. Why did you do that, Doctor?

A. Because I was an idiot.

Q. Is that your only explanation, Doctor?

A. I was reluctant to mention Chevalier.

Q. Yes.

A. No doubt somewhat reluctant to mention myself.

Q. Yes. But why would you tell him that Chevalier had gone to 3 people?

A. I have no explanation for that except the one already offered.

Q. Didn't that make it all the worse for Chevalier?

A. I didn't mention Chevalier.

Q. No; but X.

A. It would have.

Q. Certainly. In other words, if X had gone to 3 people that would have shown, would it not—

A. That he was deeply involved.

Q. That he was deeply involved. That it was not just a casual conversation.

A. Right.

Q. And you knew that, didn't you?

A. Yes.

Q. Did you tell Colonel Pash that X had spoken to you about the use of microfilm?

A. It seems unlikely. You have a record, and I will abide by it.

Q. Did you?

A. I don't remember.

Q. If X had spoken to you about the use of microfilm, that would have shown definitely that he was not an innocent contact?

A. It certainly would.

Q. Did you tell Colonel Pash that X had told you that the information would be transmitted through someone at the Russian consulate?

(There was no response.)

Q. Did you?

A. I would have said not, but I clearly see that I must have.

Q. If X had said that, that would have shown conclusively that it was a criminal conspiracy, would it not?

A. That is right.

Q. Did Pash ask you for the name of X?

A. I imagine he did.

Q. Don't you know he did?

A. Sure.

Q. Did he tell you why he wanted it?

A. In order to stop the business.

Q. He told you that it was a very serious matter, didn't he?

A. I don't recollect that, but he certainly would have.

Q. You knew that he wanted to investigate it, did you not?

A. That is right.

Q. And didn't you know that your refusal to give the name of X was impeding the investigation?

A. In actual fact I think the only person that needed watching or should have been watched was Eltenton. But as I concocted the story that did not emerge.

Q. That was your judgment?

A. Yes.

Q. But you knew that Pash wanted to investigate this?

A. Yes.

Q. And didn't you know, Doctor, that by refusing to give the name of X you were impeding the investigation?

A. I must have known that.

Q. You know now, don't you?

A. Well, actually—

Q. You must have known it then?

A. Actually the only important thing to investigate was Eltenton.

Q. What did Pash want to investigate?

A. I suppose the 3 people on the project.

Q. You knew, didn't you, Doctor, that Colonel Pash and his organization would move heaven and earth to find out those 3 people, didn't you?

A. It makes sense.

Q. And you knew that they would move heaven and earth to find out the identity of X, didn't you?

A. Yes.

Q. And yet you wouldn't tell them?

A. That is true.

Q. So you knew you were impeding them, didn't you?

A. That is right.

Q. How long had you known this man Chevalier in 1943?

A. For many years.

Q. How many?

A. Perhaps 5; 5 or 6, probably.

Q. How had you known him?

A. As a quite close friend.

Q. Had you known him professionally or socially?

A. He was a member of the faculty, and I knew him socially.

Q. What was his specialty?

A. He was a professor of French.

Q. How did you meet him; do you remember?

A. Possibly at one of the first meetings of the teachers union, but I am not certain.

Q. Were you a frequent visitor at his house?

A. Yes.

Q. And your wives were also friendly?

A. Right.

Q. Had you seen him at the meeting of leftwing organizations?

A. Yes. I think the first time I saw him I didn't know him. He presided at a meeting for Spanish relief at which the French writer Malraux was the speaker.

Q. Where was that meeting held?

A. In San Francisco.

Q. At whose house?

A. It was a public meeting. . . .

Q. Did you know Chevalier as a fellow traveler?

A. I so told the FBI in 1946 and I did know him as a fellow traveler.

Q. He followed the party line pretty closely, didn't he?

A. Yes, I imagine he did.

Q. Did you have any reason to suspect he was a member of the Communist Party?

A. At the time I knew him?

Q. Yes, sir.

A. No.

Q. Do you know?

A. No.

Q. You knew he was a quite a "red", didn't you?

A. Yes. I would say quite Pink.

Q. Not Red?

A. I won't quibble.

Q. You say in your answer that you still considered him a friend.

A. I do.

Q. When did you last see him?

A. On my last trip to Europe. He is living in Paris, divorced and has been re-married. We had dinner with them one evening. The origin of this, or at least part of the origin—

Q. May I interpose? That was in December 1953?

A. Yes, December.

Q. Go ahead.

A. He wrote me a note saying that he had been at UNESCO and had run into Professor Bohr who told him I was coming to Europe—we were coming to Europe.

Q. Professor who?

A. B-o-h-r. He asked us to look him up if we got to Paris. We planned to do so. My wife called. He was out of town on a job. He got back and we had dinner together, the four of us.

   The next day he picked us up and drove us out to visit with Malraux, who has had rather major political changes since 1936. We had a conversation of about an hour and he drove us back to the hotel. . . .

Q. Doctor, just so the record will be complete, do you recall in 1950 getting a letter from Dr. Chevalier who was then in San Francisco asking you to assist him by telling him what you testified before the House committee about the Chevalier-Eltenton incident?

A. Yes, I remember.

Q. Do you recall answering that letter?

A. I did answer it. I think I did not tell him what I testified, because it was in executive session, but referred him to a press account of what I testified. I am not quite certain on this point.

Q. At that time he was attempting to get a passport to leave the United States, was he?

A. I thought that was later, but I am not sure.

Q. That may have been. You did hear about it when he was attempting to get a passport; did you?

A. Yes.

Q. We will come to that later.

   I will read you and ask you if this is the letter that you wrote to him. I am sorry I haven't a copy of it. On the stationery of the Institute for Advanced Study, Princeton, N.J., office of the director, February 25, 1950:

Dr. Haakon Chevalier
3127 Washington Street
San Francisco, Calif.

Dear Haakon:
Thank you for your good letter of February 21. I can understand that an account of my testimony before the House committee could be helpful to you in seeking a suitable academic position at this time. I cannot send it to you be-

cause I have never myself had a transcript, and because the committee ruled at the time that they desired to keep, and would keep, the hearings secret. But I can tell you what I said. I told them that I would like as far as possible to clear the record with regard to your alleged involvement in the atom business. I said that as far as I knew, you knew nothing of the atom bomb until it was announced after Hiroshima; and that most certainly you had never mentioned it or anything that could be connected with it to me. I said that you had never asked me to transmit any kind of information, nor suggested that I could do so, or that I consider doing so. I said that you had told me of a discussion of providing technical information to the U.S.S.R. which disturbed you considerably, and which you thought I ought to know about. There were surely many other points; but these were, I think, the highlights; and if this account can be of use to you, I hope that you will feel free to use it.

As you know, I have been deeply disturbed by the threat to your career which these ugly stories could constitute. If I can help you in that, you may call on me.

Sincerely yours,

Robert Oppenheimer.

Did you write that letter?

A. Oh, sure. I didn't recollect it.

Q. Was the account of your testimony which you gave there an accurate one?

A. I think it is fairly accurate.

Q. Dr. Chevalier thereafter used that letter in connection with his passport application.

A. I didn't know that.

Q. Did you talk to him about his passport application?

A. I did. He came to Princeton at the time and I referred him to counsel to help him with it. . . .

Q. Dr. Chevalier came to Princeton to see you about the matter?

A. He came and stayed a couple of days. I don't think it would be right to say he came to see me about the passport problem. He had just been divorced. He talked of nothing but his divorce. But he was worried about whether to use an American passport or his French passport.

Q. About when was that, Doctor?

A. Could it have been the spring of 1951?

Q. I don't know.

A. It was immediately at the time he left the country.

ROGER ROBB: "You spent the night with her, didn't you?"

[Although Oppenheimer has already alluded to his friendship with Jean Tatlock, who was at one time a member of the Communist Party, he is suddenly asked to explain why he spent a night at her apartment in June 1943. Robb's purported concern is Oppenheimer's willingness to flout security regulations, but in fact, he is raising the acutely embarrassing issue of marital infidelity.]

By Mr. Robb: . . .

Q. Doctor, may we again refer to your answer, please, sir. On page 4: "In the spring of 1936, I had been introduced by a friend to Jean Tatlock, the daughter of a noted professor of English at the university, and in the autumn I began to court her, and we grew close to each other. We were at least twice close enough to marriage to think of ourselves as engaged. Between 1939 and her death in 1944, I saw her very rarely. She told me about her Communist Party memberships. They were on-again, off-again affairs and never seemed to provide for her what she was seeking. I do not believe that her interests were really political. She was a person of deep religious feeling. She loved this country, its people, and its life. She was, as it turned out, a friend of many fellow travelers and Communists, a number of whom I later was to become acquainted with."

Doctor, between 1939 and 1944, as I understand it, your acquaintance with Miss Tatlock was fairly casual; is that right?

A. Our meetings were rare. I do not think it would be right to say that our acquaintance was casual. We had been very much involved with one another, and there was still very deep feeling when we saw each other.

Q. How many times would you say you saw her between 1939 and 1944?

A. That is 5 years. Would 10 times be a good guess?

Q. What were the occasions for your seeing her?

A. Of course, sometimes we saw each other socially with other people. I remember visiting her around New Year's of 1941.

Q. Where?

A. I went to her house or to the hospital, I don't know which, and we went out for a drink at the Top of the Mark. I remember that she came more than once to visit our home in Berkeley.

Q. You and Mrs. Oppenheimer?

A. Right. Her father lived around the corner not far from us in Berkeley. I visited her there once. I visited her, as I think I said earlier, in June or July of 1943.

Q. I believe you said in connection with that that you had to see her.

A. Yes.

Q. Why did you have to see her?

A. She had indicated a great desire to see me before we left. At that time I couldn't go. For one thing, I wasn't supposed to say where we were going or anything. I felt that she had to see me. She was undergoing psychiatric treatment. She was extremely unhappy.

Q. Did you find out why she had to see you?

A. Because she was still in love with me.

Q. Where did you see her?

A. At her home.

Q. Where was that?

A. On Telegraph Hill.

Q. When did you see her after that?

A. She took me to the airport, and I never saw her again.

Q. That was 1943?

A. Yes.

Q. Was she a Communist at that time?

A. We didn't even talk about it. I doubt it.

Q. You have said in your answer that you knew she had been a Communist?

A. Yes. I knew that in the fall of 1937.

Q. Was there any reason for you to believe that she wasn't still a Communist in 1943?

A. No.

Q. Pardon?

A. There wasn't, except that I have stated in general terms what I thought and think of her relations with the Communist Party. I do not know what she was doing in 1943.

Q. You have no reason to believe she wasn't a Communist, do you?

A. No.

Q. You spent the night with her, didn't you?

A. Yes.

Q. That is when you were working on a secret war project?

A. Yes.

Q. Did you think that consistent with good security?

A. It was, as a matter of fact. Not a word—it was not good practice.

Q. Didn't you think that put you in a rather difficult position had she been the kind of Communist that you have described . . .?

A. Oh, but she wasn't.

Q. How did you know?

A. I knew her.

Q. You have told us this morning that you thought that at times social contacts with Communists on the part of one working on a secret war project was dangerous.

A. Could conceivably be.

Q. You didn't think after spending a night with a dedicated Communist—

A. I don't believe she was a dedicated Communist.

Q. You don't?

A. No.

Q. Did she go over to Spain?

A. No.

Q. Ever?

A. Not during the time I knew her.

Q. What was the occasion of her telling you about her Communist Party membership?

A. She would talk about herself rather freely, and this was one aspect of her life. She would tell me that she had been with a medical unit—I am making it up—with some kind of a unit, and it had been frustrating.

Q. What do you mean, you are making it up?

A. I mean I don't remember what kind of a unit, but she had been with some sort of a Communist unit and had left it. It had been a waste of time, and so on.

Q. By a medical unit, you mean a medical cell?

A. That is what I would have meant.

Q. You say here she was as it turned out a friend of many fellow travelers and Communists. Who were they?

A. Well, Addis was a friend of hers. Lambert was a friend of hers.

Q. Doctor, would you break them down? Would you tell us who the Communists were and who the fellow travelers were?

A. Lambert was a Communist. Addis is reported to be a Communist in the Commission's letter. I did not know whether he was a member of the party or not.

Q. You knew he was very close, didn't you?

A. Yes. Among fellow travelers, Chevalier. Among Communists or probable Communists, a man and his wife who wrote for the People's World.

Q. Who were they?

A. John Pitman and his wife. A lawyer called Aubrey Grossman, his wife she had known.

Q. Was she a Communist?

A. I don't know in the sense of party membership.

Q. But very close.

A. Close. Is the list long enough?

[After Robb presses Oppenheimer to name other individuals whom he took to be Communist Party members or fellow travelers, the hearing adjourns.]

Thursday, April 15

General Leslie R. Groves: "I would not clear Dr. Oppenheimer today"

[General Leslie R. Groves, who headed the Manhattan District project during the war and is at the time of the hearing a vice president and director of Remington Rand, is the first to testify.]

DIRECT EXAMINATION

By Mr. Garrison: . . .

Q. You appointed Dr. Oppenheimer to be the director of the work at Los Alamos?

A. Yes, sir.

Q. You devolved great responsibility upon him?

A. Yes. . . .

Q. How would you rate the quality of his achievement as you look back on it?

A. Naturally I am prejudiced, because I selected him for the job, but I think he did a magnificent job as far as the war effort was concerned. In other words, while he was under my control—and you must remember that he left my control shortly after the war was over.

Q. If you had to make the decision again, would you make it in the same way with respect to the selection of Dr. Oppenheimer and devolving the responsibilities on him which you did?

A. I know of no reason why not. Assuming all the conditions are the same, I think I would do it.

Q. You saw him very closely during those years?

A. I saw him on the average, I would say, of anywhere from once a week to once a month. I talked to him on the phone about anywhere from 4 to 5 times a day to once in 3 or 4 days. I talked on all possible subjects of all varieties. During the time I spent a number of days, for example, on trains traveling where we might be together for 6 or 8 or 12 hours at a time.

Q. You were aware of his leftwing associations at the time—his earlier leftwing associations?

A. Was I or am I?

Q. Were you at the time you appointed him?

A. At the time I appointed him to the project, I was aware that there were suspicions about him, nothing like what were contained—and I might say I read the New York Times, the letter of General Nichols and Dr. Oppenheimer's letter. I was not aware of all the things that were brought out in General Nichols' letter at the time of the appointment, but I was aware that he was or that he had, you might say, a very extreme liberal background.

I was also aware of another thing that I think must be mentioned, that he was already in the project, that he had been in charge of this particular type of work, that is, the bomb computations, and that he knew all that there was to know about that. In general, my policy was to consider the fact that the man was already in the project, and that made it very questionable whether I should separate him and also whether I should separate him under what might be termed unpleasant conditions, because then you never know what you are going to do to him. Are you going to drive him over to the other side or not? As far as what I knew at the time of his actual selection, I knew enough to tell me that I would have considered him an extreme liberal with a very liberal background. Just how many of the details I knew at the time I don't know. I did know them all later.

Q. Based on your total acquaintance with him and your experience with him and your knowledge of him, would you say that in your opinion he would ever consciously commit a disloyal act?

A. I would be amazed if he did. . . .

Q. You had complete confidence in his integrity?

A. During the operation of Los Alamos, yes, which was where I really knew him.

Q. And you have that confidence today?

A. As far as that operation went, yes. As I say, as far as the rest of it goes, I am, you might say, not a witness. I am really ignorant on that, excepting what I read in the papers.

Q. As the war neared its end, there was an even greater urgency to produce the bomb in time to use it, was there not?

A. No, because no one in this country conceived of the Japanese war ending as soon as it did, no one in responsible positions today, no matter what they say today or said since. There is not a soul that thought that the war was going to end within a reasonable time.

Q. Did Dr. Oppenheimer work as hard as a man could to produce that bomb in accordance with the deadline dates that you had projected?

A. Oh, yes, yes. In fact, he worked harder at times than I wanted him to, because I was afraid he would break down under it. That was always a danger in our project. I think it is important to realize in the case of Dr. Oppenheimer because I had a physical taken of him when we were talking about making it a militarized affair, and I knew his past physical record, and I was always disturbed about his working too hard. But I never could slow him down in any way.

Q. Do you recall your conversation with him about the Chevalier incident?

A. Yes, but I have seen so many versions of it, I don't think I was confused before, but I am certainly starting to become confused today. I recall what I consider the essential history of that affair. As to whether this occurred this time, where I was at the moment, I can't say that I recall it exactly. I think I recall everything that is of vital interest, as far as would be necessary to draw a conclusion as to that affair.

Q. Would you say what your conclusion was?

A. My conclusion was that there was an approach made, that Dr. Oppenheimer knew of this approach, that at some point he was involved in that the approach was made to him—I don't mean involved in the sense that he gave anything—I mean he just knew about it personally from the fact that he was in the chain, and that he didn't report it in its entirety as he should have done. When I learned about it, and throughout, that he was always under the influence of what I termed the typical American schoolboy attitude that there is something wicked about telling on a friend. I was never certain as to just what he was telling me. I did know this: That he was doing what he thought was essential, which was to disclose to me the dangers of this particular attempt to enter the project, namely, it was concerned with the situation out there near Berkeley—I think it was the Shell Laboratory at which Eltenton was supposedly one of the key members—and that was a source of danger to the project and that was the worry. I always had the very definite impression that Dr. Oppenheimer wanted to protect his friends of long standing, possibly his brother. It was always my impression that he wanted to protect his brother, and that his brother might be involved in having been in this chain, and that his brother didn't behave quite as he should have, or if he did, he didn't even want to have the finger of suspicion pointed at his brother, because he always felt a natural loyalty to him, and had a protective attitude toward him.

I felt at the time that what Oppenheimer was trying to tell me and tell our project, once he disclosed this thing at all—as I recall I had the feeling that he didn't disclose it immediately. In other words, he didn't come around the next day or that night and say to our security people, "Listen, some things are going on." I think he thought it over for some time. I am saying what I thought now, and not what we could prove, because we could never prove anything definite on this thing, because it all depended on the testimony of a man who was concerned in it. . . .

I felt that was wrong. If I had not felt it was important not to have any point of issue on what after all was a minor point with respect to the success of the project, I might have had quite an issue with him right then and there. As he told me very early in my conversation with him, he said, "General, if you order me to tell you this, I will tell you." I said, "No, I am not going to order you."

About 2 months later or some time later, after much discussion in trying to lead him into it, and having then got the situation more or less adjusted, I told him if you don't tell me, I am going to have to order you to do it. Then I got what to me was the final story. I think he made a great mistake in that. I felt so at the time. I didn't think it was great from the standpoint of the project, because I felt that I was getting what I wanted to know which, after all, I did know already, that this group was a source of danger to us. I didn't know that this group had tried to make this direct approach and pinpoint it that way, but I knew they were thoroughly capable of it, and I knew we had sources of danger in the Berkeley project.

I think that really was my impression of it, that he didn't do what he should have done. The reasons why were desire to protect friends and possibly his brother, and that he felt that he had done what was necessary in pinpointing. As far as I was concerned, while I didn't like it, after all it was not my job to like everything my subordinates did, or anybody in the project did. I felt I had gotten what I needed to get out of that, and I was not going to make an issue of it, because I thought it might impair his usefulness on the project.

I think that gives you the general story.

Mr. Garrison. I think that is all that I would like to ask.
Mr. Gray. Mr. Robb.

CROSS-EXAMINATION

By Mr. Robb: . . .

Q. General, did your security officers on the project advise against the clearance of Dr. Oppenheimer?

A. Oh, I am sure that they did. I don't recall exactly. They certainly were not in favor of his clearance. I think a truer picture is to say that they reported that they could not and would not clear him.

Q. General, you were in the Army actively for how many years?

A. I don't know. 1916 to 1948, and of course raised in it, also.

Q. And you rose to the rank of lieutenant general?

A. That is right.

Q. During your entire Army career, I assume you were dealing with matters of security?

A. Never before this thing started. We didn't deal with matters of security in the Army, really, until this time. The Army as a whole didn't deal with matters of security until after the atomic bomb burst on the world because it was the first time that the Army really knew that there was such a thing, if you want to be perfectly frank about it.

Q. Certainly with your work in the Manhattan project you dealt intensively with matters of security?

A. I would say I devoted about 5 percent of my time to security problems.

Q. You did become thoroughly familiar with security matters.

A. I think that I was very familiar with security matters.

Q. In fact, it could be said that you became something of an expert in it?

A. I am afraid that is correct.

Q. I believe you said that you became pretty familiar with the file of Dr. Oppenheimer?

A. I think I was thoroughly familiar with everything that was reported about Dr. Oppenheimer; and that included, as it did on every other matter of importance, personally reading the original evidence if there was any original evidence. In other words, I would read the reports of the interviews with people. In other words, I was not reading the conclusions of any security officer. The reason for that was that in this project there were so many things that the security officer would not know the significance of that I felt I had to do it myself. Of course, I have been criticized for doing all those things myself and not having a staff of any kind; but, after all, it did work, and I did live through it.

Q. General, in the light of your experience with security matters and in the light of your knowledge of the file pertaining to Dr. Oppenheimer, would you clear Dr. Oppenheimer today?

A. I think before answering that I would like to give my interpretation of what

Leslie R. Groves with J. Robert Oppenheimer at Los Alamos, August 1945.
Marie Hansen/TimePix.

the Atomic Energy Act requires. I have it, but I never can find it as to just
what it says. Maybe I can find it this time.

Q. Would you like me to show it?

A. I know it is very deeply concealed in the thing.

Q. Do you have the same copy?

A. I have the original act.

Q. It is on page 14, I think, where you will find it, General. You have the same
pamphlet I have.

A. Thank you. That is it. The clause to which I am referring is this: It is the
last of paragraph (b) (i) on page 14. It says:

"The Commission shall have determined that permitting such person to
have access to restricted data will not endanger the common defense or security," and it mentions that the investigation should include the character,
associations, and loyalty.

My interpretation of "endanger"—and I think it is important for me to
make that if I am going to answer your question—is that it is a reasonable
presumption that there might be a danger, not a remote possibility, a tortured interpretation of maybe there might be something, but that there is
something that might do. Whether you say that is 5 percent or 10 percent or
something of that order does not make any difference. It is not a case of
proving that the man is a danger. It is a case of thinking, well, he might be a
danger, and it is perfectly logical to presume that he would be, and that
there is no consideration whatsoever to be given to any of his past performances or his general usefulness or, you might say, the imperative usefulness. I don't care how important the man is, if there is any possibility other

than a tortured one that his associations or his loyalty or his character might endanger.

In this case I refer particularly to associations and not to the associations as they exist today but the past record of the associations. I would not clear Dr. Oppenheimer today if I were a member of the Commission on the basis of this interpretation.

If the interpretation is different, then I would have to stand on my interpretation of it.

MR. ROBB. Thank you, General. That is all.

J. ROBERT OPPENHEIMER: "One can be mistaken about anything"

[When Oppenheimer resumes his testimony, Robb picks up where he left off the previous afternoon, cross-examining him on his involvement in radical causes in the 1930s and on friends and associates from that era. Robb has alluded to more than a dozen of Oppenheimer's acquaintances by the time he comes to Dr. Joseph W. Weinberg.]

CROSS-EXAMINATION (resumed)

By Mr. Robb: . . .

Q. How did you come to know Dr. Weinberg?

A. In the most normal way. I knew all the graduate students who studied theoretical physics in the department of physics in Berkeley. I believe I called them all by their first names.

Q. Did you have any relationship with Weinberg other than that of professor and student?

A. I think I need to say several things in answer to that. The first simple answer is "No," until after the war when he was not a student but an instructor and when he and his wife—we saw them once or twice as was proper for dinner or tea or something.

The second thing is that with most of my students it would not be an uncommon thing for me to have dinner with them or to have lunch with them while we were working. I think my relations to Weinberg were much less close than with most of my graduate students.

Q. What was the occasion for you meeting with him and his wife after the war?

A. He was an instructor in the physics department in Berkeley. I think we probably had dinner or tea or something with every member of the department. . . .

Q. When did you first hear that Weinberg had been a Communist?

A. At the time of the 1946 interview with the FBI, the agents told me—they questioned me about Weinberg, Lomanitz and so on—and I said, "What is wrong with them?" He said, "There is a question of their membership in the Communist Party."

Q. Were you surprised to hear that?

A. A little bit but not much in the case of Weinberg.

Q. You are quite sure that is the first time you ever heard or had been told he was a Communist?

A. No. I had heard an earlier rumor.

Q. When?

A. When he came to Berkeley that he had been a member of the YCL, the Young Communist League in Madison, but it was hearsay.

Q. Who told you that?

A. I don't remember.

Q. Did you hear anything more about him at that time?

A. No.

Q. Did Weinberg and Lomanitz come to you to talk about Lomanitz' draft deferment?

A. No.

Q. Are you sure?

A. Let's see. The only time this might have been would have been at the time I talked to Lomanitz at the same time we talked so much of yesterday in the summer of 1943. I have no recollection of Weinberg being involved in that.

Q. Do you recall an occasion in Dr. Lawrence's office when you talked to both Weinberg and Lomanitz?

A. No, I don't.

Q. In all events, doctor, you are sure that until 1946, except for the rumor that you mentioned, you had no information to the effect that Weinberg was or had been a Communist?

A. No. I think that is right.

Q. You could not be mistaken about that?

A. One can be mistaken about anything. This is my best recollection. . . .

Q. When did you first meet Steve Nelson?

A. I don't know whether it was before my marriage to my wife or not. I think it was. She thinks that it was after our marriage.

Q. When did you think you met him, and what were the circumstances under which you met him?

A. I think it may have been in connection with a big Spanish party in the fall of 1939.

Q. Where?

A. In San Francisco.

Q. Do you recall talking to him on that occasion?

A. No.

Q. What is there about the occasion that makes Steve Nelson stand out in your mind?

A. He was a hero and there was either talk of him or I saw him, I don't know.

Q. What was he a hero for?

A. For his alleged part in the Spanish War.

Q. You knew he was a Communist Party functionary?

A. I knew he was a Communist and an important Communist.

Q. Thereafter, Steve Nelson was at your home on various occasions, was he not?

A. That was much later.

Q. When was that?

A. The times I remember—and I think they are the only times—were in the winter of 1941–42.

Q. What is the last date that you recall him being at your home?

A. I don't recall the dates. It probably was in 1942.

Q. 1942?

A. Yes.

Q. Summer, fall, spring, or when?

A. I don't know.

Q. Were you at that time working on the secret war project?

A. I was thinking about it if it was in the winter, and I was employed on it if it was the summer.

Q. I beg your pardon?

A. If it was in the winter I was thinking about it, and consulting about it; if it was in the summer, I was actually employed on it.

Q. In all events whether it was in the winter or summer, at the time Steve Nelson was at your house you had some connection with this project, did you not?

A. Oh, yes.

Q. How many times did Steve Nelson come to your house?

A. I would say several, but I do not know precisely.

Q. Did you ever go to his house?

A. I am not clear. If so, it was only to call for him or something like that.

Q. Call for him?

A. Yes.

Q. Why would you have called for him?

A. To bring him up to our house.

Q. Who else was present at your house on the occasions when Nelson was there?

A. I have no memory of this. These were very often Sundays and people would drop in.

Q. The occasions when he was there were not occasions when there was a large group of people?

A. No. We would be out in the garden having a picnic or something like that. It is quite possible that my brother and sister-in-law would come, but I have no memory of this.

Q. Can you give us any idea how long these visits were with Nelson?

A. A few hours.

Q. Each time?

A. The ones I am thinking of, and I think they are the ones you are referring to, and the only ones that occurred, are when he and his wife and his baby would come up.

Q. What did you have in common with Steve Nelson?

A. Nothing, except an affection for my wife.

Q. Did you find his conversation interesting?

A. The parts about Spain, yes.

Q. Was he a man of any education?

A. No.

Q. What did you talk about?

A. We didn't talk about much. Kitty and he reminisced.

Q. Reminisced about what?

A. My wife's former husband, people they had known in the party.

Q. Communist Party activities?

A. Past Communist friendships.

Q. Did Nelson tell you what he was doing in California?

A. No. I knew he was connected with the Alameda County organization.

Q. Did Nelson ever ask what you were doing?

A. No.

Q. Are you sure?

A. Positive. He knew I was a scientist.

Q. He knew that?

A. Yes.

Q. How did he know that?

A. It was well known in the community and we talked about it.

Q. Did you call him Steve?

A. I think so.

Q. Did he call you Oppy?

A. I don't remember.

Q. Probably?

A. I don't remember. He and my wife—she will tell you about it. They had close affectionate relationships and I was a natural bystander. . . .

Q. Who are the Morrisons?

A. Philip Morrison was a student of mine and was very far left.

Q. He was very far left?

A. Yes.

Q. Was he a Communist?

A. I think it probable.

Q. Did he go to work on the project?

A. He did.

Q. With your approval?

A. With no relation to me.

Q. Did you ever make known to anyone that you thought that Philip Morrison was probably a Communist?

A. No.

Q. Why not?

A. Well, let me say he was on the project in another branch quite independent of me. When he came to Los Alamos, General Groves let me understand that he knew Morrison had what he called a background and I was satisfied that the truth was known about him.

Q. Morrison came to Los Alamos?

A. That is right. When he came to Los Alamos we had this discussion.

Q. He was so far left-wing that you thought that the mere fact that Hawkins was a friend of his stigmatized Hawkins, too, did you not?

A. Not stigmatized him; gave him a left-wing association.

Q. What did Morrison do at Los Alamos? I don't mean in detail but in general.

A. He came late and he worked in what was called the bomb physics division. He worked with the reactor we had there. Then after the war he built a quite ingenious new kind of reactor.

ROGER ROBB AND J. ROBERT OPPENHEIMER: "Your memory is not refreshed by what I read you?" "No, on the whole it is confused by it"

[Robb now turns to the transcript of a September 12, 1943, interview, 26 pages in length, between Oppenheimer and Lt. Col. John Lansdale, who was in charge of security at Los Alamos. Only after insistent protests from Garrison is he permitted to have a copy of the transcript as the questioning proceeds. Oppenheimer faces especially awkward moments when indiscreet, off-the-cuff remarks made in a supposedly confidential setting more than a decade earlier are exhumed, and he is asked about them.]

Q. Doctor, we spoke yesterday of your interview with Colonel Lansdale. I want to read you some extracts from the transcript of that interview, sir. Colonel Lansdale said to you, according to this transcript—

MR. GARRISON. May we have the date?

MR. ROBB. September 12, 1943. This is the interview that took place at the Pentagon. Colonel Lansdale said to you:

"We know, for instance, that it is the policy of the Communist Party at this time that when a man goes into the Army his official connections with the Party are thereupon ipso facto severed."

You answered: "Well, I was told by a man who came from my—a very prominent man, who was a member of the Communist Party in the Middle

West, that it was the policy of the party there that when a man entered confidential war work, he was not supposed to remain a member of the party."
  Who told you that?

A. I have no recollection at all, I will think, if you wish.

Q. I wish you would, sir.

A. From the Middle West.

MR. GRAY. "Read that again.

MR. ROBB. I was told by a man who came from my—a very prominent man
who was a member of the Communist Party in the Middle West that it was
the policy of the party there that when a man entered confidential war work
he was not supposed to remain a member of the party."

By Mr. Robb:

Q. Who was that man?

A. I recollect nothing about it. I will be glad to think about it.

Q. Do you want to think now?

A. I would prefer not to. If I can think about it and tell you tomorrow. It simply rings no bell.

Q. You don't recall anybody ever told you that?

A. No, I said yesterday I didn't recollect.

Q. I know you did. Does this serve to refresh your recollection in any way?

A. Quite to the contrary. From the Middle West?

Q. You then spoke about your brother.

MR. MARKS. May I inquire, Mr. Chairman, if these transcripts are taken from
recordings, just so we can understand what is being read?

MR. ROBB. Yes. I have every reason to believe it is accurate.

MR. MARKS. I don't question that, I just wondered what the origin was.

MR. ROBB. I don't think that is necessarily a question counsel should have to
answer.

MR. MARKS. I asked the Chairman, sir.

MR. GRAY. My answer is "I don't know." If you wish to discuss it further I
would be glad to.

MR. MARKS. I thought it was a matter that could be answered simply.

By Mr. Robb:

Q. You spoke of your brother and said, "It is not only that he is not a member,
I think he has no contact." Do you recall that?

A. No; I don't recall it, but that I can imagine saying.

Q. Lansdale said: "Do you know about his wife, Jackie?"
  You answered: "I know I overwhelmingly urged about 18 months ago
when we started that she should drop social ones which I regarded as dangerous. Whether they have in fact done that, I don't know.
  Lansdale said, "Well, I am quite confident that your brother Frank has no
connection with the Communists. I am not so sure about his wife."

You answered, "I am not sure either, but I think it likely some of its importance has left her. Also, I believe it to be true that they do not have any— I don't know this for a fact—but if they had, I didn't know it, any well established contacts in Berkeley. You see they came from Palo Alto, and they had such contacts there. Then my brother was unemployed for three very, very salutory months, which changed his ideas quite a lot, and when they started in Berkeley it was for this war job. I do not know but think it quite probable that his wife Jackie had never had a unit or group to which she was attached in any way. The thing that worried me was that their friends were very left wing and I think it is not always necessary to call a unit meeting for it to be a pretty good contact."

Doctor, who were the friends and social contacts that you might have had in mind when making that statement?

A. My sister-in-law in Berkeley?

Q. And your brother.

A. I am not sure who I did have in mind. My sister-in-law had a very old friend called Winona Nedelsky.

Q. Who was she?

A. She was the wife of a physicist who left here—quite Russian—who had once been my student. She was a good friend of Jackie's. She earned her living in some Federal Housing Agency or Social Security Agency.

Q. Was she a Communist?

A. I believe so.

Q. Was she a friend of your sister-in-law in 1943?

A. I would think so. She was a friend. I don't know how much they saw each other.

Q. But in all events, you thought it cause for worry.

A. I would not have thought that a special cause for worry. I am having trouble in remembering what I could have had in mind and what I did have in mind.

Q. Can you think of anyone else that you might have had in mind as dangerous social contacts of your sister-in-law and your brother?

A. I don't know much about the life in Berkeley. I am afraid I can't.

Q. Lansdale said again, "To refer again to this business concerning the party, to make it clear the fact a person says they have severed connections with the party, the fact that they have at present no apparent interest or contact in it does not show where they have unquestionably formerly been members that they are dangerous to us."

You said, "I agree with that."

You still agree with that, do you?

A. Yes.

MR. GARRISON. Mr. Chairman, I repeat the same request I made with respect to the previous transcript, that we would like to see a copy of the full transcript.

MR. GRAY. May I say with respect to that that Dr. Oppenheimer will be given an opportunity to see documents reflecting conversations. They cannot be taken from the building.

MR. GARRISON. We appreciate that. When may we have that opportunity?

MR. GRAY. When the board and counsel have finished with the questioning.

MR. GARRISON. You mean this afternoon?

MR. GRAY. Whenever this is concluded.

By Mr. Robb:

Q. Lansdale said to you, according to this transcript, speaking of your reluctance to disclose the name of Professor X: "I don't see how you can have any hesitancy of disclosing the name of the man who has actually been engaged in an attempt of espionage in time of war. I mean my mind does not run along those channels."

You said, "I know it is a tough problem and I am worried about it a lot."

That was a correct statement of your attitude, wasn't it?

A. I would assume so.

Q. Lansdale, referring again to your reluctance to disclose the name, says, "Well, if you won't do it, you won't do it, but don't think I won't ask you again. Now I want to ask you this, And again, for the same reason which implies you're here, you may not answer. Who do you know on the project in Berkeley who are now, that's probably a hypothetical question, or have been members of the Communist Party?"

You answered, "I will try to answer that question. The answer will, however, be incomplete. I know for a fact, I know, I learned on my last visit to Berkeley that both Lomanitz and Weinberg were members. I suspected that before, but was not sure. I never had any way of knowing. I will think a minute, but there were other people. . . .

"Oppenheimer. In the case of my brother it is obvious that I know. In the cases of the others, it's just things that pile up, that I look at that way. I'm not saying that I couldn't think of other people, it's a hell of a big project. You can raise some names."

Doctor, having heard me read those lines, will you now concede that you knew at that time that both Lomanitz and Weinberg had been members of the Communist Party?

A. Evidently. Was I told by the security officers?

Q. I don't know. I have just read what you said. So when you wrote that letter of October 19, 1943, forwarding Lomanitz's request to be a transferred back to the project from military service, you knew that he had been a Communist Party member, didn't you?

A. So it appears.

Q. And you knew as early as 1943 that Weinberg had been, too.

A. So it appears.

Q. Yes, sir.

MR. GARRISON. Mr. Chairman, what troubles me about this whole method of examination is that counsel is reading from a transcript bits and parts without the full course of the conversation which took place to a witness whose memory at best, as anyone of ours would be, is very, very hazy upon all these things, and picking here a sentence and there a sentence out of context, and then holding him to the answer. I do think that this is a method of questioning that seems to me to be very unfair.

MR. ROBB. Mr. Chairman, I don't mean to make any argument about the matter, but I assume that this Board is following this transcript. If the Board feels I am being unfair at any point, I suppose the Board will interpose.

MR. GARRISON. Why shouldn't counsel be allowed to follow as any court of law, and this is not even a trial?

MR. ROBB. As you no doubt know, I have tried a good many cases, and I don't think it would be in the ordinary course of a trial.

MR. GARRISON. I disagree with you.

MR. ROBB. I resent counsel's statement that I am trying to be unfair with this witness, because I assure you that I have made every attempt to be fair with him. In fact, were I trying to be unfair, I would not ask this witness any of these questions, but would leave it in the file for the Board to read. I am giving this witness a chance to make whatever explanation he wishes to make.

MR. GARRISON. I still think that the fair thing would be to read the whole conversation and ask him what parts you want, instead of to pick isolated questions.

MR. GRAY. On the point of picking isolated questions, without trying to look at this whole question at this moment, I think it is clear that this interview concerned itself with matters which are involved in the questions Mr. Robb has been putting to the witness, and which are generally, I think, not new material. General Nichols' letter of December 23, and Mr. Oppenheimer's reply of March 4, I think both address themselves in one way or another to these individuals, Lomanitz, Weinberg, Bohm, which have been the subject of these questions.

I would say, Mr. Garrison, that I don't think it would be helpful to you at this point to have the transcript. I have said, however, that Dr. Oppenheimer and his counsel will be entitled to examine it and certainly after examination if you wish to reopen any of this testimony, you will be given every opportunity to do so. I think it is the feeling of the chairman of the board that things are not taken here out of context in a way which is prejudicial. I think also that the board has heard Dr. Oppenheimer say that with respect to some of these matters he has no recollection, which at least to me is perfectly understandable, many of these things having taken place many years ago. I do not think that it is the purpose of counsel to develop anything beyond what the facts are in this case. At least that is my interpretation.

MR. ROBB. That is my endeavor, Mr. Chairman. . . .

(Brief recess.)

MR. GARRISON. Mr. Chairman, forgive me for coming back to the same point, but during the recess I discussed this problem with my partner, Mr. Silverman, who has spent his life trying cases in the State of New York—I am not a trial lawyer, sir—our practice I am informed up there universally is that when counsel is cross examining a witness on a transcript he has never seen, counsel for the other side, if he asks the court for a copy, so he may read along with it, that request is granted. So if nothing else—I would not think of impugning this to Mr. Robb, and I hope he won't misunderstand me—I think it is the basis of the rule. That is the only reason I mention it. In other words, to make sure that the questions are in fact being read accurately from the transcript, and there are no interlineations or marks or matters of that sort that might perhaps raise a question as to the accuracy of what is there quite apart from the method by which the transcript was arrived at, and also to understand what the thread and continuity of the matter is. I merely report that to the Chairman. I don't want to put this on the basis of rules of law, because God knows, it is the rule here that this not a trial, but an inquiry, and I should suppose that a fortiori, what is proper in court of law would be accorded to us here in an inquiry. I do not labor the point. I present it to you and I will rest upon it.

THE WITNESS. May I make a comment?

MR. GRAY. Surely.

THE WITNESS. This last quotation . . . strikes me as so bizarre that I am troubled about the accuracy of the document. I am not certain—

MR. GARRISON. Do you know, Mr. Robb, whether this was taken down by a stenographer or was it from a tape?

MR. ROBB. Colonel Lansdale will be here. I might ask him. He is the one who conducted the interview.

MR. GRAY. I would like to be excused with counsel for the Board for a moment, if you please.

MR. ROBB. Mr. Chairman, I don't agree at all with the statement of law which has been made by Mr. Garrison although I confess I am not a New York trial lawyer. It has always been my understanding that when a witness is questioned about inconsistent statements, he is read the statements and he is asked if he made them. However, it is entirely immaterial to me whether counsel follows this statement or not. If the Chairman wants to have counsel have a copy of it, it is all right with me.

MR. GARRISON. We would appreciate that.

MR. ROBB. Very well.

MR. GRAY. I am about to make the ruling that Mr. [Garrison] follow reading this transcript as Mr. Robb reads it. Have you got a copy of it, Mr. Rolander?

MR. ROLANDER. I just went out and asked the secretary to try to locate a copy from the original files. I though that might be most helpful.

MR. ROBB. May the record now show, Mr. Chairman, that we are handing to Mr. Garrison the photostat copy of the interview with Dr. Oppenheimer by Lt. Col. Lansdale, 12 September 1943, consisting of 26 pages.

MR. GARRISON. Thank you, Mr. Chairman.

By Mr. Robb: . . .

Q. The next question and answer:
   "Now, have you yourself ever been a member of the Communist Party?"
   You answered, "No."
   "Lansdale. You've probably belonged to every front organization on the coast.
   "Oppenheimer. Just about."
   Doctor, do you recall that question and answer?

A. No, I don't. I don't recall this interview.

Q. If you said that to Colonel Lansdale, were you jocular?

A. I don't think I could have been jocular during this interview.

Q. "Lansdale. Would you in fact have considered yourself at one time a fellow traveler?
   "Oppenheimer. I think so. My association with these things was very brief and very intense."
   Do you recall that at all?

A. I am not recollecting anything. You may find a phrase that I do recollect.

Q. In all events, Doctor, your answer, "I think so. My association with these things was very brief and very intense," it is now your testimony that was a correct statement of fact?

A. It was very intense; brief is a relative word.

Q. Colonel Lansdale said: "I should imagine the latter anyway."
   Now, on page 11, you said, "It was historically quite brief and quite intense, and I should say I was—"
   "Lansdale. Now I have reason to believe that you yourself were felt out, I don't say asked, but felt out to ascertain how you felt about it, passing a little information, to the party.
   "Oppenheimer. You have reason?"
   "Lansdale. I say I have reason to believe, that's as near as I can come to stating it. Am I right or wrong?
   "Oppenheimer. If it was, it was so gentle I did not know it.
   "Lansdale. You don't know. Do you have anyone who is close to you, no that's the wrong word, who is an acquaintance of yours, who may have perhaps been a guest in your house, whom you perhaps knew through friends or relatives who is a member of the Communist Party. By that I mean—
   "Oppenheimer. My brother, obviously.
   "Lansdale. Well, no, I don't mean him.
   "Oppenheimer. I think probably you mean someone who just visited for a few hours.
   "Lansdale. Yes.
   "Oppenheimer. Yes, certainly, the answer to that is certainly, yes. . . .
   "Lansdale. Now, you have stated to me and also I think to General Groves that in your opinion membership in the party was incompatible with work on the project from a loyalty standpoint.

"Oppenheimer. Yes."

That was your viewpoint, wasn't it?

A. Yes.

Q. "Lansdale. Now, do you also go so far as to believe that persons who are not actually members but still retain their loyalty to the party or their adherence to the party line are in the same category?

"Oppenheimer. Let me put it this way. Loyalty to the party, yes, adherence to the party line, maybe no. In that it need not necessarily, although it often is, be the sign of subservience. At the present time I don't know what the party line is in too much detail, but I've heard from Mrs. Tolman, Tolman's wife, that the party line at present is not to discuss postwar affairs. I would be willing to say that anyone who, well let me put it this way, whose loyalty is above all else to the party or to Russia obviously is incompatible with loyalty to the United States. This is, I think, the heart of it. The party has its own discipline."

Do you recall saying that?

A. No, I don't recollect much about this. This, however sounds like what I thought.

Q. You have no doubt that was your view at that time?

A. Substantially that was my view.

Q. Is there any difference between what I have read and what your view was at that time?

A. I don't know. It is a long couple of paragraphs. It is a long time ago. I think it is substantially what I then thought.

Q. Lansdale then continued: "Now, I was coming to that. I would like to hear from you your reasons as to why you believe, let's stick to membership in the party, is incompatible to complete loyalty to the project. When, to state something a little bit foolishly membership in the Democratic Party certainly wouldn't be.

"Oppenheimer. It's an entirely different party. For one thing * * * I think I'd put it this way. The Democratic Party is the framework of the social customs * * * of this country, and I do not think that is true of the Communist Party. At least, I think that there are certainly many Communists who are above all decent guys, but there are also some that are above all Communists. It's primarily that question of personal honor that I think is involved. I don't know whether that answers the question but my idea is that being a Democrat doesn't guarantee that you're not a four-flusher, and also it has no suggestion just by virtue of your being a Democrat that you would think it would be all right to cheat other people for a purpose, and I'm not too sure about this with respect to the Communist Party."

Do you recall saying anything like that?

A. I don't.

Q. Would you say that did represent your views at that time?

A. I find nothing incompatible between it and what I remember. This is for me not a very easy line of questioning because I don't recollect what I said and I remember what I thought only in general terms. . . .

Q. And your memory is not refreshed by what I read you?
A. No, on the whole it is confused by it.

J. ROBERT OPPENHEIMER: "Of the known leakages of information, Fuchs is by far the most grave"

[After Robb raises other issues, including the unproven allegation that Oppenheimer attended a closed Communist Party meeting at his home in Berkeley in July 1941, chairman Gordon Gray asks a follow-up question just prior to adjourning the day's proceedings.]

MR. GRAY. I don't know whether you know the answer to this question, Dr. Oppenheimer, but in reading the files, there appear references to closed meetings of the Communist Party. There also appear many references to meetings of people who were Communists or fellow travelers, which were referred to as social gatherings. Without implying that you are an expert in these matters, but from conversations with your brother, perhaps, or Mrs. Oppenheimer and others, is there any real difference between a closed meeting and a social gathering if the same people are involved?

THE WITNESS. Let me tell you what I mean by the words. The words "closed meeting" mean to me one to which only members of the Communist Party can come. I think that is a rather sharp distinction if you are trying to identify who is and who isn't a member of the Communist Party. I should suppose that the difference between a meeting and social gathering was rather wide. In a meeting it was business and it was transacted and there was probably a chairman and there might be dues collected and there might be literature. Anyway, this happened at the little meeting I saw at my brother's. I should think that a social gathering would be a lot of talk which could indeed be very bad talk, but which would not be organized or programmatic. This is the sense in which I would interpret the words.

MR. GRAY. So these two meetings which have been the subject of some discussion at both of which I believe Mr. Schneiderman spoke, in the terms of the definitions which you have given, they would really have been social gatherings?

THE WITNESS. I would say they were neither. They were social gatherings ornamented by a special feature, namely, this lecture or speech. An ordinary social gathering I don't think has a lecture even in Communist jargon.

MR. GRAY. I just had the impression about these functions that many of those that we referred to were social gatherings may have been meetings. That doesn't concern your attendance at all.

There is one question I have which relates to the security of the project itself. Very early in your testimony in some discussion about procedures or security measures which were taken after very careful thought, you made the observation obviously they did not succeed. Again this is not a direct quote. Do you mind amplifying on that just a moment?

THE WITNESS. Yes. I think of the known leakages of information, Fuchs is by far the most grave. It occurred out of Los Alamos. I won't attempt to assess responsibility for the surveillance of personnel who moved around there. Facilities for surveillance were available, and they could well have been used in following Fuchs rather than somebody else. That would not have prevented his prior espionage, but it would have prevented the espionage at that time. I can't imagine any more pinpointed leakage than if Fuchs had simply communicated what he was working on. I don't mean that this was the only secret, but I can't imagine any single little point that would be more helpful to an enemy than the job he had himself. While not wishing to debate with General Groves either the necessity, the desirability, or the dangers of compartmentalization, I would like to record that if Fuchs had been infinitely compartmentalized, what was inside his compartment would have done the damage.

Friday, April 16

J. ROBERT OPPENHEIMER: "I would have done anything that I was asked to do . . . if I had thought it was technically feasible"

[Robb now turns to the charge that Oppenheimer opposed the hydrogen bomb in 1949, and that his opposition slowed down the weapon's development. To lay the groundwork, Robb queries Oppenheimer about his enthusiastic support for the atomic bomb, and his willingness, even during the war, to facilitate research on a thermonuclear device at Los Alamos. The obvious insinuation is that Oppenheimer's opposition to a crash program for building a hydrogen bomb in 1949 reflected pro-Soviet sympathies rather than moral qualms.]

CROSS-EXAMINATION (resumed)

By Mr. Robb: . . .

Q. Did you subsequent to the President's decision in January 1950 ever express any opposition to the production of the hydrogen bomb on moral grounds?

A. I would think that I could very well have said this is a dreadful weapon, or something like that. I have no specific recollection and would prefer it, if you would ask me or remind me of the context or conversation that you have in mind.

Roger Robb at a Senate hearing, July
1958. Paul Schutzer/TimePix.

Q. Why do you think you could very well have said that?
A. Because I have always thought it was a dreadful weapon. Even from a
   technical point of view it was a sweet and lovely and beautiful job, I have
   still thought it was a dreadful weapon.
Q. And have said so?
A. I would assume that I have said so, yes.
Q. You mean you had a moral revulsion against the production of such a
   dreadful weapon?
A. This is too strong.
Q. Beg pardon?
A. That is too strong.
Q. Which is too strong, the weapon or my expression?
A. Your expression. I had a grave concern and anxiety.
Q. You had moral qualms about it, is that accurate?
A. Let us leave the word "moral" out of it.
Q. You had qualms about it.
A. How could one not have qualms about it? I know no one who doesn't have
   qualms about it. . . .

Q. Doctor, in your work and discussions in 1942, in your work on the thermonuclear weapon at Los Alamos in 1943 to 1945 and in your application for the patent of 1944, and in your advice which you as chairman of the GAC gave to the Commission to get on with the work on this thermonuclear, at all those times and on all of those occasions, were you suffering from or deterred by any moral scruples or qualms about the development of this weapon?

A. Of course.

Q. You were?

A. Of course.

Q. But you still got on with the work, didn't you?

A. Yes, because this was a work of exploration. It was not the preparation of a weapon.

Q. You mean it was just an academic excursion?

A. It was an attempt at finding out what things could be done.

Q. But you were going to spend millions of dollars of the taxpayers' money on it, weren't you?

A. It goes on all the time.

Q. Were you going to spend millions if not billions of dollars of the taxpayers' money just to find out for yourself satisfaction what was going on?

A. We spent no such sums.

Q. Did you propose to spend any such sums for a mere academic excursion?

A. No. It is not an academic thing whether you can make a hydrogen bomb. It is a matter of life and death.

Q. Beginning in 1942 and running through at least the first year or the first meeting of the GAC, you were actively and consciously pushing the development of the thermonuclear bomb, weren't you? Isn't that your testimony?

A. Pushing is not the right word. Supporting and working on it, yes.

Q. Yes. When did these moral qualms become so strong that you opposed the development of the thermonuclear bomb?

A. When it was suggested that it be the policy of the United States to make these things at all costs, without regard to the balance between these weapons and atomic weapons as a part of our arsenal.

Q. What did moral qualms have to do with that?

A. What did moral qualms have to do with it?

Q. Yes, sir.

A. We freely used the atomic bomb.

Q. In fact, Doctor, you testified, did you not, that you assisted in selecting the target for the drop of the bomb on Japan?

A. Right.

Q. You knew, did you not, that the dropping of that atomic bomb on the target you had selected will kill or injure thousands of civilians, is that correct?

A. Not as many as turned out.

Q. How many were killed or injured?

A. 70,000.

Q. Did you have moral scruples about that?

A. Terrible ones.

Q. But you testified the other day, did you not, sir that the bombing of Hiroshima was very successful?

A. Well, it was technically successful.

Q. Oh, technically.

A. It is also alleged to have helped end the war.

Q. Would you have supported the dropping of a thermonuclear bomb on Hiroshima?

A. It would make no sense at all.

Q. Why.

A. The target is too small.

Q. The target is too small. Supposing there had been a target in Japan big enough for a thermonuclear weapon, would you have opposed dropping it?

A. This was not a problem with which I was confronted.

Q. I am confronting you with it now, sir.

A. You are not confronting me with an actual problem. I was very relieved when Mr. Stimson removed from the target list Kyoto, which was the largest city and the most vulnerable target. I think this is the nearest thing that was really to your hypothetical question.

Q. That is correct. Would you have opposed the dropping of a thermonuclear weapon on Japan because of moral scruples?

A. I believe I would, sir.

Q. Did you oppose the dropping of the atom bomb on Hiroshima because of moral scruples?

A. We set forth our—

Q. I am asking you about it, not "we."

A. I set forth my anxieties and the arguments on the other side.

Q. You mean you argued against dropping the bomb?

A. I set forth arguments against dropping it.

Q. Dropping the atom bomb?

A. Yes. But I did not endorse them.

Q. You mean having worked, as you put it, in your answer rather excellently, by night and by day for 3 or 4 years to develop the atom bomb, you then argued it should not be used?

A. No; I didn't argue that it should not be used. I was asked to say by the Secretary of War what the views of scientists were. I gave the views against and the views for.

Q. But you supported the dropping of the atom bomb on Japan, didn't you?

A. What do you mean support?

Q. You helped pick the target, didn't you?

A. I did my job which was the job I was supposed to do. I was not in a policy-making position at Los Alamos. I would have done anything that I was asked to do, including making the bombs in a different shape, if I had thought it was technically feasible.

Q. You would have made the thermonuclear weapon, too, wouldn't you?

A. I couldn't.

Q. I didn't ask you that, Doctor.

A. I would have worked on it.

Q. If you had discovered the thermonuclear weapon at Los Alamos, you would have done so. If you could have discovered it, you would have done so, wouldn't you?

A. Oh, yes.

Q. You were working toward that end, weren't you?

A. Yes. I think I need to point out that to run a laboratory is one thing. To advise the Government is another.

Q. I see.

A. I think I need to point out that a great deal that happened between '45 and '49—I am not supposed to say to what extent—but to a very, very massive extent, we had become armed atomically. The prevailing view was that what we had was too good—too big—for the best military use, rather than too small.

Q. Doctor, would you refer to your answer, please, sir? One further question before we get into that.

Am I to gather from your testimony, sir, that in your opinion your function as a member and chairman of the GAC included giving advice on political policies as well as technical advice?

A. I have testified as to that.

Q. Would you repeat it for me, sir?

A. I will repeat it. Our statutory function was to give technical advice.

Q. Yes, sir.

A. We were often asked questions which went outside of this narrow frame, sometimes we responded, sometimes we didn't. The reason why the general advice, I would call it, editorializing rather than political advice, contained in our annexes was in the annexes and not in the report because it did not seem a proper function for the General Advisory Committee to respond in these terms to the question that had been put to them.

Q. Doctor, is it a fair summary of your answer—and I refer you to page 37, and the following pages of your answer—that what the GAC opposed in its October 29, 1949, meeting was merely a crash program for the development of the super?

A. Yes. I think it would be a better summary to say we opposed this crash program as the answer to the Soviet atomic bomb.

Q. What did you mean by a crash program?

A. On the basis of what was then known, plant be built, equipment be procured and a commitment be made to build this thing irrespective of further study and with a very high priority. A program in which alternatives would not have an opportunity to be weighed because one had to get on and because we were not going to sacrifice time.

Q. Doctor, isn't it true that the report of the GAC you wrote, didn't you—

A. I wrote the main report; yes.

Q. Isn't it true that the report of the GAC and the annex to which you sub-scribed unqualifiedly opposed the development of the super at any time?

A. At that time.

Q. At any time?

A. No. At least, let us say we were questioned about that in a discussion with the Commission, and we made it quite clear that this could not be an un-qualified and permanent opposition. I think that in the reading of the report without the later discussions and reports it could be read that way. But in the light of what was later said, it could not be read that way.

Q. Didn't the annex to which you subscribed say in so many words, "We be-lieve a superbomb should never be produced"?

A. Yes; it did.

Q. It did say that?

A. Yes.

Q. Do you interpret that as opposing only a crash program?

A. No. It opposed the program. Obviously if we learned that the enemy was up to something, we could not prevent the production of a super bomb.

Q. What did you mean by "never"?

A. I didn't write those words.

Q. You signed it, though, didn't you?

A. I believe what we meant—what I meant was that it would be a better world if there were no hydrogen bombs in it. That is what the whole con-text says.

Q. Doctor, don't you think a fair interpretation of the record and the annex which you signed was an unqualified opposition to the production of super at any time or under any circumstances?

A. No. I don't.

Q. That is your view?

A. Yes.

Q. In all events, Doctor, you did say in your report that no one could tell with-out an actual test whether the super would work or whether it wouldn't, is that right?

A. Yes.

J. ROBERT OPPENHEIMER: "I am not sure the miserable thing will work . . . [but it] would be folly to oppose the exploration of this weapon"

[Oppenheimer's assertion that he had no communication from Glenn T. Seaborg prior to the October 1949 GAC meeting provides another opening for Robb, who has proof that Seaborg had indeed expressed his view in a letter; the implication is that Oppenheimer, by withholding the letter, had deceived the other members of the committee.]

Q. You testified that you had no intimation from Dr. Seaborg prior to the GAC meeting of October 29, 1949, as to what his views on the subject were. I am going to show you a letter taken from your files at Princeton, returned by you to the Commission, dated October 14, 1949, addressed to you, signed Glenn Seaborg, and ask you whether you received that letter prior to the meeting of October 29, 1949.

A. I am going to say before I see that that I had no recollection of it.

Q. I assumed that. May I interrupt your reading of it a moment?

A. Yes.

MR. ROBB. Mr. Chairman, I have been told by the classification officer that there are two words here that I must not read. They are bracketed, and I am showing them to Dr. Oppenheimer, and when I read the letter I shall leave them out, but I want Dr. Oppenheimer to see them.

THE WITNESS. I would be sure of one thing, and that is if that letter reached me before the meeting, I read it to the committee.

By Mr. Robb:

Q. The letter was dated October 14, 1949.

A. So it almost certainly reached me.

Q. So presumably unless it came by wagon train, it reached you, didn't it?

A. Right.

Q. I will read this letter:

University of California,
Radiation Laboratory,
Berkeley 4, Calif., October 14, 1949.

Dr. J. Robert Oppenheimer,
The Institute for Advanced Study,
Princeton, N. J.
Dear Robert:

I will try to give you my thoughts for what they may be worth regarding the next GAC meeting, but I am afraid that there may be more questions than answers. Mr. Lilienthal's assignment to us is very broad; and it seems to me that conclusions will be reached, if at all, only after a large amount of give and take discussion at the GAC meeting.

A question which cannot be avoided, it seems to me, is that which was raised by Ernest Lawrence during his recent trip to Los Alamos and Washington. Are we in a race along this line and one in which we may already be somewhat behind so far as this particular new aspect is concerned?

He was talking about the thermonuclear, wasn't he?

A. It would be obvious to me he was.

Q. Continuing:

Apparently this possibility has begun to bother very seriously a number of people out here, several of whom came to this point of view independently. Although I deplore the prospects of our country putting a tremendous effort into this, I must confess that I have been unable to come to the conclusion that we should not. Some people are thinking of a time scale of the order of 3 to 5 years which may, of course, be practically impossible and would surely involve an effort of greater magnitude than that of the Manhattan project. My present feeling would perhaps be best summarized by saying that I would have to hear some good arguments before I could take on sufficient courage to recommend not going toward such a program.

If such a program were undertaken, a number of questions arise which would need early answers. How would the National Laboratories fit into the program? Wouldn't they have to reorient their present views considerably? The question as to who might build neutron producing reactors would arise. I am afraid that we could not realistically look to the present operators of Hanford to take this on. It would seem that a strong effort would have to be made to get the duPont Company back into the game. It would be imperative that the present views of the reactor safeguard committee be substantially changed.

I just do not know how to comment, without further reflection, on the question of how the present 'reactor program' should be modified, if it should. Probably, after much discussion, you will come to the same old conclusion that the present four reactors be carried on, but that an effort be made to speed up their actual construction. As you probably know, Ernest is willing to take on the responsibility for the construction near Berkeley of a— and then I omit the two words—heavy water natural uranium reactor primarily for a neutron source and on a short time scale. I don't know whether it is possible to do what is planned here, but I can say that a lot of effort by the best people here is going into it. If the GAC is asked to comment on this proposal, it seems to me clear that we should heartily endorse it. So far as I can see, this program will not interfere with any of the other reactor building programs and will be good even if it does not finally serve exactly the purpose for which it was conceived; I have recently been tending toward the conviction that the United States should be doing more with heavy water reactors (we are doing almost nothing). In this connection, it seems to me that there might be a discussion concerning the heavy water production facilities and their possible expansion.

Another question, and one on which perhaps I have formulated more of a definite opinion, is that of secrecy. It seems to me that we can't afford to continue to hamper ourselves by keeping secret as many things as we now do. I think that not only basic science should be subject to less secrecy regulation but also some places outside of this area. For example, it seems entirely pointless now to hamper the construction of certain types of new piles by keeping secret certain lattice dimensions. In case anything so trivial as the conclusions reached at the recent international meeting on declassification with the British and Canadians at Chalk River is referred to the GAC I might just add that I participated in these discussions and thoroughly agree with the changes suggested, with the reservation that perhaps they should go further toward removing secrecy.

I have great doubt that this letter will be of much help to you, but I am afraid that it is the best that I can do at this time.

Sincerely yours, Glenn

Glenn T. Seaborg.

So, Doctor, isn't it clear to you now that Dr. Seaborg did express himself on this matter before the meeting?

A. Yes, it is clear now. Not in unequivocal terms, except on one point, and on that point the General Advisory Committee I think made the recommendation that he desired.

Q. But he did express himself, didn't he?

A. Absolutely.

Q. In a communication to which he apparently had given some thought, is that correct?

A. Right, and to which no doubt at the time I gave some thought.

Q. That is right. You have no doubt that you received this before the General Advisory Committee meeting, is that correct?

A. I don't see why I should not have.

Q. Why did you tell the Joint Congressional Committee on Atomic Energy when you testified on January 29, 1950, that Dr. Seaborg had not expressed himself on the subject prior to the meeting?

A. I am sure because it was my recollection.

Q. That testimony was given in January 1950, wasn't it?

A. That is right.

Q. And this letter had been received by—

A. Let me add one point. We had a second meeting on the hydrogen bomb which Seaborg attended and we asked him how he felt about it, and he said he would prefer not to express his views.

Q. But weren't you asked, Doctor, or didn't you tell the joint committee that Dr. Seaborg had not expressed himself on this subject prior to the meeting of October 29, 1949?

A. I would have to see the transcript. I don't remember that question and the answer.

Q. If you did make that statement, it was not true, was it?

A. It is clear that we had an expression, not unequivocal, from Seaborg, before the meeting of October 29.

Q. Doctor, did you hear my question?

A. I heard it, but I have heard that kind of question too often.

Q. I am sure of that, Doctor, but would you answer it, nevertheless?

MR. MARKS. Isn't Dr. Oppenheimer entitled to see the testimony which is being referred to, instead of answering a hypothetical question?

MR. ROBB. It is not a hypothetical question.

By Mr. Robb:

Q. If you told the joint committee, sir, that Dr. Seaborg had not expressed himself prior to the meeting of October 29, 1950, that was not true, was it?

A. It would depend, entirely.

Q. Yes or no.

A. I will not say yes or no. It would depend entirely on the context of the question. The only two things in this letter that Seaborg is absolutely clear about is that we ought to build certain kinds of reactors and we ought to have less secrecy. On the question of the thermonuclear program he can't find good enough arguments against it, but he does have misgivings.

Q. All right, Doctor. You told this Board this morning that Dr. Seaborg did not express himself prior to the meeting of October 29, 1949.

A. That is right. That was my recollection.

Q. Was that true?

A. No, that was not true.

Q. You told the board this morning—

MR. GRAY. Are you pursuing the Seaborg matter now?

MR. ROBB. I thought I would come back to it, sir.

MR. GARRISON. Mr. Chairman, I think it would be fair since the question was raised, because of the implications that may be left that the actual questions put to Dr. Oppenheimer by the joint committee about Dr. Seaborg should be read into the record with sufficient context to show what it was about. Otherwise, we are left with a possible misapprehension as to what really did take place. I don't know. I have never seen the transcript.

MR. ROBB. Mr. Chairman, that is impossible unless we have a meeting of the joint committee and they authorize that to be done. But Dr. Oppenheimer this morning as the board no doubt heard, recalled that he had so testified before the joint committee.

THE WITNESS. I had testified; I had not so testified.

MR. ROBB. The record will show what the doctor testified.

THE WITNESS. If I testified that I recall so testifying, I would like to correct the transcript.

MR. ROBB. That was not correct, either?

MR. SILVERMAN. He didn't say it.

MR. ROBB. All right. The record will show what he testified to.

MR. GARRISON. What is the procedural requirement for reading into the record the questions from that transcript?

MR. ROBB. That transcript will not be released, as I understand it, without the vote of the committee to do so, Mr. Garrison, which is why I was not able to read Dr. Oppenheimer what he said.

THE WITNESS. I think a lot depends on the nature of the question. Had Dr. Seaborg made up his mind, had he concurred with your view, or so on. It is clear from this letter he wanted to hear a discussion about it. That he saw it was a very tough question.

MR. ROBB. May I ask the doctor one more question before we take a break on this Seaborg matter.

MR. GRAY. Yes.

By Mr. Robb:

Q. Doctor, are you sure that you read Dr. Seaborg's letter to your committee, the GAC committee, at the meeting of October 29, 1949?

A. Since I forgot the existence of the letter, obviously I cannot remember reading it. I always read communications on matters before us to the committee.

Q. Is there any reflection in the report of the committee that Dr. Seaborg had expressed himself in any way about this matter?

A. No, there certainly is not.

Q. I beg your pardon?

A. There isn't.

MR. ROBB. All right.

MR. GARRISON. May I ask the chairman whether the board has before it the transcript of the joint committee testimony? I ask merely because of the fact that if it has been released to the board—

MR. GRAY. Let me respond to your question this way, Mr. Garrison, and say that after recess, which I propose to call in a moment, I should like to respond to that.

We will now recess.

(Brief recess.)

MR. GRAY. I would like to pursue the question which Mr. Garrison raised just before the recess.

The board does not have before it a complete transcript of the testimony which was under discussion.

(Mr. Marks not present in the room.)

MR. GRAY. However, I can say to Dr. Oppenheimer and his counsel that the board does understand from a source it believes to be reliable that Dr. Oppenheimer was asked a question with respect to the extent of unanimity of the views of the members of the GAC with respect to what we have been describing as the crash program. I am not sure whether it was so referred to in the testimony, but there was this question.

In response to the question Dr. Oppenheimer stated that he thought it was pretty unanimous view, that one member of the committee, Dr. Seaborg, was away when the matter was discussed, and that he had not expressed himself on it, and further saying that the other members will agree with what he has said.

THE WITNESS. That is a little different from what I was told I said. I was told I said explicitly that Seaborg had said nothing about the matter before the meeting. This was several months after the meeting and I was asked whether Seaborg had expressed his views in connection with this meeting. I would think that the proper answer to that was not so far from what you quoted me as saying.

MR. GRAY. We are trying to develop what actually the facts were in the case, and I believe you did testify that you had no communication with respect to this matter from Dr. Seaborg or at least you said you did not recall a communication, I believe.

THE WITNESS. Is that what it says in the transcript?

MR. GRAY. No; I think that is what you said earlier this morning.

THE WITNESS. I would like to make a general protest. I am told I have said certain things. I don't recall it. I am asked if I said these what would that be. This is an extremely difficult form for me to face a question. I don't know what I said. It is of record. I had it in my own vault for many years. It is not classified for reasons of national security, this conversation, and I have no sense that I could have wished to give any impression to the joint congressional committee other than an exposition because when I testified I knew for a fact that the decision had been taken. I testified in order to explain as well as I could to the committee the grounds for the advice, the color of the advice, the arguments that we had in mind. It was not an attempt to persuade them. It was not in any way an attempt to alter the outcome. It was an attempt to describe what we had in mind. A few minutes after I testified, I believe, or shortly after I testified, the Presidential announcement came out, and I knew what it was going to be. So this was not a piece of advocacy. It was a piece of exposition.

I would like to add one other thing. Having no recollection of the Seaborg letter, I cannot say that I did this. But it would have been normal practice for me at one of the meetings with the Commission not merely to read the letter to the committee, but to read the letter or parts of it relevant to our discussion to the Commission and the committee.

By Mr. Robb:

Q. In other words, Doctor, if you didn't read this Seaborg letter to your committee, it would have been quite unusual?

A. Yes. . . .

Q. Doctor, I want to show you a copy of a letter also taken from your files that you had at Princeton and turned back to the Commission. This is a copy of a letter dated October 21, 1949, bearing the typewritten signature Robert Oppenheimer, addressed to Dr. James B. Conant, president, Harvard University: . . .

Dear Uncle Jim:

We are exploring the possibilities for our talk with the President on October 30th. All members of the advisory committee will come to the meeting Saturday except Seaborg, who must be in Sweden, and whose general views we have in written form. Many of us will do some preliminary palavering on the 28th.

There is one bit of background which I would like you to have before we meet. When we last spoke, you thought perhaps the reactor program offered the most decisive example of the need for policy clarification. I was inclined to think that the super might also be relevant. On the technical side, as far as I can tell, the super is not very different from what it was when we first spoke of it more than 7 years ago: a weapon of unknown design, cost, deliberability and military value. But a very great change has taken place in the climate of opinion. On the one hand, two experienced promoters have been at work, i.e., Ernest Lawrence and Edward Teller. The project has long been dear to Teller's heart; and Ernest has convinced himself that we must learn from Operation Joe that the Russians will soon do the super, and that we had better beat them to it.

What was Operation Joe, the Russian explosion?
A. Right.
(Mr. Marks entered the room.)

By Mr. Robb:

Q. Of September 1949?
A. Right.
Q. Continuing your letter: "On the technical side, he proposes to get some neutron producing heavy water reactors built; and to this, for a variety of reasons, I think we must say amen since"—now would you paraphrase?
A. There were three military applications other than the super which these reactors would serve.

Q. * * * and many other things will all profit by the availability of neutrons.
But the real development has not been of a technical nature. Ernest spoke to Knowland and McMahon, and to some at least of the joint chiefs. The joint congressional committee, having tried to find something tangible to chew on ever since September 23d, has at least found its answer. We must have a super, and we must have it fast. A subcommittee is heading west to investigate this problem at Los Alamos, and in Berkeley. The joint chiefs appear informally to have decided to give the development of the super overriding priority, though no formal request has come through. The climate of opinion among the competent physicists also shows signs of shifting. Bethe, for instance, is seriously considering return on a full time basis; and so surely are some others. I have had long talks with Bradbury and Manley, and with von Neumann. Bethe, Teller, McCormack, and LeBaron are all scheduled to turn up within the next 36 hours. I have agreed that if there is a conference on the super program at Los Alamos, I will make it my business to attend.
What concerns me is really not the technical problem. I am not sure the miserable thing will work, nor that it can be gotten to a target except by ox cart. It seems likely to me even further to worsen the unbalance of our present war plans. What does worry me is that this thing appears to have caught the imagination, both of the congressional and of military people, as the answer to the

problem posed by the Russian advance. It would be folly to oppose the exploration of this weapon. We have always known it had to be done; and it does have to be done, though it appears to be singularly proof against any form of experimental approach. But that we become committed to it as the way to save the country and the peace appears to me full of dangers.

We will be faced with all this at our meeting; and anything that we do or do not say to the President, will have to take it into consideration. I shall feel far more secure if you have had an opportunity to think about it.

I still remember my visit with gratitude and affection.

Robert Oppenheimer

Doctor, would it appear to you from that letter that you were in error in your previous testimony that you had not expressed your views to Dr. Conant before the meeting of October 29, 1949?

A. Yes.

Q. Beg pardon?

A. Yes.

Q. Do you wish now to amend your previous answer that Dr. Conant reached the views he expressed to you without any suggestion on your part?

A. I don't know which preceded which.

Q. Is there any indication to you in this letter which I have just read that Conant had previously expressed any views to you?

A. I would say there is an indication that there had been discussion between us. I am not clear.

Q. Why were you writing to Dr. Conant before the GAC meeting on this thing?

A. I think the letter explains that.

Q. You were not trying to propagandize him, were you?

A. No.

Q. Do you agree with me that this letter is susceptible of that interpretation that you were trying to influence him?

A. Not properly; not properly so susceptible.

Q. You notice in this letter, Doctor, that you referred to Dr. Seaborg's letter, so you had it at that time, didn't you?

A. Right.

Q. And that must have been the letter we read this morning, is that correct?

A. I would assume so.

Q. Would you agree, Doctor, that your references to Dr. Lawrence and Dr. Teller and their enthusiasm for the super bomb, their work on the super bomb, that your references in this letter are a little bit belittling?

A. Dr. Lawrence came to Washington. He did not talk to the Commission. He went and talked to the joint congressional committee and to members of the Military Establishment. I think that deserves some belittling.

Q. So you would agree that your references to those men in this letter were belittling?

A. No. I pay my great respects to them as promoters. I don't think I did them justice.

Q. You used the word "promoters" in an invidious sense, didn't you?

A. I promoted lots of things in my time.

Q. Doctor, would you answer my question? When you use the word "promoters" you meant it to be in a slightly invidious sense, didn't you?

A. I have no idea.

Q. When you use the word now with reference to Lawrence and Teller, don't you intend it to be invidious?

A. No.

Q. You think that their work of promotion was admirable, is that right?

A. I think they did an admirable job of promotion.

Q. Do you think it was admirable that they were promoting this project?

A. I told you that I think that the methods—I don't believe Teller was involved, Lawrence promoted it—were not proper.

Q. You objected to them going to Knowland and McMahon?

A. I objected to their not going to the Commission.

Q. Knowland and McMahon, by that you meant Senator Knowland and Senator McMahon.

A. Of course. . . .

J. ROBERT OPPENHEIMER: "The program in 1951 was technically so sweet that you could not argue about that"

[As Robb tries unsuccessfully to get Oppenheimer to admit that he impeded work on the hydrogen bomb, Gordon Gray pursues his own line of questioning in the same area.]

MR. GRAY: . . . .

My next question is one which was not fully developed, I think, in the questioning of counsel. I don't think it is a new matter, and I think it is pertinent to the whole problem.

Is it your opinion, Doctor, that the Russians would not have sought to develop a hydrogen bomb unless they knew in one way or another, or from one source or another, that this country was proceeding with it?

THE WITNESS. That was my opinion in 1949. As of the moment I have no opinion. I don't know enough about the history of what they have been doing.

MR. GRAY. I don't think my question relates so much to historical events as to a view of the international situation and the problems with which this country was confronted. Would it not have been reasonable to expect at any time since the apparent intentions or the intentions of the U.S.S.R. were clear to us that they would do anything to increase their military strength?

THE WITNESS. Right.

Mr. Gray. Whatever it might be.

The Witness. Oh, sure.

Mr. Gray. So you don't intend to have this record suggest that you felt that if those who opposed the development of the hydrogen bomb prevailed that would mean that the world would not be confronted with the hydrogen bomb?

The Witness. It would not necessarily mean—we thought on the whole it would make it less likely. That the Russians would attempt and less likely that they would succeed in the undertaking.

Mr. Gray. I would like to pursue that a little bit. That is two things. One, the likelihood of their success would we all hope still be related to their own capabilities and not to information they would receive from our efforts. So what you mean to say is that since they would not attempt it they would not succeed?

The Witness. No. I believe what we then thought was that the incentive to do it would be far greater if they knew we were doing it, and we had succeeded. Let me, for instance, take a conjecture. Suppose we had not done anything about the atom during the war. I don't think you could guarantee that the Russians would never have had an atomic bomb. But I believe they would not have one as nearly as soon as they have. I think both the fact of our success, the immense amount of publicity, the prestige of the weapon, the espionage they collect, all of this made it an absolutely higher priority thing, and we thought similar circumstances might apply to the hydrogen bomb. We were always clear that there might be a Russian effort whatever we did. We always understood that if we did not do this that an attempt would be made to get the Russians sewed up so that they would not either.

Mr. Gray. Further with respect to the hydrogen bomb, did in the end this turn out to be a larger weapon than you felt it might be when it was under discussion and consideration in 1942 and 1943?

The Witness. We were much foggier in 1942 and 1943. I think your imaginations ranged to the present figures.

Mr. Gray. I think I should disclose to you what I am after now. I am pursuing the matter of the moral scruples. Should they not have been as important in 1942 as they might have been in 1946 or 1948 or 1949?

The Witness. Yes.

Mr. Gray. I am trying to get at at what time did your strong moral convictions develop with respect to the hydrogen bomb?

The Witness. When it became clear to me that we would tend to use any weapon we had.

Mr. Gray. Then may I ask this: Do you make a sharp distinction between the development of a weapon and the commitment to use it?

The Witness. I think there is a sharp distinction but in fact we have not made it.

Mr. Gray. I have gathered from what you have said, this was something that underlay your thinking. The record shows that you constantly, with greater intensity at varying times perhaps, encouraged the efforts toward some sort of development, but at the point when it seemed clear that we would use it if we developed it, then you said we should not go ahead with it. I don't want to be unfair, but is that it?

THE WITNESS. That is only a small part of it. That is a part of it. The other part of it is, of course, the very great hope that these methods of warfare would never have to be used by anybody, a hope which became vivid in the fall of 1949. The hope that we would find a policy for bringing that about, and going on with bigger and bigger bombs would move in the opposite direction. I think that is apparent in the little majority annex to the GAC report.

MR. GRAY. Was it your feeling when you were concerned officially and otherwise with a possible disarmament program that the United States and its allies would be in a better bargaining position with respect to the development of some sort of international machinery if it did not have the hydrogen bomb as a weapon in the arsenal, or is that relevant at all?

THE WITNESS. The kind of thing we had in mind is what one would do in 1949 and 1950.

MR. GRAY. This is quite a serious line of questioning as far as I am concerned, because it has been said—I am not sure about the language of the Nichols letter—at least in this proceeding and later on in the press, that you frustrated the development of the hydrogen bomb. That has been said. There have been some implications, I suppose, that there were reasons which were not related to feasible, to cost, et cetera.

THE WITNESS. Right. I think I can answer your question.

MR. GRAY. Very well.

THE WITNESS. Clearly we could not do anything about the nonuse or the elimination of atomic weapons unless we had nonatomic military strength to meet whatever threats we were faced with. I think in 1949 when we came to this meeting and talked about it, we thought we were at a parting of the ways, a parting of the ways in which either the reliance upon atomic weapons would increase further and further or in which it would be reduced. We hoped it would be reduced because without that there was no chance of not having them in combat.

MR. GRAY. Your deep concern about the use of the hydrogen bomb, if it were developed, and therefore your own views at the time as to whether we should proceed in a crash program to develop it—your concern about this— became greater, did it not, as the practicabilities became more clear? Is that an unfair statement?

THE WITNESS. I think it is the opposite of true. Let us not say about use. But my feeling about development became quite different when the practicabilities became clear. When I saw how to do it, it was clear to me that one had to at least make the thing. Then the only problem was what would one do about them when one had them. The program we had in 1949 was a tortured thing that you could well argue did not make a great deal of technical sense. It was therefore possible to argue also that you did not want it even if you could have it. The program in 1951 was technically so sweet that you could not argue about that. It was purely the military, the political and the humane problem of what you were going to do about it once you had it. . . .

MR. GRAY. I suppose my final question on that is related to the view you held at one time that a cessation—correct me if I mistake this—of Communist activities, as distinguished from Communist sympathies, was important in considering a man for important classified work. Is that your view today?

THE WITNESS. No; I have for a long time been clear that sympathy with the enemy is incompatible with responsible or secret work to the United States.

MR. GRAY. So it would not be sufficient to say to a man, stop making speeches, stop going to meetings; that would not be enough?

THE WITNESS. It was not in fact sufficient before. It was sufficient only if it was a man whose disengagement was dependable.

MR. GRAY. Disengagement as far as activities are concerned.

THE WITNESS. And to some extent conduct. Today it is a very simple thing it seems to me, and has been for some years. We have a well-defined enemy. Sympathy for him may be tolerable, but it is not tolerable in working for the people or the Government of this country.

JOHN LANSDALE: "We kept him under surveillance whenever he left the project. We opened his mail. We did all sorts of nasty things"

[Two witnesses, associates of Oppenheimer, testify briefly as to his loyalty: Thomas Keith Glennan, president of Case Institute of Technology in Cleveland, who served on the Atomic Energy Commission from 1950 to 1952; and Karl T. Compton, who first met Oppenheimer in 1926 and who was chairman of the Research and Development Board in the Department of Defense in 1947 and 1948. Then, former security officer John Lansdale, whose September 1943, interview with Oppenheimer has already been introduced into evidence, is called to testify. A graduate of the Virginia Military Institute and Harvard Law School, Landsale is at the time of the hearing a member of a Cleveland law firm.]

DIRECT EXAMINATION

By Mr. Garrison: . . .

Q. Will you tell the board about your discussions with General Groves about Dr. Oppenheimer's background and about his clearance?

A. I cannot recall precisely when we first began to discuss Dr. Oppenheimer. . . .

In any event, Dr. Oppenheimer had been on the project prior to the time that the Army took over. When the Army took it over, the security was virtually nonexistent and the program of personnel clearance was practically nonexistent. I won't say it did not exist because it did, but it was very incomplete. One of the first things that we did was to attempt to get some investigation and set up some program for the clearance of the personnel that were received with the project, as it were. . . .

General Groves' view, as I recall expressed, was (a) that Dr. Oppenheimer was essential; (b) that in his judgment—and he had gotten to know Dr. Oppenheimer very well by that time—he was loyal; and (c) we would clear him for this work whatever the reports said.

I will confess that I myself at that time had considerable doubts about it. Because of our worry, or my worry, let us say, about Dr. Oppenheimer, we continued to the best of our ability to investigate him. We kept him under surveillance whenever he left the project. We opened his mail. We did all sorts of nasty things that we do or did on the project.

I interviewed him myself a number of times. As I recall, the recommendations of the security organization headed up by Captain Calvert were adverse to Dr. Oppenheimer. They recommended against clearance.

By Mr. Garrison:

Q. Who was Captain Calvert?
A. I think his official title was District Security Officer. He was on General Nichols', then Colonel Nichols, staff. In any event, I fully concurred with General Groves as our investigation went on with the fact that Dr. Oppenheimer was properly cleared. . . .
THE WITNESS. I remember that I asked General Groves early in the game what would he do if it turned out that Dr. Oppenheimer was not loyal and that we could not trust him? His reply was that he would blow the whole thing wide open.

I do not mean to imply by that, that our conclusions as to clearance were necessarily dictated by indispensability. I wish to emphasize it for myself. I reached the conclusion that he was loyal and ought to be cleared.

By Mr. Garrison:

Q. You did have certain employees, did you not, that the project had at Los Alamos who were kept on the basis of what might be called a calculated risk?
A. Yes; that is true. That is true of Los Alamos and other parts of the project.
Q. Certain people who were known or believed to be Communists?
A. Yes, sir.
Q. Why did the project employ some people of that character?
A. My only answer to that is that we continually had to exercise judgment as between obvious all out security and the necessities of the project. It must be remembered that the Germans were far ahead of us in the development of an atomic bomb. We believed that the nation which first obtained one would win the war. We were under, believe me, very terrible feeling of pres-

sure. Every security decision we made with reference to important people was made in that background.

We had a number of persons who we believed were very likely to be Communists, who we were persuaded were doing such useful work and such important work, that good judgment required that we keep them and let them do their work and surround them and insulate them to the best extent of our ability. That is what we did in a number of cases.

I can't answer it any better than that.

Q. Dr. Oppenheimer was not in that category of calculated risk, I take it?

A. Not in my judgment, no.

Q. Did you ever know of any leakage of information from any of the persons of the sort you have mentioned to the outside?

A. We never discovered any leakage of information from those persons that we deliberately kept as a calculated risk. I don't mean to assert that there was none. We discovered none and we used every effort we could to make it difficult for them.

For example, with many of them we made it perfectly obvious that we were watching their every move so as to be sure that if they desired to pass information they would go to extraordinary lengths to do so and thus make it easier to detect.

Q. Did you know of any leakage from the Los Alamos project, apart from that which has become public property?

A. Apart from the inexcusable Greenglass case, I now recall none that we know of. Oh, we had a mail censorship program set up and we were continually picking up the things in letters that we thought ought not to go out and which we intercepted. Those were the kind of things which my recollection is that we didn't regard as deliberate attempts at security violation. . . .

Q. Was the job of administering this community a difficult one in your judgment as you observed it?

A. It certainly was. The commanding officers were changed very rapidly.

Q. What would you say as to the nature of the scientists and their human characteristics, as you saw them at work on the project in relations to the problem of administration?

A. The scientists en masse presented an extremely difficult problem. The reason for it, as near as I can judge, is that with certain outstanding exceptions they lacked what I called breadth. They were extremely competent in their field but their extreme competence in their chosen field lead them falsely to believe that they were as competent in any other field.

The result when you got them together was to make administration pretty difficult because each one thought that he could administer the administrative aspects of the Army post better than any Army officer, for example, and didn't hesitate to say so with respect to any detail of living or detail of security or anything else.

I hope my scientist friends will forgive me, but the very nature of them made things pretty difficult.

Q. They were slightly restive under the confinement of the isolated city.

A. Very. As time went on, more so. Toward the latter stages it became increasingly difficult to sit on the lid out there. During the early stages, no.

Q. What was Dr. Oppenheimer's policy as an administrator in relation to keeping the morale going and keeping the natural restiveness of these people within bounds? Was he helpful?

A. So far as I observed it, he was very helpful. The difficulty primarily arose from those that were one step below him, let us say, in the scientific side. Dr. Oppenheimer himself so far as security matters with which I was particularly concerned was extremely cooperative. . . .

Q. What do you recall of your interview with Dr. Oppenheimer on what we call here the Chevalier incident, if you know what I have reference to?

A. Yes. That is one of the things which I have had the advantage of reading the transcript of some weeks ago and glancing at one page of it again last night.

I should say that I talked to Dr. Oppenheimer many times. In that particular case the interview was when he was in Washington and I now believe that the interview took place in General Groves' office, although that is a reconstruction. I have no precise recollection of it except that it was in Washington.

Do you wish me to relate the substance of it?

Q. Yes.

A. The substance of it was that Dr. Oppenheimer had advised our people on the west coast that an approach had been made to someone on the project to secure information concerning the project, and that the approach had been made by one Eltenton who was well known to us—from Eltenton to a third person and from the third person to the project.

From reading the transcript and having my attention called to memoranda by Mr. Robb and Mr. Rolander, the information was that the contact was with three persons. It is perfectly obvious that was the story. It is a curious trick of memory but my recollection was one and that the one person was Dr. Oppenheimer's brother, Frank Oppenheimer. I have no explanation as to how I translate it from three into one.

I called General Groves last night and discussed it with him in an attempt to fathom that and I can't figure it out. But the record shows clearly that there were three.

My effort was to get Dr. Oppenheimer to tell me the identity of the person that was later identified as Chevalier. In that I was unsuccessful. Perhaps I was not as resourceful a questioner as I might have been. In any event I could not get him to tell me. That is the sum and substance of it.

I came back and told the general that it was up to him, that he just had to get the information for us, which the general undertook to do and later reported back the information. That goes on for pages. I am quite sure that I interrogated him concerning other persons on the project. I am quite sure it is a long statement as I read it in the transcript. Our discussion covered a wide range. That is my present recollection.

Q. Was there any other instance in which Dr. Oppenheimer did not give you information that you asked for?

A. I don't recall any.

Q. Would you class this incident as an illustration of the characteristic of the scientific mind that you spoke of a while back as deciding in their own minds what properly they should do, what was required to be done in the public interest?

A. Yes, I think that is a fair statement. I think this whole incident is a good illustration of that. I will confess that I was pretty fed up with Dr. Oppenheimer at that moment . . .

Dr. Oppenheimer then told us that Eltenton had made this approach. It was perfectly plain that Dr. Oppenheimer believed that it was quite unnecessary to our security problem to know the names of the person or persons—the one who later turned out to be Chevalier—got this contact with.

To my mind it was a sad exhibition of judgment, and an exhibition of ego that is quite unwarranted, but nevertheless quite common. That is the way I regarded it then. It did not endear him to me at the time. That is the sort of incident that it appeared to me to be.

Q. He did regard it as important and in the national interest for him to impart information that had come to him about Eltenton?

A. I assume that he did, otherwise he would not have done it.

Q. He took the initiative in doing that?

A. That is my recollection. . . .

Q. You had many interviews with both Dr. Oppenheimer and his wife during the course of the work on the project?

A. Yes.

Q. Did you endeavor in these interviews to form the most accurate and thorough going judgment possible as to his political orientation? I will come to Mrs. Oppenheimer later. Did you search to find out what you could about his attachment or lack of attachment to Communist ideology?

A. Yes, sir; that was the purpose of my talks with him. I was working on that all the time.

Q. What judgment did you form as to his political convictions at this time, that is, at the time of the project?

A. May I qualify your question? You asked me as to my judgment as to his political convictions. I formed the judgment that he was not a Communist.

Q. How did you form that judgment?

A. I would like to continue with that. My working definition of a Communist is a person who is more loyal to Russia than to the United States. That is the definition I formed very early during my work on the Communist problem in the War Department, and which I still think is a sound definition. You will note that has nothing to do with political ideas.

Unquestionably Dr. Oppenheimer was what we would characterize—and as hide bound a Republican as myself characterizes—as extremely liberal, not to say radical. Unfortunately, in this problem of determining who is and who is not a Communist, determining who is loyal and who is not, the signs which point the way to persons to be investigated or to check on are very frequently political liberalism of an extreme kind. The difficult judgment is to distinguish between the person whose views are political and the person who is a Communist, because communism is not a political thing at all.

Q. You had an extensive experience in that kind of interrogation throughout the war, did you?

A. Yes, sir; I certainly did.

Q. Did you have enough experience at it to feel as confident as men can be about their judgments?

A. I believe so. I was a lot younger then than I am now, and I am sure I had more confidence in my judgment then than I have now.

Q. About many things?

A. About many things. But my job in the War Department and up until the time I officially moved over to the atomic bomb project and severed all connections with the War Department in January 1944, was primarily concerned with the formation of judgment as to who were or were not Communists in the loyalty sense in the Army.

Q. You were satisfied on the basis of these interrogations and of all that you knew about Dr. Oppenheimer from surveillance and all other sources that he was not a Communist as you have defined one in the sense of being more loyal to Russia than to the United States?

A. Yes.

Q. You were satisfied that he was a loyal American citizen?

A. Yes.

Q. Putting the interests of his country first?

A. I believed that. . . .

Q. If you had the decision to clear or not to clear Dr. Oppenheimer today, based upon your experience with him during the war years and up until the time when your association with him ended, would you do so?

A. I will answer that, yes, based upon the same criteria and standards that we used then. I am making no attempt to interpret the present law. Those criteria were loyalty and discretion.

Q. What would you have to say as to his discretion as you saw it?

A. I think it was very good. We always worried a little bit about how much he talked during his recruitment efforts. Certainly there were times when as a security officer I would have judged the amount of information that he felt he had to give to induce somebody to come on to the project to have been indiscreet. That is always a question of judgment and it was in the line of duty, so to speak.

Q. Apart from the problem of recruitment, what would you say?

A. Yes; I believed him to be discreet. I thought it was indiscreet of him to visit Miss Tatlock.

MR. GARRISON. That is all at the moment, Mr. Chairman.

MR. GRAY. Mr. Robb.

CROSS-EXAMINATION

By Mr. Robb:

Q. As I understand it, Mr. Lansdale, you are not offering any opinion as to whether or not you would clear Dr. Oppenheimer on the basis of presently existing criteria?

A. That is a standard that is strange to me. I don't know what it is. If somebody would interpret it for me—isn't it getting pretty hypothetical?

   I believed on the basis of information I had then that Dr. Oppenheimer was loyal and discreet. I have not changed my mind, although I have no knowledge of events transpiring since sometime in 1945.

Q. You said that you thought Oppenheimer's discretion was very good, is that correct?

A. Yes, sir.

Q. You had no doubt, did you, that Jean Tatlock was a Communist?

A. She was certainly on our suspect list. I know now that she was a Communist. I cannot recall at the moment whether we were sure she was a Communist at that time.

Q. Did your definition of very good discretion include spending the night with a known Communist woman?

A. No; it didn't. Our impression was that that interest was more romantic than otherwise, and it is the sole instance that I know of. . . .

Q. Mr. Garrison asked you some questions about the scientific mind in relation to that interview that you had with Dr. Oppenheimer and you responded, I think, that Dr. Oppenheimer's attitude might well have been a manifestation of the workings of a scientific mind; is that correct?

A. Oh, yes; of which I came up against many examples.

Q. Dr. Oppenheimer has testified here before this board that he lied to you in that interview. You would not say that lying was one of the manifestations of a scientific mind, would you?

A. Not necessarily, no.

Q. It is not a characteristic—

A. It was certainly a characteristic to decide that I didn't need to have certain information.

Q. No. But the question is, Mr. Lansdale, you would not say that scientists as a group are liars, would you?

A. No. I don't think persons as a group are liars.

Q. No.

A. I certainly can't over emphasize, however, the extremely frustrating, almost maddening, let me say, tendency of our more brilliant people to extend in their own mind their competence and independence of decision in fields in which they have no competence.

Q. You were undertaking at the time you interviewed Dr. Oppenheimer to investigate what you believed to be a very serious attempt at espionage, it that right?

A. Yes. Let me put it this way. No. "Yes" is a fair answer.

Q. And Dr. Oppenheimer's refusal to give you the information that you asked him for was frustrating to you?

A. Oh, certainly.

Q. You felt that it seriously impeded your investigation, didn't you?

A. Certainly. But he wasn't the first one that impeded my investigation, nor the last.

Q. Mr. Lansdale, do you have any predisposition or feeling that you want to defend Dr. Oppenheimer here?

A. I have been trying to analyze my own feelings on that.

Q. I notice you volunteered that last remark, and I wondered why.

A. I know, and it was probably a mistake. I have attempted as nearly as I can—as nearly as it is possible—to be objective.

Q. Yes, sir.

A. I do feel strongly that Dr. Oppenheimer at least to the extent of my knowledge is loyal. I am extremely disturbed by the current hysteria of the times of which this seems to be a manifestation.

Q. You think this inquiry is a manifestation of hysteria?

A. I think—

Q. Yes or no?

A. I won't answer that question "Yes" or "No." If you are tending to be that way—if you will let me continue, I will be glad to answer your question.

Q. All right.

A. I think that the hysteria of the times over communism is extremely dangerous. I can only illustrate it by another dangerous attitude which was going on at the same time we were worrying about Dr. Oppenheimer's loyalty.

At the same time over in the War Department I was being subjected to pressure from military superiors, from the White House and from every other place because I dared to stop the commissioning of a group of 15 or 20 undoubted Communists. I was being vilified, being reviewed and rereviewed by boards because of my efforts to get Communists out of the Army and being frustrated by the blind, naive attitude of Mrs. Roosevelt and those around her in the White House, which resulted in serious and extreme damage to this country.

We are going through today the other extreme of the pendulum, which is in my judgment equally dangerous. The idea of what we are now doing, what so many people are now doing, are looking at events that transpired in 1940 and prior in the light of present feeling rather than in the light of the feeling existing then.

Now, do I think this inquiry is a manifestation of hysteria? No. I think the fact that so much doubt and so much—let me put it this way. I think the fact that associations in 1940 are regarded with the same seriousness that similar associations would be regarded today is a manifestation of hysteria.

Q. Now, Mr. Lansdale, it is true, is it not—

A. By golly, I stood up in front of General McNary then Deputy Chief of Staff of the Army and had him tell me that I was ruining peoples' careers and doing damage to the Army because I had stopped the commissioning of the political commissar of the Abraham Lincoln Brigade, and the guy was later commissioned on direct orders from the White House.

That stuff that went on did incalculable damage to this country, and not the rehashing of this stuff in 1940. That is what I mean by hysteria. . . .

Mr. Gray . . . . We are charged, as I understand it, to consider the problem put before us with respect to the character, loyalty, and associations of an individual. These are the criteria in the act.

The Witness. Character, loyalty, and association.

Mr. Gray. My question of you is perhaps of a philosophical nature. I think you rather suggested that this board should not concern itself with associations perhaps in the thirties or forties?

The Witness. I did not intend to convey that. Certainly the board should concern itself with that. What I intended to convey was that the appraisal or evaluation of associations in the forties must be viewed in the light of the atmosphere existing then and not in the light of the atmosphere existing at the present time.

Mr. Gray. You did not mean to suggest that it was your opinion that you would only consider current associations in determining problems of this kind?

The Witness. Of course not. Always our starting point, our leads to people who are disloyal, are such things as associations. For example, you can hardly put your finger on a scientist or a university professor or people who tend to get into civic affairs, you can hardly find one anywhere who is now in his fifties or so that has not been on at least one list of an association which was later determined to be subversive or to have leanings that way. Nevertheless, those associations are most frequently the starting point or the leads for investigation to go further. You always have the question of determining the significance of those: (a) the significance at the time of them, (b) whether, assuming that there was a sinister significance it has continued.

I have never, strongly as I have felt and acted with reference to communism, never adopted the assumption, once a Communist sympathizer, always a Communist sympathizer. One of the finest things that Soviet Russia ever did for us was the quick switch of the on again off again with Germany. That did more than anything else to tell the men from the boys in the Communist Party. It would be a terrible mistake to assume that, once having had sinister associations, a man was forever thereafter damned. Yet, once you uncover those, you must always exercise judgment. That judgment is always made up of a large body of intangibles. It is seldom you get anything concrete.

I am being a little vague, I know, but the whole subject is vague.

[Toward the end of Lansdale's testimony, Roger Robb reads into the record several memoranda, including two Lansdale received from army counterintelligence officers—Peer deSilva and Boris T. Pash—in September 1943. DeSilva claimed that Oppenheimer "is playing a key part in the attempts of the Soviet Union to secure, by espionage, highly secret information which is vital to the security of the United States"; Pash asserted that Oppenheimer "is not to be fully trusted and that his loyalty to a Nation is divided." Lansdale ends by saying that aside from the lie Oppenheimer told about the Chevalier incident, "my general impression is that his veracity is good."]

Monday, April 19

GORDON DEAN: "A very human man, a sensitive man, . . . a man of complete integrity"

[As the hearing opens, a tape recording is played of an August 27, 1943, conversation between Oppenheimer and two army security officers: Boris T. Pash and Lyall Johnson. A long, involved discussion ensues regarding what Oppenheimer actually said: whether, to take one example, he said that he would feel friendly to the idea of the commander in chief informing the Russians "who are working on this problem" (as Robb believed) or "that we were working on the problem" (as Garrison correctly maintained, noting that this rendition had less "sinister" implications). With the inaccuracies cleared up, the first witness, Gordon Dean, is called. A prominent investment banker, Dean had served on the Atomic Energy Commission from May 1949 to June 1953, the last three years as chairman.]

DIRECT EXAMINATION

By Mr. Garrison: . . .

Q. There was a meeting in June 1951 at Princeton in connection with the H-bomb program?

A. There was. . . .

Some studies had been made by Dr. Ulam at Los Alamos and he ran some samplings which made it look as though an H bomb built along the lines that were talked about in the fall of 1949 just could not be done, or if done it would be at such a great cost in A bombs that you couldn't pay the price.

These things were happening. The H-bomb program looked bad. Every result was discouraging. The A-bomb program was improving. However, in the spring of 1951, we started a series of tests. By that I mean test explosions. We opened in a [jerry] rig fashion on the Nevada proving ground. As I recall in that year we shot something like 14, 15, maybe 16 bombs altogether. Four at Eniwetok in the spring of 1951, and quite a few in Nevada. Some of these bore some relationship to a possible H program, and notably one shot which was fired in May of 1951 at Eniwetok, which I can't describe without using classified information.

After that explosion I thought it was high time that we got together all the people who had any kind of a view on H weapons. Of course, there were many views among the scientists. By views, I don't mean views as to whether you could have one, but views of whether you could have one and how you would get it.

I talked, as I recall, to 2 or 3 of the Commissioners and said wouldn't it be good if we could get them all around a table and make them all face each other and get the blackboard out and agree on some priorities.

We did do that. We asked Dr. Oppenheimer, as chairman of the Weapons Committee of the GAC, to preside at the meeting. We had at that meeting in Princeton in June of 1951 every person, I think, that could conceivably have made a contribution. People like Norris Bradbury, head of the Los Alamos laboratory, and 1 or 2 of his assistants, Dr. Nordheim, I believe, was there from Los Alamos very active in the H program. Johnny von Neumann from Princeton, one of the best weapons men in the world, Dr. Teller, Dr. Bethe, Dr. Fermi, Johnny Wheeler, all the top men from every laboratory, sat around this table and we went at it for 2 days.

Out of the meeting came something which Edward Teller brought into the meeting with his own head, which was an entirely new way of approaching a thermonuclear weapon. * * *

I would like to be able to describe that but it is one of the most sensitive things we have left in the atomic energy program * * *. It was just a theory at this point. Pictures were drawn on the board. Calculations were made, Dr. Bethe, Dr. Teller, Dr. Fermi participating the most in this. Oppy very actively as well.

At the end of those 2 days we were all convinced, everyone in the room, that at least we had something for the first time that looked feasible in the way of an idea. * * *

I remember leaving that meeting impressed with this fact, that everyone around that table without exception, and this included Dr. Oppenheimer, was enthusiastic now that you had something foreseeable. I remember going out and in 4 days making a commitment for a new plant. * * * We had no money in the budget to do it with and getting this thing started on the tracks, there was enthusiasm right through the program for the first time. The bickering was gone. The discussions were pretty well ended, and we were able within a matter of just about 1 year to have that gadget ready.

It had to be shipped to Eniwetok. We had to lay it on the task force and it was fired in November 1952.

Since then there have been many others fired out in the Pacific in this field.

That is the significance of the June meeting. It was the first time that all competent people in this program that could contribute anything sat around the same table and finally came up with something they all agreed on. That is when it began to roll and it rolled very fast then.

That is the chronology of it.

Q. Mr. Oppenheimer was the chairman of the meeting and presided?

A. He presided at the meeting and participated actively in the meeting and left the meeting enthusiastic. I recall talking with him afterward, and he was, I could say, almost thrilled that we had something here that looked as though it might work. * * * I might say, that the gadget which we originally thought of in 1949 probably never would work and would have cost in terms of A bombs a price we could never have paid. . . .

Q. Did you go through Dr. Oppenheimer's personnel file?

A. I did. This is the first occasion I ever had to look at Dr. Oppenheimer's personnel file. Ordinarily Commissioners don't go through the files of people unless there is some real reason. Here, however, was a person who was chairman of the committee; he had been cleared in 1947 by the Commission, and I for the first time picked it up and went through it personally myself. . . .

Q. Did you continue to read matters that went into his personnel file after this?

A. I told the security officer, I believe, or perhaps my secretary, that anything coming from the FBI concerning Dr. Oppenheimer I wanted to see, and file in my own mind at least.

Two or three did come in. Because here was a file with a lot of early association evidence, I thought he was too important a man for me to overlook him, and it was my responsibility as Chairman, also. So I did see, I am sure, every memorandum from the FBI. But there were only 2 or 3, and there was nothing particularly new in them, as I recall, from that point on.

Q. What was your belief as to Dr. Oppenheimer's loyalty after you had been through the file and had talked with him?

A. There was no question in my mind—I must say when I first looked at the file, I had doubts, largely growing out of these early associations—but there was never any doubt in my mind after I examined the file and based partly on my knowledge of Dr. Oppenheimer, which was very close, there was never any doubt as to his loyalty in my opinion. None. That decision had to be made one way or the other. It could not be half way. There were some very unpleasant early associations when you look at them in retrospect, but as far as his loyalty I was convinced of it, not that the file convinced me so much, but the fact that here was a man, one of the few men who can demonstrate his loyalty to his country by his performance. Most people illustrate their loyalty in negative terms. They did not see somebody. Here is a man who had an unusual record of performance. It is much broader than I have indicated so far.

Q. Would you state to the board your general impression of his character as well as his loyalty, his integrity and sense of discretion? How would you rate those qualities?

A. I would say that he is a very human man, a sensitive man, a very well educated man, a man of complete integrity in my association with him. And a very devoted man to his country, and certainly to the Commission. No question of these things in my mind. . . .

Q. In all of your contacts with Dr. Oppenheimer, has he ever underestimated the Russian threat in your opinion?

A. Never. From the very earliest times Oppenheimer has been worried very much about, first of all, the lack of reliability of the Russians. He showed some frustration in our inability in the early days to work out a system and he never underestimated the Russians. A lot of our people have, but this is one man who never did.

Q. Do you remember a discussion with Dr. Oppenheimer in the fall of 1950 about his chairmanship of the GAC?

A. Yes. This was after I was Chairman. Dr. Oppenheimer came to me one day—his term had to run until August of 1952, I think.

Q. As a member?

A. As a member. He was then Chairman. He said he knew that we had had quite a disagreement on the H-bomb program back in 1949 and whether it should have a high priority. He told me that he thought that this had perhaps hurt his effectiveness on the General Advisory Committee, and that he was prepared to get off if for one moment I thought that this effectiveness had been so hurt that he could not serve.

I thought about it for a few moments—in fact, I had thought about it before—and I told him that I thought that the General Advisory Committee would definitely lose, and so would the Commission, if we lost him from it at that time, and that I felt as one who had disagreed with him on the thermonuclear program that his effectiveness perhaps had been hurt in some quarters and some people's opinions, but not in mine. I would miss him very much if he left.

When 1952 came around, he had served his time and he said, "I have been on too long. I think newer heads should be brought into the program," and he said, "I hope you would not urge the President to reappoint me." So I sent a letter to the President saying that these three members, Conant, DuBridge, and Oppenheimer were leaving. I prepared a draft of the letter for the President to sign for each one of them thanking them for their services, and that was the end of Dr. Oppenheimer's term.

Q. Summing up your convictions about Dr. Oppenheimer, you have testified to his loyalty and to his integrity and character with full knowledge of what you told us about your reading of his personnel file. I take it, also, that it goes without saying that you have read the Commission's letter which initiated this proceeding?

A. The charges? Yes, I have.

Q. The Commission refers to them as items of derogatory information, and not as charges.

A. That is right. I read that letter.

Q. On the basis of that knowledge and your experience with him, in your opinion is he or is he not a security risk?

A. He is not a security risk in my opinion. If I had so considered him a security risk, I would have initiated such a hearing long, long ago. I think his usefulness has been impaired by all this. I don't know how much he can contribute further to his country, but I would hope we would get the maximum out of him. I am certain that he is devoted to his country and if given an opportunity to serve, will serve and effectively as always.

MR. GARRISON. That is all, Mr. Chairman.

CROSS-EXAMINATION

By Mr. Robb:

Q. Mr. Dean, Dr. Oppenheimer has testified before this board in substance that in 1943 he became aware of an attempt at Russian espionage against the atomic bomb project. He has further testified that when interviewed about this matter by intelligence officers of the United States Army, he told these officers a fabrication and tissue of lies.

He has also testified—

A. May I ask, are you quoting from some testimony?

MR. GRAY. Just a minute, please.

MR. GARRISON. Mr. Chairman, I want to object in the strongest terms to the form of the question which counsel has put. I think it is impossible to present to this witness the questions about the Chevalier incident without really thoroughly going into the whole case and incident in all its ramifications. I think the question gives an utterly false summation of what actually happened in the total Chevalier incident which is the only way that it can be looked at.

MR. ROBB. Mr. Garrison can go into it if he wishes, I think I have the right to put the question to the witness in the form of an assumption, if not otherwise.

MR. GRAY. I take it you are objecting to the question, Mr. Garrison?

MR. GARRISON. I am objecting to any question to this witness that tries to put to him the Chevalier incident without going into it in the kind of shape that the matter has come to this board. It involves the whole question of his relations with Chevalier, of his initiating the information about Eltenton, of the views of General Groves and Colonel Lansdale. This whole thing has a very long and complicated story. To say here to this witness as a fact that Dr. Oppenheimer did this and that in respect to the Chevalier incident seems to me most unfair.

MR. ROBB. Mr. Chairman, there is not the slightest doubt that Mr. Oppenheimer did testify that he lied to Colonel Pash and Colonel Lansdale, not once, but many times, and that his statements—

MR. GARRISON. Mr. Chairman—

MR. ROBB. May I finish—and his statements to those officers constituted a fabrication and tissue of lies, and he knew when he was lying, he was impeding the investigation in progress. There is no question in the world that the record shows that.

MR. GARRISON. Mr. Chairman, this whole business of the so-called lies over and over again was in fact nothing but one story. He told this story to Colonel Pash. He told part of it, that we have reference to here, to Colonel Lansdale. By breaking up the component parts of that story into separate questions counsel in his cross examination made this appear as if one lie after another had been told.

It lies heavy on my conscience that I did not at that time object to the impression that was trying to be conveyed to this board of a whole series of lies when in fact there was one story which was told.

MR. GRAY. Let me ask Mr. Garrison this question. Is it clear that the record shows that there was a fabrication?

MR. GARRISON. Yes.

MR. GRAY. I wonder if Mr. Robb can proceed from that point on his question in a way that it would not be objected to?

MR. ROBB. I can't keep Mr. Garrison from objecting, Mr. Chairman. Just so we have no doubt about it, I will read from the record at page 488:

"Isn't it a fair statement today, Dr. Oppenheimer, that according to your testimony now you told not one lie to Colonel Pash, but a whole fabrication and tissue of lies?

"A. Right.

"Q. In great circumstantial detail, is that correct?

"A. Right."

I submit my question on the basis of that is perfectly fair.

THE WITNESS. I don't know what the question is at this point.

MR. ROBB. Of course you don't.

MR. GARRISON. Mr. Chairman, it really does not convey at all what this was about. The question of whether Chevalier told 3 men or 1, whether Eltenton had a contact at the consulate or didn't, whether the consulate had some microfilm or didn't, all that was of an irrelevant character of what the security officer wanted to find out, which was Chevalier's name. The substance of this whole thing is that Dr. Oppenheimer did not for a long time, and he has regretted and has said so explicitly, revealed the name of Chevalier, which was what the security officers wanted. These incidental details about whether there were 3 men or 1 had nothing to do with the problem that the security officers were faced with. I think that is the question that counsel has put to Dr. Oppenheimer in that form was an unfair one which distorted the record, and I should have objected to it at that time.

MR. GRAY. I would like to say, Mr. Garrison, that frankly the Chairman of the Board does not know what the question is, and I have heard the witness observe that he does not. I don't know what the question is. The argument to the Chairman by counsel in the presence of the witness pretty well established a background perhaps to which you are objecting to in the first place. There has been a discussion of this incident. I should like to ask if Mr. Robb will put his question, and I will give Mr. Garrison an opportunity to object to the question.

By Mr. Robb:

Q. Mr. Dean, I am going to ask you to assume that Dr. Oppenheimer testified before this board that in 1943 he became aware of an attempt at Russian espionage against the atomic energy project, and assume that he further testified that when interviewed about this matter by intelligence officers of the United States Army, he told these officers a fabrication and tissue of lies, and assume that he further testified that when he told these lies, he knew that by telling them, he was impeding the investigation of Russian espionage.

Now, if Dr. Oppenheimer so testified in substance, would that cause you to change your opinion about him?

A. As a security risk, then, or a security risk today?

Q. Now.

A. None. There must have been some reason for it. . . .

MR. GRAY. I would gather the witness' answer was favorable to Dr. Oppenheimer. It was so intended, was it not?

THE WITNESS. Yes. My answer was, do you mean a security risk then or now. The questioner said "A security risk now," and I said none. . . .

HANS A. BETHE: "Only . . . when the bomb dropped on Japan, . . . did we start thinking about the moral implications"

[Hans A. Bethe, a professor of physics at Cornell University, emigrated from Nazi Germany to England in 1933 and to the United States in 1935. He met Oppenheimer in 1929 and the two became good friends. Oppenheimer recruited Bethe to head the theoretical division at Los Alamos. His testimony deals in part with his reservations about working on the hydrogen bomb in 1949, reservations Bethe only put aside after the outbreak of the Korean War in June 1950.]

DIRECT EXAMINATION

By Mr. Marks: . . .

Q. Dr. Bethe, have you read the letter of General Nichols and Dr. Oppenheimer's reply?

A. Yes, I have.

Q. How far back does your own familiarity with Dr. Oppenheimer's political associations and activities go?

A. I—

Q. And what do you know about them?

A. I heard about his political inclination in 1938 from some good friends of ours, Dr. Weisskopf and Dr. Placzek, who is mentioned in Dr. Oppenheimer's answer letter, and I understood from them that he was inclined rather far to the left.

Q. Coming to the work on the atomic bomb, would you tell us briefly about the part that you and he played in the work on this subject before Los Alamos was formed and then subsequently during the Los Alamos days?

A. Our association began in 1942, on this matter. Dr. Oppenheimer called together a group of theoretical physicists, to discuss the way how an atomic bomb could be assembled. This was a small group of about seven people or so. We met in Berkeley for the summer of 1942. We first thought it would be a very simple thing to figure out this problem and we soon saw how wrong we were.

Q. What about Los Alamos? When did you join the Los Alamos group?

A. Between that time and Los Alamos, the first was the time when Los Alamos was being created. It was a very hard task to create this laboratory. Most scientists were already involved in war work very deeply and it required somebody of very great enthusiasm to persuade them to leave their jobs and to join the new enterprise of Los Alamos. I think nobody else could have done this than Dr. Oppenheimer. He was successful in getting together a group of really outstanding people.

At Los Alamos, as I mentioned before, we had very close relations because I was the leader of one of the divisions, one I believe of seven divisions. We met almost daily, certainly at least once a week.

In Los Alamos again I want to say how difficult a job it was and it seems to me that no enterprise quite as hard as this had ever been attempted before. I believe that Oppenheimer had absolutely unique qualifications for this job and that the success is due mostly to him and mostly to his leadership in the project.

Q. What were some of the factors that made it so difficult?

A. There were many. One was in the technical work itself.

Q. I simply wanted to indicate the nature of the difficulty.

A. It was that all the time new difficulties came up in different connections, new technical difficulties which had to be solved.

Q. Apart from technical difficulties.

A. Apart from that, one great difficulty was that scientists are great individualists, and many of the scientists there had very different ideas how to proceed. We needed a unifying force and this unification could only be done by a man who really understood everything and was recognized by everybody as superior in judgment and superior in knowledge to all of us. This was our director. It was also a matter of character, of devotion to the job, of the will to succeed. It was a matter of judgment of selecting the right one among many different approaches. It was a matter of keeping people satisfied that

Hans A. Bethe, January 1957. Photograph by Bob Davis, courtesy AIP Emilio Segrè Visual Archives, Physics Today Collection.

they had a part in the laboratory, and we all had the feeling that we had a part in the running of the laboratory, and that at the same time at the head of the laboratory somebody who understood more than we did.

Q. Was there any notable exceptions to this?

A. There were a few notable exceptions. There were people who were dissatisfied. Among them was Dr. Teller.

Q. Why was he dissatisfied?

A. He had—

Q. By the way, am I right that he was on your staff?

A. He was on my staff. I relied—and I hoped to rely very heavily on him to help our work in theoretical physics. It turned out that he did not want to cooperate. He did not want to work on the agreed line of research that everybody else in the laboratory had agreed to as the fruitful line. He always suggested new things, new deviations. He did not do the work which he and his group was supposed to do in the framework of the theoretical division. So that in the end there was no choice but to relieve him of any work in the general line of the development of Los Alamos, and to permit him to pursue his own ideas entirely unrelated to the World War II work with his own group outside of the theoretical division.

This was quite a blow to us because there were very few qualified men who could carry on that work.

Q. Turning to another subject, Dr. Bethe, what was the attitude of Dr. Oppenheimer with respect to the requirements of security at Los Alamos?

A. He was very security minded compared to practically all the scientists. He occupied a position very much intermediate between the Army and the scientists. The scientists generally were used to free discussion and free discussion of course was allowed in the laboratory completely and this was one of the reasons for putting it at the remote place. However, many of us did not see sometimes the need for the strictness of the requirements and Dr. Oppenheimer was, I think, considerably more ready to see this need and to enforce security rules.

Q. Is that what you mean by occupying a position intermediate between the scientists and the Army.

A. That is what I mean.

Q. Let me ask you, Dr. Bethe, if you can speak of it, what views did the scientists have about the moral or humane problems that many people have discerned in the atomic bomb program at Los Alamos.

A. I am unhappy to admit that during the war—at least—I did not pay much attention to this. We had a job to do and a very hard one. The first thing we wanted to do was to get the job done. It seemed to us most important to contribute to victory in the way we could. Only when our labors were finally completed when the bomb dropped on Japan, only then or a little bit before then maybe, did we start thinking about the moral implications.

Q. What did you think about that or what did the scientists generally think about it?

A. There was a general belief that this was a tremendous weapon that we had brought into the world and that we might have been responsible for incredible destruction in the future. That we had to do whatever we could to tell people, especially the people of the United States, what an atomic bomb meant, and that we should try as much as possible to urge an international agreement on atomic weapons in order to eliminate them as weapons from war if this could be agreed to by all the major nations. . . .

Q. Dr. Bethe, let me go back for a moment. I think you said that you had been told in the late thirties that Dr. Oppenheimer's, I think you used the phrase "extreme" left-wing political views. That was between the time when you first met him in 1929 and your later closeness to him?

A. Yes.

Q. When you again met Dr. Oppenheimer, after this brief meeting that you described in 1929, what were your own observations about his political orientation?

A. They were very surprising to me.

Q. When would this have been?

A. That was in 1940. At the Physical Society meeting in Seattle, Wash., we had a long evening in which political matters were discussed. This was in late June, I believe, of 1940. It was just after the fall of France, and I felt very deeply that a great catastrophe had happened to the world. At this conversation, Dr. Oppenheimer talked for quite a long time in this same sense.

(Mr. Garrison entered the room.)

THE WITNESS. He told all of us how much France meant to the western world, and how the fall of France meant an end of many things that he had considered precious and that now the western civilization was really in a critical situation, and that it was very necessary to do something to save the values of western civilization.

By Mr. Marks: . . .

Q. After the explosion of the Russian A bomb, was there any change in the character of your work?

A. Yes.

Q. Would you describe what happened?

A. Should I—

Q. As to yourself.

A. In October of 1949 I had a visit from Dr. Teller at Los Alamos.

Q. You were at Los Alamos?

A. No, he was at Los Alamos. I was in Ithaca. He came to visit me as he was also visiting several other scientists, and he tried to persuade me to come to Los Alamos full time, and to help evolve full scale thermonuclear weapons.

Q. Dr. Bethe, there has been some talk in these proceedings about the General Advisory Committee meeting towards the end of October of 1949.

A. May I go on?

Q. I beg your pardon. I am sorry.

A. At the time Dr. Teller visited me, I had very great internal conflicts what I should do. Dr. Teller was presenting to me some of his technical ideas which seemed to make technically more feasible one phase of the thermonuclear program. I was quite impressed by his ideas.

On the other hand, it seemed to me that it was a very terrible undertaking to develop a still bigger bomb, and I was entirely undecided and had long discussions with my wife.

Q. When did this occur?

A. This was early in October, as far as I remember. It may have been the middle of October, but some time between early and middle of October. What I should do? I was deeply troubled what I should do. It seemed to me that the development of thermonuclear weapons would not solve any of the difficulties that we found ourselves in, and yet I was not quite sure whether I should refuse.

Q. Did you consult Dr. Oppenheimer about what to do and if so, approximately when?

A. I did consult Dr. Oppenheimer. In fact, I had a meeting with him together with Dr. Teller. This was just a few days later, I think only 2 days later, or 3, than my first meeting with Dr. Teller. So this would again be around the middle of October, and perhaps a little earlier. I found Dr. Oppenheimer equally undecided and equally troubled in his mind about what should be done. I did not get from him the advice that I was hoping to get. That is, I did not get from him advice from either direction to decide me either way.

He mentioned that one of the members of the General Advisory Committee, namely Dr. Conant, was opposed to the development of the hydrogen bomb, and he mentioned some of the reasons which Dr. Conant had given. As far as I remember, he also showed me a letter that he had written to Dr. Conant. As far as I remember, neither in this letter nor in his conversation with us did he take any stand.

Q. What did you do about the invitation that Teller had extended you?

A. About 2 days after talking to Dr. Oppenheimer I refused this invitation. I was influenced in making up my mind after my complete indecision before by two friends of mine, Dr. Weisskopf and Dr. Placzek. I had a very long and earnest conversation with Dr. Weisskopf what a war with the hydrogen bombs would be. We both had to agree that after such a war even if we were to win it, the world would not be such, not be like the world we want to preserve. We would lose the things we were fighting for. This was a very long conversation and a very difficult one for both of us.

I first had a conversation with Dr. Weisskopf alone and then with Weisskopf and Placzek together on the drive from Princeton to New York. In this conversation essentially the same things were confirmed once more. Then when I arrived in New York, I called up Dr. Teller and told him that I could not come to join his project.

Q. When would this have been, approximately?

A. I still can't give you any much better date than before. It was certainly quite some time before the General Advisory Committee meeting. I don't know whether it was 2 weeks before or 10 days before. It may have been 3 weeks before. I could establish the date if this is important.

Q. Since that time, however, you have done work on the thermonuclear program, on the H bomb?

A. I have indeed.

Q. When did that begin?

A. This began after the outbreak of the Korean war.

Q. What have you done since then, describing it just in general terms?

A. In June of 1950, when the Korean war broke out, I decided that I should put a full effort on Los Alamos work and in particular should work also on thermonuclear weapons. I offered to Los Alamos to do active work at times when I was at Los Alamos, but also when I was at Cornell. This offer was accepted. I have done work with an assistant who I supplied from among my own students. I believe this work has been recognized as contributing.

Q. Are you saying that continuously from the outbreak of the Korean trouble—

A. Essentially continuously. I worked of course only part time as long as I was at Cornell. Then I was at Los Alamos at more frequent intervals since then. I mentioned before that I spent a whole 8 months there from February 1952 to September, which was a critical period in the development of the first full scale thermonuclear test which took place in November of 1952, as you well know.

  I also went there at other times during the summer. I went usually for a month in the winter, and I worked in between at Ithaca.

Q. When you did finally decide in the summer of 1950 to go to work on the thermonuclear program, what became of the inner troubles that you had previously that contributed to turning down Teller's original offer?

A. I am afraid my inner troubles stayed with me and are still with me, and I have not resolved this problem. I still feel that maybe I have done the wrong thing, but I have done it.

Q. You have done the wrong thing in what?

A. The wrong thing in helping to create a still more formidable weapon, because I don't think it solves any of our problems.

Q. During the early part of 1950, that is, after you turned down Teller's invitation, but before you went to work at Los Alamos, on the thermonuclear program, you made some public statements, I believe, in the press. You wrote an article which I believe was published in the Scientific American, and the Bulletin of Atomic Scientists, setting forth your views about the thermonucléar problem.

  Would you describe briefly what you regarded as the alternative to going ahead with the thermonuclear program?

A. Yes, sir.

Q. I am speaking now of the period from the end of 1949 to the middle of 1950.

A. Yes. I thought that the alternative might be or should be to try once more for an agreement with the Russians, to try once more to shake them out of their indifference or hostility by something that was promising to be still bigger than anything that was previously known and to try once more to get an agreement that time that neither country would develop this weapon. This is enough of an undertaking to develop the thermonuclear weapon that if both countries had agreed not to do so, that it would be very unlikely that the world would have such a weapon.

Q. Can you explain, Dr. Bethe, how you reconciled that view just described of wanting to make another try at agreement with Russia, with the view that you described a little while ago in which you expressed the feeling that negotiations with Russia on the A-bomb were hopeless?

A. Yes. I think maybe the suggestion to negotiate again was one of desperation. But for one thing, the difference was that it would be a negotiation about something that did not yet exist, and that one might find it easier to renounce making and using something that did not yet exist than to renounce something that was actually already in the world. For this reason, I thought that maybe there was again some hope. It also seemed to me that it was so evident that a war fought with hydrogen bombs would be destruction of both sides that maybe even the Russians might come to reason.

Q. Didn't you feel that there was a risk involved in taking the time to negotiation which might have given the Russians the opportunity to get a head start on the H-bomb?

A. There had to be a time limit on the time that such negotiations would take, maybe a half year or maybe a year. I believe we could afford such a head start even if there were such a head start. I believed also that some ways could have been found that in the interim some research would go on in this country. I believed that also our armament in atomic bombs as contrasted to hydrogen bombs was strong enough and promised to be still stronger by this time, that, is, by the time the hydrogen could possibly be completed, so that we would not be defenseless even if the Russians had the hydrogen bomb first.

Q. Do you have any opinion, Dr. Bethe, on the question of whether there has been in fact any delay in the development and the perfection of thermonuclear weapons by the United States?

A. I do not think that there has been any delay. I will try to keep this unclassified. I can't promise that I can make myself fully clear on this.

Q. Try to, will you?

A. I will try. When President Truman decided to go ahead with the hydrogen bomb in January 1950, there was really no clear technical program that could be followed. This became even more evident later on when new calculations were made at Los Alamos, and when these new calculations showed that the basis for technical optimism which had existed in the fall of 1949 was very shaky, indeed. The plan which then existed for the making of a hydrogen bomb turned out to be less and less promising as time went on.

Q. What interval are you now speaking of?

A. I am speaking of the interval from January 1950 to early 1951. It was a time when it would not have been possible by adding more people to make any more progress. The more people would have to do would have to be work on the things which turned out to be fruitful.

Finally there was a very brilliant discovery made by Dr. Teller. * * * It was one of the discoveries for which you cannot plan, one of the discoveries like the discovery of the relativity theory, although I don't want to compare the two in importance. But something which is a stroke of genius, which does not occur in the normal development of ideas. But somebody has to suddenly have an inspiration. It was such an inspiration which Dr. Teller had * * * which put the program on a sound basis.

Only after there was such a sound basis could one really talk of a technical program. Before that, it was essentially only speculation, essentially only just trying to do something without having really a direction in which to go. Now things changed very much * * *. After this brilliant discovery there was a program.

Q. Dr. Bethe, if the board and Mr. Robb would permit me, I would like to ask you somewhat a hypothetical question. Would your attitude about work on the thermonuclear program in 1949 have differed if at that time there had been available this brilliant discovery or brilliant inspiration, whatever you call it, that didn't come to Teller until the spring of 1951?

A. It is very difficult to answer this.

Q. Don't answer it if you can't.

A. I believe it might have been different.

Q. Why?

A. I was hoping that it might be possible to prove that the thermonuclear reactions were not feasible at all. I would have thought that the greatest security for the United States would have lain in the conclusive proof of the impossibility of a thermonuclear bomb. I must confess that this was the main motive which made me start work on thermonuclear reactions in the summer of 1950.

With the new * * * (idea) [In transcript, footnote reads: "supplied for clarity."] I think the situation changed because it was then clear, or almost clear—at least very likely—that thermonuclear weapons were indeed possible. If thermonuclear weapons were possible, I felt that we should have that first and as soon as possible. So I think my attitude might have been different.

Q. One final question, Dr. Bethe. I should have asked you this. I have referred you to the press statements and the article that you published in the late winter and spring of 1950, expressing critical views of the H-bomb program. Did you ever discuss those moves, that is to make such statements and write such articles, with Dr. Oppenheimer?

A. I never did. In fact, after the President's decision, he would never discuss any matters of policy with me. There had been in fact a directive from President Truman to the GAC not to discuss the reasons of the GAC or any of the procedures, and Dr. Oppenheimer held to this directive very strictly.

Q. Did you consult him about the article?

A. I don't think I consulted him at all about the article. I consulted him about the statement that we made. As far as I remember, he gave no opinion.

Q. On the basis of your association with him, your knowledge of him over these many years, would you care to express an opinion about Dr. Oppenheimer's loyalty to the United States, about his character, about his discretion in regard to matters of security?

A. I am certainly happy to do this. I have absolute faith in Dr. Oppenheimer's loyalty. I have always found that he had the best interests of the United States at heart. I have always found that if he differed from other people in his judgment, that it was because of a deeper thinking about the possible consequences of our action than the other people had. I believe that it is an expression of loyalty—of particular loyalty—if a person tries to go beyond the obvious and tries to make available his deeper insight, even in making unpopular suggestions, even in making suggestions which are not the obvious ones to make, are not those which a normal intellect might be led to make.

I have absolutely no question that he has served this country very long and very well. I think everybody agrees that his service in Los Alamos was one of the greatest services that were given to this country. I believe he has served equally well in the GAC in reestablishing the strength of our atomic weapons program in 1947. I have faith in him quite generally.

Q. You and he are good friends?

A. Yes.

Q. Would you expect him to place his loyalty to his country even above his loyalty to a friend?

A. I suppose so.

MR. MARKS. That is all.

CROSS-EXAMINATION

By Mr. Robb:

Q. Doctor, when Dr. Teller came to see you in 1949, were you at Ithaca then, sir?

A. Yes.

Q. And then you and Dr. Teller went down to Princeton to see Dr. Oppenheimer?

A. We went down separately, but we met again in Princeton.

Q. May I ask, Doctor, why did you pick Dr. Oppenheimer to consult about this matter?

A. Because we had come to rely on his wisdom.

Q. Doctor, you spoke of Dr. Teller at Los Alamos as always suggesting new * * * (ideas).

A. Yes.

Q. It was a new * * * (idea) suggested by Dr. Teller which resulted in your success in producing the thermonuclear; wasn't it?

A. This may be true, and some of his suggestions certainly were extremely valuable.

Q. Yes, sir.

A. There were other suggestions which turned out to be very much to the contrary. Dr. Teller has a mind very different from mine. I think one needs both kinds of minds to make a successful project. I think Dr. Teller's mind runs particularly to making brilliant inventions, but what he needs is some control, some other person who is more able to find out just what is the scientific fact about the matter. Some other person who weeds out the bad from the good ideas.

     * * * as soon as I heard of Dr. Teller's new invention, I was immediately convinced that this was the way to do it, and so was Dr. Oppenheimer. I should mention a meeting which took place in 1951, in June, at which Dr. Oppenheimer was host. At this meeting the final program for the thermonuclear reactions was set up. At this meeting Dr. Oppenheimer entirely and wholeheartedly supported the program.

Q. Doctor, how many divisions were there at Los Alamos?

A. It changed somewhat in the course of time. As far as I could count the other day, there were 7, but there may have been 8 or 9 at some time.

Q. Which division was Klaus Fuchs in?

A. He was in my division which was the Theoretical Division.

MR. ROBB. Thank you. That is all.

MR. GRAY. . . . I am addressing myself to the point that it has been said in many places that the attitude of the GAC did in fact delay successful work. I believe this has been said. You are familiar with that.

THE WITNESS. I am familiar with that.

MR. GRAY. I am trying to address myself to that point.

THE WITNESS. It is awfully hard to answer. It is true certainly that a stroke of genius does not come entirely unprepared and that you get ideas only on the subjects that you are working on. If you are working on other subjects, let us say fission weapons, you probably won't have any inspiration about thermonuclear weapons. It is true on the other hand that two quite important suggestions or discoveries were made on thermonuclear problems during the time when Los Alamos was not actively working on these. I cannot name them in an unclassified session.

     One of them was the thing that I mentioned repeatedly, the minor application, as I call it, of thermonuclear principles. I think it is quite obvious that only when there is a concerted effort can there be the atmosphere in which you can have big ideas. Whether we would be farther ahead or less far ahead, I don't know.

MR. GRAY. I was aware that was a difficult question. I have only two more, Doctor.

You testified that at one period you were hoping that it might be possible to prove that thermonuclear weapons were just simply not possible.

THE WITNESS. Yes.

MR. GRAY. I assume, then, that you were hoping that if they were not possible in this country they could not be possible in the U.S.S.R.?

THE WITNESS. Precisely.

MR. GRAY. Did you have any reason to hope that the Russians were not taking a contrary view to yours? You were hoping that it could not be possible.

THE WITNESS. Yes.

MR. GRAY. Would it be unreasonable to suppose that the Russians might have been taking the contrary view?

THE WITNESS. That they were hoping that it was possible?

MR. GRAY. Yes.

THE WITNESS. I am quite prepared to assume that, but I don't know.

MR. GRAY. So that there was a double hope that we couldn't do it and also that they couldn't, but we had no basis for believing that they would not make every effort, I assume?

THE WITNESS. That is true. In the times when everybody was very pessimistic about the outcome of our own effort, that is, in the year 1950 essentially, I was often hoping that the Russians would spend their efforts on this problem and that they would waste their efforts on this problem.

MR. GRAY. My final question, I think, relates to Mr. Marks' last question to you.

In the light of your intimate personal acquaintanceship with Dr. Oppenheimer and within the framework of the Atomic Energy Act of 1946, you have no doubts about him with respect to his loyalty, his character, his discretion, which were the three areas which Mr. Marks put the question to you.

THE WITNESS. Yes.

MR. GRAY. In order to complete the record, because there is another consideration which the act imposes and that is, associations, would you answer also affirmatively to the question including the test of associations?

THE WITNESS. Those associations that I personally know about I certainly heartily approve. The associations which I mentioned—

DR. EVANS. What was that?

THE WITNESS. I said that—

MR. GRAY. The associations he knows about he would heartily approve.

THE WITNESS. The associations in the dim past of the late 1930's and maybe early 1940's I certainly cannot approve, but I think they are superseded by a long record of faithful service and that one has to judge a man according to his actions, recent actions, which are, as far as I know, all in the public domain and all perfectly known and open to scrutiny.

MR. GRAY. Thank you.

REDIRECT EXAMINATION

By Mr. Marks:

Q. I would like to be sure, Dr. Bethe, that I understand the sense in which you made the statement about which the chairman has also questioned you, I believe, that the motivation you had in going back to work in the summer of 1950 on the thermonuclear problem was the hope that you could prove it would not work. Did you mean that you hoped you could prove by argument that it would not work, or that you could discover it as a law of nature in the sense of the theory of relativity or another scientific theory that it was impossible?

A. Hardly quite as conclusively as the theory of relativity, but rather that I could make an argument that the methods that we could conceive of for such development would all not work. That there were laws of nature which doomed such an attempt to failure.

Q. Would that process which you now describe of work on which you launched have been an indispensable part of discovering what would work?

A. I think so; yes. I don't know whether it was indispensable because Teller dispensed with it. Teller was able to make his invention without having had a conclusive discussion of all the possibilities. . . .

Q. Dr. Bethe, you said, as I understood your remarks, that you disagree . . . about the desirability of relying exclusively on thermonuclear weapons?

A. I did not say exclusively. Predominantly.

Q. Was this because of moral considerations?

A. Yes. It was my belief that if and when war ever comes that it is most important not to overdestroy the enemy country, but to fit the weapon in each case to the target and to attempt the best accuracy that one can on bombing so as to make a minimum of destruction compatible with gaining the objective. It was on this that we disagreed.

Q. I am afraid I don't understand you. Did you mean atomic weapons could do the job?

A. Yes, sir. Supposing you have, for instance, a city which contains two industrial plants which you want to bomb, each of which could be knocked out by a 100 kiloton atomic weapon correctly placed, you could also use a 5 million ton thermonuclear weapon to hit them both, which would reduce the problem for the Air Forces because they would have to fly only 1 plane instead of 2.

It seemed to me that both from moral considerations and for the consideration of the state of the enemy country after the war, which we traditionally take care of in some way, it was important to choose the former alternative and not the latter.

MR. MARKS. That is all.

[Lloyd K. Garrison calls two additional witnesses who testify briefly. James B. Fisk, vice president for research at the Bell Telephone Laboratories, who met Oppenheimer when he was director of the AEC's Division of Research in 1947–1948, said he knew of "no more devoted citizen in this country." Frederick Osborne, who represented the United States on the United Nations Atomic Energy Commission from 1947 to 1950 spoke of Oppenheimer's "real patriotism." The hearing then adjourns.]

Tuesday, April 20

GEORGE F. KENNAN: "It is only the great sinners who become the great saints"

[The first witness in what will be a long, exhausting day of hearings is George F. Kennan. Formerly director of the State Department's policy planning staff and also ambassador to Russia, Kennan was widely regarded as one of the chief architects of United States "containment" policy during the cold war. At the time of the hearing in residence at the Institute for Advanced Study in Princeton, he is well acquainted with Oppenheimer, the institute's director.]

DIRECT EXAMINATION

By Mr. Marks: . . .

Q. In what connections have you known Dr. Oppenheimer?

A. I first met Dr. Oppenheimer so far as I can recall when I was Deputy for Foreign Affairs. That is equivalent to Deputy Commandant for Foreign Affairs at the National War College here in Washington in 1946. Dr. Oppenheimer lectured there. I was in charge of political instruction generally. I heard the lecture and was very much impressed by the eminence, clarity and precision and scrupulousness of thought by which it was characterized.

I then took over this responsibility as head of the Policy Planning Staff in the Department of State, and in the ensuing years until the summer of 1950, when I left the Department of State, I met Dr. Oppenheimer on numbers of occasions in the course of my work. Those occasions were practically all ones or almost all ones on which we had to work on the formulation of foreign policy in fields that required the collaboration of other departments of Government and notably the Atomic Energy Commission and the Department of Defense. . . .

Q. As a result of your experience with Dr. Oppenheimer in the cases that you have reference to, what convictions, if any, did you form about him?

A. I formed the conviction that he was an immensely useful person in the councils of our Government, and I felt a great sense of gratitude that we had his help. I am able to say that in the course of all these contacts and deliberations within the Government I never observed anything in his conduct or his words that could possibly, it seemed to me, have indicated that he was animated by any other motives than a devotion to the interests of this country.

Q. Did you ever observe anything that would possibly have suggested to you that he was taking positions that the Russians would have liked?

A. No. I cannot say that I did in any way. After all, the whole purpose of these exercises was to do things which were in the interest of this country, not in the interests of the Soviet Union, at least not in the interests of the Soviet Union as their leaders saw it at that time. Anyone who collaborated sincerely and enthusiastically in the attempt to reach our objectives, which Dr. Oppenheimer did, obviously was not serving Soviet purposes in any way.

Q. Have you said that he contributed significantly to the results?

A. I have, sir.

Q. Mr. Kennan, is there any possibility in your mind that he was dissembling?

A. There is in my mind no possibility that Dr. Oppenheimer was dissembling.

Q. How do you know that? How can anybody know that?

A. I realize that is not an assertion that one could make with confidence about everyone. If I make it with regard to Dr. Oppenheimer it is because I feel and believe that after years of seeing him in various ways, not only there in Government, but later as an associate and a neighbor, and a friend at Princeton, I know his intellectual makeup and something of his personal makeup and I consider it really out of the question that any man could have participated as he did in these discussions, could have bared his thoughts to us time after time in the way that he did, could have thought those thoughts, so to speak, in our presence, and have been at the same time dissembling.

I realize that is still not wholly the answer. The reason I feel it is out of the question that could have happened is that I believed him to have an intellect of such a nature that it would be impossible for him to speak dishonestly about any subject to which he had given his deliberate and careful and professional attention.

That is the view I hold of him. I have the greatest respect for Dr. Oppenheimer's mind. I think it is one of the great minds of this generation of Americans. A mind like that is not without its implications.

Q. Without its what?

A. Implications for a man's general personality. I think it would be actually the one thing probably in life that Dr. Oppenheimer could never do, that is to speak dishonestly about a subject which had really engaged the responsible attention of his intellect. My whole impression of him is that he is a man who when he turns his mind to something in an orderly and responsible way, examines it with the most extraordinary scrupulousness and fastidiousness of intellectual process.

I must say that I cannot conceive that in these deliberations in Government he could have been speaking disingeniously to us about these matters. I would suppose that you might just as well have asked Leonardo da Vinci to distort an anatomical drawing as that you should ask Robert Oppenheimer to speak responsibly to the sort of questions we were talking about, and speak dishonestly.

Q. Mr. Kennan, in saying what you have just said, are you saying it with an awareness of the background that Dr. Oppenheimer has, the general nature of which is reflected in the letter which General Nichols addressed to him, which is the genesis of these proceedings, and his response?

A. I am, sir.

Q. How do you reconcile these two things?

A. I do not think that they are necessarily inconsistent one with the other. People advance in life for one thing. I saw Dr. Oppenheimer at a phase of his life in which most of these matters in General Nichols' letter did not apply. It seems to me also that I was concerned or associated with him in the examination of problems which both he and I had accepted as problems of governmental responsibility before us, and I do not suppose that was the case with all the things that were mentioned in General Nichols' letter about his early views about politics and his early activities and his early associations.

I also think it quite possible for a person to be himself profoundly honest and yet to have associates and friends who may be misguided and mislead and for who either at the time or in retrospect he may feel intensely sorry and concerned. I think most of us have had the experience of having known people at one time in our lives of whom we felt that way.

Q. I think one might interpret this correspondence that I have referred to as going even further than that. I won't go into what has been testified here or a characterization of that which has been said in this room, but in the correspondence itself, an incident is referred to—I assume you have read the correspondence?

A. I have in a cursory way as a newspaper reader reads it in the newspapers.

Q. An incident is referred to in 1943, in which it is said that an approach to Dr. Oppenheimer was made under circumstances suggesting that the approach was somehow connected with a possible effort by the Russians to secure information or to secure information in their behalf, and that for some months thereafter he failed to report this incident.

What effect does that failure on his part which he freely admits was wrong have on your present thinking about it?

A. Mr. Marks, I have testified about him here as I have known him. I can well understand that at earlier periods in his life conflicts of conscience might have arisen as I think they could with any sensitive person between his feelings about his friends—perhaps his pity for them—and his governmental duties. On the other hand, I would also be inclined to bear in mind the fact that in 1943 the Soviet Union was hardly regarded by our top people in our Government as an enemy. That great masses of American materials were being prepared for shipment to the Soviet Union, many of them I assume involving the transmission of official secrets. I could imagine that the implications of this may not at that time have appeared to be so sinister as they do today in retrospect, and I could also imagine if after all the information was not given in this particular instance, the man in question might have felt that no damage had been done to the Government interest, and that the question of the men who had initiated such a request might be better perhaps left to their own consciences and to the process of maturity in their own development.

I don't know. I can imagine those things. For that reason I would hesitate to make definite judgments on the basis simply of what I read in the letter of indictment.

Q. Would it change your opinion if I were to suggest to you that when Dr. Oppenheimer did report this incident to security officers on his own initiative, as it turned out, he didn't tell them everything about it. He still withheld the name of the friend and told them a story that was not the whole truth.

A. Mr. Marks, I do not think that that would alter anything on the statement that I just made prior to your question. I might only add to it that I could well conceive that Dr. Oppenheimer might have done things which he would think in retrospect were mistakes or which others would conclude in retrospect were mistakes, but that would not preclude in his own instance any more than it would in the case of any of the others the process of growth and the ability to recognize mistakes and to learn from them and to make fewer in the future. What I have said about his activities, his personality, the cast of his mind during the years when I knew him would I think not be affected.

Q. These convictions that you have expressed about him, the confidence that you have expressed in him, what part is played in that judgment by the experience that you had as a Soviet expert?

A. I think a considerable part. One of the convictions that I have carried away from such experience as I have had with these matters in the field of Soviet work concerning the Soviet Union is that these things cannot really be judged in a fully adequate way without looking at the man as an entirety. That is I am skeptical about any security processes that attempt to sample different portions of a man's nature separate from his whole being. I must say as one who has seen Robert Oppenheimer now over the course of several years, and more latterly outside of Government, that I have these feelings and entertain them on the basis of my estimate of his personality and his character as a whole.

Q. Are they feelings or are they convictions?

A. They are on my part convictions, sir. . . .

CROSS-EXAMINATION

By Mr. Robb: . . .

Q. I would like to ask you a question as an expert on diplomacy, Mr. Kennan. Supposing the Russians had developed the hydrogen bomb, and had got it and we didn't have it; what would then be our position vis-à-vis the Russians in any negotiations?

A. That, of course, is a key question and a very penetrating one. It is one which I have had occasion to argue many times with my friends here in Washington. I do not think that the position would have been so much different from what it is today. The Russians have for reasons which I don't think include any altruism or any thing like that, or idealism, but they have been very, very careful not to use the weapons of mass destruction as a threat to other people. I don't recall any time that the Russians have ever threatened as a means of political pressure to use these weapons, to use these weapons against anybody else. On the contrary, their position has been consistently all along that they were holding them—whether this is true or not, it has been their public position—that they were holding them for purposes only of retaliation and deterrents and would not use them unless they were used against them.

It would be a change of Soviet policy if they were to attempt to use any of these weapons as a means of pressure. I have also always held doubts—I realize this is a very difficult thing to express—as to whether the fact that perhaps one party had weapons of this sort a little more destructive or greatly more destructive than the other would nevertheless change this situation so vitally. We did, after all, have the old type of bomb. We had some means of delivery. I think the world would have gone along pretty much the same. I have in mind in making that judgment the fact that atomic weapons are not the only weapons of mass destruction that exist. There are also extremely ugly and terrible biological and chemical weapons, at least we have been allowed to think there are, and if the Russians want to create destruction in this country solely for the sake of destruction, I think there are other means by which they can do it than the hydrogen bomb.

Q. You don't feel, then, that we would have been at any disadvantage as against the Russians if they had the hydrogen bomb and we had not?

A. I am not absolutely certain. I cannot give you a flat negative answer to that. Perhaps we would have been. Perhaps I have been wrong about this. But I think that our position with regard to them has depended much less on the mathematical equation of who has this and who has that in the way of weapons of mass destruction than we think it has. After all our problems with them as I have seen them on the political side were very much the same in the days when we had the monopoly of the atomic weapon as they are today to my way of thinking. They are pretty much the same old problems. I really do not suspect these people, Mr. Robb, of a desire to drop this thing on us just out of some native contrariness or desire to wreak destruction for destructions' sake in this country. I think they are people who fight wars for very specific political purposes, and usually to get control over some area or territory contiguous to what they already have.

I have often had occasion to say that there is only one real question that interests these people, I mean the Soviet leaders, and that is the question of who has the ability to haul people out of bed at three in the morning and cause them to disappear without giving any accounting for them, and where. In other words, who can exercise totalitarian police power over a given territory, and where can you do it. That is what they are interested in knowing. They think that everybody else rules the way they rule. They are always interested in the territorial problem. For that reason I don't think that these weapons play such a part in their thinking as they play in ours. They want to know not only how to destroy territory, but how to get control of it, and dominate it and run people.

Q. Of course, you will agree that if you were mistaken in that evaluation, it would be a very serious mistake.

A. I agree and for that reason I have, I believe, always had a certain caution with regard to my own views.

Q. Yes, sir. Mr. Kennan, you spoke of the Russian policy as manifested to you. Do you believe the Russians were sincere in their manifestations to you of their policy?

A. Oh, no. We have never drawn our judgments of their policy from a literal interpretation of their words. There is no reason why these people should ever have been sincere in anything that they said to a capitalist government. They may have been on occasions, but there is no real reason for it.

Q. Putting it in the language of the ordinary man, you just can't trust them, isn't that right?

A. That is correct. They do not really expect to be trusted.

MR. ROBB. Thank you very much.

MR. GRAY. May I ask you some questions, Mr. Kennan? . . .

If you were today director of the policy planning staff and there came to you from a staff member or from some other source, perhaps even the Secretary of State, that a certain individual had been made a member of the policy planning staff who had had close Communist associations as late as the late thirties or perhaps early forties, would you seriously consider adding such a person to your staff today?

THE WITNESS. It would depend, Mr. Chairman, on what I would think were his possibilities for contribution to the staff and to what extent the negative points on his record had been balanced out by a record of constructive achievement and loyalty. . . .

MR. GRAY. I assume that if it were a secretary, for example, or clerical assistant, that it would be easier for you to decide that the person should not be employed.

THE WITNESS. I would think that would be correct.

MR. GRAY. So I gather that you feel that perhaps the application of individual judgment increases with the stature and importance of the individual concerned. That is perhaps not a clear question.

The WITNESS. I do feel this, that the really gifted and able people in Government are perhaps less apt than the others to have had a fully conventional life and a fully conventional entry, let us say, into their governmental responsibilities. For that reason I think that while their cases have to be examined with particular care, obviously for the reasons of the great responsibilities they bear and the capabilities for damage in case one makes a mistake, nevertheless it is necessary to bear in mind in many cases, especially people who have great intellectual attainments—because those attainments often it seems to me do not always come by the most regular sort of experience in life, they are often the result of a certain amount of buffeting, and a certain amount of trial and error and a certain amount of painful experience—I think that has to be borne in mind when one uses people of that sort.

I agree it presents a special problem, not an easy one for the Government. I have the greatest sympathy for the people who have to face it. . . .

MR. GRAY. I would like to move back to the question of your attitudes toward the development of the hydrogen bomb in the period before the President's decision to proceed in January of 1950. Had you been told, Mr. Kennan, in 1949, for example, by a scientist whose judgment and capability you respected that it was probable that a thermonuclear weapon could be developed which would be more economical in terms of the use of material and cost and the rest of it than the equivalent number of atom bombs, would you have then been in favor of developing the hydrogen bomb?

THE WITNESS. I would not have favored developing it at least until a real decision had been made in this Government about the role which atomic weapons were to play generally in its arsenal of weapons. I would have had great doubts then about the soundness of doing it. That comes from philosophic considerations partly which I exposed to the Secretary of State, which did not I might say meet with his agreement or with that of most of my colleagues and the future will have to tell, but it seemed to me at the end of this atomic weapons race, if you pursued it to the end, we building all we can build, they building all they can build, stands the dilemma which is the mutually destructive quality of these weapons, . . . the public mind will not entertain the dilemma, and people will take refuge in irrational and unsuitable ideas as to what to do.

For that reason I have always had the greatest misgivings about the attempt to insure the security of this country by an unlimited race in the cultivation of these weapons of mass destruction and have felt that the best we could do in a world where no total security is possible is to hold just enough of these things to make it a very foolish thing for the Russians or anybody else to try to use them against us.

MR. GRAY. So you would have been in favor of stopping production of the A bomb after we had reached a certain point with respect to the stockpile?

THE WITNESS. That is correct.

MR. GRAY. Whatever that might have been?

THE WITNESS. No; and I didn't consider myself competent to determine exactly what that point was. I have never known the number of our bombs nor the real facts of their destructiveness or any of those things.

MR. GRAY. Knowing the Russians as you do—perhaps as well as any American—would you have expected them to continue to improve whatever weapons they may have within limitations of economy, scientific availability and so forth?

THE WITNESS. My estimate is that they would have cultivated these weapons themselves primarily for the purpose of seeing that they were not used, and would have continued to lay their greatest hopes for the expansion of their power on the police weapons, the capacity to absorb contiguous areas, and on the conventional armaments as a means of intimidating other people and perhaps fighting if they have to fight. . . .

DR. EVANS. Mr. Kennan, there are a couple of questions I want to ask you. You will admit, I suppose, that at one time in his career, Dr. Oppenheimer displayed that he was a rather naive individual. You will admit that, won't you?

THE WITNESS. That I think is apparent from the exchange of correspondence that I read in the papers. . . .

DR. EVANS. Now, just one other question. You opposed this hydrogen bomb on two grounds—on moral grounds and on the fact it was so big it would be like using a sledge hammer to kill a mosquito. Is that true?

THE WITNESS. I have never conceived them really as just the moral ground because I didn't consider that. After all, we are dealing with weapons here, and when you are dealing with weapons you are dealing with things to kill people, and I don't think the considerations of morality are relevant. I had real worries, sir, about the effects of this on our future policy and suitability of our future policy.

DR. EVANS. That is all.

REDIRECT EXAMINATION

By Mr. Marks:

Q. Mr. Kennan, I would like to follow up briefly the question that you were asked by Dr. Evans about the problem which this board faces, and the test it has to apply in discharging its rather awesome responsibility, is one in which it has to assess, as I read the act, character, associations and loyalty of the individual, advise the Commission whether the Commission should determine that permitting the individual to have access to restricted data—a term which I believe you understand—will not endanger the common defense and security. . . .

I would like to explore your own views about what standards you had in mind when you said that in relation to gifted individuals, it was common to find that they had unconventional backgrounds, and that therefore, as I understood it, a different type of inquiry was required for evaluation. Could you explain a little bit more fully what you had in mind?

A. It is simply that I sometimes think that the higher types of knowledge and wisdom do not often come without very considerable anguish and often a very considerable road of error. I think the church has known that. Had the church applied to St. Francis the criteria relating solely to his youth, it would not have been able for him to be what he was later. In other words, I think very often it is in the life of the spirit; it is only the great sinners who become the great saints and in the life of the Government, there can be applied the analogy.

I have often said it is the people who have come to their views through the questioning of other things who have the highest and firmest type of understanding in the interests of the Government. At any rate, it seems to me that the exceptional people are often apt not to fit into any categories of requirements that it is easy to write into an act or a series of loyalty regulations.

I feel that one ought to bear that in mind. I realize the problem for the Government as to how it is to do it, and technically it is not always easy. It is a dangerous thing to talk exceptions because nobody can define again by category who is an exceptionally gifted person and who is not. The attempt is often invidious and involves the creation of an invidious distinction.

I am not sure it can be formalized, but I have always felt that the United States Government has to realize that it has a real problem here, particularly with the people who have the greater capacities. There is need here for considerable flexibility, and as I say at the outset, I think for a looking at the man as a whole and viewing his entire personality and not judging portions of it.

I am afraid that may not be a very clear answer to what you asked. . . .

MR. GRAY. Dr. Evans I believe has 1 or 2 questions.

DR. EVANS. Mr. Kennan, in answer to one of the questions that was asked you, I think you stated in effect, or at least you implied that all gifted individuals were more or less screwballs.

THE WITNESS. Let me say that they apt to be, if I may.

DR. EVANS. Would you say that a large percentage of them are?

THE WITNESS. No, sir; I would not say that they are screwballs, but I would say that when gifted individuals come to a maturity of judgment which makes them valuable public servants, you are apt to find that the road by which they have approached that has not been as regular as the road by which other people have approached it. It may have had zigzags in it of various sorts.

DR. EVANS. I think it would be borne out in the literature. I believe it was Addison, and someone correct me if I am wrong, that said, "Great wits are near to madness, close allied and thin partitions do their bounds divide."

Dr. Oppenheimer is smiling. He knows whether I am right or wrong on that. That is all.

JAMES B. CONANT: "Dr. Oppenheimer's appraisal of the Russian menace . . . was hard headed, realistic, and thoroughly anti-Soviet"

[The examination of the next witness, David E. Lilienthal, is interrupted so that the board may hear from James B. Conant and Enrico Fermi (after which, Lilienthal resumes testifying). Formerly president of Harvard University, at the time of the hearing United States high commissioner to Germany, Conant served as a scientific adviser to General Groves during the war and remained in close touch with Oppenheimer afterward. Conant appears on the physicist's behalf despite being told by Secretary of State John Foster Dulles that "it would be a good deal better if you did not become publicly involved," and being warned by Dulles, as Conant wrote in his diary, that "this might destroy my usefulness to govt."]

DIRECT EXAMINATION

By Mr. Garrison: . . .

Q. You have read the Commission's letter of December 23, 1953, which initiated these proceedings containing the derogatory information about Dr. Oppenheimer?

A. Yes, I have read it.

Q. Have you a comment to make on it?

A. Yes, I have. I would like to comment on it. I would like to comment on one section particularly. Somewhere in the letter it says that the substance of the information which raises the question concerning your eligibility for employment, referring to Dr. Oppenheimer, on atomic energy work, is as follows, and then later it says that it was further reported that in the autumn of 1949 and subsequently you strongly opposed the development of the hydrogen bomb; one, on moral grounds; two, by claiming it was not possible; three, by claiming that there were insufficient facilities and scientific personnel to carry on the development; and four, that it was not politically desirable.

Well, it seems to me that letter must have been very carelessly drafted, if I may say so, because if you take those two statements together, of course, it would indicate that anybody who opposed the development of the hydrogen bomb was not eligible for employment on atomic energy work later.

I am sure that no one who drew that letter could have intended that, because such a position would be an impossible position to hold in this country; namely, that a person who expressed views about an important matter before him, as a member of the General Advisory Committee, could then be ineligible because of a security risk for subsequent work in connection with the Government. I am sure that argument would not have been intended. If it did, it would apply to me because I opposed it strongly, as strongly as anybody else on that committee, that is, the development of the hydrogen bomb. Not for the reasons that are given there.

If I might say so they are a rather caricature of the type of argument which was used in the committee in which I participated. I should say I opposed it as strongly as anybody on a combination of political and strategic and highly technical considerations. I will go into that later to some degree although I don't think this is the place to justify the conclusions of the General Advisory Committee. It would be a long story.

It seems to me that clearly the question before you here is the question rather, is the implied indictment, I submit, namely, because of the information in the first part of this letter—Dr. Oppenheimer's association with alleged Communist sympathizers in the early days in his youth—that that somehow created a state of mind in Dr. Oppenheimer so that he opposed the development of the hydrogen bomb for what might be said reasons which were detrimental to the best interests of the United States, because they were interests of the Soviet Union which he in one way or another had at heart.

That, I take it, is the issue which I take it is before you in part in considering this letter. It is to that that I would like to speak for, I think, I have some evidence that convinces me that any such charge is completely ill founded.

If it were true that Dr. Oppenheimer's opposition to the development of the hydrogen bomb were in any way connected with a sympathy which he might have had with the Soviet Union, or communism, then surely many other actions and decisions which he was involved in over the period of years in which I was associated with him would have likewise been influenced by any such point of view.

The record is quite the contrary. I just call your attention to a few facts probably already before you—actions of Dr. Oppenheimer, participation in decisions, all of which were strongly detrimental to the interests of the Soviet Union after the close of the war.

We can start with the time shortly after the Acheson-Lilienthal report when an attempt was made through the United Nations to get an agreement with Russia on the control of atomic bombs.

As I recall it, Dr. Oppenheimer was early associated with Mr. Baruch and then later with Mr. Osborne in that series of negotiations. I was only tangentially associated, I was called in from time to time by Mr. Osborne. I remember sitting in one or two meetings. I can't give you the dates because I haven't had time to look any of this up, and I don't keep records.

At that time we had a number of discussions which were early, you see, in the development of the postwar period, with Dr. Oppenheimer and with others. At that time it seemed to me that Dr. Oppenheimer's appraisal of the Russian menace, of the Soviet situation, was hard headed, realistic, and thoroughly anti-Soviet, designs which even then were quite clear with their expansion into the free world.

That would be my first basis for believing that his attitude at that time was thoroughly loyal to the United States and thoroughly opposed to the Soviet Union and communism in every way.

Then coming to the period when he became chairman of the General Advisory Committee. Again this is probably well known to you. There is no restricted information here. I am going to speak in general terms.

Yet, as Winston Churchill later said, it was the possession of the atomic bombs in our hands that prevented, so he believes, Russia being at the channel ports during that period of history. There was a great deal to be done. Dr. Oppenheimer was a vigorous proponent as chairman of the committee of getting ahead and putting that shop in order.

Los Alamos was revivified. From then on all the decisions of the committee, with possibly the exception of this controversial thing about the hydrogen bomb would, I think, be shown entirely on the side of arming the United States. There was only one possible enemy against whom it was being done—it was the Soviet Union.

There are many other matters if I had a chance to go over the records of the General Advisory Committee.

As seems implied in this indictment that Dr. Oppenheimer was influenced by pro-Soviet and anti-United States views, he would not have taken the views he did. I named just two that come to me.

One is a matter on which I think I can take some credit of calling to the attention of the Advisory Committee of getting ahead rapidly on methods of detecting any explosion that might occur in the atomic field by the Russians. I remember Dr. Oppenheimer may have picked that up before I did; he may have had the suggestion before I did, although I don't think so, and taking steps in the committee to see that something would be done in that regard.

Clearly anybody that was influenced by any point of view in favor of the Soviet Union could hardly have done that.

Another matter—the development of smaller atomic bombs which could be used for tactical purposes; support of the ground troops which in my judgment of military strategy seemed to me of great importance. That was a matter which I know he pushed vigorously in the committee. He made strong statements about it. I think he was very active.

There again it seems to me is an illustration of a definite action taken by this man which contradicts what seems to me the implied thesis in this part of the indictment. . . .

MR. GRAY. A summary of your testimony might be that so far as you have any knowledge about anything and on the basis of your best judgment you consider that Dr. Oppenheimer's character, loyalty and associations are such that he should have access to restricted data.

THE WITNESS. Quite so. And I would give the specific items in which his judgment was such that if he had been influenced by pro-Communist views, or pro-Soviet views, he would not have taken those actions or decisions, and they were quite serious. In other words, this is not a general expression of belief based on casual conversations, but participating in a great many, I would say, fairly powerful anti-Soviet actions. . . .

By Mr. Garrison:

Q. Just one question, Dr. Conant. Supposing that you were told that early in 1943 during the wartime project on which Dr. Oppenheimer served he had been approached by a friend—I think you have heard of the Chevalier incident?

A. It is in the letter.

Q. That this friend had told him of Eltenton's channel for transmitting information to Russians, that Dr. Oppenheimer rejected emphatically any suggestion that activity of this sort should be engaged in and spoke of it as treasonous; supposing that some months later, after a delay of some months, Dr. Oppenheimer volunteered the information about Eltenton to security officers but refused to disclose at their request and their urging the name of his friend who was the intermediary and indeed suggested that the intermediary might have been some unnamed other people; that later when he, having persisted in this refusal to name this friend, knowing that the security officers were very anxious to ascertain who it was, General Groves asked him to tell him, that he declined to tell General Groves, that unless General Groves ordered it and General Groves said he didn't want to order it, but to think it over and later General Groves did tell him that he would order him unless he told him, and that Dr. Oppenheimer then revealed the name of Chevalier; would the judgment which you have expressed here about Dr. Oppenheimer's loyalty, about his character, be altered?

A. It seems to me if I followed this hypothetical—I assume it is hypothetical, the way you are stating it—incident, if I sum it up, in that case the question would have been that he had been negligent in taking steps necessary to bring into prosecution somebody who had attempted to get information? Is that roughly what the charge would have been?

This is a fairly complicated story you are telling me with a good many yeses, ands, and buts in it.

Q. There was the element of delay in reporting it; there was the delay of not frankly stating it and the circumstances when he did report it; there was the element of declining to name the friend after he had been pressed to do so; but there was the element finally of his revealing the name and also of his having initiated the whole business of revealing Eltenton's name.

A. Of course, any such thing like that would depend on the number of instances. You are assuming this is the one instance.

Q. For the purpose of the question, yes.

A. I would suppose that the question that would be presented then with that is, What were the motives at that time, and what did that show about his subsequent attitude in regard toward the Soviet Union? Did he do that at that time for reasons of trying to protect the Soviet Union agent who was trying to get information and did that indicate that he would continue to have an attitude from then on about various matters connected with atomic energy which would be not in the interest of the United States?

In view of all the things I mentioned, I would say that it didn't change it for that reason. It stood by itself and had nothing else but conversation with the man. You have to take the summation of evidence as you see it. If I were merely testifying here that I had known Dr. Oppenheimer in talks over these years, and so on, and I thought he was a loyal citizen, I don't think my evidence would be of the sort that I hope it is. By having participated with him in what I believe to have been effective actions against the Soviet Union. . . .

Mr. Gray. May I pursue this hypothetical question of Mr. Garrison's for a moment, Dr. Conant? You suggested what issue that hypothetical situation might raise, namely, that this might be an indication of an interest in protecting the Soviet Union. I am not sure these were your remarks.

The Witness. Or an act of the Soviet Union, if I got the quick summary of it correctly.

Mr. Gray. Or it might be interpreted as simply a desire to protect a friend.

The Witness. Yes. I would say a mistaken idea that you had to protect a friend in those circumstances.

Mr. Gray. If in this hypothetical situation as I think Mr. Garrison indicated, the security officer was pressing for this information, very important perhaps to the security officer who was charged with the security and who would not have any reason to believe that perhaps friendship was involved, the question again—and I am relating this to the present and to the act—or I suppose a question is: In any situation involving a divided loyalty or a conflicting loyalty, the protection of a friend, and to the obligation one owes to one's government, is there any question as to which should be—

The Witness. Not in my mind. That is why as you recall, I said I wanted to answer that question in the context that this was one incident and not many. I think we all recognize in reviewing a long history of a person, people can make errors. If they are single, they are one thing; if they are multiplied, they are quite a different picture.

Dr. Evans. Dr. Conant, if you had been approached by someone for security information, wouldn't you have reported it just as quickly as you could?

The Witness. I think I would have, yes. I hope I would have; let us put it that way.

Dr. Evans. That is all.

MR. ROBB. May I ask one more question?
MR. GRAY. Yes.

By Mr. Robb:

Q. When you did report it, Doctor, you would have told the whole truth about it?
A. I hope so.
Q. I am sure you would. Thank you.

ENRICO FERMI: "My opinion . . . was that one should try to outlaw the thing before it was born"

[After receiving the Nobel Prize for physics in 1938, Enrico Fermi (whose wife, Laura, also a physicist, was Jewish) left Fascist Italy for the United States. A professor of physics at the University of Chicago, he served as Oppenheimer's associate director at Los Alamos, and then on the General Advisory Committee from 1947 through 1950.]

DIRECT EXAMINATION

By Mr. Marks: . . .

Q. Were you a member of the General Advisory Committee of the Atomic Energy Commission?
A. I was a member of the General Advisory Committee for a period of a little bit short of 4 years, until December of 1950.
Q. You participated then in the deliberations of that committee concerning the advice to the Commission on the thermonuclear program in the fall of 1949?
A. I did.
Q. Would you tell the board briefly what you can in an unclassified way about those deliberations, the positions taken, the reasons for them?
A. Yes. I should perhaps mention the matter goes back to about 5 years, and my recollection is partly vivid, partly a little bit uncertain, but I think I remember the essentials, which are about this way: That the committee was confronted with forming an opinion whether it was the right time to start an all out program for developing the hydrogen bomb.
Q. This would have been the meeting of October 29, 1949?
A. That I understand is the date, although I don't remember it on my own. So we were confronted with this decision. I can testify naturally to my feelings in this matter better than I can to those of other people. As far as I could see the situation, I had the concern that the pressure for this development was extremely inordinate, or at least so it seemed to me. I was concerned that it

might weaken the development of conventional atomic weapons which was then picking up and essentially set it back for what seemed to me at the time a not quite decided advantage on the other side. For that reason, and I believe that these views must have been shared more or less by everybody in our group, because a decision that it was not the right time to go in an absolutely overriding way in that direction was, as far as I remember, unanimous.

There was a subsequent point on which some difference of opinion arose, and I found myself in this connection in the minority together with Rabi. Again I have no absolutely clear recollection. I have no doubt that the board has available the records of those meetings presumably where things are spelled out in full detail. My recollection is that this divergence of opinion was on whether to essentially declare or establish the policy not to go ahead with the program or whether some circumstances could make us go ahead.

My opinion at that time was that one should try to outlaw the thing before it was born. I sort of had the view at that time that perhaps it would be easier to outlaw by some kind of international agreement something that did not exist. My opinion was that one should try to do that, and failing that, one should with considerable regret go ahead.

Q. Do you remember, Dr. Fermi, whether or not there was opportunity at those meetings late in October 1949 with the freest and fullest discussion among you—consistent with the rather brief time, few days?

A. Yes, I think so. I think everybody had a right to his own opinion and to defend his own opinion.

Q. Was there a great deal of discussion and debate?

A. No doubt there was. I think we had some trouble and some soul searching, all of us. . . .

My general impression is that we all had the concern that the conventional weapons program should not be weakened and we tried to see that the various provisions that were taken for furthering the hydrogen program would not be of such a nature of interfering seriously with the conventional weapons program. Actually I believe that this could be done and I am not aware that there has been such a weakening.

Q. Do you have any impression that these actions that you took had the effect of interfering with the program for the thermonuclear development?

A. No.

Q. Going back to the earlier period when you were a member of the GAC, prior to the meeting on the thermonuclear device, would you describe very briefly the position that Dr. Oppenheimer took with respect to the development, perfection and refinement of atomic weapons?

A. Yes. I think I can say very definitely that I always saw him push for all the measures that could improve our positions in conventional atomic weapons, and this includes seeing to it that exploration of ores would go ahead vigorously, that production of primary materials would be expanded, that all the various gadgets that go into this weapon would be streamlined as much as possible, that varieties of weapons that could conceivably improve our military position would be investigated and developed. I don't in fact in this respect remember any instance in which I disagreed on essential points. We always found ourselves very much together pushing in that direction together with the help of our colleagues. But perhaps Oppenheimer first and I, in somewhat second line, knew perhaps more about the technical details of weapons than most other people of the board knew, so that this task naturally fell more precisely in our province.

Q. Would you say that these measures with respect to which you and Oppenheimer had a primary concern and role have had any significant effect on the military power of the United States?

A. I would think so.

Q. Could you amplify that at all?

A. It is very hard to know what would have happened if something had not happened. Still I feel that this action certainly has contributed, I think, in focusing the attention of the Commission on the importance of certain actions, in breaking certain bottlenecks that were retarding or limiting the production. Advice I don't suppose is comparable to action in importance, but as far as advice is of importance, I think it was in that direction definitely.

Q. One final question. In his role as chairman of the General Advisory Committee and conducting the meetings and the affairs of that committee, what opportunity did Dr. Oppenheimer afford to the other members of the committee to express fully their views and to exert their influence?

A. I think perfect opportunity. Of course, he is a person who knows a great deal about these things and knows how to express what he knows with extreme efficacy, so naturally many questions just because of this preeminence and not because so much of his sitting in the chair, he would naturally take a leading role. But certainly everybody had a perfect freedom to act with his own mind and according to his conscience on any issue. . . .

MR. GRAY. Would you guess now on the basis of recollection that most of the people who came to that meeting had their minds pretty well made up about this issue, or do you think that they arrived at the conclusions which were reflected in the various reports they signed as a result of the meeting?

THE WITNESS. I would not know. I had and I imagine that many other people had sort of grave doubts. It was a difficult decision. Even now with the benefit of 5 years of hindsight, I still have doubts as to what really would have been wise. So I remember that I had in my own mind definite doubts, and I presume my ideas and I imagine those of other people, too, must have gradually been crystallizing as the discussion went on. However, I have no way of judging.

MR. GRAY. I know it is difficult to answer that question. The fact is that in this particular case, Dr. Conant did not take your advice. . . .

DR. EVANS. You were at Columbia University when the first knowledge came out about the fission of uranium.

THE WITNESS. Yes, that is right.

DR. EVANS. Do you believe, Dr. Fermi, that scientific men should be sort of circumscribed in regard to scientific information that they may discover?

THE WITNESS. I am sorry, I am not sure I got the question.

DR. EVANS. Do you believe in circumscribing the scientific men in regard to scientific information that they discover, that is, not permitting them to publish it?

THE WITNESS. I see. The matter was this. In ordinary times, I would say that scientific discoveries should be made public. At that particular time with the war impending and critical political situations and so on, I joined with a group of others, the leader of the group or the most active member of that group was Leo Szilard, in a voluntary censorship to keep certain results that could lead in the direction of the atomic bomb.

DR. EVANS. Do you believe it is actually possible to conceal this kind of information?

THE WITNESS. Well, for a very limited time, yes. Forever, no.

DR. EVANS. That is, you could have guessed a lot of this stuff if you had been over in Rome?

THE WITNESS. I think I might possibly have guessed some things, at least.

DAVID E. LILIENTHAL: "Here is a man of good character, integrity, and of loyalty to his country"

[David E. Lilienthal, who headed the Tennessee Valley Authority during the 1930s and 1940s, served as chairman of the Atomic Energy Commission from October 1946, to February 1950. To prepare for testifying, he requested access to the AEC file on Oppenheimer's 1947 security clearance, but, as he later noted, "vital parts of these records had been removed without my knowledge." Those very documents, he believed, were then used by Roger Robb to cast doubt on his trustworthiness. The session is not adjourned until 7:45 P.M., and that night, Lilienthal wrote in his diary, he could hardly sleep, "so steamed up was I over the 'entrapment' tactics . . . and sadness and nausea at the whole spectacle."]

DIRECT EXAMINATION

By Mr. Silverman: . . .

Q. When did you say you became Chairman of the AEC?

A. I think it was the 28th of October 1946.

Q. Some time after you became Chairman was the question of Dr. Oppenheimer's past associations and his left wing activities and so on called to your attention?

A. Yes, it was.

Q. Will you tell us the circumstances of that, please?

A. The board will recall that there is a kind of grandfather clause in the Atomic Energy Act, by which those who had been cleared under the Manhattan District continued to hold their clearances—I have not looked at this provision for some time—but the effect is to hold their clearances until a reexamination by the FBI was made, and the question is reexamined on the basis of new additional information, or something to that effect. So we had a number of such reexaminations coming to us.

I have located the date of March 8 as being the date on which I appeared—give or take a day or so—a call from Mr. Hoover saying he was sending over by special messenger an important file involved in this reexamination.

I received this file. It related to Dr. Oppenheimer. It contained in it a great deal of information from the Manhattan District, and perhaps some subsequent investigation. I called the commissioners together on the 10th. The day of Mr. Hoover's call appears to be Saturday. In any event, I called the commissioners together on a Monday, March the 10th, in the morning, I believe. . . .

Q. Will you tell us what happened at that Commission meeting?

A. Commission conference would be the best description because it continued for some time. It was very informal. We had this file which I requested all the commissioners to read. It was not necessary to request them to because it was obviously a matter of great interest and importance. Instead of delegating this to someone else, it seemed clear that we should do the evaluating, since the responsibility of deciding what should be done, if anything, was ours. So we did begin a reading of this file around the table in my office in the New State Building, and then later as time went on, members would take all or parts of their file to their offices and so on.

One of the first things that was observed was that although this file did contain derogatory information going back a number of years, it did not contain any reference, as far as I recall, or at least any significant reference, to the work that Dr. Oppenheimer had done as a public servant. . . .

Q. You were saying that you found that the file contained derogatory information, but did not contain affirmative matter, shall we say?

A. It did not contain any information about those who worked with Dr. Oppenheimer in the Manhattan District. So we asked Dr. Vannevar Bush, who we knew had been active in the pre-Manhattan District enterprise, as well as since that time, and Dr. James Conant, both who happened to be in town, to come in and visit us about this file. They expressed themselves about Dr. Oppenheimer and his loyalty and character and associations and particularly the degree to which he had contributed to the military strength of the United States.

I called Secretary Patterson, or someone did, to ask him to request General Groves, under whom Dr. Oppenheimer had served, be asked to supply

a statement about his opinion about Dr. Oppenheimer and the circumstances under which he was selected and kept as director of the laboratory.

We discussed this with Dr. Bush and Dr. Conant during that day and I
think into the next day.

Q. Did you ask Dr. Bush or Dr. Conant for anything in writing?

A. I don't know whether they volunteered or whether we asked, but certainly
they did provide written statements more or less following the line of their
oral statements.

Yesterday I had an opportunity to read these and refresh my recollection
on them. I take it they are in the files. . . .

Q. As a result of your experience with Dr. Oppenheimer and your knowledge
of him, have you formed an opinion as to his loyalty, his integrity, his character, all the other factors that go into forming a judgment as to his loyalty,
security?

A. Yes, I have.

Q. What is your opinion?

A. I have no shadow of a doubt in my mind that here is a man of good character, integrity and of loyalty to his country.

Q. How would you assess him as a security risk?

A. I did not regard him up until the time my knowledge of the program
ceased, and had no occasion to regard him as a security risk.

Q. I think you already indicated that in March 1947 you consciously assayed
the situation and came to the conclusion that he was not a security risk?

A. Yes. At that time we had this file before us and that was my conclusion,
that in the light of the overall picture, taking everything into account, the
minus signs were very few indeed, and the plus signs very great indeed,
and I thought he was a contribution to the security of the country. I have
had no occasion since that time to change that view.

Q. Has your experience with him confirmed that view?

A. My experience from that time did confirm that view. I am sure that it is
clear that he has made great contributions to the security of the country. . . .

By Mr. Robb: . . .

Q. Now, may I, sir, go back to the beginning of your testimony in which you
gave an account of the events which took place in March 1947? I believe
you said that the file was delivered to you on a Saturday, March 8, is that
right?

A. That is my recollection, yes. . . .

Q. What did that consist of?

A. I can't recall except that was a very substantial file, that it contained the
kind of—a great deal of material from the Manhattan District, Intelligence
Division, or whatever it was called, counterintelligence. It was a typical FBI
file. A typical FBI personnel file.

Q. I have before me what you received, Mr. Lilienthal. It appears to be a 12-
page summary memorandum on J. Robert Oppenheimer, and a 15-page

summary memorandum on Frank Oppenheimer. Is that in accord with your recollection of what you received?

A. No, it is not. I am sure you are obviously correct. My recollection was that we had a big file. I didn't recall that there was a summary from the FBI. . . .

Q. The letter from Mr. Hoover, Mr. Lilienthal, see if this refreshes your recollection, dated March 8, 1947, addressed to you:

"My Dear Mr. Lilienthal: In view of developments to date I thought it best to call to your attention the attached copies of summaries of information contained in our files relative to Julius Robert Oppenheimer, who has been appointed as a member of the General Advisory Committee, and his brother, Frank Friedman Oppenheimer, who was employed in the Radiation Laboratory at Berkeley, Calif., until recently. It will be observed that much of the material here contained in the attached memoranda was obtained from confidential sources."

Having heard that, do you agree that what you got was the two summaries?

Mr. Garrison. Is that the whole letter?

The Witness. I don't know the distinction between the summary and the report. But whatever you have there, if you have it, I received. In order to refresh my recollection of this hearing, I asked for this file yesterday and was told it was an FBI file and I could not see it. If I had seen it, my recollection would have been refreshed.

By Mr. Robb:

Q. You know, don't you, Mr. Lilienthal, that the rules for security hearings, which I believe were adopted while you were chairman, provide that the contents of FBI reports may not be disclosed?

A. Yes, but the rules of the Commission, as I understand, permit Commissioners to have access to anything they had access to during the period of their commissionership.

Q. I don't want to debate that with you.

A. I apparently am wrong if that is the regulation now, but that is what I asked for. . . .

Q. Now, after you received this material from Mr. Hoover, on Monday morning, do I understand your testimony that you presented it to the Commission, is that right?

A. That is my recollection.

Q. And each of them read the material, is that correct?

A. During the course of succeeding hours, or a couple of days, each of them did read it.

Q. Didn't they read it right then?

A. That was my recollection.

Q. That they did?

A. They sat down and began passing it around, and took it to their offices, and so on. . . .

Q. After you had digested this material that Mr. Hoover had sent you, did you form any opinion as to whether or not the information contained in Mr. Hoover's material was true or false?

A. Well, I don't know how to answer that. The information was like other information and we had no way of determining whether it was true or false and we did not see the people and the informants were anonymous and so on, and so I don't know how to answer that question.

Q. Well, from that point on, did you proceed on the assumption it was true, or did you proceed on the assumption it was false?

A. Well, I proceeded on the assumption, we proceeded to try to evaluate it, some of it having a ring of veracity and some of it—for example as I recall one of the reports, and I think it is in this report, the informant turned out to be a nine-year-old boy. If that is true in this case, it may not be, then obviously you would say, "Well, this probably is not anything to rely on." But in other cases the report would say that the informant "X" is someone the bureau has great confidence in, and you would assume that that was true.

Q. Was the nine-year-old boy referred to in the material Mr. Hoover sent you on March 8?

A. I had an impression, but this may have been some other file and as I remember that as an illustration of how you have to evaluate these things.

Q. Well, now, having this material before you, I assume that contained certain allegations against Dr. Oppenheimer, didn't it?

A. It constituted derogatory information about Dr. Oppenheimer, that is right.

Q. And you say you proceeded to evaluate it?

A. We did our best to evaluate it. . . .

Q. And I believe you have testified there were some items that you accepted as true, and some you had doubt about?

A. Yes. I can't remember which was which, but I have the recollection that some of these things were stronger and more clear than others, but the whole picture was that of derogatory information about the man's past associations, and one episode that was worse than that.

Q. Which was that?

A. Involving Chevalier.

Q. What do you mean, "worse than that," Mr. Lilienthal?

A. Well, this struck me as being the only thing, the thing in the whole record, that would give the gravest concern, and for that, and the thing that dismissed that concern from my mind was the fact that General Groves and Mr. Lansdale, the security officer, at the time this happened examined this man on the question, and were apparently satisfied that this was not or did not endanger the national security, and the evidence to that was they kept him on. I can't add anything to that. That seemed to me a very conclusive kind of a judgment about whether he was dangerous or not. . . .

Q. Isn't it true, Mr. Lilienthal, that that very day, March 10, 1947, after talking with Dr. Bush and Dr. Conant, that you concluded that there was no doubt as to Dr. Oppenheimer's loyalty?

A. I don't recall whether it was that day, I am satisfied as to what the ultimate conclusion was, but we did not entertain any doubts for any length of time, and I for one entertained no doubt, speaking for myself, entertained no doubts at all.

Q. Now, thereafter, I believe you testified you talked to Mr. Clifford at the White House about it?

A. Yes.

Q. And what was the purpose of your conference with him?

A. Well, we had in mind that Dr. Oppenheimer was an appointee of the President, and unlike employees of the Commission he was an appointee of the President as a member of the General Advisory Committee, and we ought to make sure the President knew of the existence of this derogatory information, and so as I recall Dr. Bush and I conveyed this information to him, and I believe it was on the following day. . . .

Q. Did you suggest to Mr. Clifford that a special board be convened to review this material?

A. No, we did not.

Q. Was that ever discussed with Mr. Clifford?

A. No, I believe not.

Q. Are you sure about that?

A. I am not sure, but I have no recollection of it.

Q. Was there any reason that you knew of for the appointment of a board of any kind to review this material?

A. No. It didn't seem to me and I don't recall it seemed to anyone that there was that much question about it. The reason for that of course is that this man subsequent to the time of these events and these associations had done a great deal for his country and to prove by his conduct that he was a loyal citizen of the country. He wasn't just an ordinary unknown individual whose achievements were not well known to us and to the people we consulted.

Q. As to the creation of a board of any sort to evaluate this material, it was never discussed between you and Mr. Clifford?

A. I don't recall, it could be, but I don't recall that. Mr. Clifford, my impression is Mr. Clifford said he would advise the President, but Mr. Clifford did not seem to take this seriously, and to the extent of requiring procedure of that kind, but I could be quite wrong about that. . . .

By Mr. Robb:

Q. Now, was Mr. Carroll Wilson present at the meetings which were held concerning this matter?

A. I don't recall. My recollection is that these were executive meetings and those Mr. Wilson would not attend, but he might have attended. I don't really recall.

Q. I have before me, taken from the files, the original of the memorandum from Carroll L. Wilson, general manager, to the file, and I will read it to you. . . .

"March 11, 1947: The Commission met this morning for further consideration of the matters discussed yesterday in connection with Dr. Oppenheimer. The Commission concluded tentatively (1) that on the basis of the—

MR. GARRISON. What is that?

MR. ROBB (reading), "The Commission concluded tentatively, (1) that on the basis of the information supplied by Dr. Bush and Dr. Conant concerning Dr. Oppenheimer's outstanding contributions in this project and his consistent concern for the security of this country in connection with his services as a member of the JRDB Committee on Atomic Energy and as an adviser to the Department of State, Dr. Oppenheimer's loyalty was prima facie clear despite material contained in the FBI summary; (2) that as a result of his work for the Government during the last 4 years he is now 1 of the best, if not the best-informed scientist in regard to 'restricted data' concerning atomic energy; (3) that while under these circumstances the questions raised by the summary did not create an issue or any immediate hazard, it was essential to undertake promptly a full and reliable evaluation of the case so that it could be promptly disposed of in one way or another.

"As a first step, it was decided to secure as promptly as possible written expression of views from Dr. Bush, Dr. Conant, and General Groves as to Dr. Oppenheimer's loyalty. As a second step, it was decided that the chairman should confer with Dr. Bush and Mr. Clifford of the White House concerning the establishment of an evaluation board of distinguished jurists to make a thorough review and evaluation of the case. Inasmuch as Dr. Oppenheimer is a Presidential appointee to the General Advisory Committee to the Commission, the case is one in which the White House has a definite interest. In addition, the matter is of interest to the Department of State inasmuch as Dr. Oppenheimer has served as an adviser to the Department of State on many phases of atomic energy, including serving as a member the Board of Consultants to the Department of State in the preparation of a plan for the international control of atomic energy, and subsequently as an adviser to Mr. Baruch and more recently as adviser to Mr. Frederick Osborne.

"At 3 p.m. today Dr. Bush and the chairman"—that was you, wasn't it?

THE WITNESS. Yes, sir.

MR. ROBB (reading), "Dr. Bush and the chairman met with Mr. Clifford and advised him of the circumstances in connection with this case and discussed with him the desirability of having a review of this case by a board of distinguished jurists or other citizens. The chairman proposed that there be considered for membership on this board judges of the Supreme Court. Mr. Clifford stated that he was decidedly opposed to any move which would draw members of the court into outside activities and felt that this case did not warrant an exception to that policy. This policy would not preclude selection of other jurists for temporary service on such an evaluation board if it were deemed desirable that such a board be established. Mr. Clifford stated that he would discuss the matter with the President and communicate with the chairman and Dr. Bush on Wednesday.

"The results of the discussion with Mr. Clifford were reported to the Commission at a meeting at 5 p.m. this afternoon. At that meeting the general manager reported that a detailed analysis of the FBI summary was in process of preparation by the Commission's security staff as an aid to evaluation."

Have you any comment on that, Mr. Lilienthal?

THE WITNESS. No. I haven't. It is quite evident that Mr. Clifford in the end did not favor the idea of such a board, or perhaps we changed our minds, but I had forgotten that recommendation.

By Mr. Robb:

Q. You had forgotten that?

A. Yes. I think the thing that this does confirm is that the initial reaction of the Commissioners was as stated, on the whole case, in view of the record of service to his country, this did not raise questions in our minds but was a case or matter that should be very carefully dealt with, and dealt with very carefully in the evaluation process.

Q. But you would agree, would you not, sir, that in 1947 you and the Commission seriously considered, and in fact were of the view that a board should be impaneled to consider this matter?

A. It is quite evident from this memorandum that this was considered.

Q. And you thought enough of it to go to Mr. Clifford at the White House and so recommend?

A. That is right.

Q. In other words, you recommended in 1947 that the exact step which is now being taken, be taken then?

A. We suggested it, and I think perhaps that is the import of the memorandum as I recall, we suggested this to the White House.

Q. That step did not strike you as fantastic or unreasonable, did it?

A. No.

Q. Now, did you talk with Mr. Clifford again about that matter of the board?

A. I don't recall, and I really don't.

Q. I will show you the original of a memorandum, on March 12, 1947, 11:25 a.m., report of telephone conversation, at 11:20 with Clark M. Clifford, Special Counsel for the President. That is dated March 12, and it has "DEL" on the bottom. Did you write that, Mr. Lilienthal?

(Whereupon, the document was handed to the witness.)

MR. GARRISON. Did you say, "Did he write it?"

MR. ROBB. Did he dictate it?

MR. GARRISON. This is a record that he purportedly made?

By Mr. Robb:

Q. Your answer is that you did dictate it?

A. Yes, it would appear that I did . . .

Q. Now, Mr. Lilienthal, this was a matter of grave import to you, wasn't it?

A. Yes it was an important matter, one of many important matters, that is right.

Q. It was of sufficient importance, and important to you, that you took short-hand notes on this conversation, and then dictated a memorandum about it, is that right?

A. That is right.

Q. But it is now your testimony that you had completely forgotten any discussion with Mr. Clifford about a board of review?

A. It is.

Q. And you had completely forgotten that you even considered such a board?

A. It is. I must say it just entirely escaped my mind.

MR. GARRISON. Mr. Chairman, I would like to point out that it seems to me that the practice that is adopted here of asking, this was the same case with Dr. Oppenheimer on his cross-examination, the Government in possession of documents taken from here and there, including from their own files, in Dr. Oppenheimer's case in Princeton, and knowing that they had, first asking them to testify about something quite a while ago, without warning and without reading the documents, and presenting them and saying, "Tell us what happened," and it seems to me that this is designed to try to make the witness look to the board in as unfavorable a light as possible, and to make what is a lapse of memory seem like a deliberate falsification. I regret that this kind of procedure which is quite suitable in criminal prosecution and a court of law, when that attempt is being made before a jury, I am sorry that it has to be made here.

MR. ROBB. Mr. Chairman, may I reply to that, as I take it to be some reflection upon my professional integrity and my professional methods. Let me say—

MR. GARRISON. I have not questioned your integrity.

MR. ROBB. I have no apology to make for the methods I am pursuing in the cross-examination of these witnesses. It is an axiom that the greatest invention known to man for the discovery of truth is cross-examination, and I am pursuing what Mr. Garrison should know are orthodox, entirely proper and entirely legitimate methods of cross-examination. I make no apology to Mr. Garrison or anyone else for the method I am pursuing, and I submit that I have been entirely fair.

I asked the witness and I have taken him over these matters which I submit are matters which, well, I won't make an argument on that point, and he has said he did not remember them, and now I have read him these papers, and he says that he forgot them.

THE WITNESS. Mr. Chairman, may I make this comment, that in the great multiplicity of things that went on at that time, it is not at all impossible that I should not remember even as important a matter as this, but a simple way to secure the truth and accuracy would have been to have given me these files yesterday, when I asked for them, so that when I came here, I could be the best possible witness and disclose as accurately as possible what went on at that time. I am a little confused about the technique. The board wants the facts, and the facts are in the file, and I asked for the file so I could be a better witness, and it was denied me. So I just have to rely on memory during a very troubled and difficult time on matters that are obviously important, but they are not as important as many other things we were concerned with at that time. It would help me a good deal, and I could be a much better witness if I saw the files that I helped to contribute to make.

MR. ROBB. Mr. Chairman, I think Mr. Garrison would agree that it is an entirely fair comment to make that it is demonstrated that the memory of the witness was not infallible.

THE WITNESS. I would be the first to insist on that.

MR. ROBB. Since we are depending largely on memory, I think it is a fair test.

MR. SILVERMAN. Why, when we have documents.

MR. GARRISON. I thought the notion of an inquiry and not trial was to get at the truth by the shortest possible route, and it seems to me the attempt to make a witness seem to be not telling the truth, or his memory is not to be relied on by this board, by the surprise production of documents, is not the shortest way to arrive at the truth. It seems to me more like a criminal trial than it does like an inquiry and I just regret it has to be done here.

MR. GRAY. Well, the board certainly will take cognizance of the comments of counsel in respect to this matter, and I think that if counsel is not permitted to engage in cross-examination and simply relies on notes the witnesses may take from documents in a file, there may be some difficulty in arriving at some evaluations, and now on this particular point, it seems to me pertinent at least against general and public discussions, with which counsel cannot be unaware, including the New York Times story, the information for which was furnished by counsel, it is repeatedly and publicly stated that the Commission and others cleared Dr. Oppenheimer at the time that these were old charges rehashed, and completely considered and evaluated at the time. It does seem important to me, at least as chairman of this board, to find out exactly what did take place at that time.

MR. GARRISON. I agree with you, Mr. Chairman, in full. I want nothing but the truth brought out here. And all of the truth about all of the things, and I want complete cross-examination, and I raise only the question of surprising the witnesses with documents they themselves prepared which are in the file and which the Government has, and it seems to me a shorter way of arriving at the truth and a fairer way where a witness has prepared a document which the Government has in its possession is to ask him if he prepared that document, and to read it into the record, rather than confuse him first by asking him about things that he doesn't remember. That is the only point I make, and that limited point, and I wish in no way to confine this inquiry. But it is an important point though limited.

Wednesday, April 21

[The board hears from two witnesses who testify in Oppenheimer's behalf. Sumner T. Pike, a member of the AEC from 1946 to the end of 1951, is head of the Maine Public Utilities Commission. He says that he never doubted Oppenheimer's loyalty: "I think he is a man of essential integrity. I think he has been a fool several times, but there was nothing in there that shook my feeling." Norman Foster Ramsey Jr., a professor of physics at Harvard University, who was at Los Alamos from 1943 to 1945 as a consultant to the Secretary of War, similarly testifies to the widespread respect in which Oppenheimer was held.]

> ISIDOR I. RABI: "He is a consultant, and if you don't want to consult the guy, you don't consult him period. . . . We have an A-bomb . . . * * * and what more do you want, mermaids?"

[Isidor I. Rabi, professor of physics at Columbia University, is then called. A friend of Oppenheimer's for a quarter of a century, Rabi succeeded him as chairman of the General Advisory Committee. Ten days earlier, as the hearing was about to begin, Samuel Silverman, an associate of Garrison's, had warned Rabi not to telephone Oppenheimer since his phone was sure to be tapped, as indeed it was. Midway through Rabi's appearance, Oppenheimer briefly left the hearing room and permitted the questioning to continue in his absence.]

DIRECT EXAMINATION

By Mr. Marks: . . .

Q. Dr. Rabi, if you will indulge me I would like to skip around somewhat because as nearly as possible I would like to avoid too much repetition of things that have already been gone into by others.

Isidor I. Rabi (left) and Lee A. DuBridge, Washington, D.C. AIP Emilio Segrè Visual Archives, Segrè Collection.

Will you describe to the extent that you can what took place in the fall of 1949 insofar as the GAC was concerned or you are concerned in respect of the question of thermonuclear program for the Atomic Energy Commission?

A. I can only give my own view and my own recollection. I have not prepared myself for this by studying the minutes. I intended to, but I am on in the morning rather than the afternoon. So I can give you just my own recollection.

The thermonuclear reaction or as it was called the super was under intense study from my very first contact with Los Alamos.

Q. When was that?

A. About April 15, 1943. At the establishment of the laboratory, Dr. Oppenheimer called together a group of people to discuss the policy and technical direction of the laboratory, and I was one of those who was invited to that discussion. All through the war years and following that, that was a subject of discussion and consideration by some of the very best minds in physics.

The problem proved to be an extremely difficult, very recalcitrant problem, because of the many factors which were involved where the theory, the understanding of the thing, was inadequate. It was just a borderline. The more one looked at it, the tougher it looked.

Following announcement of the Russian explosion of the A bomb, I felt that somehow or other some answer must be made in some form to this to regain the lead which we had. There were two directions in which one could look; either the realization of the super or an intensification of the effort on fission weapons to make very large ones, small ones, and so on, to get a large variety and very great military flexibility.

Furthermore, a large number, a large increase in the production of the necessary raw materials, the fissionable materials and so on, or one could consider both. There was a real question there where the weight of the effort should lie.

Q. When would you say that this question that you are now describing began to become acute in your thinking?

A. Right away.

Q. You mean with the Russian explosion?

A. As soon as I heard of the Russian explosion. I discussed it with some colleagues. I know I discussed it with Dr. Ernest Lawrence, with Luis Alvarez, and of course with the chairman of our committee, Dr. Oppenheimer. In fact, I discussed it with anybody who was cleared to discuss such matters, because it was a very, very serious problem.

That question then came up at the meeting of the General Advisory Committee.

Q. That would have been the meeting that began on October 29, 1949?

A. Yes. I do not recollect now whether this was the first meeting after the announcement of the Russian explosion or whether there was an intervening meeting.

Q. To refresh your recollection, Dr. Rabi, I think it has been in the record here that there was a regular meeting of the General Advisory Committee just after or just at the time when the Russian explosion was being evaluated.

A. Yes. I recollect now. . . .

Q. This meeting which you identified was more or less contemporaneous by the official announcement of this Government that there had been a Russian explosion, was there any discussion at that time of the thermonuclear?

A. I would have to refresh my memory on that. I cannot say. I would be astonished if there were not. I cannot say. I could go back and look. In fact, we talked about it at every meeting.

Q. In all events, the interval between that meeting and the one on the 29th, was very much on your mind?

A. Yes, sir.

Q. Do you have any recollection or impression as to the form in which the question of what to do about the thermonuclear problem came up in your meeting that began on October 29? . . .

A. As I recollect it now—it is 5 years ago—the chairman, Dr. Oppenheimer, started very solemnly and as I recall we had to consider this question. The question came not whether we should make a thermonuclear weapon, but whether there should be a crash program. There were some people, and I myself was of that opinion for a time, who thought that the concentration on the crash program to go ahead with this was the answer to the Russian thermonuclear weapon. The question was, should it be a crash program and a technical question: What possibilities lay in that? What would be the cost of initiating a crash program in terms of the strength of the United States because of the weakening of the effort on which something which we had in hand, namely, the fission weapons, and the uncompleted designs of different varieties, to have a really flexible weapon, the question of interchangeability of parts, all sorts of things which could be used in different military circumstances.

Then there was the question of the military value of this weapon. One of the things which we talked about a great deal was that this weapon as promised which didn't exist and which we didn't know how to make, what sort of military weapon was it anyway? What sort of target it was good for. And what would be the general political effect.

In other words, we felt—and I am talking chiefly about myself—that this was not just a weapon. But by its very nature, if you attacked a target, it took in very much more. We felt it was really essential and we discussed a great deal what were you buying if you got this thing. That was the general nature of the discussion.

Technical, military, and the combination of military political. . . .

Q. To the extent that you can tell it without getting into any classified material, what was the outcome of the GAC meeting of October 1949?

A. I will try to give it as best I can.

Q. Let me break it down. First, is it fair to say that the committee was in agreement with respect or essentially in agreement with respect to the technical factors involved in the thermonuclear situation?

A. It was hard to say whether there was an agreement or not because what we are talking about was such a vague thing, this object, that I think different people had different thoughts about it. You could just give a sort of horseback thing and say, maybe something would come out in 5 years. It is that sort of thing. I know in my own case I think I took the dimmest technical view of this, and there are others who were more optimistic.

Q. I think it has been indicated here that there was some statement in the report of the GAC at that time to the effect that it was the opinion that a concerted imaginative effort might produce—that there was a 50–50 chance of success in 5 years.

MR. ROBB. In the interest of accuracy, I think the report says a better than even chance. Let me check it to make sure.

MR. GARRISON. That is correct.

By Mr. Marks:

Q. Was that supposed to be a consensus of the views?

A. More or less. When you are talking about something as vague as this particular thing, you say a 50–50 chance in 5 years, where you don't know the kind of physical factors and theory that goes into the problem. I just want to give my own impression that it was a field where we really did not know what we were talking about, except on the basis of general experience. We didn't even know whether this thing contradicted the laws of physics.

Q. You didn't know what?

A. Whether it contradicted the laws of physics.

Q. In other words, it could have been altogether impossible.

A. It could have been altogether impossible. The thing we were talking about. I want to be specific.

Q. I understand.

A. We were talking within a certain definite framework of ideas.

Q. To the extent that you can describe them now and confining yourself to that meeting, to the extent that you can describe them without trespassing on classified material, what were the recommendations of the GAC?

A. They were complicated. We divided into two groups. No, there were some recommendations to which I think we all agreed, which were specific technical recommendations.

Q. Can you say what they had to do with in general terms?

A. Certain improvements in weapons, the production of certain material which would be of great utility in weapons and which we felt at the time might be fundamental if a super were to be made. We recommend sharply a go-ahead on that. We recommended certain directions of weapons and there was a third important recommendation which I don't recollect now of a technical nature.

Q. You have spoken of a division. What had you reference to there?

A. In addition to that there were supplementary reports on which Dr. Fermi and I formed a minority, and the other six members present the majority. That had more to do with this sphere where the political and the military impinge. One group felt—I don't like to speak for them because the record is there, but my impression was—that this projected weapon was just no good as a weapon.

Q. You mean the particular weapon?

A. I am not talking from the technical but the military opinion. That it was not of great military utility. The possible targets were very few in number, and so on. I could elaborate on that if I should be asked, but I am speaking for somebody else, and there is a record.

Q. That was the group with which you did not join?

A. Yes. Of this specific design, Dr. Fermi and I as I recollect it now felt that in the first place as far as we could see from the question of having a deliverable weapon one did not gain a tremendous amount. Secondly, we felt that the whole discussion raised an opportunity for the President of the United States to make some political gesture which would be such that it would strengthen our moral position, should we decide to go ahead with it. That our position should be such that depending on the reaction, we would go ahead or not, whatever going ahead were to mean.

Q. What made you think that it was appropriate for you to speak about these rather nontechnical but more political, diplomatic and military considerations?

A. That is a good question. However, somehow or other we didn't feel it was inappropriate. In our whole dealing with the Commission, we very often, or most often, raised the questions to be discussed. In other words, we would say we want to discuss this and this thing. Would you please provide us with documents, would you bring individuals to talk to us on this, and we would address the Commission on questions.

On the other hand, we didn't feel badly if they didn't act on our suggestions. Sometimes they did and sometimes they didn't. So we did not feel that this was inappropriate. It would be very hard for me to tell you now why we thought it was appropriate, but we thought so. . . .

Q. After the President announced the decision to go ahead with the hydrogen bomb in January of 1950, what attitude and what steps, if any, did the GAC take with respect to the subject from then on?

A. I think we started talking about the best ways and means to do it. It was a very difficult question, because here is a statement from the President to do something that nobody knew how to do. This was just a ball of wax. So we were really quite puzzled except insofar as to try to get people to go and look at the problem.

Q. In that connection, did the GAC itself try to look into the problem?

A. Insofar as we could; yes. We had people who were quite expert and actually worked on it, chiefly of course Dr. Fermi, who went back to Los Alamos, summers and so on, and took a lot of time with it. So we had a very important expert right on the committee. Of course, Dr. Oppenheimer knew very well the theoretical questions involved.

Q. Do you think the GAC had any usefulness in helping the work on this particular subject?

A. I think it did; I think it had a great usefulness some way indirect and some way direct, ways of trying to bring out the solid facts. It is awfully hard to get at those facts. I recall particularly one meeting, I think it was in the summer of 1950 at Los Alamos, I am sure of the dates, where we actually got together all the knowledgeable people we could find, I think Dr. Bethe was there and Fermi, to try to produce some kind of record which would tell us where we stood. This was before the Greenhouse test.

Q. You mean what the state of the art was at that time?

A. What the state of the art was, and where do we go from here.

Q. How many of the laws of nature on the subject were available?

A. What ideas and what technical information was available. We got this report and it was circulated by the Commission in various places because there was some kind of feeling that here the President is given the directive and somehow something is going to appear at the other end and it was not appearing.

Q. If you can tell, Dr. Rabi, what was the connection or relation between the meeting you have just described at Los Alamos and another meeting that has been testified here which took place, I believe, in 1951, in the late spring at Princeton?

A. That was an entirely different meeting. At that meeting we really got on the beam, because a new invention had occurred. There we had a situation where you really could talk about it. You knew what to calculate and so on, and you were in the realm where you could apply scientific ideas which were not some extrapolation very far beyond the known. This is something which could be calculated, which could be studied, and was an entirely different thing.

Q. Why did it take that long?

A. Just the human mind.

Q. There was the President's directive in January 1950.

A. Why it took this long? One had to get rid of the ideas that were and are probably no good. In other words, there has been all this newspaper stuff about delay. The subject which we discussed in the 1949 meeting, that particular thing has never been made and probably never will be made, and we still don't know to this day whether something like that will function.

This other thing was something quite different, a much more modest and more definite idea on which one could go. . . .

Q. Doctor, it can be gathered from the nature of these proceedings that this board has the function of advising the Commission with respect to a determination that the Commission must make on whether permitting Dr. Oppenheimer to have access to restricted data will not endanger the common defense and security.

In formulating this advice, the considerations suggested by the Atomic Energy Act to be taken into account are the character, associations, and loyalty of the individual concerned.

Do you feel that you know Dr. Oppenheimer well enough to comment on the bearing of his character, loyalty and associations on this issue?

A. I think Dr. Oppenheimer is a man of upstanding character, that he is a loyal individual, not only to the United States, which of course goes without saying in my mind, but also to his friends and his organizations to which he is attached, let us say, to the institutions, and work very hard for his loyalties; an upright character, very upright character, very thoughtful, sensitive feeling in that respect. . . .

MR. MARKS. It is agreeable to Dr. Oppenheimer that the proceedings continue this afternoon without his presence.

MR. GRAY. I just want to make it clear that it is a matter of his own choosing, and of Mr. Garrison, that they are not present this afternoon for the remainder of these proceedings.

MR. MARKS. That is correct. He may be back before we finish, but this is a matter of his own choosing.

MR. GRAY. Would you proceed, Mr. Robb.

CROSS-EXAMINATION

By Mr. Robb:

Q. Dr. Rabi, you testified that in the fall of 1949, the problem of the super program had your attention quite considerably.

A. Yes.

Q. And I believe you said that you talked with Dr. Lawrence and Dr. Alvarez about it.

A. Yes.

Q. Could that have been in October, just before the meeting of the GAC.
    (Dr. Oppenheimer entered the room.)

MR. GRAY. You are back now, Dr. Oppenheimer.

DR. OPPENHEIMER. This is one of the few things I am really sure of.

THE WITNESS. I can't remember the exact date. I think it was in the fall. It was before the GAC meeting.

By Mr. Robb:

Q. It was before the GAC meeting?

A. I am quite sure.

Q. Did Dr. Alvarez and Dr. Lawrence come to see you in New York?

A. That is right.

Q. Together or did they come separately?

A. Together.

Q. What was the purpose of their visit to you, sir?

A. Well, we are old friends. I don't remember what the purpose was that they wanted to come up which I didn't find extraordinary. Physicists visit one another. Both are people I have known for a long time. But we did talk on this thing which was in our mind.

Q. Yes. To save time, didn't they come to see you with special reference to the thermonuclear question or the super question?

A. That may have been in their minds. It may have been in their minds. We got going on it right away.

Q. In all events, you talked about it?

A. That is right. What was in their minds, I don't know.

Q. Do you recall what their views were on it as they expressed them to you then?

A. Their views were that they were extremely optimistic. They are both very optimistic gentlemen. They were extremely optimistic about it. They had been to Los Alamos and talked to Dr. Teller, who gave them a very optimistic estimate about the thing and about the kind of special materials which would be required. So they were all keyed up to go bang into it.

Q. They thought we ought to go ahead with it?

A. I think if they had known then what we knew a year later, I don't think they would have been so eager. But at that time they had a very optimistic estimate.

Q. To help you fix the time, was that after the Russian explosion?

A. After the Russian explosion.

Q. Was that the main reason why they thought we ought to get along with the thermonuclear program?

A. I don't know.

Q. Beg pardon?

A. I would suppose so. As I testified before, what I testified was that we felt we had to do something to recover our lead.

Q. Did you express your view to them on that subject?

A. Yes, that we had to do something, and I think that I may have inclined— this is something which I kept no notes and so on.

Q. I understand, doctor.

A. I think I may have inclined toward their view on the basis of the information they said they had from Dr. Teller.

Q. Did you find yourself in any substantial disagreement with their views as they expressed them then?

A. It wasn't the case of agreement or disagreement. I generally find myself when I talk with these two gentlemen in a very uncomfortable position. I like to be an enthusiast. I love it. But those fellows are so enthusiastic that I have to be a conservative. So it always puts me in an odd position to say, "Now, now. There, there," and that sort of thing. So I was not in agreement in the sense that I felt they were as usual, which is to their credit—they have accomplished very great things—overly optimistic.

Q. Except for that you agreed with their thought that we ought to do something, as you put it, to regain our position?

A. That is right. I felt very strongly. I spoke to everybody I could properly speak to, as I said earlier, talking about what we could do to get back this enormous lead which we had at that time. This of course was one of the possibilities.

Q. Was it before that or after that you talked to Dr. Oppenheimer?

A. I really don't remember the sequence of events at that time and when I saw Dr. Oppenheimer, whether he was away for the summer or I was, or what, I wish I could testify. I don't keep a diary.

Q. I understand. All I want is your best recollection, doctor. Whenever you talked to Dr. Oppenheimer, did he express his views on this matter?

A. It is very hard to answer. I just don't recollect to tell you a specific time at a specific place where I spoke to Oppenheimer.

Q. May I help you a little bit? It is difficult to separate what he might have told you before the meeting with what he said at the meeting.

A. To which meeting are you talking?

Q. The meeting of October 29.

A. I don't really remember that we met before the meeting or immediately before the meeting, or that he told me something of that sort. I just don't remember. My actual recollection is that I learned the purpose of the meeting at the meeting, but I am not certain. I just can't tell.

Q. At all events, the views expressed by Dr. Oppenheimer at the meeting were not in accord with those expressed to you by Alvarez and Lawrence, were they?

A. No, the meeting was a very interesting one. It was a rather solemn meeting. I must say that Dr. Oppenheimer as chairman of the meeting always conducted himself in such a way as to elicit the opinions of the members and to stimulate the discussion. He is not one of these chairmen who sort of takes it their privilege to hold the floor; the very opposite. Generally he might express his own view last and very rarely in a strong fashion, but generally with considerable reservations. When he reported to the Commission, it was always a miracle to the other members on the committee how he could summarize three days of discussions and give the proper weight to the opinion of every member, the proper shade, and it rarely happened that some member would speak up and say, "This isn't exactly what I meant." It was a rather miraculous performance. . . .

Q. Do you recall any mention at that meeting of October 29, 1949, of a communication from Dr. Seaborg about the problem under discussion?

A. I can't recollect. I don't know. I might add it would not have been very significant, because my feeling is now that we came into the meeting without any clear ideas, that in the course of an extremely exhausting discussion to and fro, examining all the possibilities we each became clearer as to what this thing meant. So anybody who didn't participate in the discussion wouldn't have gotten what we conceived at that time to be that kind of clarity. . . .

MR. GRAY. I have one other question. You testified very clearly, I think, as to your judgment of Dr. Oppenheimer as a man, referring to his character, his loyalty to the United States, and to his friends and to institutions with which he might be identified, and made an observation about associations.

As of today would you expect Dr. Oppenheimer's loyalty to the country to take precedence over loyalty to an individual or to some other institution?

THE WITNESS. I just don't think that anything is higher in his mind or heart than loyalty to his country. This sort of desire to see it grow and develop. I might amplify my other statement in this respect, and that is something we talked of through the years. When we first met in 1929, American physics was not really very much, certainly not consonant with the great size and wealth of the country. We were very much concerned with raising the level of American physics. We were sick and tired of going to Europe as learners. We wanted to be independent. I must say I think that our generation, Dr. Oppenheimer's and my other friend that I can mention, did that job, and that 10 years later we were at the top of the heap, and it wasn't just because certain refugees came out of Germany, but because of what we did here. This was a conscious motivation. Oppenheimer set up this school of theoretical physics which was a tremendous contribution. In fact, I don't know how we could have carried out the scientific part of the war without the contributions of the people who worked with Oppenheimer. They made their contributions very willingly and very enthusiastically and single-mindedly.

MR. GRAY. Perhaps I could get at my question this way. You are familiar, if you have read the Nichols letter and read the summary of a file which Chairman Strauss handed you, with the Chevalier episode to some extent, I take it.

THE WITNESS. I know of the episode, yes.

MR. GRAY. Would you expect Dr. Oppenheimer today to follow the course of action he followed at that time in 1943?

THE WITNESS. You mean refuse to give information? Is that what you mean?

MR. GRAY. Yes.

THE WITNESS. I certainly do. At the present time I think he would clamp him into jail if he asked such a question.

MR. GRAY. I am sorry.

THE WITNESS. At the present time if a man came to him with a proposal like that, he would see that he goes to jail. At least that is my opinion of what he would do in answer to this hypothetical question.

MR. GRAY. Do you feel that security is relative, that something that was all right in 1943, would not be all right in 1954?

THE WITNESS. If a man in 1954 came with such a proposal, my God—it would be horrifying.

MR. GRAY. Supposing a man came to you in 1943.

THE WITNESS. I would have thrown him out.

MR. GRAY. Would you have done anything more about it?

THE WITNESS. I don't think so. Unless I thought he was just a poor jackass and didn't know what he was doing. But I would try to find out what motivated him and what was behind it, and get after that at any time. If somebody asked me to violate a law and an oath— . . .

Mr. Gray. In any event, I believe you did testify that you would be quite convinced—I am not sure you did—are you quite convinced that as of today Dr. Oppenheimer's course of action would be in accord with what you would do, rather than what he did in respect to the matter of this sort. I can't say what a man will do, but we only can apply subjective tests in these matters as far as your testimony as to character, loyalty and so forth, are concerned. So this is all subjective, but would you expect without any real question in your mind that today Dr. Oppenheimer would follow the kind of course that you would approve of today with respect to this matter?

The Witness. I think I can say that with certainty. I think there is no question in my mind of his loyalty in that way. You know there always is a problem of that sort. I mean the world has been divided into sheep and goats. I mean the country has been divided into sheep and goats. There are the people who are cleared and those who are not cleared. The people against whom there has been some derogatory information and whatnot. What it may mean and so on is difficult. It is really a question in one's personal life, should you refuse to enter a room in which a person is present against whom there is derogatory information. Of course, if you are extremely prudent and want your life circumscribed that way, no question would ever arise. If you feel that you want to live a more normal life and have confidence in your own integrity and in your record for integrity, then you might act more freely, but which could be criticized, either for being foolhardy or even worse.

In one's normal course at a university, one does come across people who have been denied clearance. Should you never sit down and discuss scientific matters with them, although they have very interesting scientific things to say?

Mr. Gray. No, I would not think so. . . .

REDIRECT EXAMINATION

By Mr. Marks: . . .

Q. Dr. Rabi, Mr. Robb asked you whether you had spoken to Chairman Strauss in behalf of Dr. Oppenheimer. Did you mean to suggest in your reply—in your reply to him you said you did among other things—did you mean to suggest that you had done that at Dr. Oppenheimer's instigation?

A. No; I had no communication from Dr. Oppenheimer before these charges were filed, or since, except that I called him once to just say that I believed in him, with no further discussion.

Another time I called on him and his attorney at the suggestion of Mr. Strauss. I never hid my opinion from Mr. Strauss that I thought that this whole proceeding was a most unfortunate one.

Dr. Evans. What was that?

THE WITNESS. That the suspension of the clearance of Dr. Oppenheimer was a very unfortunate thing and should not have been done. In other words, there he was; he is a consultant, and if you don't want to consult the guy, you don't consult him, period. Why you have to then proceed to suspend clearance and go through all this sort of thing, he is only there when called, and that is all there was to it. So it didn't seem to me the sort of thing that called for this kind of proceeding at all against a man who had accomplished what Dr. Oppenheimer has accomplished. There is a real positive record, the way I expressed it to a friend of mine. We have an A-bomb and a whole series of it, * * * and what more do you want, mermaids? This is just a tremendous achievement. If the end of that road is this kind of hearing, which can't help but be humiliating, I thought it was a pretty bad show. I still think so. . . .

RE-CROSS-EXAMINATION

By Mr. Robb: . . .

Q. Dr. Rabi, getting back to the hypothetical questions that have been put to you by the Chairman and Dr. Evans about the Chevalier incident, if you had been put in that hypothetical position and had reported the matter to an intelligence officer, you of course would have been told the whole truth about it, wouldn't you?

A. I am naturally a truthful person.

Q. You would not have lied about it?

A. I am telling you what I think now. The Lord alone knows what I would have done at that time. This is what I think now.

Q. Of course, Doctor, as you say, only God knows what is in a man's mind and heart, but give us your best judgment of what you would do.

A. This is what I think now I hope that is what I would have done then. In other words, I do not—I take a serious view of that—I think it is crucial.

Q. You say what?

A. I take a serious view of that incident, but I don't think it is crucial.

Q. Of course, Doctor, you don't know what Dr. Oppenheimer's testimony before this board about that incident may have been, do you?

A. No.

Q. So perhaps in respect of passing judgment on that incident, the board may be in a better position to judge than you?

A. I have the highest respect for the board. I am not going to make any comment about the board. They are working very hard, as I have seen.

Q. Of course, I realize you have complete confidence in the board. But my point is that perhaps the board may be in possession of information which is not now available to you about the incident.

A. It may be. On the other hand, I am in possession of a long experience with this man, going back to 1929, which is 25 years, and there is a kind of seat of the pants feeling which I myself lay great weight. In other words, I might even venture to differ from the judgment of the board without impugning their integrity at all. . . .

Thursday, April 22

NORRIS E. BRADBURY: "A scientist wants to know. He wants to know correctly and truthfully and precisely"

[Norris E. Bradbury met Oppenheimer in the early 1930s when he entered the University of California at Berkeley as a graduate student in physics. During the war he served as a commander in the naval reserve, and in June 1944, was assigned to Los Alamos. The following year, when Oppenheimer left, Bradbury took over as director of the Los Alamos Scientific Laboratory, a position he still holds as he testifies.]

DIRECT EXAMINATION

By Mr. Silverman: . . .

Q. What would you say as to the cooperation or lack of cooperation that was evidenced by specifically Dr. Oppenheimer and generally by the General Advisory Committee with respect to the thermonuclear program?

A. Both the General Advisory Committee and Dr. Oppenheimer, I always found from my personal knowledge extremely helpful and cooperative—I am seeking an appropriate word—actively cooperative with the Los Alamos Laboratory in this field. This was, of course, not a unique thing in the thermonuclear field. The GAC and Dr. Oppenheimer had always to my knowledge been an active friend and been active friends of the laboratory, and had been helpful and had worked closely with us in all our discussions relevant to Los Alamos, or many discussions relative to Los Alamos. They invited the staff of the laboratory to meet with them. I met with them myself on many occasions.

Their comments were always helpful. Their advice was always helpful. I never knew them or Dr. Oppenheimer to take a stand or a position or to give advice which was other than useful and helpful to the laboratory. . . .

Q. Do you recall a meeting at Princeton in the spring or summer of 1951?

A. Yes, I do.

Q. You were present at that meeting?

A. I was present.

Q. Would you care to say something about the role played by Dr. Oppenheimer there, particularly in connection with what it may indicate to the board as to his cooperation in the thermonuclear program?

A. The meeting of the General Advisory Committee in June, I believe it was, of 1951, was called following an Eniwetok operation. It was called following, let me say, the discovery at Los Alamos of some extremely promising ideas in this field, and at that time the exploitation of these ideas seemed to us at Los Alamos and to others of our consultants and associated with us in the field warrant some attention by the Commission to certain decisions, let me say, of production, which were extremely important, and could well be quite expensive.

We as the laboratory made this proposal. We found the General Advisory Committee and Dr. Oppenheimer extremely enthusiastic both about this idea and about the general proposals which were needed to implement this idea, particularly insofar as they required Commission action. Indeed, I think it fair to say that the General Advisory Committee and Dr. Oppenheimer were willing to go further than the laboratory in support of this, let us say, new approach to the problem, and that their recommendations to the Commission were at least as enthusiastic as ours, and actually went somewhat beyond, in terms of support, what we had originally drafted.

I would regard this myself as very positive evidence of the interest and enthusiasm which the GAC was showing and showed in this field. . . .

Q. You have seen the portion of the Commission's letter in which the statement is made, "It was further reported that you, Dr. Oppenheimer, were instrumental in persuading other outstanding scientists not to work on the hydrogen project, and the opposition of the hydrogen bomb of which you are the most experienced, most powerful and most effective member has definitely slowed down its development."

What would you say about the statement that the program was slowed down because of Dr. Oppenheimer's opinion or activities?

A. It is not my opinion that the program was slowed down, as I have said. Of course, if he himself had been in a position or wished to work on it directly and personally, this would undoubtedly have been a great help. However, it is my opinion that the program went and has gone with amazing speed, particularly in view of the predictions made regarding the difficulty of this program throughout the years 1945 to 1949. I know of no case, if you wish me to pursue these remarks, where Dr. Oppenheimer persuaded anyone not to work in this field.

As I have remarked, scientists of this caliber generally make up their own minds about wishing to work or not to work in this field. A number of outstanding people whom we would like to have brought into this program felt that their best contribution to the country was to remain in university circles and contribute to the training of graduate students.

With this point of view, one can hardly differ. Of course, Los Alamos Laboratory had a selfish approach to it.

Q. Would you say that Dr. Oppenheimer's attitude, opinions, activities with respect to the development of thermonuclear weapons in any way indicated that there were some malevolent or sinister motives about it?

A. Absolutely not. As I have remarked, from 1946 on, I have never known him to act in a way other than was a help to the laboratory. . . .

He has given us frequently prospects, outstanding young individuals, whom we might be able to approach particularly in the field of theoretical physics to join the laboratory.

With me personally he has never been other. From October 1945 on and during the war years, other than encouraging, helpful, congratulatory, and generally both a personal friend and a friend of the laboratory.

Q. How long have you known Dr. Oppenheimer?

A. I knew him as an instructor when I was a graduate student at Berkeley in 1931–32, probably, somewhere through there. I knew him as director of Los Alamos Scientific Laboratory from June of 1944 until October 1945. I knew him thereafter as chairman of the General Advisory Committee and saw him regularly, I would say, several times a year, in that capacity. He visited Los Alamos, I would again say, at least once a year or perhaps twice, in connection with his responsibilities as chairman of the General Advisory Committee.

Q. How well do you think you know him as a man, his character, and so on, the kind of person he is?

A. I would think I would know him as well as one knows any individual with whom one has had friendly and professional contact over quite a long number of years, and perhaps better than the average having seen him in his capacity as director of the laboratory, in which I then had an assisting subordinate position.

Q. Do you have an opinion as to Dr. Oppenheimer's loyalty to the country, and as to whether he would be a security risk?

A. I do have such an opinion and it is a very strong one.

Q. Would you state it, please?

A. I would regard him from my observation as completely loyal to this country. In fact, I would make a statement of this sort, I think, that while loyalty is a very difficult thing to demonstrate in an objective fashion, if a man could demonstrate loyalty in an objective way, that Dr. Oppenheimer in his direction of Los Alamos Laboratory during the war years did demonstrate such loyalty. I myself feel that his devotion to that task, the nature of the decisions which he was called upon to make, the manner in which he made them, were as objective a demonstration of personal loyalty to this country as I myself can imagine.

Q. As to this business of a security risk, which I take it is perhaps a little different from loyalty, do you have an opinion on that?

A. I do not regard him as a security risk.

Mr. Silverman. I have no further questions.

Mr. Gray. Mr. Robb.

CROSS-EXAMINATION

By Mr. Robb: . . .

Q. Doctor, what was your position after the Russian explosion on the question of whether or not we should develop the thermonuclear bomb? Were you for it or against it?

A. I was under the impression I had made some remarks on that subject. When you say develop the thermonuclear bomb, may I qualify my remarks to this extent. I felt, as I believe I said earlier, extremely strongly that the laboratory must undertake all possible attacks upon the thermonuclear system to see what there was of utility in this field. Now, it seems easy now to say thermonuclear bomb has been developed by public announcement; it seems obvious that there must always have been such a device in the obvious cards. This was not the case. The state of knowledge of thermonuclear systems during the war, and thereafter, and really up until the spring of 1951, was such as to make the practical utility or even the workability in any useful sense of what was then imagined as a thermonuclear weapon extremely questionable. This does not mean that—in fact, it meant very much to us that one must find out what is there in this field. Only by work in it will one find out. It is possible that we would have explored the field and out it was not, that we could not find a useful military system in it. But without this exploration, it is clear you wouldn't know.

We felt very strongly that we had to know the fact. In 1949–50 the state of knowledge at that time would certainly permit one to be very pessimistic about the practical utility of what was called a hydrogen bomb.

Q. Did you think that the Russians would certainly try to find out?

A. I was personally certain that no group of people knowing the energy which was available in the so-called fusion type of reaction would fail to explore this field.

Q. Therefore you thought we ought to also?

A. I certainly feel this way, yes, felt and feel.

Mr. Robb. Thank you, Doctor. That is all I care to ask the Doctor. . . .

Mr. Gray. Dr. Bradbury, I don't want you or anyone else to misunderstand the next question I am going to ask. It points to no conclusion certainly in my mind about anything at all. It has to do with perhaps the most serious underlying implication involved in these proceedings. That has to do with loyalty to country.

I think your statement in response to a question from counsel was that you had no question about Dr. Oppenheimer's loyalty, and you based it at least in part on his very remarkable accomplishments during the war years as Director of the Laboratory. I think there are those perhaps who questioned Dr. Oppenheimer's loyalty and who might argue that an individual who was sympathetic to the U.S.S.R. could very consistently have gone far beyond the call of normal duty in his war work, which was beneficial to the interests of the United States, and still have felt that sympathetic interests for the Soviet Union were also being served. That is at least an argument can be made, and I am sure you are familiar with it.

THE WITNESS. Yes.

MR. GRAY. In your testimony about Dr. Oppenheimer's loyalty, are you prepared to give your judgment to the war years? In other words, do you think that his actions since the war are of the same character and nature as to lead you to a conclusion about his loyalty?

THE WITNESS. I do, and I have the same opinion. I think it can be supported by the same sort—perhaps not quite the same sort of objective evidence. I am well aware that it is possible to attribute ulterior motives to almost any human action. It is possible to argue these questions in perpetuity along those lines. Referring to my statement about his behavior as Director of Los Alamos Laboratory, in my own opinion, this to me constitutes as strong objective evidence as one can hope for, of loyalty. I have to base this not only upon the technical accomplishments of the laboratory, but upon the way in which these accomplishments were done, upon the manner in which he sought and made use of advice from his senior staff, essentially upon a sort of subjective impression which you can only get by seeing a man look worried, that indeed the success of this laboratory and its role in the war that was then going on were objectives which were uppermost and surpassed all others in his mind. I was not looking in his mind, and I cannot say this of course from definite knowledge. You can never say anything about a man's loyalty by looking at him except what you feel. I would feel from everything that I could see of his operation at Los Alamos during the war years that here is a man who is completely and unequivocally loyal to the best interests of this country.

I would make the same remark about the associations I had with him after the war years. I suppose it is true, although he can say this better than I, that he had deep personal concerns about the actual role of atomic weapons in the national security. I think anyone is entitled and should have this same sort of concern. What personal decisions one makes in the long run is of course a personal matter. But certainly his chairmanship of the GAC after the war years never questioned the fact or never questioned the assertion that the Los Alamos Laboratory should continue, should be strengthened, should proceed along lines of endeavor which were of military effectiveness. Every decision that I can recall that the GAC made with respect to the laboratory, with the possible exception of what may have been their opinion regarding thermonuclear development, seemed to me to be the right decision. In other words, there was never to my knowledge any degree of difference of opinion between myself, my senior staff, and the positions taken by the GAC.

This was particularly the case that the laboratory felt extremely strongly that actual test of nuclear weapons were a fundamental part of the progress in this field. We still feel that way extremely strongly. The GAC supported us in this. Had they not done so, our progress would have been enormously slower or almost zero. This could have been a point where one might have taken a contrary position perhaps. The GAC did not do so.

I believe the question which I tend to believe was exaggerated at the time in the public press and got into erroneous importance at the time through the efforts of a number of people—it assumed an erroneous stature in public debate—was on a case where we might have found ourselves in a difference of opinion with the GAC. Whether this difference was real or not, I am not prepared to say. But I have stated what the opinion of the laboratory was as strongly as I can.

I do not personally believe that if there was this difference of opinion, and I presume there was some difference of opinion here, that it was based on malevolent motives.

I believe and still believe that the apparent position of the GAC was based upon a defendable argument although one with which I might not personally agree. I might not have personally agreed with one of the conclusions of the question of policy that some members of the GAC arrived at. Nevertheless, I do not regard them as opinions which are either malevolent or subversive. I positively regard them as opinions which can be held and which were held as matters relating to the safety of the United States.

The safety of the United States I am convinced was uppermost in the minds of all members, including the chairman, of the GAC. We may have differed as to the best methods of obtaining the safety. I think such differences are an essential part of any democratic system. I never had then nor do I now have the slightest feeling that these differences were motivated by any other than a direct deep and sincere concern for the welfare of the country.

That was only substantiated by the actions of the GAC after the President's decision, which again were in strong support of this whole field which we characterize as thermonuclear. Basically the GAC supported the laboratory as a weapons laboratory in all fields. If there was a difference of opinion in 1949–50, it had to do with perhaps the technical question of emphasis on one or another line of attack in the weapons field in general.

Does that answer your question?

MR. GRAY. I think probably it does. I think your answer is in the affirmative. I think my question was that you feel that the character and nature and intensity of Dr. Oppenheimer's loyalty has been as great in postwar years as you saw it in the war years.

THE WITNESS. That is my feeling. . . .

DR. EVANS. Do you think that scientific men as a rule are rather peculiar individuals?

THE WITNESS. When did I stop beating my wife?

MR. GRAY. Especially chemistry professors?

DR. EVANS. No, physics professors.

THE WITNESS. Scientists are human beings. I think as a class, because their basic task is concerned with the exploration of the facts of nature, understanding, this is a quality of mind philosophy—a scientist wants to know. He wants to know correctly and truthfully and precisely. By this token it seems to me he is more likely than not to be interested in a number of fields, but to be interested in them from the point of view of exploration. What is in them? What do they have to offer. What is their truth. I think this degree of flexibility of approach, of interest, of curiosity about facts, about systems, about life, is an essential ingredient to a man who is going to be a successful research scientist. If he does not have this underlying curiosity, willingness to look into things, wish and desire to look into things, I do not think he will be either a good or not certainly a great scientist.

Therefore, I think you are likely to find among people who have imaginative minds in the scientific field, individuals who are also willing, eager to look at a number of other fields with the same type of interest, willingness to examine, to be convinced and without a priori convictions as to rightness or wrongness, that this constant or this or that curve or this or that function is fatal.

I think the same sort of willingness to explore other areas of human activity is probably characteristic. If this makes them peculiar, I think it is probably a desirable peculiarity.

HARTLEY ROWE: "I don't like to see women and children killed wholesale because the male element of the human race are so stupid that they can't . . . keep out of war"

[Bradbury's testimony was followed by that of Walter Gordon Whitman, head of the chemistry department at the Massachusetts Institute of Technology, and since 1950, a member of the General Advisory Committee. He stated that Oppenheimer was "completely loyal" but that he had antagonized the U.S. Air Force by suggesting that it should not have a monopoly over atomic weapons. Then Hartley Rowe—an engineer, a member of the General Advisory Committee from 1947 to 1950, and a vice president of the United Fruit Co.—is called to testify in Oppenheimer's behalf.]

DIRECT EXAMINATION

By Mr. Marks: . . .

Q. Would you give an account, as far as you can on the basis of your memory, and without getting into classified materials, of that meeting of the GAC, of its discussions and of your own views on the subject of the crash program for an H-bomb?

A. My recollection is that it was a pretty soul searching time, and I had rather definite views of my own that the general public had considered the A-bomb as the end of all wars, or that we had something that would discourage wars, that would be a deterrent to wars. I was rather loath to enter into a crash program on the H-bomb until we had more nearly perfected the military potentialities of the A-bomb, thinking that it would divert too large a portion of the scientific world and too large a portion of the money that would be involved to something that might be good and it might be bad.

Q. As far as you yourself were concerned, did you have any qualms about the development of an H-bomb or the use of it if it could be developed?

A. My position was always against the development of the H-bomb.

Q. Could you explain that a little?

A. There are several reasons. I may be an idealist but I can't see why any people can go from one engine of destruction to another, each of them a thousand times greater in potential destruction, and still retain any normal perspective in regard to their relationships with other countries and also in relationship with peace. I had always felt that if a commensurate effort had been made to come to some understanding with the nations of the world, we might have avoided the development of the H-bomb.

Q. Did you oppose the actions that the Atomic Energy Commission was taking and with respect to which the General Advisory Committee was advising during the period between 1947 and 1950 to realize the full potential of the A-bomb?

A. Will you state the question again?

Q. Did you oppose the efforts that were made to realize the full potential of the A-bomb during the period 1947 onward?

A. Not knowingly, no. We were in that, and my earnest opinion was that we should make the best of it.

Q. If you can, would you explain why on the one hand you supported the development of A-bombs to their full potential, but at the same time held views that were in opposition to the H-bomb?

A. I thought the A-bomb might be used somewhat as a military weapon in the same order as a cannon or a new device of that sort, and that we perhaps could use it as a deterrent to war, and if war came, if we had all the potentialities of it developed, we would be in a stronger position than if we only had the bomb itself without any of the other characteristic military weapons that were developed later.

Q. Why did you distinguish between that and the H-bomb?

A. Purely as a matter of the order of destruction. The H-bomb, according to the papers, this is not classified, is a thousand times more destructive than the A-bomb, and you haven't yet reached the potentiality of it.

Q. I am not clear whether you are saying that you felt that the H-bomb was big enough for our needs.

A. I think the A-bomb was exploited to its full capacity, yes. I don't like to step up destructiveness in the order of 1,000 times. . . .

Mr. Gray. Mr. Rowe, I was very much interested in your description of your feelings in late 1949 about the development of the H-bomb. I think you made it very clear how you felt about it.

I would like to ask you whether you ever, in thinking about our problem and what we should do in this country, whether it was a source of concern to you that the Soviet Union might be working and perhaps successfully, towards the development of this kind of weapon. Perhaps my question is does that make any difference to you at all?

The Witness. It makes some difference, yes; but I would place more reliance on the proper use of the A-bomb without the H-bomb unless it developed as it did later that we had to go into it as a deterrent. I don't think it will ever be used against our enemies. I am quite concerned as to whether we would ever use the A-bomb or the A-bomb artillery or other military weapons.

Mr. Gray. Some witnesses who have come before this board have testified that the news of the Soviet success in early fall, whenever it was, September, announced in September—

The Witness. You mean last year?

Mr. Gray. No; I mean in 1949, the A-bomb of the Soviet.

The Witness. Yes.

Mr. Gray. Some witnesses have testified that at that point they felt that we should do something to regain our lead, is the way it has been expressed, I believe; that we had a margin of advantage we thought over a possible enemy, and the one with whom we would most likely be engaged in conflict if we became so engaged, that with the announcement of the Soviet explosion it appeared that the lead we had might dwindle and perhaps not continue to be a lead, and therefore something should be done to regain it. Do I understand your testimony correctly in thinking that you felt that proper exploitation of the weapon we already had and the knowledge we already had would have enabled us to maintain the lead, or was that important?

The Witness. I wasn't thinking so much of the lead, but I thought it would be more effective, and we would have a better balanced military arm, the Army, the Navy, and the Air Force. Whatever you take away from any one of those three is going to unbalance them. A trade of the effort being put on the H-bomb would detract from the things that needed to be done to get new weapons so that in the next world war we would not be fighting the war with the weapons of the previous war, as we have in the last two. It seemed to me we had a much better chance militarywise in perfecting our A-bomb weapons. You understand what I mean by the different kind of weapons?

Mr. Gray. Yes, sir.

The Witness. Than it would be to devote that effort to producing something that was a thousand times worse in explosive power at least, and can only be used in my opinion in retaliation. I don't think it has any place in a military campaign at all. Then if you used it in retaliation, you are using it against civilization, and not against the military.

I have that distinction very clearly in my mind. I don't like to see women and children killed wholesale because the male element of the human race are so stupid that they can't get out of war and keep out of war.

MR. GRAY. I would like to turn to something else for a moment. You have read General Nichols' letter and Dr. Oppenheimer's reply?

THE WITNESS. Yes, sir.

MR. GRAY. Do you feel that your present conviction about Dr. Oppenheimer's character, loyalty and associations, would be the same if you knew that the information contained in the Nichols letter by early associations was true? Would your reply still be the same?

Let me repeat, Mr. Rowe, I am not saying that it is or is not true. Can you assume that derogatory information and still arrive at the answer you gave to Mr. Marks' question?

THE WITNESS. I think my answer to that would be I would make it just that much stronger because people make mistakes and people in the climate of public opinion in those days which was quite different than it is now—we know a great deal more than we did then—I think a man of Dr. Oppenheimer's character is not going to make the same mistake twice. I would say he was all the more trustworthy for the mistakes he made.

LEE A. DUBRIDGE: "Dr. Oppenheimer . . . was a natural and respected and at all times a loved leader"

[The final witness of the day, Lee A. DuBridge, is president of the California Institute of Technology and chairman of the Science Advisory Committee of the Office of Defense Mobilization. He went to Los Alamos as a consultant in May 1945, and later served on the General Advisory Committee, from 1946 to 1952, when Oppenheimer was chairman. Two weeks before the hearing began, DuBridge spoke with Oppenheimer on the telephone. To Oppenheimer's assertion that the hearing was "damn nonsense," DuBridge replied: "It's more troublesome than that; if it were only nonsense we might fight it, but it is deeper than that."]

DIRECT EXAMINATION

By Mr. Garrison: . . .

Q. I want to ask you a little about the work of the General Advisory Committee from its inception up to the October 1949 meeting. I want to ask you a few questions about that meeting and then a few questions about what happened in the GAC after President Truman gave the go-ahead on the all-out program for the H-bomb.

We have a good deal of testimony already on these subjects. I don't expect an exhaustive discussion from you, but I would like you to tell the board a few of the things that stand out in your memory during the period from the beginning of the GAC up to October 1949 in the way of recommendations made by the GAC to the Commission and what part Dr. Oppenheimer played in that effort. . . .

A. Even if Dr. Oppenheimer had not been officially elected Chairman each year, and if I may say so, he resigned or attempted to resign each year, feeling that a new Chairman should be elected, the Committee unanimously rejected his recommendation every year, and asked him to continue to serve as Chairman. He was so naturally a leader of our group that it was impossible to imagine that he should not be in the chair. He was the leader of our group first because his knowledge of the atomic energy work was far more intimate than that of any other member of the Committee. He had obviously been more intimately involved in the actual scientific work of the Manhattan project than any other person on our Committee. He was a natural leader because we respected his intelligence, his judgment, his personal attitude toward the work of the Commission, and the Committee. Of course, without saying we had not the faintest doubt of his loyalty. More than that, we felt, and I feel that there is no one who has exhibited his loyalty to this country more spectacularly than Dr. Oppenheimer. He was a natural and respected and at all times a loved leader of that group.

At the same time I should emphasize that at no time did he dominate the group or did he suppress opinions that did not agree with his own. In fact, he encouraged a full and free and frank exchange of ideas throughout the full history of the Committee. That is the reason we liked him as a leader, because though he did lead and stimulate and inform us and help us in our decisions, he never dominated nor suppressed contrary or different opinions. There was a free, full, frank exchange, and it was one of the finest Committees that I ever had the privilege to serve on for that reason.

Q. Coming now to the October 29, 1949, meeting at which the question of the crash program for the H-bomb was discussed at great length, do you recall how the topic of the so-called crash program for the H-bomb came up to the GAC?

A. This is a matter of recollection of a particular thing that happened. I will have to tell it in rather general terms though I am sure the records of the Committee must be available to you. . . .

I think it went something like this. May I go back just a moment? After this question was posed by Dr. Oppenheimer to the Committee for its consideration—and I will not attempt to state the full technical content of that question at the moment—Dr. Oppenheimer asked the members of the Committee if they would in turn around the table express their views on this question. The way in which the Committee happened to be seated at the table, I was either the last or the next to last to express my views.

The Chairman, Dr. Oppenheimer, did not express his point of view on this question until after all of the rest of the members of the Committee had expressed themselves. It was clear, however, as the individual members did express their opinions as we went around the table, that while there were differing points of view, different reasons, different methods of thinking, different methods of approach to the problem, that each member came essentially to the same conclusion, namely, there were better things the United States could do at that time than to embark upon this super program. . . .

If we made any mistake in our reports, the mistake was in not amplifying and giving our views. I think we made our reports too brief, and therefore they were not understood. Therefore, much of what I am saying is opinion I held as I recall it, and I am not sure just how much was written down. Only a small part of that actually. Therefore, there were technical reasons for not thinking that the super was ready for production. There were important reasons for thinking that there were more fruitful things at Los Alamos, and the other laboratories could proceed on the fission program.

The fission weapon program was such that a very large destructive power was in our hands, and it was not clear to me that the thermonuclear weapons would add in significant ways to that destructive power.

Finally, there was a question of whether the United States could not find a better way of strengthening, rather than deteriorating its moral position with the rest of the world. It seemed to me and to some other members—I think all of the members of the Committee—that if the United States, instead of making a unilateral announcement that it was proceeding with this new and terribly destructive weapon, should instead say to the world that such a weapon may be possible, but we would like to discuss methods of reaching agreements where no nation would proceed with the design and construction of such a weapon.

It seemed to me at the time that the moral position of the United States in the face of the rest of the world would be better if we took that kind of a stand rather than making a unilateral announcement that we were proceeding with this new weapon of mass destruction. That as I recollect it was the background of my thinking at that time.

I must say that I cannot claim credit for originality in these thoughts. These thoughts evolved from my discussions with the other members of the Committee. But as nearly as I can reconstruct my thoughts at that time, that is it. . . .

Q. May I just for a moment remind you that the Atomic Energy Act requires the board to consider character, associations, and loyalty. Having this frame of reference that the board here must consider, the character, associations and loyalty of Dr. Oppenheimer, in determining whether or not his continuance of his clearance would endanger the national safety, having in mind the past associations set forth in the letter, having in mind what you know about Dr. Oppenheimer's character, having in mind what you say that the continuance of his clearance would to any degree endanger the national safety?

A. In no degree whatsoever.

Q. On what do you base this judgment?

A. In the first place, these associations that are mentioned were those of many, many years ago. As I understand it, they have largely long since been terminated, in at least one case by death. In the second place, these were rather natural associations of a person who had strong human interests, interests in human rights and human liberties and human welfare, who had strong revulsions against the growth of dictatorship in Germany, Spain, and Italy, and who wanted to express his opposition to such violations of human liberty as he regarded these dictatorships. He therefore found himself among others of like minds, some of whom it turned out were possible members of the Communist Party. But this was only a natural exhibition of his deep interest in human beings and in human liberty and had nothing to do with his devotion to this country, or nothing adverse to do with this country.

In the second place, it seems to me that to question the integrity and loyalty of a person who has worked hard and devotedly for his country as Dr. Oppenheimer has on such trivial grounds is against all principles of human justice. It seems to me whatever his ideas and associations were in 1935, is quite irrelevant in view of the last years since 1941–42, during which he has shown such a devoted interest to the welfare, security and strength of the United States. Whatever mistakes, if they were mistakes, and I do not suggest that they were, that were made in the thirties have well been washed out and the value of a man like Dr. Oppenheimer to his country has been adequately and repeatedly proved.

It would be in my opinion against all principles of justice to now not recognize the way in which his loyalty has been proved in a positive way through positive contributions. Furthermore, this country needs men of that kind, and should not deprive itself of their services.

Q. I think I should put this question to you because it is something that I want you to bear in mind when I ask you to give me your final judgment.

You are familiar with the Chevalier incident as recited in the Commission's letter.

A. That is my only familiarity, what I read in the letter. . . .

Q. . . . You would regard that seriously, I take it?

A. I would want to examine this situation very seriously. . . . I assume therefore you wish me to answer this from the point of view of my knowledge of Dr. Oppenheimer's character and integrity, and my statement would be without hesitation that I would say that these acts which he is supposed to have committed in no case stem from any disloyalty to the United States, but possibly a mistaken but nevertheless a sincere and honest belief that this was the best thing to do at the time. I just know that Dr. Oppenheimer is loyal to his friend and loyal to his country, that he is honest, but has a humane feeling, that if he did these things it was with a sense that a loyalty to a friend was important but was not in conflict with any loyalty to the country at that time.

Q. Do you think that today if he were asked by security officers to reveal information which they believe to be important for the security of the country, that he would decline to do so even if a friend were involved?

A. I am sure that at any time if he had felt a loyalty to his country was involved, he would have done what seemed to be the proper thing to reinforce that loyalty.

Q. I am asking you today, leaving aside whether he thought that his friend was innocent or not, if he were told by security officers that in their judgment the interests of the country required knowledge which he had about a friend, would he put the interests of his country ahead of the friendship?

A. I am confident that he would. We have all learned a great deal about security problems in the last 10 years.

MR. GARRISON. That is all.

CROSS-EXAMINATION

By Mr. Robb:

Q. Doctor, do you think that loyalty to a friend justifies the giving of false information to a security officer?

A. I would not wish to do that myself.

Q. You would not do it, would you?

A. I don't think so.

Q. In fact, you can't conceive of any circumstances under which you would not?

A. I wouldn't say that.

Q. It is hard to think of any?

A. First, it is hard to project ourselves back 10 years as to what the situation was like then. None of us had any very keen appreciation of the problems of security and secrecy at that time or what was involved. I cannot say under no circumstances would I be reluctant to give away or give information about a friend if I were personally convinced that this information had nothing to do with the country's welfare. I would try to cooperate with security officers under all conditions but I cannot say that under no conditions would I be reluctant to give such information.

Q. That was not quite my question. My question was whether or not you would feel that loyalty to your friend justified you in lying to a security officer.

A. No, I would not feel so.

Q. The standards of honesty were the same in 1943 as they are now, weren't they?

A. Presumably. . . .

Mr. Gray. Dr. Evans, do you have any questions.

Dr. Evans. Dr. DuBridge, let us go back again to that Chevalier incident. You remember about it. I want to ask you this question. Was it Dr. Oppenheimer's job to decide whether the security of his country was involved, rather than to report the incident?

The Witness. Would you repeat that?

Dr. Evans. Yes. Was it Dr. Oppenheimer's job to decide for himself whether the security of the country was involved rather than report the incident immediately?

The Witness. I think possibly Dr. Oppenheimer was mistaken in his judgment at that time. I am sure it is a mistake he will not repeat.

Dr. Evans. You would not have done it the way Dr. Oppenheimer did?

The Witness. Knowing what I do now, today, I would not. What I would have done in 1940, I cannot say.

Dr. Evans. That is all.

Mr. Gray. Mr. Garrison.

REDIRECT EXAMINATION

By Mr. Garrison: . . .

Q. I just wanted to make sure—and I think it is probably sure by now, but perhaps not—that with respect to the items of information about the H-bomb in the Commission's letter, do you have any opinion with regard to those particular items? . . .

A. I would like to make a report about the first part.

First, it seems to me that those statements about his opinions, even insofar as they are true, could perfectly possibly and indeed I believe were the opinions of a perfectly loyal American seeking to increase and not decrease the military establishment of his country.

"Further reported that even after it was determined as a matter of national policy to proceed with the development of a hydrogen bomb, you continued to oppose the project and not cooperate fully in the project."

To the best of my knowledge that statement was false. "It was reported that you departed from your proper role in the distribution of the reports of the General Advisory Committee for the purpose of trying to turn such top personnel against the development of the hydrogen bomb." To the best of my knowledge that is false.

I think it is quite probable that copies of GAC reports did reach the top people of Los Alamos as all our reports did by normal channels, but that the chairman of the committee departed from his proper role or did this with the purpose of trying to turn personnel against the hydrogen bomb is in my opinion false.

"It was further reported that you were instrumental in persuading other outstanding scientists not to work on the hydrogen project, and your opposition to the hydrogen bomb of which you are the most experienced and most powerful has definitely slowed down its development," that is also false. Quite the contrary, I believe Dr. Oppenheimer's efforts and the efforts of the GAC were intended solely to improve the position of this country, with no other objective, purpose or result.

MR. GARRISON. That is all.

Friday, April 23

ROGER ROBB: "Mr. Chairman, unless ordered to do so by the board, we shall not disclose to Mr. Garrison in advance the names of the witnesses we contemplate calling"

[As the hearing opens, Lloyd K. Garrison requests that Roger Robb follow the usual trial procedure and provide the defense lawyers with the names of the witnesses he intends to call, as, in fact, Garrison had done for Robb.]

MR. GARRISON. Mr. Chairman, I was informed by you yesterday afternoon that some witnesses would be called this coming week by the board. I had assumed from prior discussions that we would be informed of the names of these witnesses, but whether or not that assumption was correct, I asked you at the close of the session yesterday for the names of the respective witnesses in order that we might have time to prepare for cross-examination, if cross-examination seemed to be indicated with respect to one or more of them.

I would like to state very briefly the reasons why it seemed to me this request is a proper one to make on behalf of Dr. Oppenheimer.

The purpose of this inquiry which is not a trial is to arrive at the truth as nearly as truth can be arrived at. I don't think it takes any argument to point out that cross-examination is one of the ways of bringing out the truth. I appreciate fully that there is no question here of denying the right of cross-examination, but there is, as I am sure the board knows, oftentimes a need of preparation in cases where there may be an element of surprise in the calling of a witness, or in cases where a witness who one might perhaps think it possible the board might call we would know in advance would require a great deal of preparation, and in the press of other work, we would not want to undertake that uselessly if the person were not to be called. But in the main it is to have an opportunity to consider who is going to be called and to inform ourselves as to what we need to do.

With respect to our own witnesses, we have I think from the very first day, and from time to time gladly supplied the board with a list of people whom we expected to call. There have been changes in the schedule. Some inevitable additions and some who could not make it because of conflict of things and so forth, but in general I have tried to keep the board as accurately informed as I could.

It is quite clear that in the case of at least some of these witnesses substantial preparation for cross-examination was made ahead of time and in the case of several others opportunity was had for the representatives of the board to discuss matters with these witnesses themselves, a process to which we had not the slightest objection at all.

Now, it seems to me that the same kind of notice and the same opportunity for preparation both in fairness to Dr. Oppenheimer and in the interest of developing the true state of affairs be accorded to Dr. Oppenheimer.

Therefore, on his behalf I request that we be informed of the witnesses whom the board proposes to call.

MR. ROBB. Mr. Chairman, unless ordered to do so by the board, we shall not disclose to Mr. Garrison in advance the names of the witnesses we contemplate calling.

I should like briefly to state the reasons which compel me to this conclusion in the very best of spirit, and I am sure Mr. Garrison will take it that way.

In the first place, I might say, Mr. Chairman, that from the very inception of this proceeding, I think Dr. Oppenheimer has had every possible consideration. Going back to December, subsequent to the receipt by him of the letter from General Nichols, the time for his answer to be sent in was extended several times at his request, and without any objection whatever, because it was thought that was a reasonable request.

At the proceedings before this board, I am sure the record will show that the board has extended every courtesy and consideration to Dr. Oppenheimer and his witnesses. The board has permitted the testimony of several witnesses to be interrupted in order that others might be called to suit their convenience. The board has sat long hours for that purpose. One evening, as I recall, we sat until 7:45, and I cross-examined the witness for the last 2 hours of that session. On one occasion we adjourned early so that Mr. Garrison might confer with his client with a view to putting him on for redirect examination.

Counsel has made no objection to any questions, although I say frankly that some questions might have been objectionable, but witnesses have been permitted to argue from the witness stand without objection, and tell the board in rather forceful terms about what the board ought to do about the problem, without objection.

Mr. Rolander has worked late at night and on Saturday and Sunday in order to get the record in shape so that it might be taken by Mr. Garrison and his associates.

I mention all these things, Mr. Chairman, only to illustrate what I think the record abundantly shows, which is every effort has been made to make this a full and a fair hearing, and to accord Dr. Oppenheimer every right, and I am sure that has been done.

Mr. Chairman, the public has an interest in this proceeding also, and of course the public has rights which must be looked out for. In my opinion, and it is a very firm opinion, the public interest requires that these witnesses be not identified in advance. I will say frankly that I apprehend, and I think reasonably apprehend, that should that be done, the names of these witnesses would leak, and the result then would be the embarrassment and the pressure of publicity.

I think furthermore, and I will be frank about it, that in the event that any witnesses from the scientific world should be called, they would be subject to pressure. They would be told within 24 hours by some friends or colleagues what they should or should not say. I say specifically and emphatically I am not suggesting that would be done by Dr. Oppenheimer, his counsel or anybody representing him. But I think the record abundantly shows here the intense feeling which this matter has generated in the scientific world. I think it perfectly reasonable to believe that should there appear here today that Scientist Y was to testify, inside of 24 hours that man would be subject to all sorts of pressure.

Now, Mr. Garrison has said there would be no leak. Perhaps so, Mr. Chairman, but the New York Times of the day after this hearing began, and the column which appeared in the Washington Post this morning do not lead me to rely with any great assurance upon any such statements. I think it would be a serious danger that the orderly presentation of testimony, the truthful presentation of testimony would be impeded were these witnesses to be identified.

Mr. Garrison speaks of the preparation for cross-examination. In the first place, I didn't ask Mr. Garrison for the names of his witnesses in advance. It was entirely immaterial to me whether he gave them to me or not. We talked, of course, to General Groves, Mr. Lansdale—I think that is all of the witnesses—because both of them wanted to look at the files to refresh their recollection. Most of the witnesses who were called here I never saw before in my life.

I will let Mr. Garrison in on a little trade secret. In the case of almost all of the witnesses, my only advance preparation for cross-examination was a thorough knowledge of this case. I am sure that Mr. Garrison has an equally thorough knowledge of the case. He has been working on it, I am sure, as long as I have. He has the assistance of Dr. Oppenheimer. Dr. Oppenheimer is the one man in the world who knows the most about Dr. Oppenheimer, his life, and his works. He also knows as much, I think, as anybody else about the subject of nuclear physics, which has been under discussion.

Mr. Garrison also has the assistance of three able counsel in this room, and I believe one other lawyer who is reading the transcript and making a digest of it for him.

As for surprise, I am sure any witness who testifies here within the scope of the issues of this case will not be unfamiliar to Mr. Garrison, nor will the subject matter of his testimony be unfamiliar to Mr. Garrison.

I am sure Mr. Garrison can do just as well as I did, however well that may have been. Maybe he wants to do better, if he can, fine.

Mr. Chairman, to sum up, my position is simply dictated by the public interest which I think would not be served by a disclosure in advance of the names of these witnesses for the reasons I have stated. I think that fairness to Dr. Oppenheimer does not require such a disclosure.

MR. GRAY. Do you care to respond to any of that?

MR. GARRISON. Mr. Chairman, I don't want to make an argument. I just want to make one or two observations.

First, with regard to the procedure of the board, the only thing that I have objected to that I still regard with all due respect as not in keeping with the spirit of the regulations is the questioning of witnesses, particularly Dr. Oppenheimer, as to their recollection of things past when the Government had in its possession papers, some of them taken in Dr. Oppenheimer's case from his own file as classified, and then declassified and read to him after the questions had been put in a way that could be calculated to make the witness appear in as poor a light as possible. The sort of thing I can make no objection to on orthodox legal rules of trial behavior in a court room, but which seem to me not appropriate here. I simply have to say that lest by silence I seem to acquiesce.

I also might say that in a court room that state of affairs can scarcely arise because of the nature of the documents and the source from which they came in this case. So it is perhaps an altogether novel situation and all the more I think not in keeping in the spirit of inquiry as distinct from a trial. . . .

MR. GRAY. I can respond on behalf of the board, because we have had some discussion of it this morning. I am going to advert to several things that counsel said here, so my statement may be in the nature of random observations in part. . . .

Now, it is true, Mr. Garrison, that you have at all times attempted to keep the board and Mr. Robb informed as to your general course of action with respect to witnesses. It is a courtesy which has been appreciated. It was not something that was required by the board.

I would like to say a little bit about this matter of calling witnesses. In our earlier discussion, I think I have loosely used the phrase witnesses to be called by the board. Actually I don't think at this moment that the board intends to call any witnesses. I do not consider that we have called those who have testified to this point, and the witnesses whom Mr. Robb will examine in direct examination will be called by him. For that purpose, this board considers you the attorney for Dr. Oppenheimer, Mr. Robb the attorney for the Atomic Energy Commission. He was appointed by the Atomic Energy Commission, as I understand it.

The board would be very much concerned if Dr. Oppenheimer's interests were in any way adversely affected by anything in the nature of surprise. I would guess from what Mr. Robb has told me that there probably will not be an element of surprise in the sense that we have in mind in this discussion. If, however, there is, the board will wish to be informed by counsel for Dr. Oppenheimer, and can give you assurance on behalf of the board that we will so conduct the proceeding that any disadvantage to Dr. Oppenheimer by reason of surprise as may be related to cross-examination may not continue.

The board is interested in developing the facts, and if you are unable under the circumstances to perform your functions—very important functions—as counsel for Dr. Oppenheimer, we want to hear about it, and take the necessary steps.

The proceedings under which we operate, which are familiar to you, I know, require that the board conduct the proceedings in a way which will protect the interests of the individual and of the Government. The representative of the Government in this case feels with some conviction that the interests of the Government could possibly be prejudiced by furnishing a list of witnesses at this time.

My ruling after consultation with the board is that Mr. Robb will not be ordered by the board to furnish these names. I couple to that ruling, however, a repeated assurance that we wish to hear you at any time that you think you are at a disadvantage by not having had the names of the witnesses. . . .

MR. GARRISON. I want to thank you for the courtesy with which this proceeding has been uniformly conducted. I know the spirit of fairness which animates the members of the board. What you have said about considering any request we might make for time to prepare for cross-examination if we were disadvantaged by the calling of some particular witness meets what I was going to say after the chairman had made his ruling.

I just feel I must make one comment, not in criticism of the board, but with respect to the procedure. The notion that counsel for the Commission is to call his own witnesses in a proceeding which therefore takes on the appearance of an adversary proceeding with the board sitting as judges, and counsel for the Government on the one hand, and counsel for the employee on the other, is not quite a true picture of the actual shape of affairs. Unlike in an ordinary adversary proceeding before a judge in a courtroom, counsel here is possessed of documents taken from Dr. Oppenheimer's files in some cases which we have no opportunity to see in advance of their reading, and all the rest of which we have no opportunity ever to see.

It differs further in that the board itself is in possession of all these documents which it has had a week's opportunity to examine before the hearing began. This, then is not like an ordinary adversary proceeding. This is what we have to bear, Mr. Chairman. . . .

VANNEVAR BUSH: "Here is a man who is being pilloried because he had strong opinions, and had the temerity to express them"

[Following this exchange between attorneys for both sides, Harry A. Winne testifies. Recently retired as a vice president of General Electric, Winne explains that he met Oppenheimer early in 1946, when he was a consultant to Assistant Secretary of State Dean Acheson's Committee on Atomic Energy, and expresses confidence in Oppenheimer's loyalty and integrity. Then Vannevar Bush is called. Trained as an engineer and mathematician, Bush had taught at the Massachusetts Institute of Technology and, from 1941 to 1945, served as director of the Office of Scientific Research and Development. At the time of the hearing, he is president of the Carnegie Institution in Washington.]

DIRECT EXAMINATION

By Mr. Garrison: . . .

Q. About how long have you known Dr. Oppenheimer?

A. I have known him well since the early days of the war. I undoubtedly met him in gatherings of physicists before that time, but have no specific recollection of the first date that I met him.

Q. What was your connection with his appointment to the Manhattan District?

A. There were appointments before then. At that time General Groves, who was in charge of the Manhattan District, reported to a body of which I was chairman, . . . It was the Military Policy Committee, of which I was chairman. Dr. Conant was my deputy. General Groves took up all of his programs and policies with that group.

At the time General Groves made the appointment of Dr. Oppenheimer at Los Alamos, he took that matter up with us. In my memory he took it up informally, not in a formal meeting, and discussed it with Dr. Conant and with me.

Q. What recommendation did you make?

A. General Groves said he had in mind appointing Dr. Oppenheimer. He reviewed for us orally what he knew of Dr. Oppenheimer's prewar record. I don't remember that we looked at any file or any written records. He recited some of the previous history. Then he asked the opinion of me and Dr. Conant in regard to the appointment, and I told him I thought it was a good appointment.

Q. Did you have any discussion about any prior left-wing associations that he had?

A. Yes, we did. He recited previous associations.

Q. When you say "he," you mean whom?

A. General Groves.

Q. About when was this?

Vannevar Bush, November 1957. Hank
Walker/TimePix.

A. I noted down a few dates. I can't say, gentlemen, that my memory for dates
   and the like is good. In fact, it is a little bad. I have that date here somewhere. Oppenheimer was chosen in November of 1942.

Q. Did you have opportunity to observe his work at Los Alamos?

A. In a sense which I was responsible for it. The structure at that time, you
   remember, was this: OSRD started this work and continued it for a considerable period. It continued parts of it in fact after that date. I originally
   carried the full responsibility for it, reporting to the President. On my recommendation when the matter came to the construction of large facilities,
   the matter was transferred to the War Department. Secretary Stimson and I
   conferred, and the Manhattan District was set up. Groves was made head of
   it.

   After that the Military Policy Committee reviewed his recommendations
   on which I was chairman, and there was also a policy committee appointed
   by the President which consisted of the Vice President, Secretary Stimson,
   General Marshall, Dr. Conant and myself, I believe. That was appointed by
   Mr. Roosevelt at my request. When I was carrying the full responsibility, I
   told him I would prefer to have some group of that sort, and that committee
   was appointed. It never was formally dissolved.

Q. Would you say a word as to your view of his achievement at Los Alamos?

A. He did a magnificent piece of work. More than any other scientist that I know of he was responsible for our having an atomic bomb on time.

Q. When was your next governmental connection with him, do you recall?

A. There have been so many I am not sure which one.

Q. Let me go back a minute and ask you another question about the Los Alamos work.

What significance would you attach to the delivery of the A-bomb on time, or was it delivered on time?

A. That bomb was delivered on time, and that means it saved hundreds of thousands of casualties on the beaches of Japan. It was also delivered on time so that there was no necessity for any concessions to Russia at the end of the war. It was on time in the sense that after the war we had the principal deterrent that prevented Russia from sweeping over Europe after we demobilized. It is one of the most magnificent performances of history in any development to have that thing on time. . . .

Q. In connection with the Secretary of State's panel, did you have occasion to visit the Secretary of State in the summer of 1952?

A. I will not try to be exact on dates on that. But when the panel had gotten to a point where it was about to draft a report, we met with the full panel and the Secretary of State, and went over some of our conclusions orally, as I remember.

Q. Before that time did you have occasion to talk with the Secretary of State about the question of postponing the test of the H-bomb? . . .

A. I did.

. . . There were two primary reasons why I took action at that time, and went directly to the Secretary of State. There was scheduled a test which was evidently going to occur early in November. I felt that it was utterly improper—and I still think so—for that test to be put off just before election, to confront an incoming President with an accomplished test for which he would carry the full responsibility thereafter. For that test marked our entry into a very disagreeable type of world.

In the second place, I felt strongly that that test ended the possibility of the only type of agreement that I thought was possible with Russia at that time, namely, an agreement to make no more tests. For that kind of an agreement would have been self-policing in the sense that if it was violated, the violation would be immediately known. I still think that we made a grave error in conducting that test at that time, and not attempting to make that type of simple agreement with Russia. I think history will show that was a turning point that when we entered into the grim world that we are entering right now, that those who pushed that thing through to a conclusion without making that attempt have a great deal to answer for.

That is what moved me, sir. I was very much moved at the time. . . .

Q. Turning to another topic, at the time of the establishment of the Atomic Energy Commission and the General Advisory Committee, or several months after the establishment of them both, did the Chairman of the Atomic Energy Commission consult you about Dr. Oppenheimer's clearance?

A. Yes, I remember that he did. Mr. Lilienthal consulted me, and I wrote him a letter about it.

Q. Do you have a copy of that with you?

A. What I have is this. . . . Isn't is quicker for me to read it?

Mr. Gray. Why don't you read it?

The Witness. "At our conference yesterday you asked me to comment concerning Dr. J. Robert Oppenheimer, and I am very glad to do so. Dr. Oppenheimer is one of the great physicists of this country or of the world for that matter. Prior to the war he was on the staff of the University of California, and was regarded as the leader of theoretical aspects of atomistics and similar subjects of physics. Shortly after the Army entered into the development of atomic energy he was given a very important appointment by General Groves. This appointment made him director of the laboratory at Los Alamos, which was in all probability the most important post held by any civilian scientist in connection with the entire effort. General Groves undoubtedly made this appointment after a very careful study of the entire affair from all angles, as this was his custom on important appointments. Subsequent developments made it very clear that no error had been made in this connection, for Dr. Oppenheimer proved himself to be not only a great physicist, but also a man of excellent judgment and a real leader in the entire effort. In fact, it was due to the extraordinary accomplishments of Oppenheimer and his associates that the job was completed on time. Subsequent to the end of the war Dr. Oppenheimer has had a number of important appointments. He was invited by Secretary Stimson as one of the scientists consulted by the Secretaries of War and Navy in connection with the work of the Interim Committee. He was appointed by the State Department as a member of the board which drew up the plan on which Mr. Baruch based his program. He has recently been appointed by the President as a member of the General Advisory Committee of your organization. I have appointed him a member of the Committee on Atomic Energy of the Joint Research and Development Board. All of this has followed from his extraordinary war record in which he made a unique and exceedingly important contribution to the success of the war effort of this country.

"I know him very well indeed and I have personally great confidence in his judgment and integrity."

Mr. Robb. I have the original now.

By Mr. Garrison:

Q. At the time you wrote that letter, had you been through Dr. Oppenheimer's personnel file, the FBI reports?

A. I don't think I ever went through Dr. Oppenheimer's FBI file. If I did, I certainly do not remember.

Q. Did you understand at the time that you wrote that letter that he had left-wing associations?

A. I understood that at the time his first appointment was made at Los Alamos. I had an exposition of the entire affair from General Groves.

Q. You read the letter of General Nichols dated December 23, 1953, to Dr. Oppenheimer, containing the items of derogatory information?

A. Yes, I read that as it appeared in the press.

Q. Is there anything in that letter which would cause you to want to qualify the letter which you wrote to Mr. Lilienthal that you have just read?

A. Now, let me answer that in two parts. I had at the time of the Los Alamos appointment complete confidence in the loyalty, judgment, and integrity of Dr. Oppenheimer. I have certainly no reason to change that opinion in the meantime. I have had plenty of reason to confirm it, for I worked with him on many occasions on very difficult matters. I know that his motivation was exactly the same as mine, namely, first, to make this country strong, to resist attack, and second, if possible to fend off from the world the kind of mess we are now getting into.

On the second part of that, would I on the basis of that document, if those allegations were proved, change my judgment. That is what I understand this board is to decide. I don't think I ought to try to prejudge what they might find out.

Q. I would not want to ask you to do that, and my question is not designed to do that.

A. My faith has not in the slightest degree been shaken by that letter or anything else.

MR. GARRISON. I think that is all, Doctor.

MR. GRAY. Mr. Robb?

MR. ROBB. I have no questions, Mr. Chairman.

MR. GRAY. I have one question which relates to the development of the hydrogen bomb in general, and it is prompted by something you said in answer to a question put to you by Mr. Garrison, I think.

I believe you said that you felt that that test in the fall of 1952 was of value to the Russians in their own program. Did I understand that correctly?

THE WITNESS. I am sure it was.

MR. GRAY. And this is for technical reasons?

THE WITNESS. I am sure of it for one reason because when we reviewed the evidence of the first Russian atomic explosion, we didn't find out merely that they had made a bomb. We obtained a considerable amount of evidence as to the type of bomb, and the way in which it was made. If they had no other evidence than that from their own test and the like, they would have derived information. * * *

MR. GRAY. Would it have been your guess that the Soviets would have attempted to develop this kind of weapon?

THE WITNESS. Why, certainly, because it is very valuable indeed to them. To us, with 500 KT fission bombs we have very little need for a 10 megaton hydrogen bomb. The Russians, on the other hand, have the great targets of New York and Chicago, and what have you. It is of enormous advantage to them.

MR. GRAY. So they probably would have sought to develop this in any event unless some international control machinery had been in effect.

THE WITNESS. That is right.

MR. GRAY. And our not proceeding, as some people thought we should not, probably didn't have any relation to what the Russians might do about it.

THE WITNESS. I think it has relation to what the Russians might do about it because whether we proceeded or not determined to some extent the speed with which they could proceed. Let me interpose a word there, Mr. Chairman.

MR. GRAY. Yes, sir.

THE WITNESS. It was not a question, as I understand it, of whether we should proceed or not. It was a question of whether we should proceed in a certain manner and on a certain program. I have never expressed opinions on that. But certainly there was a great deal of opinion which seemed to me sound that the program as then presented was a somewhat fantastic one. So it was not a question of do we proceed or do we not. I think there was no disagreement of opinion as to whether we ought to be energetic in our research, whether we should be assiduously looking for ways in which such a thing could be done without unduly interfering with our regular program. The question of whether we proceeded along a certain path—may I say one more word on that, Mr. Chairman, quite frankly, and I hope you won't misunderstand me, because I have the greatest respect for this board. Yet I think it is only right that I should give you my opinion.

I feel that this board has made a mistake and that it is a serious one. I feel that the letter of General Nichols which I read, this bill of particulars, is quite capable of being interpreted as placing a man on trial because he held opinions, which is quite contrary to the American system, which is a terrible thing. And as I move about I find that discussed today very energetically, that here is a man who is being pilloried because he had strong opinions, and had the temerity to express them. If this country ever gets to the point where we come that near to the Russian system, we are certainly not in any condition to attempt to lead the free world toward the benefits of democracy.

Now, if I had been on this board, I most certainly would have refused to entertain a set of charges that could possibly be thus interpreted. As things now stand, I am just simply glad I am not in the position of the board.

MR. GRAY. What is the mistake the board has made?

THE WITNESS. I think you should have immediately said before we will enter into this matter, we want a bill of particulars which makes it very clear that this man is not being tried because he expressed opinions. . . .

DR. EVANS. Dr. Bush, you don't think we sought this job, do you?

THE WITNESS. I am sure you didn't, and you have my profound sympathy and respect. I think the fact that a group of men of this sort are willing to do as tough and as difficult a job as this augurs well for the country. It is in stark contrast with some of the things that we have seen going on about us in similar circumstances. Orderly procedure and all of that is good. I merely regret that the thing can be misinterpreted as it stands on the record, and misinterpreted in a way that can do great damage. I know, of course, that the executive branch of the United States Government had no intention whatever of pillorying a man for his opinions. But the situation has not been helped, gentlemen, recently by statements of the Secretary of Defense. I can assure you that the scientific community is deeply stirred today.

The National Academy of Science meets this next week, and the American Physical Society meets, and I hope sincerely that they will do nothing foolish. But they are deeply stirred. The reason they are stirred is because they feel that a professional man who rendered great service to his country, rendered service beyond almost any other man, is now being pilloried and put through an ordeal because he had the temerity to express his honest opinions.

MR. GRAY. Dr. Bush, are you familiar with the Atomic Energy Act of 1946 at all?

THE WITNESS. I have read it.

MR. GRAY. Are you familiar with the fact that the Commission has a published set of procedures which for these purposes have the effect of law?

THE WITNESS. Yes. I am not quarreling with the procedure, Mr. Chairman.

MR. GRAY. As I understand it, and I can be corrected by counsel, the writing of a letter to Dr. Oppenheimer with specifications is required under these procedures.

THE WITNESS. I have been a friend of General Nichols for many years. He wrote the letter. I quite frankly think it was a poorly written letter and should have been written in such a way that it made it absolutely clear that what was being examined here was not the question of whether a man held opinions and whether those were right or wrong, whether history has shown it to be good judgment or poor judgment. I think that should have been made very clear.

MR. GRAY. I would also point out just in the interest of having a record here, and I don't consider myself in any argumentation with you, for whom I have a very high regard, personally and professionally, that there were items of so-called derogatory information—and that is a term of art—in this letter, setting aside the allegations about the hydrogen bomb. There were items in this letter which did not relate to the expression and holding of opinions.

THE WITNESS. Quite right, and the case should have tried on those.

MR. GRAY. This is not a trial.

THE WITNESS. If it were a trial, I would not be saying these things to the judge, you can well imagine that. I feel a very serious situation has been created, and I think that in all fairness I ought to tell you my frank feeling that this has gotten into a very bad mess. I wish I could suggest a procedure that would resolve it.

MR. GRAY. The proceeding, of course, is taking place in accordance with procedures, and I was glad to hear you say a few moments ago that you felt that this was a fair kind of proceeding. I am not sure I am quoting you correctly.

THE WITNESS. You can quote me to that effect. I think some of the things we have seen have been scandalous affairs. I think in fact the Republic is in danger today because we have been slipping backward in our maintenance of the Bill of Rights.

MR. GRAY. Dr. Evans.

DR. EVANS. Dr. Bush, I wish you would make clear just what mistake you think the board made. I did not want this job when I was asked to take it. I thought I was performing a service to my country.

THE WITNESS. I think the moment you were confronted with that letter, you should have returned the letter, and asked that it be redrafted so that you would have before you a clearcut issue which would not by implication put you in the position of trying a man for his opinions.

DR. EVANS. I was not confronted with that letter, and I don't think it would have made any difference if I had been. I was simply asked if I would serve on the board. What mistake did I make when I did that?

MR. GARRISON. Mr. Chairman, might I make a remark for myself here, speaking for Dr. Oppenheimer? I have the deepest respect for Dr. Bush's forthright character, for his lifelong habit of calling a spade a spade as he sees it. I simply want to leave no misunderstanding on the record here that we share the view that this board should not have served when asked to serve under the letter as written.

THE WITNESS. I can assure you, Mr. Chairman, that the opinions being expressed are my own. They usually are.

MR. GRAY. I have never heard it suggested that you didn't express your own opinion, Dr. Bush.

DR. EVANS. Dr. Bush, then your idea is that suppose I was asked to serve on this board, and I didn't know anything about it—I had not seen any of this material—after I had agreed to serve, and saw this material, I should have resigned?

THE WITNESS. No, I think you simply should have asked for a revision of the bill of particulars.

DR. EVANS. I am just anxious to know what you think my procedure should have been.

THE WITNESS. That is what I think. Now, I don't see how you can get out of this mess.

MR. MORGAN. Doctor, on what ground would you ask for a bill of particulars if you didn't know the record?

THE WITNESS. I think that bill of particulars was obviously poorly drawn on the face of it, because it was most certainly open to the interpretation that this man is being tried because he expressed strong opinions. The fact that he expressed strong opinions stands in a single paragraph by itself. It is not directly connected. It does have in that paragraph, through improper motivations he expressed these opinions. It merely says he stated opinions, and I think that is defective drafting and should have been corrected.

MR. MORGAN. In other words, we want to prejudge the case before we know anything about it.

THE WITNESS. Not at all. But I think this board or no board should ever sit on a question in this country of whether a man should serve his country or not because he expressed strong opinions. If you want to try that case, you can try me. I have expressed strong opinions many times, and I intend to do so. They have been unpopular opinions at times. When a man is pilloried for doing that, this country is in a severe state. . . . Excuse me, gentlemen, if I become stirred, but I am.

Monday, April 26

KATHERINE OPPENHEIMER: "I was emotionally involved in the Spanish cause"

[The first witness is Oppenheimer's wife, Katherine. Born in Germany in 1910, she emigrated to the United States with her parents at the age of three and became a citizen by virtue of her father's naturalization in 1922. She had herself been the subject of investigative reports, although not, of course, to the same extent as her husband. In May 1944, FBI director J. Edgar Hoover informed John Lansdale that she had been "active in Youngstown, Ohio, in the Communist Party during 1934, 1935, and 1936." In this, the first of her two appearances, she explains her radical past and faces cross-examination not from Roger Robb but rather from Gordon Gray.]

DIRECT EXAMINATION

By Mr. Silverman:

Q. Mrs. Oppenheimer, you are the wife of Dr. J. Robert Oppenheimer?
A. I am.
Q. What were you doing in the autumn of 1933?
A. I was attending the University of Wisconsin.
Q. You were attending the University of Wisconsin?
A. That is right.
Q. As an undergraduate student?
A. Yes.

Q. What did you do during the Christmas holidays of 1933?

A. I went to stay with friends of my parents in Pittsburgh.

Q. Will you tell us the circumstances of your meeting Joe Dallet?

A. Yes. I have an old friend in Pittsburgh, a girl called Selma Baker. I saw quite a bit of her at that time. It was Selma who said she knew a Communist, and would we like to meet him. Everybody agreed that would be interesting. There was a New Year's party. Selma brought Joe Dallet.

Q. Did you and he fall in love during that holiday period?

A. We did.

Q. Did you decide you would be married?

A. We did.

Q. Did you fix a date for that?

A. Yes. I decided to go back and finish my semester at Wisconsin and then join Joe in Youngstown and get married there.

Q. Is that what you did?

A. Yes.

Q. The semester ended at the end of January, I suppose, of 1934, and you went to Youngstown?

A. Early February. I don't know.

Q. Joe Dallet was a member of the Communist Party?

A. He was.

Q. And you knew that he was?

A. Yes.

Q. During your life with him, did you join the party?

A. Yes, I did.

Q. Will you tell us why you joined the party?

A. Joe very much wanted me to, and I didn't mind. I don't know when I joined the party. I think it was in 1934, but I am not sure when.

Q. Did you do work for the party?

A. Yes.

Q. What kind of work?

A. I mimeographed leaflets and letters. I typed. I did generally office work, mostly for the steel union that was then in existence.

Q. What were most of your activities related to?

A. Mostly to the union at first, and later anything that came up, I was sort of general office boy.

Q. Did you pay dues to the party?

A. Yes.

Q. How much were the dues?

A. I believe mine were 10 cents a week.

Q. Would you describe the conditions under which you lived with Joe Dallet as those of poverty?

A. Yes.

Q. How much rent did you pay?

A. Five dollars a month.

Q. As time went on, did you find that you became devoted to the party or more devoted or less devoted or more attached or less attached?

A. I don't think I could ever describe it as a devotion or even attachment. What interest I had in it decreased.

Q. Did Joe's interest decrease?

A. No, not at all.

Q. Was that a cause of disagreement between Joe and yourself?

A. I am afraid so.

Q. Did you and Joe ultimately separate?

A. We did.

Q. When was that?

A. About June of 1936.

Q. Would you say that your disagreement with Joe about your lack of enthusiasm, shall we say, for the party, had something to do with the separation?

A. I think it was mostly the cause of the separation. I felt I didn't want to attend party meetings or do the kind of work that I was doing in the office. That made him unhappy. We agreed that we couldn't go on that way.

Q. Did you remain in love with him?

A. Yes.

Q. Where did you go when you separated?

A. I joined my parents in England.

Q. That was about June of 1936?

A. I think it was June.

Q. Did a time come when you wrote Joe that you were willing to rejoin him?

A. Yes. I wrote him probably very early in 1937, saying that I would like to rejoin him.

Q. Did he answer you?

A. He answered saying that would be good, but he was on his way to Spain to fight for the Republic cause, and would I please instead meet him in Paris.

Q. Where did you meet him?

A. I met him at Cherbourg aboard the Queen Mary as it docked.

Q. That was in 1937?

A. Yes. I think it was March. I am not sure.

Q. Did you go with him then to Paris?

A. We took the boat train and went to Paris.

Q. How long did you stay in Paris with him.

A. I would think about 10 days. It could have been a week, it could have been 2 weeks, but roughly—

Q. Do I understand that he had a furlough or some time off or something because of the reunion?

A. That is right.

Q. What did you do during that 10 days or so in Paris?

A. We walked around and looked at Paris, went to restaurants, the sort of thing one does in Paris. We went to the museums and picture galleries. We went to one large political meeting, a mass meeting, where they were advocating arms for Spain.

Q. Who was the speaker?

A. Thorez.

Q. He was a Communist?

A. Yes.

Q. Do you recall any other political activities if that might be called one during that period or that 10 days or so?

A. I think one should describe as a political activity that one place I saw where people who were going to Spain were being checked in and told how to do it. I went there once.

Q. As a spectator?

A. I had nothing to do.

Q. Then Joe went off to Spain.

A. Yes.

Q. During that period did you meet Steve Nelson?

A. Yes. I met him in Paris. I saw him several times. I think Joe and I had meals with him occasionally.

Q. What did you talk about with him?

A. I don't know; all kinds of things. I think among other things the only thing that interests this board is the fact that we talked of various ways of getting to Spain, which was not easy.

Q. Then Joe went to Spain at the end of that 10 days or so?

A. Yes.

Q. What did you do?

A. I went back to England.

Q. Did you try to do anything about joining Joe?

A. Yes, I wanted to very much.

Q. What was your plan as to how you would join Joe?

A. I was told that they would try to see if it were possible, and if it were, I would hear from someone in Paris and then go to Paris, and be told how to get there.

Q. Was there talk of your getting a job somewhere in Spain?

A. Yes. I don't know what, though.

Q. Were you ultimately told that it was possible?

A. I got a letter from Joe saying that he found me a job in Albacrete.

Q. Did you then go to Paris?

A. First I stayed in England and waited quite a while, until October.

Q. What year was this?

A. 1937. I then got a wire saying I should come to Paris, and I went. Do you want me to go on?

Q. What happened when you got to Paris?

A. When I got to Paris, I was shown a telegram saying that Joe had been killed in action.

Q. What did you do then?

A. I was also told that Steve Nelson was coming back from Spain in a day or two, and I might want to wait and see what Steve had to say. He had a lot to tell me about Joe.

Q. Did Steve come?

A. Yes.

Q. And met you in Paris?

A. Yes.

Q. Did you talk with Steve?

A. Yes, I spent at least a week there. I saw Steve most of the time.

Q. What did you talk about with him.

A. Joe, himself, myself.

Q. Would you say that Steve was kind to you and sort of took care of you during that period?

A. He certainly was, very.

Q. Did you discuss with Steve what you would do now?

A. I did.

Q. Will you tell us what that discussion was?

A. For a little while I had some notion of going on to Spain anyway.

Q. Why?

A. I was emotionally involved in the Spanish cause.

Q. Did Joe's death have something to do with your wanting to go on anyhow?

A. Yes, as well as if alive he would have.

Q. Did you discuss this with Steve?

A. I did, but Steve discouraged me. He thought I would be out of place and in the way. I then decided that probably I would go back to the United States and resume my university career.

Q. Is that what you did?

A. Yes.

Q. After you returned to the United States, did you continue to see any of the friends that you had with the Communists?

A. When I first got back I saw some friends of Joe's in New York who wanted to know about him and to whom I wanted to talk. I saw some other members of the Communist Party in New York. I went to Florida with three girls. I know one was a Communist. I think another one was, and the third one I don't remember.

Q. Did that relationship with Communist friends continue?

A. No, it did not.

Q. What happened?

A. I visited a friend of mine in Philadelphia. I had planned to go to the University of Chicago, and got back to the United States to go back to their second trimester. I don't know whether they still have that system. I knew no one there. I met a lot of people in Philadelphia, and they said, "You know all of us, why don't you stay here?" I stayed in Philadelphia and entered the University of Pennsylvania, the spring semester of the year 1937–38.

Q. What kind of work did you do at the university?

A. Chemistry, math, biology.

Q. Was biology your major?

A. It became my major interest.

Q. Did you continue to do professional work as a biologist?

A. I did graduate work later and some research.

Q. Ultimately you had a research fellowship or assistantship?

A. Both.

Q. Where?

A. University of California.

Q. Did you remarry?

A. Yes.

Q. Would you give us the date of your remarriage and the man whom you married?

A. I married Richard Stewart Harrison, an English physician, in 1938, in December or November.

Q. Was he a Communist?

A. No.

Q. He was a practicing physician?

A. He had been, I think, in England. He had to take all his examinations in this country and do an internship and a residency before he could practice here.

Q. Did he go to California?

A. Yes.

Q. And you went with him?

A. No. He went to California much earlier than I to take up his internship.

Q. Did you go out there to join him?

A. Yes.

Q. After graduation in June of 1939? When did you meet Dr. Oppenheimer?

A. Somewhere in 1939.

Q. When were you divorced from Dr. Harrison?

A. In the first of November 1940.

Q. You then married Dr. Oppenheimer?

A. Yes.

Q. Did there come a time after you married Dr. Oppenheimer when you again saw Steven Nelson?

A. Yes.

Q. Will you tell us the circumstances of that?

A. I will as best I can remember. I remember being at a party and meeting a girl called Merriman. I knew of her. She was in Albacrete, and her husband also got killed in action there. The reason I remembered her name is that I had been asked to bring her some sox when I came. When I met her at this party, she said did I know that Steve Nelson was in that part of the country. I said no, and then expressed some interest in his welfare. Some time thereafter Steve Nelson telephoned me, and I invited him and his wife and their small child up to our house.

Q. What did you talk about?

A. We had a picnic lunch. The Nelsons were very pleased that they finally had a child, because they tried for a long time to have one without success. We talked about the old days, family matters.

Q. Did you see him again?

A. I think that they came out to our house two times.

Q. Was it all just social?

A. Yes.

MR. GRAY. What was the date of this period, approximately? If you have said, I have forgotten.

THE WITNESS. I didn't say, Mr. Gray, because I am a bit vague.

By Mr. Silverman:

Q. Can you give it as closely as you can?

A. Yes. I would guess it was late 1941 or perhaps in 1942. I don't know.

Q. Are you fairly clear it was not later than 1942?

A. Fairly clear.

Q. Have you seen Steve Nelson since 1942?

A. Since whenever it was?

Q. Yes.

Katherine (Kitty) Oppenheimer. J. Robert Oppenheimer Memorial Committee.

A. No.

Q. You are no longer a member of the Communist Party?

A. No.

Q. When would you say that you ceased to be a member?

A. When I left Youngstown in June 1936.

Q. Have you ever paid any dues to the party since then?

A. No.

Q. Will you describe your views on communism as pro, anti, neutral?

A. You mean now?

Q. Now.

A. Very strongly against.

Q. And about how far back would you date that?

A. Quite a long time. I had nothing to do with communism since 1936. I have seen some people, the ones that I have already described.

MR. SILVERMAN. That is all.

MR. ROBB. No questions.

MR. GRAY. Mrs. Oppenheimer, how did you leave the Communist Party?

THE WITNESS. By walking away.

MR. GRAY. Did you have a card?

THE WITNESS. While I was in Youngstown; yes.

MR. GRAY. Did you turn this in or did you tear it up?

THE WITNESS. I have no idea.

MR. GRAY. And the act of joining was making some sort of payment and receiving a card?

THE WITNESS. I remember getting a card and signing my name.

MR. GRAY. Generally speaking, as one who knows something about communism as it existed at that time in this country and the workings of the Communist Party, and therefore a probable understanding of this thing, what do you think is the kind of thing that is an act of renunciation? That is not a very good question. In your case you just ceased to have any relationships with the party?

THE WITNESS. I believe that is quite a usual way of leaving the party.

MR. GRAY. When you were in the party in Youngstown, or when you were in the party at any time, did you have a party name?

THE WITNESS. No. I had my own name, Kitty Dallet.

MR. GRAY. Was that the usual thing for people to use their own name?

THE WITNESS. I knew of no one with an assumed name. I believe that there must have been such people, but I knew of none.

MR. GRAY. I think the record shows that in some cases there were people who had some other name.

THE WITNESS. I think there were people who lived under an assumed name and had that name in the party, but then that was the only name I would have known.

MR. GRAY. When you saw Steve Nelson socially in whatever year this was,

1940, 1941 or 1942, did you discuss the Communist Party with him? Did he know that you were no longer a member of the Communist Party?

THE WITNESS. Yes, that was perfectly clear to him.

MR. GRAY. Did he chide you for this or in any way seek to reenlist your sympathy?

THE WITNESS. No.

MR. GRAY. He accepted the fact that you had rejected communism?

THE WITNESS. Yes. I would like to make it clear that I always felt very friendly to Steve Nelson after he returned from Spain and spent a week with me in Paris. He helped me a great deal and the much later meeting with him was something that was still simply friendship and nothing else.

MR. GRAY. The people you dealt with in Paris or that you saw there were members of the Communist Party. I have in mind any discussions you had about going to Spain, both before and after your husband's death?

THE WITNESS. I wouldn't know who was or wasn't then. Many people were going to Spain who were not members of the Communist Party. I think, however, that probably most of the people I saw were Communists.

MR. GRAY. But at that time you were not?

THE WITNESS. No.

MR. GRAY. This was following your leaving the party in Youngstown?

THE WITNESS. That is right.

MR. GRAY. Do you suppose they were aware of the fact that you had left the Communist Party?

THE WITNESS. I am sure they were. I mean such as knew me.

MR. GRAY. This is a question not directly related to your testimony, but we have had a witness before the board recently—I might say I am sorry I didn't ask him this question—and this witness referred to Soviet communism in a general discussion here before the board. In your mind as a former member of the Communist Party in this country, can a distinction be made between the Soviet communism and communism?

THE WITNESS. There are two answers to that as far as I am concerned. In the days that I was a member of the Communist Party, I thought they were definitely two things. The Soviet Union had its Communist Party and our country had its Communist Party. I thought that the Communist Party of the United States was concerned with problems internal. I now no longer believe this. I believe the whole thing is linked together and spread all over the world.

MR. GRAY. Would you think that any knowledgeable person should also have that view today?

THE WITNESS. About communism today?

MR. GRAY. Yes.

THE WITNESS. Yes, I do.

MR. GRAY. I was puzzled by this reference to Soviet communism in April 1954. But in any event, you would not make a distinction.

THE WITNESS. Today, no; not for quite a while.

MR. GRAY. But in those days you in your own mind made the distinction?

THE WITNESS. Yes.

MR. GRAY. At that time the American Communist Party was not known to you to be taking its instructions from Russia?

THE WITNESS. No.

MR. GRAY. You testified that today you are opposed to the Communist Party and what it stands for.

THE WITNESS. Yes.

MR. GRAY. I am getting back now to whatever an action of renunciation is. Do you think these days that a person can make a satisfactory demonstration of renunciation simply by saying that there has been renunciation?

THE WITNESS. I think that is too vague for me, Mr. Gray.

MR. GRAY. All right. I am afraid it is a little vague for me, too. I won't pursue it. Do you have any questions?

DR. EVANS. Just one. Mrs. Oppenheimer, I have heard from people that there are two kinds of Communists, what we call an intellectual Communist and just a plain ordinary Commie. Is there such a distinction, do you know?

THE WITNESS. I couldn't answer that one.

DR. EVANS. I couldn't either. Thank you. I have no more questions.

MR. GRAY. Thank you very much, Mrs. Oppenheimer.

CHARLES C. LAURITSEN: "I think there is a great deal of difference between being a Communist in 1935 and being a Communist in 1954"

[Born in Denmark, Charles C. Lauritsen had received his doctorate in physics at the California Institute of Technology in 1930, and had then joined the faculty. During World War II he was a pioneer in rocket development, and in 1944 he went to Los Alamos to assist in the final stages of building the atomic bomb. There he worked closely with Oppenheimer, one of his dearest friends since they had first met at Caltech in the late 1920s.]

DIRECT EXAMINATION

By Mr. Marks: . . .

Q. Did you observe Dr. Oppenheimer during the thirties and the forties, and can you say anything about his political views and activities during that time?

A. I cannot say very much about it. I knew very little about it until, I think, about the time of the Spanish war. This was the first time that I knew that he had any political interest. Up to that time I have no recollection that we ever discussed political questions of any in interest or serious nature.

Q. What impression did you come to have of his political interests?

A. It is a little difficult to say because I think they changed a great deal with time. I would say that at one stage he was very deeply interested in the Spanish Loyalist cause, and took the attitude that was taken at that time by many liberals, the hope that they could do something about it, and that they would like to help the Spanish Loyalist cause.

Q. You spoke of his changing views. What do you mean by that?

A. I think it was probably a gradual increase in interest in social causes, a compassion for the underdog, if you like. The attitude that many liberals took at that time.

Q. Did you observe in him an identification with views that were regarded as Communist views or with which the Communists were associated?

A. I think at that time very few of us and perhaps very few Americans had very little idea about what communism was. I think most of us that were concerned about political things and international things were considerably more concerned about fascism at that time than we were about communism. Fascism seemed the immediate threat, rather than communism. Also, I think perhaps my own views were colored by the fact that I was born and raised in Denmark, where Germany was the natural enemy, rather than Russia. I think for that reason we did not pay as much attention to the evils of communism as we should have done.

Q. Were you mixed up in any communistic activity?

A. No.

MR. ROBB. Mr. Chairman, I don't think the witness quite answered the question Mr. Marks propounded to him. I wonder if we might have it read back so the witness could have it in mind.

(Question read by the reporter.)

THE WITNESS. I frankly did not know just what characterized the Communist view at that time. When they talked about improving the lot of the working people, I believe Oppenheimer and probably many other people thought this was a good beginning. But that this was not the whole story of the Communist ideology I think was not realized by very many people at that time. Does that answer the question?

MR. ROBB. Yes.

THE WITNESS. It did not occur to me at that time or at any other time that he was a Communist Party member.

Q. Dr. Lauritsen, what opinion do you have about Dr. Oppenheimer's loyalty and character? By loyalty I mean loyalty to the United States.

A. I have never had any reason to doubt it.

Q. Do you think you could be mistaken about this?

A. I suppose one can always be mistaken, but I have less doubt than any other case I know of.

Q. Less doubt than in any other case?

A. Than in any other person that I know as well.

Q. Do you know many people better?

A. Not many. I suppose I know my own son better, but I don't trust him any more.

Q. To what extent would you trust Dr. Oppenheimer's discretion in the handling of classified information, restricted data?

A. You are referring now to recent years when he understood these problems, I hope. In that case I think I would trust his discretion completely. I think in the early thirties very few of us knew anything about discretion and were not very conscious of security. Whether he had been indiscreet at that time, I don't know. It is possible. It is possible I have been indiscreet. But I am sure after he understood what security meant, and what was involved, that he has been as discreet as he knew how.

Q. What do you mean by as discreet as he knew how?

A. As discreet as it is possible to be and try to get some work done.

Q. Do you have any idea about whether your views about the needs for and the possibilities of being discreet are any different than his?

A. I think they are no different now, certainly.

Q. Let us take the period commencing in 1944, when you went to Los Alamos. Is that the span of years you are talking about?

A. During that period this would apply. At that time he knew the importance of the information we had.

MR. MARKS. That is all, Mr. Robb.

MR. GRAY. I think it would be well to break for a few minutes at this point.
(Brief recess.)

MR. GRAY. Mr. Robb, will you proceed.

CROSS-EXAMINATION

By Mr. Robb:

Q. Doctor, do I understand that you have known Dr. Oppenheimer both professionally and socially?

A. That is correct.

Q. Have you visited him from time to time at his ranch in New Mexico?

A. I have visited him I think twice.

Q. When was that, sir?

A. About the middle thirties—1935 or 1936, I believe.

Q. Do you also know Dr. Oppenheimer's brother Frank?

A. I do.

Q. When did you meet him, sir?

A. I believe I met him for the first time at the ranch in 1935 or 1936. I may have seen him once before, but I am not quite sure.

Q. Was he on the faculty at Caltech?

A. He was a graduate student.

Q. Under you?

A. Yes.

Q. Did you get to know him pretty well, too?

A. I got to know him quite well in the laboratory.

Q. And you saw him on the ranch, also, I take it?

A. Yes.

Q. Did you know him at Los Alamos?

A. Yes, I did.

Q. Have you seen him since then very frequently?

A. Not frequently. I have seen him. Most recently last year at a meeting of the physical society in Albuquerque, N. Mex.

Q. Up until the end of it, did you have any reason to belive that Frank was a Communist or had been a Communist?

A. No, I had no reason to believe that until he made that statement himself.

Q. What would you say about Frank's loyalty?

A. I have no reason to doubt his loyalty.

Q. And his character?

A. His character is very good.

Q. You would make about the same answer about him that you do about Dr. Oppenheimer?

A. Yes, I would think so. His judgment was perhaps not as good as Dr. Oppenheimer's.

Q. Yes, sir. I notice that you made some little distinction between Dr. Oppenheimer's present appreciation of security and his appreciation in the past of security.

A. I think that applies to all of us.

Q. Yes, sir. You suggested that there might have been some change in Dr. Oppenheimer's attitude on those matters.

A. On how important you think it is, how seriously you take it.

Q. Would you care to tell us, Doctor, when you think that change took place?

A. I think we all learned about it during the war.

Q. You think Dr. Oppenheimer learned about it during that period?

A. That would be my judgment. I think this was true of most of us that had had little to do with military things until that time. . . .

MR. GRAY. Dr. Lauritsen, do you feel as of today a member of the Communist Party, that is, a man who is currently a member of the Communist Party, is automatically a security risk?

THE WITNESS. I think so.

MR. GRAY. You don't have any question in your mind about that, do you?

THE WITNESS. No; not if I can believe what I have been told about the Communist Party, and I do believe it.

MR. GRAY. In testifying earlier, I think you said you considered Dr. Frank Oppenheimer loyal in every respect, and with no reservations about this character or trustworthiness?

THE WITNESS. That is right.

MR. GRAY. Are you aware that Dr. Frank Oppenheimer has stated at an earlier period in his life he was a member of the Communist Party?

THE WITNESS. Yes, sir I am aware of that now.

MR. GRAY. But still you say you have no reservations about his loyalty or character?

THE WITNESS. No, I have not.

MR. GRAY. Would you explain to the Board why you conclude that you would trust him with any secret, which I believe is the effect or import of what you say, today, although you believe that a member of the Communist Party is automatically a security risk? Would you explain that?

THE WITNESS. I believe he has resigned from the Communist Party, and he is no longer under the discipline of the Communist Party. I believe he was cleared for work on war projects during the war and including nuclear weapons work.

MR. GRAY. This was not after it was known he was a member of the Communist Party?

THE WITNESS. This I have no way of knowing. I do not know what turned up in his investigation.

MR. GRAY. Would you feel that if it had been known at the time that he was a member of the Communist Party he should have been cleared for war work?

THE WITNESS. If he had not resigned previously, I would certainly not recommend his clearance. If he had resigned previously because he no longer wanted to be a member of the Communist Party because he had found out that the Communist Party was not what it appeared to be, then I would still be inclined to say that he would be reliable.

MR. GRAY. Today on classified projects for which you have some responsibility, including a security responsibility, if a man comes to the project seeking employment, who is known to you to have been a former member of the Communist Party, would you employ him simply on his statement that he no longer was a member of the Communist Party?

THE WITNESS. No; not without appropriate clearance through official channels.

MR. GRAY. What would your recommendation be?

THE WITNESS. If he had resigned from the Communist Party when he found out what the purpose of the Communist Party really was, and had been a member only as long as he had been under misconceptions about these things, then I would not hold that against him.

MR. GRAY. You would accept as evidence of that his own statement?

THE WITNESS. Not necessarily. I think some people you can trust, and others you can't trust. I think it depends on what other activities he has been involved in and what he has been doing. In Frank's case, I think he demonstrated that he wanted to work for this country. Other people perhaps have not demonstrated that. I think there is a great deal of difference between being a Communist in 1935 and being a Communist in 1954. I don't think

very much of us knew, I certainly did not know what the Communist Party
was up to and how it operated.

MR. GRAY. Let me ask this question: Would it be a rather accurate summary of
at least parts of your testimony to say that you never really understood very
much about the Communist Party or its workings?

THE WITNESS. That I did not?

MR. GRAY. That is right.

THE WITNESS. At that time.

JERROLD R. ZACHARIAS: "I am afraid that wars are evil. . . . But the question of morality . . . you do not have time for when you are trying to think how you fight"

[Jerrold R. Zacharias had also known Oppenheimer since the 1920s. During
World War II he worked at the radiation laboratory at the Massachusetts Institute of Technology, and at the time he testifies he directs its laboratory of
nuclear science. During the summer of 1952 he participated in a study project at Lincoln Laboratory, as did Oppenheimer, Rabi, and Lauritsen. Some in
the air force regarded the Lincoln Project's recommendation for an early
warning system as a threat to the Strategic Air Command, and *Fortune* magazine referred to a dangerous—although entirely fictional—conspiracy by a
cabal known as "ZORC" (the "C" was for "Charles Lauritsen"). Just before
the hearings opened, Zacharias wrote an encouraging letter to Oppenheimer, saying, "you have nothing personal to fear—really not—and your
stand is so important for the nation. I guess all I mean is—give 'em hell.
We're all with you."]

DIRECT EXAMINATION

By Mr. Marks: . . .

Q. . . . you were about to tell the story of what happened as a result of the
summer study.

A. The Lincoln Laboratory set up to work on technological and technical aspects of continental defense. In fact, air defense of any sort. Just prior to the
summer of 1952, Dr. Lauritsen and I had a long discussion about the trend
in continental defense, whether the buildup was great enough, * * *.

Dr. Lauritsen and I decided that it might be a very good thing if we looked
into these technical, military, and economic questions again during that
summer. We decided that we should talk this over with certain others
whom we knew very well. First of all, Dr. Hill, who was then the Director
and is now the director of Lincoln Laboratory. We decided we would talk it
over with Dr. Oppenheimer and Dr. Rabi.

Q. Why did you talk to Dr. Oppenheimer?

A. In my experience it is always profitable to talk to Dr. Oppenheimer. His head is so clear on questions of this sort that when you flounder for months to try to formulate your ideas, you get to him and he can listen and help state clearly what you and he and others have decided is the germ of what you are thinking. This is true in all of my contacts with Dr. Oppenheimer on this kind of question.

We decided, then, that it would be a good idea to start such a study, that Dr. Oppenheimer, Dr. Rabi, and Dr. Lauritsen agree to work on this study in part. The reason is that it is very difficult to recruit men of stature, men of ability into any kind of study. They are doing what they think is adequate and they have some sense of urgency but they also have the feeling, why don't we let somebody else do the work.

Dr. Hill, who is the director of the Lincoln Lab, and I felt that if Dr. Oppenheimer, Dr. Rabi, and Dr. Lauritsen agreed to work on this in part, that it would be easier for us to recruit a number of very brilliant people and some of the more experienced people to do the job. Indeed, that turned out to be true. So that directly within the Lincoln Laboratory and sponsored by the Air Force, as I say, we set up a study. . . .

Q. Did you conceive the recommendations of this summer study that you have referred to as being inconsistent or to be in conflict with any national policy with respect to what is described as strategic air policy?

A. The only conflict is of a funny sort. Let me begin it this way. Certainly part of any defensive system in this country is what we call our offensive plan. One doesn't think of protecting the continent by conventional defensive means. That is, destruction of enemy bases is just as important and every bit as important as local defense. It was the feeling of a number of us who worked on this summer study that the amount of money and the amount of effort that the Government would have to put into overall defense was larger or is larger than was being put in then. Many people interpreted our strong recommendations for defense as an unfortunate method of cutting into appropriations for Strategic Air Command. This was not the case in our recommendations and we believed then and I still believe that the money is going to have to come from other sources, and not from cuts from the military except in the matter of pruning certain military things that are not terribly fruitful.

Objections to try to build up continental defense from the point of view of people who are trying to build up offensive power alone, simply that if you work with a limited number of dollars and a limited amount of effort, naturally if you build one thing up, you would have to build the other down. Whereas, I am firmly of the opinion that we are going to build the whole thing up, and our economy will have to stand it, and I am assured that it will. Does that answer your question?

Q. You mean that you had both strategic air and also continental defense?

A. Yes, sir; and other military things, too, as events of the present show. . . .

Q. The work which you described in which Dr. Oppenheimer participated on continental defense and other military and scientific affairs, who did you conceive to be the enemy that we needed to be worried about?

A. There is no question in anybody's mind, and there was no question in the mind of anyone who participated or was closely associated with any of these discussions, Soviet Union, and the word "enemy," or "Russia" and the word "enemy" are sort of interchanged freely. It is that deeply imbedded in everybody's thinking, including that of Dr. Oppenheimer.

Q. What was your general purpose in devoting yourself to this work?

A. That is a simple question. This is the only country we have, and these are tough times, and we want to help it.

Q. As a result of your association with Dr. Oppenheimer have you formed an opinion or conviction as to his character and his loyalty to the United States?

A. I am completely convinced of his loyalty to the United States. Can I add a little way of saying it?

When you are gathered in a group of men who are discussing the details on how to combat the Russians, how to contain the Russians, how to keep them from overrunning the rest of the world, and so on, the loyalties come out very, very clearly. There just is not any question in my mind that Dr. Oppenheimer's loyalty is for this country and in no way or shape by anything other than hostility toward the U.S.S.R.

Q. What about his character?

A. His character? Ethical, moral is first rate.

Q. Do you have any views as to his capacity to exercise discretion in dealing with classified and restricted data and military secrets?

A. In my opinion, he is always discreet and careful and has regarded the handling of secret documents and secret ideas and so on with discretion and understanding. You might think it is not the easiest thing in the world to carry around a head full of secrets and go about in public, too, and talk about burning questions of the day. It is difficult. I believe that Dr. Oppenheimer has showed in every instance to my knowledge that he can do this kind of thing.

MR. MARKS. That is all.

MR. ROBB. I can finish in 2 minutes, I think.

MR. GRAY. If we can, let us go ahead.

CROSS-EXAMINATION

By Mr. Robb:

Q. Doctor, are you in the group that is called ZORC?

A. Yes, except let me say that this name was never heard of by the members of that group, by any one of those four until it appeared in the national magazine.

Q. I was going to ask you if you could tell us what you know about the origin of that nomenclature.

A. I have no knowledge of the origin of that nomenclature. I do know one friend of mine went around to a meeting of the Physical Society and hunted for people who had heard of it. Found one and I would rather not mention the name because it has nothing to do with this thing. He may have heard it or it may have been the invention of the man who wrote the article.

Q. I think for our purpose, the name is not popular. Was there a group consisting of yourself, Dr. Oppenheimer, Dr. Rabi, and Dr. Lauritsen?

A. No, no more than there would be a group of any four people who respect each other despite the fact that they hold slightly different ways of looking at things—a community of interests and a slight disparity of approach. These four people, I think, are very different.

Q. Were you four people the nucleus of that Lincoln summer study?

A. No, sir. The four were not. I would say the nucleus, as I tried to clarify before, were Dr. Hill and myself. That is, the director of the Lincoln Laboratory. The first discussions were with Dr. Lauritsen. Dr. Oppenheimer and Dr. Rabi agreed that it would be a good thing to go ahead with it and they were willing to lend their prestige to help pull in some people into it, but this is far from being the nucleus of the thing.

Q. That is what I am trying to find out because it has been rather fuzzy in my mind. Were you four people—Dr. Oppenheimer, Dr. Lauritsen, Dr. Rabi, and you—peculiarly active in that summer study? Were you the leaders of it?

A. Let me say this. I ran it. I was the director of it. So, I was in it. There are no two ways about that. Dr. Rabi, Dr. Oppenheimer and Dr. Lauritsen spent a small fraction of their time. However, let me say this. We had for the first week of that study a briefing for 4 days, as I remember it, that was packed with as much meat as you can get into any 4 days of technical briefing. I wanted a summary of that technical briefing, and there were about 65 people there, all very fully informed, and the only man I could turn to give a summary, who could pull the thing together, was Dr. Oppenheimer. He did a masterful job. It was perfectly clear to everybody in that group how Oppenheimer felt about all of the issues, so that if you questioned any one of those you could find a statement of what he believed.

Q. Was there any discussion, Dr. Zacharias, about the comparative morality of a so-called fortress concept, on the one hand, and a strategic air force to wage aggressive war on the other?

A. Not in that summer study. I am afraid that wars are evil. I do not think there is anyone in the room who would take exception to that. It is not a very meaningful statement. But the question of morality, one way or the other, you do not have time for when you are trying to think how you fight.

Q. Was there any conclusion reached as to the relative importance of a strategic air force on the one hand and an impregnable air defense on the other hand and, if so, what was it?

A. I know of no one who really knows the inside of the military who believes that it is possible to have either an impregnable and all overwhelming and completely decisive strategic air command, and I know of no one in the know who thinks you can have a completely impregnable defense. What the country needs is a little of both and one has to supplement the other. That was clearly stated in the conclusion of this report.

ROBERT F. BACHER: "Dr. Oppenheimer's individual contribution was the greatest of any member of the General Advisory Committee"

[The next witness, Olliver E. Buckley, has recently retired as chairman of the board of Bell Telephone Laboratories, but continues to serve on the AEC's General Advisory Committee, to which he was appointed in 1948. He testifies that Oppenheimer's leadership was "outstandingly good." Then the board hears from Robert F. Bacher, who received his Ph.D. in physics from the University of Michigan in 1930 and headed the experimental physics division at Los Alamos. He described himself politically as "an upstate New York Republican." A member of the Atomic Energy Commission from 1946 to 1949, he is during the time of his testimony chairman of the Division of Physics, Mathematics, and Astronomy at the California Institute of Technology.]

DIRECT EXAMINATION

By Mr. Garrison: . . .

Q. As a member of the Atomic Energy Commission, did you have occasion to observe closely the work of the GAC?

A. Yes, I think that during the period I was in Washington I probably followed the work of the General Advisory Committee more closely than any other member of the Commission. This was natural because I was the only one with a scientific and technical background, and the work of the General Advisory Committee was mostly scientific and technical. I frequently attended much of their meeting and read their reports very carefully. They were very valuable to us in getting the atomic energy enterprise back on its feet and getting some of the work established that we thought ought to get established.

Q. Would you make a comment on Dr. Oppenheimer's work as chairman of that committee?

A. It was outstanding. He was appointed a member of the General Advisory Committee. The members of the General Advisory Committee themselves elected him chairman of that committee. Until he left, the committee, I believe, he continued to be chairman. He had had the closest connection with the weapons development work of any of the members of the General Advisory Committee.

In that period in early 1947 when the General Advisory Committee was set up, our greatest problem was to try to get the Los Alamos Laboratory in the development of weapons into a sound shape. The General Advisory Committee, I might add, was vigorous on this point, and very helpful in getting the laboratory into shape both by reason of the recommendations which they made, and also the direct help that they gave us in connection with personnel for the laboratory.

Q. What about Dr. Oppenheimer's individual contribution in this effort?

A. I would say in this effort Dr. Oppenheimer's individual contribution was the greatest of any member of the General Advisory Committee. He took his work on the General Advisory Committee very seriously. He usually came to Washington before the meetings to get material ready for the agenda and usually stayed afterward to write a report of the meeting.

During the course of the meeting prolonging discussion at great length so everybody would express his views, nevertheless after the views had been expressed, he had a very great clarity in focusing these views of what would be a report of the committee. . . .

Q. How well do you feel that you know Dr. Oppenheimer?

A. I feel I know him very well. I have worked very closely with him during the war, have seen him frequently since the war, and feel I know him really very well. I just don't think it would be possible to work with a man as closely as I worked with Dr. Oppenheimer during the war without knowing him very well.

Q. What is your opinion as to his loyalty to the United States?

A. I have no question at all of his loyalty.

Q. On what do you base that? Is that purely a subjective judgment?

A. I think opinions of that sort are always subjective judgments. In this case I put great credence in my own judgment, naturally, because I know him very well. But this is essentially an assessment on my part based on knowing him for a great many years. I have the greatest confidence in his loyalty.

Q. What would you say as to his sense of discretion in the use that he would make of the knowledge that has come to him and will continue to come to him assuming that he continues in Government work?

A. I found Dr. Oppenheimer to be very discreet. I can remember during the war once when we had to go out on a trip together and it was essential that he carry a memorandum, that even in note form was classified, and he was so careful and he pinned it in his hip pocket. I thought here is a man who really is very careful about these things. But to say more generally as to his discretion, I have always found Dr. Oppenheimer to be very discreet in his handling of classified information.

Q. Is there anything else you care to say to this board about his character as a man and as a citizen?

A. I have the highest confidence in Dr. Oppenheimer. I consider him to be a person of high character. I consider him to be a man of discretion, a good security risk and a person of full loyalty to the country.

MR. GARRISON. That is all, Mr. Chairman.

CROSS-EXAMINATION

By Mr. Robb:

Q. Dr. Bacher, you were asked by Mr. Garrison what you knew about Dr. Oppenheimer's political views at the time you were in Los Alamos, and you answered, I believe, that you knew him to be a Democrat.

Did you know anything about his interest in other political philosophies?

A. As I think I answered Mr. Garrison, too, we didn't have very much time to discuss politics at Los Alamos.

Q. Whether you discussed it or not, did you know?

A. Not much. I had been aware of the fact that he had leftish sympathies before the war, but I didn't really know very much about it, and I didn't discuss it with him.

Q. Did you ever state to anyone that you knew that between 1934 and 1942, Dr. Oppenheimer became interested in various political philosophies and was interested as many others were at the time in the experiment being conducted by the Soviet Government in Russia?

A. I don't know, but it sounds as if I might have.

Q. Did you know that?

A. That is a difficult question to answer, because I am not exactly sure what it would take to know that. I was aware that this was commonly discussed. . . .

DR. EVANS. Do you think that a man can be completely loyal to his country and still be a security risk?

THE WITNESS. Yes. If he is a drunkard, he might be a security risk and be completely loyal.

DR. EVANS. Just suppose because of his associates.

THE WITNESS. It seems to me that on this question of association that is a different question. If you have full confidence in a man's character and his integrity and his discretion, I don't believe that one can rule him out as a security risk on the basis of his knowing people who have in the past had connection with the Communist Party, mostly because I don't believe there would be many people left in the United States that would satisfy that criterion.

DR. EVANS. Then you are answering the question this way. You think a man can be completely loyal, and if he is completely loyal, he is not a security risk? Is that what you are saying?

THE WITNESS. I believe I specified a little more than that, Dr. Evans. I said, if I recall correctly, that if he is a person of high character, a person of integrity, and a person who is discreet, and is at the same time a person who is clearly loyal, then he is not a security risk, assuming of course that other criteria such as he is not a drunk or things of that sort are included.

DR. EVANS. You think Dr. Oppenheimer is always discreet?

THE WITNESS. I do.

DR. EVANS. Do you think he was discreet when he refused to give the name of somebody that talked to him? Do you remember that Chevalier incident?

THE WITNESS. I don't remember the point you refer to, I am afraid.

DR. EVANS. Someone approached Dr. Oppenheimer about getting security information, and Dr. Oppenheimer refused to give the name of the man that approached him.

THE WITNESS. I thought he did give the name, Dr. Evans.

DR. EVANS. He refused twice I think, and for quite a long time he didn't give it. Am I right on that?

MR. ROBB. I believe that is correct.

MR. GARRISON. That is right.

DR. EVANS. Was that discreet?

THE WITNESS. Could you ask the question again, Mr. Evans?

DR. EVANS. Yes. If you were on a project, and you had access to a lot of secret information, and I came to you and told you that there was somebody that knew that I could give information to if you would give it to me, would you have gone and told somebody that I had approached you?

THE WITNESS. I think that should have been reported.

MR. GARRISON. Mr. Chairman.

DR. EVANS. Maybe I put the question very badly.

MR. GARRISON. All right. I accept it as a hypothetical question.

DR. EVANS. You have never been approached by people?

THE WITNESS. No, never.

DR. EVANS. Do you believe a man should place loyalty to his country before loyalty to a friend?

THE WITNESS. Yes.

DR. EVANS. That is all I want to ask.

Tuesday, April 27

JOHN VON NEUMANN: "All of us in the war years . . . got suddenly in contact with a universe we had not known before . . . ; we suddenly were dealing with something with which one could blow up the world"

[The first witness to appear, James McCormack, is a major general in the air force who served as director of the AEC's Division of Military Application from 1947 to 1951. While he had favored a crash program to develop the H-bomb in 1949—"If the weapon is there, if it can be had, how can we afford not to try for it"—he saw nothing sinister in Oppenheimer's reluctance to embark on such a program, and did not consider him a security risk. McCormack's testimony is followed by that of Dr. John von Neumann. Born in Hungary, he emigrated to the United States in 1930, became a professor of mathematical physics at Princeton University, and in 1933 was appointed to the Institute for Advanced Study. Since 1952 he has been a member of the AEC's General Advisory Committee. Like McCormack, von Neumann disagreed with Oppenheimer's view of the H-bomb but defends him as a loyal American.]

DIRECT EXAMINATION

By Mr. Silverman: . . .

Q. There has been, I guess, a fair amount of testimony that would be an understatement—about the GAC report of October 1949, with respect to the hydrogen bomb and the thermonuclear program. Dr. von Neumann, did you agree with the GAC report and recommendations?

A. No. I was in favor of a very accelerated program. The GAC at that point recommended that the acceleration should not occur.

Q. Very accelerated hydrogen bomb or thermonuclear program?

A. Yes, it is all the same thing.

Q. Would it be fair to say one might say in the opposite camp on the question?

A. Yes, that is correct.

Q. Did you consider that the recommendations of the GAC and in particular Dr. Oppenheimer were made in good faith?

A. Yes, I had no doubt about that.

Q. Do you have any doubt now?

A. No.

Q. You knew, of course, that Dr. Oppenheimer was not the only person who was opposed to the program?

A. No, the whole group of scientists and military who were keenly in this matter—of course, there had been a lot of discussion and practically everyone of us knew very soon fairly precisely where everybody stood. So we know each other's opinions, and very many of us had discussed the matter with each other. Dr. Oppenheimer and I had discussed it with each other, and so we knew each other's views very precisely.

My impression of this matter was, like everybody else, I would have been happy if everybody had agreed with me. However, it was evidently a matter of great importance. It was evidently a matter which would have consequences for the rest of our lives and beyond. So there was a very animated controversy about it. It lasted for months.

That it lasted for months was not particularly surprising to my mind. I

J. Robert Oppenheimer and John von Neumann in front of an early computer, 1952. Photograph by Alan W. Richards, Princeton, N.J., courtesy AIP Emilio Segrè Visual Archives.

think it was perfectly normal that there should be a controversy about it. It was perfectly normal that emotions should run rather high.

Q. Have you yourself participated in the program of the development of thermonuclear weapons and the hydrogen bomb?

A. Yes.

Q. After the President's decision in January of 1950, is it your impression that the GAC and particularly Dr. Oppenheimer was holding back in the effort to develop the bomb?

A. My impression was that all the people I knew, and this includes Dr. Oppenheimer, first of all took this decision with very good grace and cooperated. The specific things I know were various actions which were necessary in 1951. At that time there were a number of technical decisions that had to be made about the technical program. I know in considerable detail what Dr. Oppenheimer did then, and it was certainly very constructive.

Q. Can you tell us any of that in unclassified terms?

MR. ROBB. Excuse me. Could I ask what date he is referring to?

THE WITNESS. I am referring particularly to a meeting in Princeton in June 1951.

MR. ROBB. Thank you.

By Mr. Silverman:

Q. I don't know whether you can expand on this in unclassified terms or not.

A. I think the details of why there was a need for technical decisions at that moment and exactly how far they went and so on, I assume is classified, unless I am otherwise instructed. But it is a fact. You must expect in any program of such proportions that there will be as you go along serious technical decisions that have to be made. This was one. There was a meeting at Princeton which was attended I think by part of the GAC. I think it was the weapons subcommittee of the GAC which is in fact about two-thirds of the group, plus several Commissioners, plus several experts which included Dr. Bethe, Dr. Teller, myself, Dr. Bradbury—I am not sure whether Dr. York was there—Dr. Nordheim and possibly others. This meeting was called by Dr. Oppenheimer and he certainly to the extent which anybody was directing it, he was directing it. This was certainly a very necessary and constructive operation.

Q. At that meeting did he express himself as being in favor of going ahead?

A. In all the discussions at that point there was no question of being or not being in favor. In other words, it was a decided technical policy. I didn't hear any discussions after 1950 whether it ought to be done. There certainly were no such discussions at this meeting. The question was whether one should make certain technical changes in the program or not.

All I am trying to say is that at that point there was a need for technical changes. If anybody wanted to misdirect the program by very subtle means, this would have been an occasion.

Q. Did Dr. Oppenheimer cooperate in making it easier for you and others to work at Los Alamos for Los Alamos on the hydrogen bomb program?

A. I certainly never had the slightest difficulty. One thing is that I think if Dr. Oppenheimer had wanted to create difficulties of this kind, as far as I am concerned, it would have been possible. Also, our relations would probably have deteriorated. There was absolutely nothing of that. Our personal relations stayed very good throughout. I never experienced any difficulty in going as much to Los Alamos as necessary.

Q. There was no suggestion by Dr. Oppenheimer that this was interfering with your work at the institute?

A. None whatsoever, absolutely none. . . .

Q. And I take it there was no objection to your doing any work that might be helpful to Los Alamos at Princeton?

A. Absolutely none whatsoever.

Q. Did Dr. Oppenheimer attempt to dissuade you from working on the hydrogen-bomb program?

A. No. We had a discussion. Of course, he attempted to persuade me to accept his views. I equally attempted to persuade him to accept my views, and this was done by two people who met during this period. I would say apart from the absolutely normal discussion on a question on which you happen to disagree, there was absolutely nothing else. The idea that this might be pressure I must say did not occur to me ever.

Q. Do you now think that it was pressure?

A. No. I think it was the perfectly normal desire to convince somebody else.

Q. During what period was this discussion?

A. This was in 1949, December 1949. I remember quite clearly two discussions, one which was about half an hour at which time I saw the GAC opinion and we discussed it.

Q. You had a Q clearance at that time?

A. Yes. We discussed the same subject again about a week later, again for about 20 minutes or half an hour, I don't know. We probably also talked about the subject on other occasions, but I don't recall.

Q. Wasn't the discussion about whether you personally should work on the hydrogen-bomb program?

A. Absolutely not. The only question was whether it was or was not wise to undertake that program.

Q. You have known Dr. Oppenheimer, I think you said, substantially continuously since 1943 to the present date?

A. Yes.

Q. With the exception of the period from 1945, the end of the Los Alamos days, until 1947, when Dr. Oppenheimer came to the institute as director.

A. That is correct.

Q. During that period you have really lived in the same small town?

A. Yes.

Q. And been friends and known each other quite well during all that time?

A. Yes.

Q. Both professionally and socially?

A. Yes, that is correct.

Q. Do you have an opinion about Dr. Oppenheimer's loyalty to the United States, his integrity?

A. I have no doubts about it whatever.

Q. Your opinion I take it is quite clear and firm?

A. Yes, yes.

Q. Do you have an opinion as to Dr. Oppenheimer's discretion in the handling of classified materials and classified information?

A. Absolutely. I have personally every confidence. Furthermore I am not aware that anybody has questioned that.

Q. There seems to be some question among my associates whether I asked this. Do you have an opinion about Dr. Oppenheimer's loyalty?

A. Yes.

Q. What is that?

A. I would say he is loyal.

Q. Do you have any doubt on that subject at all?

A. No.

MR. SILVERMAN. I have no further questions.

CROSS-EXAMINATION

By Mr. Robb:

Q. Dr. von Neumann, you stated that Dr. Oppenheimer attempted to persuade you to accept his views, and you attempted to persuade him to accept your views in December 1949?

A. Yes.

Q. Would you tell us briefly what his views were as you understood them?

A. Well, that it would be a mistake to undertake an acceleration of the hydrogen bomb, the thermonuclear program for the following reasons: Because it would disorganize the program of the AEC because instead of developing fission weapons further, which one knew how to do and where one could predict good results fairly reliably, one getting back on a crash program which would supersede and damage everything else, and the results of the crash program would be dubious. That furthermore, from the military point of view, making bigger explosions was not necessarily an advantage in proportion to the size of the explosion. Furthermore, that we practically had the lead in whatever we did, and the Russians would follow, and that we were probably more vulnerable than they were for a variety of reasons, one of which is that we can probably saturate them right now—I meant right then—whereas they could not at that moment. Therefore, a large increment on both sides would merely mean that both sides can saturate the other. Also, that since there was now this possibility of a large increment in destructive power, this was now for the second time, and possibly for the last time an opportunity to try to negotiate control and disarmament.

I think this was by and large the argument. There are a few other angles which are classified which I think are not very decisive.

Q. Doctor, was there anything in his argument about the immorality of developing the thermonuclear?

A. I took it for granted that it was his view. It did not appear very much in our arguments, but we knew each other quite well. My view on that is quite hard boiled, and that was known.

Q. What was Dr. Oppenheimer's view, soft boiled?

A. I assume, but look, now, I am going by hearsay. I have not discussed it with him.

Q. I understand.

A. I assume that one ought to consider it very carefully whether one develops anything of this order of destruction just per se.

Q. Yes, sir. Doctor, in response to a question from Mr. Silverman, you said you had no question about Dr. Oppenheimer's integrity, did you not?

A. Yes.

Q. By that you meant his honesty, did you not?

A. Yes.

Q. Doctor, do you recall having heard anything about an incident which occurred between Dr. Oppenheimer and a man named Chevalier?

A. Yes, but that was lately. I do not know for absolutely sure when I first heard it. I saw the letter of charges and there it occurs. When I read it, I had the vague impression that I had heard this before, but I think that this was in the last few years.

Q. You saw the letter of General Nichols and Dr. Oppenheimer's response?

A. Yes. I am not absolutely certain whether I saw the complete original or whether I saw somebody's excerpts of relevant parts.

Q. What is your present understanding about that incident that I referred to—the Chevalier incident? What do you have in mind about what happened?

A. What I understand happened was—and please correct me if my recollection is inexact—my impression is that Chevalier was a man who had been Dr. Oppenheimer's friend in earlier years, who in 1942, I think, or early 1943, when Dr. Oppenheimer was already associated with the atomic energy project which was not yet the Manhattan district, made an approach and suggested to him that somebody else, whose name I have forgotten, was working for Russia and would be able to transmit scientific and technical information to Russia.

I understood that Dr. Oppenheimer essentially told him to go to hell, but did not report this incident immediately, and that when he later reported it, he did not report it completely for some time, until, I think, ordered by General Groves to do so. . . .

Look, you have to view the performance and the character of a man as a whole. This episode, if true, would make me think that the course of the year 1943 or in 1942 and 1943, he was not emotionally and intellectually prepared to handle this kind of a job; that he subsequently learned how to handle it, and handled it very well, I know. I would say that all of us in the war years, and by all of us, I mean all people in scientific technical occupations got suddenly in contact with a universe we had not known before. I mean this peculiar problem of security, the fact that people who looked all right might be conspirators and might be spies. They are all things which do not enter one's normal experience in ordinary times. While we are now most of us quite prepared to discover such things in our entourage, we were not prepared to discover these things in 1943. So I must say that this had on anyone a shock effect, and any one of us may have behaved foolishly and ineffectively and untruthfully, so this condition is something ten years later, I would not consider too serious. This would affect me the same way as if I would suddenly hear about somebody that he has had some extraordinary escapade in his adolescence.

I know that neither of us were adolescents at that time, but of course we were all little children with respect to the situation which had developed, namely, that we suddenly were dealing with something with which one could blow up the world. Furthermore, we were involved in a triangular war . . . two of our enemies had done suddenly the nice thing of fighting each other. But after all, they were still enemies. This was a very peculiar situation. None of us had been educated or conditioned to exist in this situation, and we had to make our rationalization and our code of conduct as we went along.

For some people it took 2 months, for some 2 years, and for some 1 year. I am quite sure that all of us by now have developed the necessary code of ethics and the necessary resistance.

So if this story is true, that would just give me a piece of information on how long it took Dr. Oppenheimer to get adjusted to this Buck Rogers universe, but no more. I have no slightest doubt that he was not adjusted to it in 1944 or 1945.

Q. Had you completed your answer?

A. Yes.

Q. In 1943, Dr. Oppenheimer was the director of the Los Alamos Laboratory, wasn't he?

A. Yes.

Q. I believe at that time he was 39 years old?

A. Yes.

Q. You wouldn't say he was at that time an adolescent, would you?

A. No. I was trying to make this clearer. There are certain experiences which are new for an adolescent, and where an adolescent will behave in a silly way. I would say these experiences were new for a man of 39, if he happened to be 39 at that moment in history.

Q. Do you think, Doctor, that honesty, the ability and the desire to tell the truth, depends upon the international situation?

A. It depends on the strain under which you are.

Q. The strain?

A. Yes.

Q. You mean a man may lie under certain strains when he would not under ordinary circumstances?

A. Yes, practically everybody will lie under anesthesia.

Q. Do you think, Doctor, if you had been placed in the same situation that Dr. Oppenheimer was in 1943, in respect of this matter, that you would have lied to the security officers?

A. Sir, I don't know how to answer this question. Of course, I hope I wouldn't. But—you are telling me now to hypothesize that somebody else acted badly, and you ask me would I have acted the same way. Isn't this a question of when did you stop beating your wife?

Q. I don't think so, Doctor, since you asked me. . . .

MR. GRAY. Suppose at Los Alamos someone had come to you—this is purely hypothetical—and said, although the British are our allies and the official policy of the United States Government is to share military information of the highest degree of secrecy with the British, this policy is being frustrated in Washington, now I have a way of getting to the British scientists information about what we are doing here in Los Alamos, and don't you think it is up to us to make sure that official policy is not frustrated, and you knew that this person was interested in the British, what would your position have been at that time, Dr. von Neumann?

THE WITNESS. For one thing, I would certainly not have given him information, but I asume that the main question is would I have reported him right away.

MR. GRAY. Yes; let me ask that question. The British were allies, it was official policy, this man frankly said that then if the information were made available, it could be transmitted through channels which were not official channels.

THE WITNESS. I would probably have reported him. I realize, however, that this can lead to a bad conflict. If I am convinced that the man is honest in his own benighted way, that is an unpleasant conflict situation, I would probably have reported him anyway.

MR. GRAY. The reason I asked the question is not to get an answer from you on the basis of a hypothetical question, but to really ask next whether you would have made a distinction at that time between an approach on behalf of the Russians and an approach on behalf of the British.

THE WITNESS. Yes. I think the probability of being at war with Russia in the next 10 years was high, and the probability of being at war with England in the next 10 years was low. . . .

DR. EVANS. If someone had approached you and told you he had a way to transport secret information to Russia, would you have been very much surprised if that man approached you?

THE WITNESS. It depends who the man is.

DR. EVANS. Suppose he is a friend of yours.

THE WITNESS. Well; yes.

DR. EVANS. Would you be surprised?

THE WITNESS. Yes.

DR. EVANS. Would you have reported it immediately?

THE WITNESS. This depends on the period. I mean before I got conditioned to security, possibly not. After I got conditioned to security, certainly yes.

DR. EVANS. You would.

THE WITNESS. I mean after quite an experience with security matters and realizing what was involved; yes.

DR. EVANS. I am sure you would now, Dr. von Neumann.

THE WITNESS. There is no doubt now.

DR. EVANS. You don't know some years ago whether you would have or not?

THE WITNESS. What I am trying to say is this, that before 1941, I didn't even know what the word "classified" meant. So God only knows how intelligently I would have behaved in situations involving this. I am quite sure that I learned it reasonably fast. But there was a period of learning during which I may have made mistakes or might have made mistakes. I think I didn't.

DR. EVANS. Would you put loyalty to a friend above loyalty to your country at any time?

THE WITNESS. No.

REDIRECT EXAMINATION

By Mr. Silverman: . . .

Q. Do you think that Dr. Oppenheimer would place loyalty to a friend above loyalty to his country?

A. I would not think so.

Q. Dr. Evans asked you about whether it is possible for a man to be loyal to his country, and yet be a security risk because of his associations.

A. Yes.

Q. I think you answered "Yes." Do you feel you know Dr. Oppenheimer's associations reasonably well?

A. I rather think so.

Q. Do you think that Dr. Oppenheimer is a security risk because of his present associations?

A. No, I don't think so.

MR. SILVERMAN. That is all.

MR. ROBB. One further question.

CROSS-EXAMINATION

By Mr. Robb:

Q. Doctor, you have never had any training as a psychiatrist, have you?

A. No.

MR. ROBB. That is all.

MR. GRAY. Thank you very much, Dr. von Neumann.

WENDELL M. LATIMER: "I kept turning over in my mind . . . what was in Oppenheimer that gave him such tremendous power over these men"

[The first witness to be called by Roger Robb is Wendell M. Latimer, a professor of chemistry at the University of California at Berkeley where he has taught since 1919. He serves as associate director of the Berkeley Radiation Laboratory, which is headed by Ernest O. Lawrence. Since Robb had not had to provide a list of witnesses in advance, Samuel Silverman requests a few minutes to prepare his cross-examination, a request that Gordon Gray rejects.]

DIRECT EXAMINATION

By Mr. Robb: . . .

Q. Doctor, did there come a time when you began thinking about a weapon which is called the H-bomb?

A. Yes.

Q. When was that?

A. I suspected I started worrying about the H-bomb before most people. Just as soon as it became evident to me that the Russians were not going to be cooperative and were distinctly unfriendly.

Q. Would you keep your voice up just a bit, Doctor?

A. I felt that it was only a question of time that the Russians got the A-bomb. I haven't much confidence in secrecy keeping these things under control very long. It seemed to me obvious that they would get the A-bomb. It also seemed to me obvious that the logical thing for them to do was to shoot immediately for the super weapon, that they knew they were behind us in the production of a bomb. It seemed to me that they must conclude shooting ahead immediately in making the super weapons. So I suspect it was around 1947 that I started worrying about the fact that we seemed to be twiddling our thumbs and doing nothing.

   As time passed, I got more and more anxious over this situation that we were not prepared to meet, it seemed to me, a crash program of the Russians. I talked to a good many people about it, members of the General Advisory Committee.

Q. Do you recall who you talked to about it?

A. I talked to Glenn Seaborg for one. I didn't get much satisfaction out of the answers. They seemed to me most of them on the phony side.

Q. Doctor, may I interpose right here before we go on to ask you a couple of questions, first, why did it seem obvious to you that the Russians would proceed from the A-bomb to the H-bomb?

A. They knew they were behind us on the A-bomb, and if they could cut across and beat us to the H-bomb or the super weapons, they must do it. I could not escape from the conclusion that they must take that course of action. It was the course of action that we certainly would have taken if we were behind. I could not escape from that conclusion.

Q. The second question is, you said that we seemed to be twiddling our thumbs in the matter. What was the basis for that feeling on your part?

A. In the period between 1945 and 1949 we didn't get anywhere in our atomic energy program in any direction. We didn't expand our production of uranium much. We didn't really get going on any reactor program. We didn't expand to an appreciable extent our production of fissionable material. We just seemed to be sitting by and doing nothing.

I felt so certain that the Russians would get the A-bomb and shoot for the H-bomb that all during that period I probably was overanxious, at least compared to most of the scientists in the country. But it seemed to me that such an obvious thing would happen.

Q. Reverting again to your narrative, you said you talked to Dr. Seaborg and others about going ahead with the H-bomb, and their answers, you said, seemed to be phony. What did you mean by that?

A. I can't recall all the details during that period. When the Russians exploded their first A-bomb, then I really got concerned.

Q. What did you do?

A. In the first place, I got hold of Ernest Lawrence and I said, "Listen, we have to do something about it." I think it was after I saw Ernest Lawrence in the Faculty Club on the campus, the same afternoon he went up on the Hill and Dr. Alvarez got hold of him and told him the same thing. I guess the two of us working on him at once with different impulses got him excited, and the three of us went to Washington that weekend to attend another meeting, and we started talking the best we could, trying to present our point of view to various men in Washington.

On that first visit the reception was, I would say, on the whole favorable. Most people agreed with us, it seemed to us, that it should be done.

Q. Could you fix the approximate date of this?

A. I would say within 2 or 3 weeks after the explosion of the Russian bomb. I don't remember the date of that.

Q. That was in September 1949.

A. Shortly after that. . . .

Q. What was the reception of your suggestions received at that period of time? I am speaking of the time 2 or 3 weeks after the Russian explosion.

A. It was favorable, I would say. We met practically no opposition as I recall.

Q. Will you tell us whether or not that situation changed?

A. It definitely changed.

Q. When?

A. Within a few weeks. There had been a lot of back pressure built up, I think primarily from the Advisory Committee.

Q. Would you explain that to us a bit?

A. I don't remember now all the sources of information I had on it, but we very quickly were aware of the fact that the General Advisory Committee was opposed.

Q. What was the effect of that opposition by the Committee upon fellow scientists, if you know?

A. There were not many scientists who knew the story. I frankly was very mystified at the opposition.

Q. Why?

A. Granted at that time the odds of making a super weapon were not known, they talked about 50–50, 10 to 1, 100 to 1, but when the very existence of the Nation was involved, I didn't care what the odds were. One hundred to one was too big an odd for this country to take, it seemed to me, even if it was unfavorable. The answers that we kept getting were that we should not do it on moral grounds. If we did it, the world would hate us. If we didn't do it, the Russians wouldn't do it. It was too expensive. We didn't have the manpower. These were the types of argument that we got and they disturbed me.

Q. Did you ascertain the source of any of this opposition?

A. I judge the source of it was Dr. Oppenheimer.

Q. Why?

A. You know, he is one of the most amazing men that the country has ever produced in his ability to influence people. It is just astounding the influence that he has upon a group. It is an amazing thing. His domination of the General Advisory Committee was so complete that he always carried the majority with him, and I don't think any views came out of that Committee that weren't essentially his views.

Q. Did you have any opinion in 1949 on the question of the feasibility of thermonuclear weapons?

A. Various calculations seemed to show that it might go if you could just get the right conditions or the right mechanical approach to it. The odds didn't look good, but as I say, I didn't care what the odds were, if there was a possibility of it going, I thought we must explore it, that we could not afford to take a chance not to. The stakes were too big. The very existence of the country was involved and you can't take odds on such things.

Q. Was there any way that you knew of to get the answer without experiment and tests?

A. No, I am sure all the calculations showed that the only way it could ever be settled was by trying it.

Q. Have you followed the progress of the thermonuclear program since 1949?

A. In a rough way, yes. In the past 2 years, we have been working on some of the problems at the Radiation Laboratory.

Q. At Berkeley?

A. At Berkeley.

Q. Dr. Latimer, this board is required within the framework of the statute to determine upon its recommendation to the general manager as to whether or not the security clearance of Dr. Oppenheimer should be continued and the standards set up by the statute for the board are the character, the associations and the loyalty of Dr. Oppenheimer. Would you care to give the board, sir, any comments you have upon the basis of your knowledge of Dr. Oppenheimer as to his character, his loyalty and his associations in that context?

A. That is a rather large order.

Q. I know it is, Doctor.

A. His associations at Berkeley were well known. The fact that he did have Communist friends. I never questioned his loyalty. There were elements of the mystic in his apparent philosophy of life that were very difficult to understand. He is a man of tremendous sincerity and his ability to convince people depends so much upon this sincerity. But what was back of his philosophy I found very difficult to understand.

A whole series of events involved the things that started happening immediately after he left Los Alamos. Many of our boys came back from it pacifists. I judged that was due very largely to his influence, this tremendous influence he had over those young men. Various other things started coming into the picture.

For example, his opposition to the security clause in the atomic energy contracts, opposition on the floor of the National Academy which was very intense and showed great feeling here. These various arguments which were used for not working on the H-bomb, the fact that he wanted to disband Los Alamos. The fact of the things that weren't done the 4 years that we twiddled our thumbs. All these things seemed to fit together to give a certain pattern to his philosophy. A man's motives are just something that you can't discuss, but all his reactions were such as to give me considerable worry about his judgment as a security risk.

Q. I will put it in very simple terms, Doctor. Having in mind all that you have said, and you know, would you trust him?

A. You mean in matters of security?

Q. Yes, sir.

A. I would find—trust, you know, involves a reasonable doubt, I would say.

Q. That is right.

A. On that basis I would find it difficult to do so. . . .

CROSS-EXAMINATION

By Mr. Silverman: . . .

Q. Did you know what General Groves' views were as to whether it was desirable in the years 1947 on—in the early years there—as to whether it was desirable to concentrate on fission weapons rather than on thermonuclear?

A. I suppose I heard his views. They seemed to coincide with that of the General Advisory Committee pretty much. I suspect again under the influence of Dr. Oppenheimer.

Q. You don't of course question General Groves' patriotism or his good faith?

A. I don't question the patriotism of any of the members on that committee. Of course, he was not on the committee. Not only General Groves, but the other members on the committee, Conant and the other members, they were under the influence of Dr. Oppenheimer, and that is some influence, I assure you.

Q. Were you under Dr. Oppenheimer's influence?

A. No, I don't believe I was close enough contact to be. I might have been if I had been in closer contact.

Q. You think that General Groves was under Dr. Oppenheimer's influence?

A. Oh, very definitely.

Q. Have you ever spoken to General Groves?

A. About this problem?

Q. At all.

A. Oh, yes; I saw him frequently during the war.

Q. On what do you base your judgment that General Groves was under Dr. Oppenheimer's influence?

A. I wouldn't go too far in answering that question, because I don't know how much General Groves' opinions have changed in recent years. The statements that I have heard attributed to him seemed to follow the same—at least for a while, I have not seen his statements very recently—but during part of this period he seemed to be following the Oppenheimer line.

Q. What I am curious about is how do you know that Dr. Oppenheimer was not following the Groves line?

A. That is ridiculous.

Q. Pardon?

A. Knowing the two men, I would say that is ridiculous. Oppenheimer was the leader in science. Groves was simply an administrator. He was not doing the thinking for the program.

Q. I am trying to arrive upon what it is that you base your—I think you said it was a suspicion, but perhaps I am wrong, that General Groves was under Dr. Oppenheimer's influence. Is it simply the fact of your knowledge of Dr. Oppenheimer and the fact that he is a leading scientist and a man of great gifts.

A. I know these things were overwhelming to General Groves. He was so dependent upon his judgment that I think it is reasonable to conclude that most of his ideas were coming from Dr. Oppenheimer.

Q. How do you know he was so dependent?

A. I don't. I don't know, but I have seen the thing operate.

Q. There were other scientists at Los Alamos, weren't there?

A. Yes, there were.

Q. And General Groves has had contact with other scientists.

A. Yes, but there were no other scientists there with the influence that Dr. Robert Oppenheimer had and moreover this close association with Groves certainly one would normally conclude that he still had tremendous influence over him. It may be an unreasonable conclusion, but it doesn't seem so to me.

Q. Forgive me, but no man considers his own view unreasonable.

A. That is right. You must accept these as my personal opinions and nothing more than that.

Q. I am trying to arrive on what you base these personal opinions.

A. Various things that go into a man's judgment are sometimes difficult to analyze.

Q. I am trying to find out to what extent objective facts—

A. I had studied this influence that Dr. Oppenheimer had over men. It was a tremendous thing.

Q. When did you study this influence?

A. All during the war and after the war. He is such an amazing man that one couldn't help but try to put together some picture.

Q. Tell us about these studies that you made about Dr. Oppenheimer's influence. You said after the war.

A. He has been a most interesting study for years. Unconsciously, I think one
tries to put together the elements in a man that make him tick. Where this
influence comes from, what factors in his personality that give him this
tremendous influence. I am not a psychoanalyst. I can't give you how my
picture of this thing was developed, but to me it was an amazing study, just
thinking about these factors.

Q. For a long time you have been thinking about Dr. Oppenheimer's influence
on people.

A. Yes, particularly during this period when he was able to sway so many
people, so many of his intimate—

Q. What is the period here?

MR. ROBB. Wait a minute. He has not finished.

MR. SILVERMAN. Sorry.

THE WITNESS. During this period of discussion as to whether one should work
on the H-bomb and the super weapons. I was amazed at the decision that
the committee was making, and I kept turning over in my mind how they
could possibly come to these conclusions, and what was in Oppenheimer
that gave him such tremendous power over these men. . . .

Q. You said some of the boys came back from Los Alamos pacifists, and you
judged that to be due to Dr. Oppenheimer's influence. On what did you base
that judgment?

A. Their great devotion to him. They were capable of independent judgment,
but it looked to me like a certain amount of indoctrination had taken place.
That matter I would not put too much weight on, but it was just an observation that they had. . . .

Q. Dr. Latimer, let me put it to you as frankly as I can, and I would like you
honestly, and I know you will, to consider this point of view. Would you say
that your judgment that these boys were influenced to become pacifists by
Dr. Oppenheimer is based essentially on your judgment that Dr. Oppenheimer is a very persuasive person, and that very few people come in contact with Dr. Oppenheimer without being influenced by him?

A. That is certainly an important factor in my decision.

Q. And that therefore if someone comes back after having a contact with Dr.
Oppenheimer with a view which to you appears to be Dr. Oppenheimer's
view, it is in your judgment reasonable to suppose that Dr. Oppenheimer influenced them?

A. I would conclude from the devotion of these boys to him that would not be
contrary to his own opinions and probably expressed.

Q. Did you know what his opinions were on the question of pacifism?

A. Let me phrase this a little differently. Let us not put the general pacifism,
but an unwillingness to build weapons or to work on any research involving weapons. I believe that was a more careful statement of the opinions
they voiced.

Q. Dr. Latimer, that is a very different thing from being pacifists, is it not?

A. It amounts to the same thing, I would say. We have to have weapons to fight. If we don't have weapons, we don't fight.

Q. Wasn't it true that many scientists after the explosion at Hiroshima and perhaps even before that—many scientists after the explosion at Hiroshima were terribly troubled by this weapon?

A. Oh, yes.

Q. Weren't you, sir?

A. I was more troubled by what the Russians might do along the same line.

Q. I would like to ask you whether you were troubled by this weapon.

A. No.

Q. Were you troubled by the fact that 70,000 people were killed at Hiroshima?

A. I felt that you might even have saved lives. I had been in the Pacific and I had seen something of the difficulty of getting the Japanese out of caves. I went over there on a special mission that involved that problem. I felt that if we had to land our boys on the coast of Japan, and knowing what I knew about the difficulty of getting Japanese out of underground positions, that the loss of life might be very much greater.

Q. I think we all understand that consideration, Dr. Latimer, and I think we all share it. What I would like to know is whether you were troubled by the fact that 70,000 people were killed at Hiroshima.

A. I suppose I was troubled to the same extent that I was troubled by the great loss of life which occurred in our fire bombs over Tokyo. The two things were comparable in my mind. I am troubled by war in general.

Q. Don't you think that perhaps boys who had worked on the atom bomb and who perhaps felt some responsibility for the bomb might have felt that trouble in perhaps even more acute form?

A. I grant that is correct; they might have. . . .

[Following Latimer's testimony, Lloyd Garrison submits several brief documents, including an affidavit by James R. Killian Jr., president of the Massachusetts Institute of Technology, attesting that Oppenheimer was "deeply devoted to strengthening the security of the Nation." Then the day's hearing is adjourned.]

Wednesday, April 28

ROSCOE C. WILSON: "My feeling is that the masters in the Kremlin cannot risk the loss of their base. This base is vulnerable only to attack by air power"

[Roger Robb explains that Ernest O. Lawrence will be unable to appear because of illness, and then calls Roscoe Charles Wilson, a major general in the air force, who has just completed a two-year stint as head of the Air War College in Montgomery, Alabama, and is on his way to England to become commander of the Third Air Force. He first met Oppenheimer at Los Alamos, which he visited as a liaison officer to General Groves. Candidly describing himself as "first of all a big-bomb man," Wilson replies to a question about a report, made in February 1950, by an AEC long-range objectives panel on which he served.]

DIRECT EXAMINATION

By Mr. Robb:

Q. Can you tell us about that report, General?

A. This panel was composed of a group of military people, of which I was one, and the chairman was Dr. Oppenheimer. Another member was Dr. Bacher, and another Dr. Luis Alvarez. The panel contained some conservative statements on the possibility or the feasibility of an early production of a thermonuclear weapon. These reservations were made on technical grounds. They were simply not challengeable by the military. They did, however, cause some concern in the military.

It is hard for me to explain this, except to say that most of us have an almost extravagant admiration for Dr. Oppenheimer and Dr. Bacher as physicists, and we simply would not challenge any technical judgment that they might make. But I must confess, and I find this exceedingly embarrassing, sir, that as a result of this panel and other actions that had taken place in the Committee on Atomic Energy, that I felt compelled to go to the Director of Intelligence to express my concern over what I felt was a pattern of action that was simply not helpful to national defense.

Q. Action by whom?

A. By Dr. Oppenheimer.

Q. Would you explain what that pattern was?

A. I would like first to say that I am not talking about loyalty. I want this clearly understood. If I may, I would like to say that this is a matter of my judgment versus Dr. Oppenheimer's judgment. This is a little embarrassing to me, too. But Dr. Oppenheimer was dealing in technical fields and I was dealing in other fields, and I am talking about an overall result of these actions.

First, I would like to say, sir, that I am a dedicated airman. I believe in a concept which I am going to have to tell you or my testimony doesn't make sense.

The U.S.S.R. in the airman's view is a land power. It is practically independent of the rest of the world. I feel that it could exist for a long time without sea communications. Therefore, it is really not vulnerable to attack by sea. Furthermore, it has a tremendous store of manpower. If you can imagine such a force, it could probably put 300 to 500 divisions in the field, certainly far more than this country could put into the field. It is bordered by satellite countries upon whom would be expended the first fury of any land assault that would be launched against Russia, and it has its historical distance and climate. So my feeling is that it is relatively invulnerable to land attack.

Russia is the base of international communism. My feeling is that the masters in the Kremlin cannot risk the loss of their base. This base is vulnerable only to attack by air power. I don't propose for a moment to say that only air power should be employed in case of a war with Russia, but I say what strategy is established should be centered around air power.

I further believe that whereas air power might be effective with ordinary weapons, that the chances of success against Russia with atomic weapons or nuclear weapons are far, far greater.

It is against this thinking that I have to judge Dr. Oppenheimer's judgments. Once again, his judgments were based upon technical matters. It is the pattern I am talking about.

I have jotted down from my own memory some of these things that worried me.

First was my awareness of the fact that Dr. Oppenheimer was interested in what I call the internationalizing of atomic energy, this at a time when the United States had a monopoly, and in which many people, including myself, believed that the A-bomb in the hands of the United States with an Air Force capable of using it was probably the greatest deterrent to further Russian aggression. This was a concern.

To do this the Air Force felt that it required quite an elaborate system of devices. Some were relatively simple to produce, some of them were exceedingly difficult to produce, and some of them were very costly. Dr. Oppenheimer was not enthusiastic about 2 out of 3 of these devices or systems. I do not challenge his technical judgment in these matters, but the overall effect was to deny to the Air Force the mechanism which we felt was essential to determine when this bomb went off. In our judgment, this was one of the critical dates, or would be at that time, for developing our national-defense policy.

Dr. Oppenheimer also opposed the nuclear-powered aircraft. His opposition was based on technical judgment. I don't challenge his technical judgment, but at the same time he felt less strongly opposed to the nuclear-powered ships. The Air Force feeling was that at least the same energy should be devoted to both projects.

The approach to the thermonuclear weapons also caused some concern. Dr. Oppenheimer, as far as I know, had technical objections, or, let me say, approached this conservatism for technical reasons, more conservatism than the Air Force would have liked.

The sum total of this, to my mind, was adding up that we were not exploiting the full military potential in this field. Once again it was a matter of judgment. I would like to say that the fact that I admire Dr. Oppenheimer so much, the fact that he is such a brilliant man, the fact that he has such a command of the English language, has such national prestige, and such power of persuasion, only made me nervous, because I felt if this was so it would not be to the interest of the United States, in my judgment. It was for that reason that I went to the Director of Intelligence to say that I felt unhappy.

MR. ROBB. That is all I care to ask. Thank you, General.

CROSS-EXAMINATION

By Mr. Silverman:

Q. General, you said you are not raising a question of loyalty?

A. No, sir.

Q. You do not question Dr. Oppenheimer's loyalty?

A. I have no knowledge in this area at all, sir.

Q. Do you—

MR. ROBB. Wait a minute. Let him finish his answer.

THE WITNESS. I have no knowledge one way or another.

By Mr. Silverman:

Q. Have you any information to indicate that Dr. Oppenheimer has been less than discreet in the handling of classified information?

A. No, sir; I haven't. Maybe I talk probably too much. . . .

MR. GRAY. You stated, General Wilson, on the basis of your association—I believe you stated—with Dr. Oppenheimer, you did not doubt his loyalty to the United States?

THE WITNESS. I have no knowledge of this at all, sir. I certainly have observed nothing nor have I heard him say anything that I personally would say was disloyal. In fact, sir, it seems to me that he has demonstrated his loyalty, once again in a private opinion, in the tremendous job he has done for this country. I have just no knowledge of this.

MR. GRAY. I should like to ask you another question on this point. It may be a difficult one to answer. Is it possible, do you think, for an individual to be completely loyal to the United States, and yet engage in a course of conduct which would be detrimental to the security interests of the United States?

THE WITNESS. Yes; I do.

MR. GRAY. I would like to refer now to what you described as a pattern of conduct. You mentioned several things. The internationalization of atomic energy has not been accomplished. With respect now to the long-range detection system, have these other two that have been under discussion here been developed, and are they now in use?

THE WITNESS. Yes, sir; they have been developed and are in use. It was a bitter wrangle to get them developed, but they are in use.

MR. GRAY. With respect to nuclear powered aircraft—I don't know what the security problem is in this next question—may I ask you whether this is a promising field at the present time? I suppose I should state frankly the purpose of this series of questions. You have stated that you do not question Dr. Oppenheimer's technical judgment and competence.

THE WITNESS. Yes.

MR. GRAY. You made that very clear. I am trying to find out really whether in these several things that you referred to as constituting what might be a pattern of conduct, whether events have shown technical judgment in this case to have been faulty. Let me say for the record this board is not asked to pass upon the technical judgment of anybody, and is not competent to pass upon it. But it seems to me an answer to my question is pertinent to the part of the inquiry that we are engaged in. So I ask whether in these areas subsequent events have proved the validity or otherwise of these technical judgments which you accepted more or less without question, I believe you said, from Dr. Oppenheimer. We know that internationalization of atomic energy has not been accomplished. With respect to the others—

THE WITNESS. Of course, the long-range detection program has been accomplished. I don't recall that Dr. Oppenheimer ever said that this couldn't be done. It was just perhaps that we ought to concentrate on the portions that could be done readily and quickly. I don't remember exactly the argument. It was essentially that—do what we can and perhaps that is the best we can do, this sort of thing, and for the rest let us experiment. The Air Force was frantic because it was charged with the job of detecting this first explosion and it felt all three methods had to be developed and put in place or it would fall down on its job.

MR. GRAY. I think I won't press you on the answer to the question as I asked it, because it is not a good question.

THE WITNESS. Yes, sir; I am sorry.

MR. GRAY. General Wilson, with respect to what might be called the philosophy of strategy in a conflict with the Soviet Union, is it your view, as a dedicated airman today, knowing what you know about our capabilities in the field of nuclear weapons, that these weapons are important?

THE WITNESS. Vastly, yes, sir.

MR. GRAY. And as an airman, would you feel that even with improvements in the atomic weapons, which may have taken place in these years we have been discussing, these are still important weapons, that is, the thermonuclear?

THE WITNESS. Yes, sir.

MR. GRAY. You feel as an airman, knowing air capabilities, that they have direct useful application in the course of a conflict with the Soviet Union in particular?

THE WITNESS. I think that they are vital, sir, to deterring a war, and I think that they are vital to winning a war should such a thing come. Further than this, it would seem intolerable to me that the Russians have such a weapon and the United States not. This is to get back to this area again. I would have reversed essentially our position when we had a monopoly on the atomic bomb—not entirely, but to a large degree. Involved as we are in a nonshooting war, this could have been a tremendous defeat for the United States.

MR. GRAY. We have had testimony given to this board by scientists who were involved in some of these discussions to the effect that thermonuclear weapons are more useful to the enemy than they are to us. By that I believe they meant to say that we are more vulnerable, assuming that both powers have these weapons, than are the Russians. Do you share that view?

THE WITNESS. Of course, it depends on the perimeters of our problem. Stated just as you have stated it, I would share that view. But think what would happen if we did not have the bomb and they did. The fact that we are troubled does not mean we should [not] have this weapon in my view. . . .

KENNETH S. PITZER: "I would not rate Dr. Oppenheimer's importance in this field very high for the rather personal reason . . . that I have disagreed with a good many of his important positions"

[Kenneth S. Pitzer, dean of the college of chemistry at the University of California at Berkeley, served from 1949 to 1951 as director of the AEC's research division. In April 1952, he requested an interview with the FBI. He explained that he "now is doubtful" as to Oppenheimer's loyalty. He claimed that Oppenheimer had opposed the development of the H-bomb, and had then impeded its progress by "persuading other outstanding scientists not to work on the H-bomb Project." In the event the FBI decided to forward his views to the AEC, Pitzer added, "he desired that suitable precautions be taken to conceal his identity."]

DIRECT EXAMINATION

By Mr. Robb: . . .

Q. Doctor, would you say that you are pretty familiar with the nuclear scientists, physicists, and chemists in the country? Are you generally familiar with them?

A. I have reasonably wide acquaintanceship, more of course on the chemical side, but I am acquainted with many nuclear physicists.

Q. Given Dr. Oppenheimer's attitude and feelings as you have described them, what can you tell us about what would be the effect in your opinion upon the scientific world of such attitudes and feelings so far as either increasing or decreasing enthusiasm for the thermonuclear program? That is a long question. I hope it is clear. I am trying not to lead you.

A. I hope you will permit me to make a statement of my general impressions of that time. After the President made the decision and announced it to the papers, I was rather surprised to find that Dr. Oppenheimer did not in some manner or another disqualify himself from a position of, shall we say, technical leadership of the program. I had the feeling that if my advice on a major subject of this sort had been so—if the decision had been so much in reverse from my advice, let us put it that way—that I would not have wanted to be in a position of responsibility with respect to the subsequent pursuit of the program.

As to just what course of action would have been most appropriate, there are various alternatives. I think this would have led to a clearer and more vigorous program had some other arrangement of this sort been had.

Q. Why do you think that, Doctor?

A. It would have been clear that the Commission was by this time thoroughly behind the program and that the fullest support was going to be given to it because special arrangements had been made to be sure that the leadership would be vigorous.

Q. Do you think the fact that Dr. Oppenheimer stayed on entertaining the views which you have told us about discouraged other physicists from going ahead on the program with vigor?

A. I can only say to this that I am afraid it may have. I am not aware of detailed negotiations or influences on particular individuals, but I do know there was difficulty in that early period in obtaining the staff that would have seemed desirable to me and as I believe Dr. Teller felt was desirable at that time, particularly in the theoretical physics area. To have had other advisory leadership that was known to be enthusiastic for the program would, I think, have assisted.

Q. You suggested other advisory leadership. Did you have in mind a specific step that might have been taken either by Dr. Oppenheimer or by the Commission to get such leadership?

A. As I said before, it seemed to me that there were several alternatives there. If the most extreme change had seemed desirable, there was a possibility of full changes of membership in the Statutory Advisory Committee. Other possibilities could have been the appointment of some special panel in this field, and of course a marked and clearcut change in the viewpoints of certain individuals would have assisted the program.

Q. In your opinion did Dr. Oppenheimer do everything he might have to further the program after the President's decision?

A. Again in an inferential sense, I am afraid I must say that he did not.

Q. Would you explain that to us a little bit?

A. As I indicated earlier, it seemed to me that had he enthusiastically urged men in the theoretical physics field to go to Los Alamos or other points as indicated for this program that the difficulties in staffing it would have not arisen. I am sure he had great influence over individuals in that field.

On the other hand, as I say, this is simply an inference, and not something that I know from day to day and man to man.

Q. I understand. What was Dr. Oppenheimer's influence in the physics field during that period to your knowledge?

A. He was unquestionably a most influential individual in dealings with other physicists, particularly theoretical physicists, but also experimental men. . . .

Q. What can you tell us about the importance or the essentiality to the atomic weapons and the thermonuclear weapons program today of Dr. Oppenheimer, in your opinion?

A. Let me develop this in a number of facets.

Q. That is why I asked the broad question so you can answer it in your own way.

A. I would like to discuss these briefly from three points of view. One is in terms of immediate scientific work. That is the calculations, theoretical derivations and this sort of thing. This by and large is done by younger people, particularly in the field of theoretical physics. I haven't the slightest doubt that Dr. Oppenheimer would be valuable to such work but, by and large, from that tradition and experience in theoretical physics, this sort of thing is done by people in their twenties or thirties.

The second aspect is that of leadership among men in this field. I have no doubt that Dr. Oppenheimer's influence and importance in the sense of leadership among men is of the highest order. He would have a great deal of influence and could be of a great deal of assistance in persuading able people to work at certain places and at certain times and in selecting people for this.

The third phase that I would mention would be that on what might be called policy advice. This is the sort of thing that the Commission and other nontechnical management people need. Personally, I would not rate Dr. Oppenheimer's importance in this field very high for the rather personal reason, I suspect, that I have disagreed with a good many of his important positions and I personally would think that advisers in the policy field of greater wisdom and judgment could be readily obtained.

Q. You say very honestly that you personally disagree. Let me ask you whether or not events have proved that you were right or Dr. Oppenheimer was right.

A. That is a difficult question. I think personally that we were right in going into a vigorous thermonuclear program at the time we did. I would not want to question the possibility of a perfectly sincere and reasonable judgment to the contrary at that time. I want to make it perfectly clear that I am emphasizing here essentially need, or in the extreme, indispensability of the advice than some other feature. Possibly it would be just fair to say that in the policy area I certainly do not regard Dr. Oppenheimer as having any indispensability. . . .

CROSS-EXAMINATION

By Mr. Silverman: . . .

Q. I think you said you were rather surprised that Dr. Oppenheimer did not disqualify himself from a position of technical leadership of a program with which he apparently disagreed. Do you know whether Dr. Oppenheimer did in fact offer to resign from the chairmanship of the General Advisory Committee at that time?

A. I have no information on that.

Q. You have not heard that he offered to the Chairman, Mr. Dean, to resign?

A. I don't believe I heard that; no.

Q. And you don't know what Mr. Dean's reaction was. You just never heard of it?

A. I never heard about it.

Q. I think there has been testimony here about it, so I think the record is clear enough on it.

A. At least, if I heard of it, I do not recall at this time.

Q. I take it you would be less critical of Dr. Oppenheimer's attitude if that were the fact, if he offered to resign and was urged to remain?

A. Certainly so. I think, however, that his position today would be better if he had insisted on at least some degree of disqualification in this field at that time.

Q. I wish you would elaborate on that.

A. Let me put it this way. I am extremely sorry to see this issue concerning advice which on hindsight proved not too good brought up in connection with a security clearance procedure. I feel very strongly that scientists should feel free to advise the Government and not be held to account if their advice proves not the best afterward. This should have no relevance to security clearance procedure. If Dr. Oppenheimer had seen fit to insist upon stepping out of the position of advising on the hydrogen program, this could not be introduced into this argument at this time. I am very sorry to see that it does have to come up at this time.

Q. I need hardly say that I entirely agree with you. . . .

EDWARD TELLER: "I feel that I would like to see the vital interests of this country in hands which I understand better, and therefore trust more"

[If there was a turning point in the hearings, it occurred when Edward Teller testified. As the driving force behind the development of the hydrogen bomb, Teller's opinion, Roger Robb knew, could be decisive. The problem, however, was that Teller did not believe Oppenheimer should lose his security clearance. Interviewed by Robb and Rolander in Berkeley on March 15, Teller said that Oppenheimer had given "bad advice in the matter of the H-bomb, and that in the future his advice should not be taken and he should never have any more influence." Nevertheless, according to Rolander's memorandum of the talk, "he said he hoped Oppenheimer's clearance would not be lifted for a mere mistake of judgment." In an effort to ensure that Teller would bolster his case, Robb met with him the evening before he testified and showed him the portion of Oppenheimer's testimony in which he conceded he had lied to security officers about the Chevalier incident.]

DIRECT EXAMINATION

By Mr. Robb:

Q. Dr. Teller, may I ask you, sir, at the outset, are you appearing as a witness here today because you want to be here?

A. I appear because I have been asked to and because I consider it my duty upon request to say what I think in the matter. I would have preferred not to appear.

Q. I believe, sir, that you stated to me some time ago that anything you had to say, you wished to say in the presence of Dr. Oppenheimer?

A. That is correct. . . .

Q. Dr. Teller, you know Dr. Oppenheimer well; do you not?

A. I have known Dr. Oppenheimer for a long time. I first got closely associated with him in the summer of 1942 in connection with atomic energy work. Later in Los Alamos and after Los Alamos I knew him. I met him frequently, but I was not particularly closely associated with him, and I did not discuss with him very frequently or in very great detail matters outside of business matters.

Q. To simplify the issues here, perhaps, let me ask you this question: Is it your intention in anything that you are about to testify to, to suggest that Dr. Oppenheimer is disloyal to the United States?

A. I do not want to suggest anything of the kind. I know Oppenheimer as an intellectually most alert and a very complicated person, and I think it would be presumptuous and wrong on my part if I would try in any way to analyze his motives. But I have always assumed, and I now assume that he is loyal to the United States. I believe this, and I shall believe it until I see very conclusive proof to the opposite.

Q. Now, a question which is the corollary of that. Do you or do you not believe that Dr. Oppenheimer is a security risk?

A. In a great number of cases I have seen Dr. Oppenheimer act—I understood that Dr. Oppenheimer acted—in a way which for me was exceedingly hard to understand. I thoroughly disagreed with him in numerous issues and his actions frankly appeared to me confused and complicated. To this extent I feel that I would like to see the vital interests of this country in hands which I understand better, and therefore trust more.

Edward Teller (left) and Enrico Fermi, Chicago, 1951. AIP Emilio Segrè Visual Archives.

In this very limited sense I would like to express a feeling that I would feel personally more secure if public matters would rest in other hands. . . .

Q. Did you work during the war at Los Alamos?

A. I did.

Q. When did you go there, sir?

A. In April 1943.

Q. What was the nature of your work there?

A. It was theoretical work connected with the atomic bomb. Generally speaking—I do not know whether I have to go into that in any detail—I was more interested by choice and also by directive in advanced development, so that at the beginning I think my work was perhaps more closely connected with the actual outcome or what happened in Alamagordo, but very soon my work shifted into fields which were not to bear fruition until a much later time.

Q. Will you tell the board whether or not while you were in Los Alamos in 1943 or 1944, you did any work or had any discussions about the so-called thermonuclear weapon? . . .

A. I hope that I can keep my answer in an unclassified way. I hope I am not disclosing a secret when I say that to construct the thermonuclear bomb is not a very easy thing, and that in our discussions, all of us frequently believed it could be done, and again we frequently believed it could not be done. I think Dr. Oppenheimer's opinions shifted with the shifting evidence. To the best of my recollection before we got to Los Alamos we had all of us considerable hopes that the thermonuclear bomb can be constructed. It was my understanding that these hopes were fully shared by Dr. Oppenheimer.

Later some disappeared and perhaps to counterbalance some things that might have been said, I think I have made myself some contributions in discovering some of these difficulties.

I clearly remember that toward the end of the war Dr. Oppenheimer encouraged me to go ahead with the thermonuclear investigations. I further remember that in the summer of 1945, after the test at Alamogordo it was generally understood in the laboratory that we are going to develop thermonuclear bombs in a vigorous fashion and that quite a number of people, such as the most outstanding, like Fermi and Bethe, would participate in it.

I also know that very shortly after the dropping of bombs on Japan this plan was changed and to the best of my belief it was changed at least in good part because of the opinion of Dr. Oppenheimer that this is not the time to pursue this program any further.

I should like to add to this, however, that this also thoroughly responded to the temper of the people in the laboratory, most of whom at that time understandably and clearly and in consonance with the general tempo of the country, wanted to go home.

Q. Did you have any conversations with Dr. Oppenheimer at or about September 1945 about working on the thermonuclear?

A. We had around that period several conversations and in one of them, to the best of my recollection, Oppenheimer and Fermi and Allison and I were present. Oppenheimer argued that this is not the time at which to pursue the business further, that this is a very interesting program, that it would be a wonderful thing if we could pursue it in a really peaceful world under international cooperation, but that under the present setup this was not a good idea to go on with it.

I perhaps should also like to mention that to the best of my knowledge at that time there was a decision by a board composed of several prominent people, one of them Dr. Oppenheimer, which decided in effect that thermonuclear work either cannot or should not be pursued that it at any rate was a long-term undertaking requiring very considerable effort. To my mind this was in sharp contrast to the policy pursued a short time before.

But I also should say that this sharp contrast was at least in part motivated by the fact that in Los Alamos there was a crew of exceedingly able physicists who could do a lot and at the end of the war were trying to get back to their purely academic duties, and in this new atmosphere it might have appeared indeed hard to continue with such an ambitious program.

One member of the board which made this decision, Fermi, and who concurred in that decision, told me about that decision and told me that he knew that I am likely to disagree with it, and asked me to state my opinion in writing. This I did, and I gave my written statement to Oppenheimer, and therefore, both the opinion that the thermonuclear bomb at that time was not feasible, and my own opinion that one could have proceeded in this direction are documented.

Q. Did there come a time when you left Los Alamos after the war?

A. That is right. As I mentioned, I left in February 1946. May I perhaps add something here if we are proceeding in a chronological manner?

Q. Yes.

A. Perhaps if I might interject this not in response to one of your questions.

Q. That is perfectly all right, sir.

A. I would like to say that I consider Dr. Oppenheimer's direction of the Los Alamos Laboratory a very outstanding achievement due mainly to the fact that with his very quick mind he found out very promptly what was going on in every part of the laboratory, made right judgments about things, supported work when work had to be supported, and also I think with his very remarkable insight in psychological matters, made just a most wonderful and excellent director.

Q. In that statement were you speaking of Dr. Oppenheimer's ability as an administrator or his contribution as a scientist or both?

A. I would like to say that I would say in a way both. As an administrator he was so busy that his purely scientific contributions to my mind and in my judgment were not outstanding, that is, not insofar as I could see his original contributions. But nevertheless, his scientific contributions were great by exercising quick and sound judgment and giving the right kind of encouragement in very many different cases. I should think that scientific initiative came from a great number of other excellent people whom Oppenheimer not let alone but also to a very great extent by his able recruiting effort he collected a very considerable number of them, and I should say that purely scientific initiatives and contributions came from many people, such like, for instance, von Neumann, Bethe, Segrè, to mention a few with whom I am very closely connected, and very many others, and I cannot begin to make a complete list of them. . . .

Q. Doctor, let me ask you for your opinion as an expert on this question. Suppose you had gone to work on thermonuclear in 1945 or 1946—really gone to work on it—can you give us any opinion as to when in your view you might have achieved that weapon and would you explain your opinion?

A. I actually did go to work on it with considerable determination after the Russian bomb was dropped. This was done in a laboratory which at that time was considerably behind Los Alamos at the end of the war. It is my belief that if at the end of the war some people like Dr. Oppenheimer would have lent moral support, not even their own work—just moral support—to work on the thermonuclear gadget, I think we could have kept at least as many people in Los Alamos as we then recruited in 1949 under very difficult conditions.

I therefore believe that if we had gone to work in 1945, we could have achieved the thermonuclear bomb just about 4 years earlier. This of course is very much a matter of opinion because what would have happened if things had been different is certainly not something that one can ever produce by any experiment.

Q. That is right.

A. I think that statements about the possible different course of the past are not more justified but only less hazardous than statements about the future. . . .

Q. Do you recall when the Russians exploded their first bomb in September 1949? Do you recall that event?

A. Certainly.

Q. Will you tell the board whether or not shortly thereafter you had a conversation with Dr. Oppenheimer about the thermonuclear or about what activity should be undertaken to meet the Russian advance?

A. I remember two such conversations. One was in the fall and necessarily superficial. That was just a very few hours after I heard, returning from a trip abroad, that the Russians had exploded an A-bomb. I called up Oppenheimer who happened to be in Washington, as I was at that time, and I asked him for advice, and this time I remember his advice literally. It was, "Keep your shirt on."

Perhaps I might mention that my mind did not immediately turn in the direction of working on the thermonuclear bomb. I had by that time quite thoroughly accepted the idea that with the reduced personnel it was much too difficult an undertaking. I perhaps should mention, and I think it will clear the picture, that a few months before the Russian explosion I agreed to rejoin Los Alamos for the period of 1 year on leave of absence from the University of Chicago.

I should also mention that prior to that Oppenheimer had talked to me and encouraged me to go back to Los Alamos, and help in the work there. I also went back to Los Alamos with the understanding and with the expectation that I shall just help along in their normal program in which some very incipient phases of the thermonuclear work was included, but nothing on a very serious scale.

I was quite prepared to contribute mostly in the direction of the fission weapons. At the time when I returned from this short trip abroad, and was very much disturbed about the Russian bomb, I was looking around for ways in which we could more successfully speed up our work and only after several weeks of discussion did I come to the conclusion that no matter what the odds seemed to be, we must at this time—I at least must at this time put my full attention to the thermonuclear program.

I also felt that this was much too big an undertaking and I was just very scared of it. I was looking around for some of the old crew to come out and participate in this work. Actually if anyone wanted to head this enterprise, one of the people whom I went to visit, in fact the only one where I had very strong hopes, was Hans Bethe.

Q. About when was this, Doctor?

A. To the best of my recollection it was the end of October.

Q. 1949?

A. Right. Again I am not absolutely certain of my dates, but that is the best of my memory. I can tie it down a little bit better with respect to other dates. It was a short time before the GAC meeting in which that committee made a decision against the thermonuclear program.

After a somewhat strenuous discussion, Bethe, to the best of my understanding, decided that he would come to Los Alamos and help us. During this discussion, Oppenheimer called up and invited Bethe and me to come and discuss this matter with him in Princeton. This we did do, and visited Oppenheimer in his office.

When we arrived, I remember that Oppenheimer showed us a letter on his desk which he said he had just received. This letter was from Conant. I do not know whether he showed us the whole letter or whether he showed us a short section of it, or whether he only read to us a short section. Whichever it was, and I cannot say which it was, one phrase of Conant's sticks in my mind, and that phrase was "over my dead body," referring to a decision to go ahead with a crash program on the thermonuclear bomb.

Apart from showing us this letter, or reading it to us, whichever it was, Oppenheimer to the best of my recollection did not argue against any crash program. We did talk for quite awhile and could not possibly reproduce the whole argument but at least one important trend in this discussion—and I do not know how relevant this is—was that Oppenheimer argued that some phases of exaggerated secrecy in connection with the A-bomb was perhaps not to the best interests of the country, and that if he undertook the thermonuclear development, this should be done right from the first and should be done more openly.

I remember that Bethe reacted to that quite violently, because he thought that if we proceeded with thermonuclear development, then both—not only our methods of work—but even the fact that we were working and if possible the results of our work should be most definitely kept from any public knowledge or any public announcement.

To the best of my recollection, no agreement came out of this, but when Bethe and I left Oppenheimer's office, Bethe was still intending to come to Los Alamos. Actually, I had been under the impression that Oppenheimer is opposed to the thermonuclear bomb or to a development of the thermonuclear bomb and I don't think there was terribly much direct evidence to base this impression on. I am pretty sure that I expressed to Bethe the worry, we are going to talk with Oppenheimer now, and after that you will not come. When we left the office, Bethe turned to me and smiled and he said, "You see, you can be quite satisfied. I am still coming."

I do not know whether Bethe has talked again with Oppenheimer about that or not. I have some sort of a general understanding that he did not, but I am not at all sure that this is true.

Two days later I called up Bethe in New York, and he was in New York at that time, and Bethe then said that he thought it over, and he had changed his mind, and he was not coming.

I regretted this very much, and Bethe actually did not join work on the thermonuclear development until quite late in the game, essentially to put on the finishing touches.

I do not know whether this sufficiently answers your question. . . .

Q. In January 1950, the President decided that we should go ahead with the thermonuclear program. Do you recall that?

A. I do.

Q. After that decision was announced, did you go to work on the thermonuclear?

A. I most certainly did.

Q. Was the program accelerated?

A. It was.

Q. What was done in general to accelerate it?

A. A committee was formed which for a strange and irrelevant reason was called a family committee.

Q. Who was on that committee?

A. I was the chairman and there were a number of people representing various divisions in the laboratory, and this committee was in charge of developing some thermonuclear program and within a very short time this committee made a number of proposals directed toward some tests which were to give us information about the behavior of some phenomena which were relevant.

At the same time I exerted all possible effort and influence to persuade people to come to Los Alamos to work on this, particularly serious because theoretical work was very badly needed.

Q. What was done in respect of the number of personnel working on the thermonuclear? Was it increased, and if so, how much?

A. It was greatly increased. As I say prior to that there was at most half a dozen people working on it. I am not able to tell you how many people worked on the thermonuclear program in that period. I would say that very few people worked on it really full time. I am sure I didn't work on it full time although in that time the major portion of my effort was directed toward the thermonuclear work. I believe that Los Alamos has prepared an official estimate in response to a question, and that would be, I think, the best source of how many people worked on the thermonuclear program at that time. I would guess, but as a very pure guess, and I should not be surprised if that document would disprove me, that the number of people working on the thermonuclear program increased then to something like two, three, or four hundred, which still was something like 10, 20, or perhaps a little more percent of the laboratory's effort. Perhaps it was closer to 20 percent. I might easily be mistaken.

Q. At all events it was a very large increase.

A. It was a very large increase. As compared to the previous one it was just between standing still and starting to go.

Q. Did you at or about that time, that is, shortly after the President's decision, have any discussion with Oppenheimer as to whether or not he would assist you?

A. I had two discussions with him, but one was shortly before. I would like to quote it a little. Actually the time when President Truman made the announcement I happened to be in Los Angeles and was planning to stay there, in fact had accepted an appointment at UCLA which I at that time had to postpone at any rate because I saw this in the paper. You see, I was not going to stay in Los Alamos much longer, and the fact that there came this announcement from President Truman just changed my mind. Prior to the announcement, preceding it perhaps by 2 or 3 days, I saw Dr. Oppenheimer at an atomic energy conference concerning another matter, and during this meeting it became clear to me that in Dr. Oppenheimer's opinion a decision was impending and this decision would be a go-ahead decision.

At that time I asked Oppenheimer if this is now the decision, would he then please really help us with this thing and help us to work, recalling the very effective work during the war. Oppenheimer's answer to this was in the negative. This was, however, very clearly before President Truman's decision. However, I also should say that this negative reply gave me the feeling that I should not look to Oppenheimer for help under any circumstances.

A few months later, during the spring, I nevertheless called up Oppenheimer and I asked him not for direct help, but for help in recruiting people, not for his own work but for his support in recruiting people. Dr. Oppenheimer said then, "You know in this matter I am neutral. I would be glad, however, to recommend to you some very good people who are working here at the Institute," and he mentioned a few. I wrote to all of these people and tried to persuade them to come to Los Alamos. None of them came.

Q. Where were those people located?

A. At the Institute of Advanced Study in Princeton. . . .

Q. Except for giving you this list of names that you have told us about of people all of whom refused to come, did Dr. Oppenheimer, after the President's decision in January 1950, assist you in any way in recruiting people on the thermonuclear project?

A. To the best of my knowledge not in the slightest.

Q. After the President's decision of January 1950, did Dr. Oppenheimer do anything so far as you know to assist you in the thermonuclear project?

A. The General Advisory Committee did meet, did consider this matter, and its recommendations were in support of the program. Perhaps I am prejudiced in this matter, but I did not feel that we got from the General Advisory Committee more than passive agreement on the program which we evolved. I should say passive agreement, and I felt the kind of criticism which tended to be perhaps more in the nature of a headache than in the nature of enlightening.

I would like to say that in a later phase there is at least one occurrence where I felt Dr. Oppenheimer's reaction to be different.

Q. Would you tell us about that?

A. I will be very glad to do that. In June of 1951, after our first experimental test, there was a meeting of the General Advisory Committee and Atomic Energy Commission personnel and some consultants in Princeton at the Institute for Advanced Study. The meeting was chaired by Dr. Oppenheimer. Frankly I went to that meeting with very considerable misgivings, because I expected that the General Advisory Committee, and particularly Dr. Oppenheimer, would further oppose the development. By that time we had evolved something which amounted to a new approach, and after listening to the evidence of both the test and the theoretical investigations on that new approach, Dr. Oppenheimer warmly supported this new approach, and I understand that he made a statement to the effect that if anything of this kind had been suggested right away he never would have opposed it.

Q. With that exception, did you have any indication from Dr. Oppenheimer after January 1950 that he was supporting and approving the work that was being done on the thermonuclear?

A. My general impression was precisely in the opposite direction. However, I should like to say that my contacts with Oppenheimer were infrequent, and he might have supported the thermonuclear effort without my knowing it.

Q. When was the feasibility of the thermonuclear demonstrated?

A. I believe that this can be stated accurately. On November 1, 1952. Although since it was on the other side of the date line, I am not quite sure whether it was November 1 our time or their time.

Q. What?

A. I don't know whether it was November 1 Eniwetok time or Berkeley time. I watched it in Berkeley.

Q. Did you have a conversation with Dr. Oppenheimer in the summer of 1950 about your work on the thermonuclear?

A. To the best of my recollection he visited Los Alamos in the summer of 1950 and then in the early fall the General Advisory Committee met in Los Alamos—I mean he visited in Los Alamos early in the summer, and then they met in Los Alamos sometime, I believe, in September, and on both occasions we did talk.

Q. What did Dr. Oppenheimer have to say, if anything, about the thermonuclear?

A. To the best of my recollection he did not have any very definite or concrete advice. Whatever he had tended in the direction that we should proceed with the theoretical investigations, which at that time did not look terribly encouraging, before spending more money or effort on the experimental approach, which I think was at that time not the right advice, because only by pursuing the experimental approach, the test approach, as well as the theoretical one did we face the problem sufficiently concretely so as to find a more correct solution. But I also should like to say that the opinion of Dr. Oppenheimer given at that time to my hearing was not a very decisive or not a very strongly advocated opinion, and I considered it not helpful, but also not as anything that need worry us too much.

I must say this, that the influence of the General Advisory Committee at that time was to the best of my understanding in the direction of go slow, explore all, completely all the designs before looking into new designs, do not spend too much on test programs, all of which advice I consider as somewhat in the nature of serving as a brake rather than encouragement.

Q. Doctor, I would like to ask for your expert opinion again.

In your opinion, if Dr. Oppenheimer should go fishing for the rest of his life, what would be the effect upon the atomic energy and the thermonuclear programs?

A. You mean from now on?

Q. Yes, sir.

A. May I say this depends entirely on the question of whether his work would be similar to the one during the war or similar to the one after the war.

Q. Assume that it was similar to the work after the war.

A. In that case I should like to say two things. One is that after the war Dr. Oppenheimer served on committees rather than actually participating in the work. I am afraid this might not be a correct evaluation of the work of committees in general, but within the AEC, I should say that committees could go fishing without affecting the work of these who are actively engaged in the work.

In particular, however, the general recommendations that I know have come from Oppenheimer were more frequently, and I mean not only and not even particularly the thermonuclear case, but other cases, more frequently a hindrance than a help, and therefore, if I look into the continuation of this and assume that it will come in the same way, I think that further work of Dr. Oppenheimer on committees would not be helpful. . . .

CROSS-EXAMINATION

By Mr. Silverman: . . .

Q. Did Mr. Oppenheimer oppose the Livermore Laboratory as it was finally set up?

A. No. To the best of my knowledge, no.

Q. His opposition was to another Los Alamos?

A. It was to another Los Alamos, and when the Atomic Energy Commission, I think, on the advice from the military did proceed in the direction, the General Advisory Committee encouraged in particular setting up a laboratory at the site where it was set up. But prior to that, I understand that the General Advisory Committee advised against it.

Q. That is when there was a question of another Los Alamos?

A. Right. . . .

MR. GRAY. Dr. Teller, I think earlier in your testimony you stated that in August 1945, Dr. Oppenheimer talked with you and indicated his feeling that Los Alamos would inevitably disintegrate. I believe those were your words, and that there was no point in your staying on there. Is my recollection correct?

THE WITNESS. Yes. I am not sure that my statement was very fortunate, but I am pretty sure that this is how I said it.

MR. GRAY. Would you say that his attitude at that time was that it should disintegrate?

THE WITNESS. I would like to elaborate on that for a moment. I think that I ought to say this: I do not like to say it. Oppenheimer and I did not always agree in Los Alamos, and I believe that it is quite possible, probably, that this was my fault. This particular discussion was connected with an impression I got that Oppenheimer wanted me particularly to leave, which at first I interpreted as his being dissatisfied with the attitude I was taking about certain questions as to how to proceed in detail. It became clear to me during the conversation—and, incidentally, it was something which was quite new to me because prior to that, while we did disagree quite frequently, Oppenheimer always urged no matter how much we disagreed in detail I should certainly stay and work. He urged me although on some occasions I was discouraged and I wanted to leave. On this occasion, he advised me to leave. I considered that at first as essentially personal matters. In the course of the conversation, it became clear to me that what he really meant at that time—I asked him—we disagreed on a similar thing and I forget the thing, but I do remember asking him in a similar discussion that, 3 months ago—"You told me by all means I should stay. Now you tell me I should leave." He said, "Yes," but in the meantime we had developed these bombs and the work looks different and I think all of us would have to go home—something to that effect. It was at that time that I had the first idea that Oppenheimer himself wanted to discontinue his work very rapidly and very promptly at Los Alamos. I knew that changes were due but it did not occur to me prior to that conversation that they were due quite that rapidly and would affect our immediate plans just right then and there. I do not know whether I have made myself sufficiently clear or not.

I failed to mention this personnel element before. I am sorry about that. I think it is perhaps relevant as a background. . . .

MR. GRAY. Dr. Teller, you are familiar with the question which this board is called upon to answer, I assume.

THE WITNESS. Yes, I believe so.

MR. GRAY. Let me tell you what it is and invite counsel to help me out if I misstate it. We are asked to make a finding in the alternative, that it will or will not endanger the common defense and security to grant security clearance to Dr. Oppenheimer.

I believe you testified earlier when Mr. Robb was putting questions to you that because of your knowledge of the whole situation and by reason of many factors about which you have testified in very considerable detail, you would feel safer if the security of the country were in other hands.

THE WITNESS. Right.

MR. GRAY. That is substantially what you said?

THE WITNESS. Yes.

MR. GRAY. I think you have explained why you feel that way. I would then like to ask you this question: Do you feel that it would endanger the common defense and security to grant clearance to Dr. Oppenheimer?

THE WITNESS. I believe, and that is merely a question of belief and there is no expertness, no real information behind it, that Dr. Oppenheimer's character is such that he would not knowingly and willingly do anything that is designed to endanger the safety of this country. To the extent, therefore, that your question is directed toward intent, I would say I do not see any reason to deny clearance.

If it is a question of wisdom and judgment, as demonstrated by actions since 1945, then I would say one would be wiser not to grant clearance. I must say that I am myself a little bit confused on this issue, particularly as it refers to a person of Oppenheimer's prestige and influence. May I limit myself to these comments?

MR. GRAY. Yes. . . .

DR. EVANS. You understand, of course, that we did not seek the job on this board, do you not?

THE WITNESS. You understand, sir, that I did not want to be at this end of the table either. . . .

RE-CROSS-EXAMINATION

By Mr. Silverman:

Q. I would like you, Dr. Teller, to distinguish between the desirability of this country's or the Government's accepting Dr. Oppenheimer's advice and the danger, if there be any, in Dr. Oppenheimer's having access to restricted data. As to this latter, as to the danger in Dr. Oppenheimer's having access to restricted data without regard to the wisdom of his advice, do you think there is any danger to the national security in his having access to restricted data?

A. In other words, I now am supposed to assume that Dr. Oppenheimer will have access to security information?

Q. Yes.

A. But will refrain from all advice in these matters which is to my mind a very hypothetical question indeed. May I answer such a hypothetical question by saying that the very limited knowledge which I have on these matters and which are based on feelings, emotions, and prejudices, I believe there is no danger.

MR. GRAY. Thank you very much, Doctor.

Thursday, April 29

JOHN J. McCLOY: **"He used the graphic expression like two scorpions in a bottle, that each could destroy the other"**

[Formerly assistant secretary of war, at the time of the hearing chairman of the board of Chase National Bank, John J. McCloy was a veritable pillar of the establishment. He had last seen Oppenheimer in January at a meeting of the Council on Foreign Relations' Study Group on Soviet–U.S. Relations. Shortly before he testified on Oppenheimer's behalf, McCloy told one friend, Supreme Court Justice Felix Frankfurter: "Knowing firsthand the tremendous contributions that this man made to the development of our position in atomic weapons, I can't conceive of any real disloyalty on his part no matter what his early associations were." He told another friend, President Dwight Eisenhower, that to investigate a man like Oppenheimer "is somewhat like inquiring into the security risk of a Newton or a Galileo. Such people are themselves always 'top secret.'"]

DIRECT EXAMINATION

By Mr. Garrison: . . .

Q. Coming down to the Soviet study group which you mentioned in the Council of Foreign Relations, you were the presiding officer of that group?

A. Yes, I was the presiding officer.

Q. And Dr. Oppenheimer was a member of the group?

A. Yes. . . .

Q. When did the group begin?

A. It began at the beginning of 1953. It has been going for a year, and it will probably go for another year. He was selected at the outset and attended one or two meetings and then he went to lecture abroad so we didn't have him present at a substantial number of meetings. Then he did give us a picture of where he thought we stood generally in relation to the Soviets in respect to atomic development.

Q. Without going into the details of what he said, what impression did his talk leave on you about his general attitude toward the situation?

A. The impression that I gathered from him was one of real concern that although we had a quantitative superiority, that that didn't mean a great deal. * * * We were coming to the point where we might be, he used the graphic expression like two scorpions in a bottle, that each could destroy the other, even though one may have been somewhat larger than the other, and he was very much concerned about the security position of the United States. He pressed vigorously for the continued activity in this field, and not letting down our guard, so to speak. Taking advantage of any opportunity that really presented itself that looked as if it was substantial, but if there was to be any negotiation, be certain that we were armed and well prepared before we went to such a conference. Indeed, I have the impression that he, with one or two others, was somewhat more, shall I say, militant than some of the other members of the group. I think I remember very well that he said, for example, that we would have to contemplate and keep our minds open for all sorts of eventualities in this thing * * *.

In the course of this, I think I should say that he was questioned by the members of the group from time to time. In a number of cases, he refused to reply, saying that he could not reply because in doing so that would involve some security information. His talk was generally in generalities, to some extent following the line that he took in an article which I saw later on published in Foreign Affairs.

I got the very strong impression of Dr. Oppenheimer's sensitivity to what he considered to be the interests of the United States and to the security of the United States.

Q. Based on your acquaintance with Dr. Oppenheimer, and your experiences with him, would you give the board your opinion as to his loyalty and as to his security risk or want of risk?

A. In the first place, just to get it out of the way, let me say that there is nothing that occurred during the entire period of my contact with Dr. Oppenheimer which gave me any reason to feel that he was in any sense disloyal to the United States. But I would want to put it more positively than that, and also add that throughout my contacts with him, I got the impression, as one who has had a good bit of contact and experience with defense matters, that he was very sensitive to all aspects of the security of the United States.

I gathered the impression that he was deeply concerned about the consequences of this awful force that we had released, anxious to do what he could toward seeing that it was not used or did not become a destroyer of civilization. He was somewhat puzzled as to what form that would take and still be consistent with the interests of the United States. That perhaps more than a number of others who were, so to speak, laymen in this field, who were members of that study group, were aware of the techniques of the defense of the United States. He was a little more aware than those who had not been really associated with the Defense Department of the military position of the United States somewhat apart from the atomic situation. So much for loyalty.

I can't be too emphatic as to my impression of Dr. Oppenheimer in this regard. I have the impression of his being a loyal, patriotic citizen, aware of his responsibilities and that I want to accent.

As to his security risk—to use the current phrase—I again can state that negatively certainly. I know of nothing myself which would make me feel that he was a security risk. I don't know just exactly what you mean by a security risk. I know that I am a security risk and I think every individual is a security risk. You can always talk in your sleep. You can always drop a paper that you should not drop, or you can speak to your wife about something, and to that extent no human being is an absolutely secure person. I don't suppose we are talking about that.

I never heard of any of Dr. Oppenheimer's early background until very recently, and so that has never been an element in my thinking. I have only thought of him as being a figure whom I feel I know, and I feel I am somewhat knowledgeable in this field, and one I feel I know is as much responsible as anybody else if perhaps not more than anybody else in this particular field of the weapon for our preeminence in that field. Too many reports came in to us as to the work that he was doing, the difficulties under which he was laboring, and they were difficulties because there had to be very great security precautions and a lot of barbed wire and what not which introduced serious human problems in connection with the plants where he was operating, and the reports all were that in spite of all this, and in spite of the little squabbles that took place among this confined group of scientists, there was a certain inspiration to their work and enthusiasm and a vigor and energy that many ascribed to Dr. Oppenheimer, and which I am quite clear played a major part in bringing about the achievement of the weapon at the critical point, and time that it was achieved. . . .

As I try to look back to that period, I think we would have taken pretty much anybody who had certainly the combination of those qualities, the theoretical ability, plus the practical sense, to advance our defense position in that field. In those days we were on guard against the Nazis and the Germans. I think we would have grabbed one of them if we thought he had that quality, and surrounded him with as much security precautions as we could. Indeed, I think we would have probably taken a convicted murderer if he had that capacity. There again is this question of the relative character of security. It depends somewhat on the day and age that you are in.

I want to emphasize particularly this affirmative side of it. The names we bandied about at that time included a number of refugees and a number of people that came from Europe. I have the impression—I may be wrong about it—but I have the impression that a very large element of this theoretical thinking did emanate from the minds of those who immigrated from this country, and had not been generated here as far as it had been in Europe. There were names like Fermi and Wigner and Teller, Rabi, another queer name, Szilard, or something like that—but I have the impression they came over here, and probably imbued with a certain anti-Nazi fervor which tended to stimulate thinking, and it is that type of mind that we certainly needed then.

We could find, so to speak, practical atomic physicists, and today there are great quantities of them being trained, and whether we are getting this finely balanced imagination which can stretch beyond the practicalities of this thing is to my mind the important aspect of this problem. The art is still in its infancy and we still are in need of great imagination in this field.

In a very real sense, therefore, I think there is a security risk in reverse. If anything is done which would in any way repress or dampen that fervor, that verve, that enthusiasm, or the feeling generally that the place where you can get the greatest opportunity for the expansion of your mind and your experiments in this field is the United States, to that extent the security of the United States is impaired.

In other words, you can't be too conventional about it or you run into a security problem the other way. We are only secure if we have the best brains and the best reach of mind in this field. If the impression is prevalent that scientists as a whole have to work under such great restrictions and perhaps great suspicion, in the United States, we may lose the next step in this field, which I think would be very dangerous for us. . . .

I will say that as far as I have had any acquaintance with Dr. Oppenheimer, I have no doubt as to his loyalty, and I have absolutely no doubt about his value to the United States and I would say he is not a security risk to the United States.

MR. GARRISON. Thank you.

MR. GRAY. Do you have any questions, Mr. Robb?

CROSS-EXAMINATION

By Mr. Robb:

Q. How long have you been president of the Chase National Bank?

A. A little over a year.

Q. Had you previously had experience in the banking business?

A. I was president of the so-called International Bank for Reconstruction and Development, which is known as the World Bank.

Q. Chase is the largest bank in the world?

A. No; it is the third. The Bank of America and National City are larger.

Q. Have you a great many branches?

A. Yes; 28.

Q. As far as you know, Mr. McCloy, do you have any employee of your bank who has been for any considerable period of time on terms of rather intimate and friendly association with thieves and safecrackers?

A. No; I don't know of anyone.

Q. I would like to ask you a few hypothetical questions, if I might, sir.

Suppose you had a branch bank manager, and a friend of his came to him one day and said, "I have some friends and contacts who are thinking about coming to your bank to rob it. I would like to talk to you about maybe leaving the vault open some night so they could do it," and your branch manager rejected the suggestion. Would you expect that branch manager to report the incident?

A. Yes.

Q. If he didn't report it, would you be disturbed about it?

A. Yes.

Q. Let us go a little bit further. Supposing the branch bank manager waited 6 or 8 months to report it, would you be rather concerned about why he had not done it before?

A. Yes.

Q. Suppose when he did report it, he said this friend of mine, a good friend of mine, I am sure he was innocent, and therefore I won't tell you who he is. Would you be concerned about that? Would you urge him to tell you?

A. I would certainly urge him to tell me for the security of the bank.

Q. Now, supposing your branch bank manager, in telling you the story of his conversations with his friend, said, "My friend told me that these people that he knows that want to rob the bank told me that they had a pretty good plan. They had some tear gas and guns and they had a car arranged for the getaway, and had everything all fixed up," would you conclude from that it was a pretty well-defined plot?

A. Yes.

Q. Now, supposing some years later this branch manager told you, "Mr. Mc-Cloy, I told you that my friend and his friends had a scheme all set up as I have told you, with tear gas and guns and getaway car, but that was a lot of bunk. It just wasn't true. I told you a false story about my friend." Would you be a bit puzzled as to why he would tell you such a false story about his friend?

A. Yes; I think I would be.

MR. ROBB. That is all. . . .

MR. GRAY. Mr. McCloy, following Mr. Robb's hypothetical question, for the moment, let us go further than his assumption. Let us say that ultimately you did get from your branch manager the name of the individual who had approached him with respect to leaving the vault open, and suppose further that your branch manager was sent by you on an inspection trip of some of your foreign branches, and suppose further that you learned that while he was in London he looked up the man who had made the approach to him some years before, would this be a source of concern to you?

THE WITNESS. Yes; I think it would. It is certainly something worthy of investigation, yes. . . .

MR. GRAY. So that you would say as of today that it is appropriate and proper to have this kind of an inquiry?

THE WITNESS. As far as I know, certainly if you have something there that trips your mind, you ought to make an inquiry about it.

MR. GRAY. I meant this proceeding that we are involved in.

THE WITNESS. Yes.

MR. GRAY. Would you take a calculated risk with respect to the security of your bank?

THE WITNESS. I take a calculated risk every day in my bank.

MR. GRAY. Would you leave someone in charge of the vaults about whom you have any doubt in your mind?

THE WITNESS. No, I probably wouldn't.

MR. GRAY. My question I can put in a more straightforward way, and it is one of the basic issues before the country, and certainly one involved in this country. And that is, when the paramount concern is the security of the country, which I believe is substantially the language of the Atomic Energy Act, can you allow yourself to entertain reasonable doubts?

Before you answer, let me say if this leads you to think that I or the members of the board have any conclusions about this matter at this point, I wish you would disabuse yourself of that notion.

THE WITNESS. Surely.

MR. GRAY. What I am trying to get at is this relates yourself in your discussion about the other things you have to take into consideration.

THE WITNESS. Surely. That brings me back again on this problem which I was checked a little because I was going a little far afield, and I don't think I can get the pat analogy to the bank vault man. But let me say, suppose that the man in charge of my vaults knew more about protection and knew more about the intricacies of time locks than anybody else in the world, I might think twice before I let him go, because I would balance the risks in this connection. . . .

One of my tasks in Germany was to pick up Nazi scientists and send them over to the United States. These Nazi scientists a few years before were doing their utmost to overthrow the United States Government by violence. They had a very suspicious background. They are being used now, I assume—whether they are still, I don't know, because I am not in contact with it—on very sensitive projects in spite of their background. The Defense Department has been certainly to some extent dependent upon German scientists in connection with guided missiles. I suppose other things being equal, you would like to have a perfectly pure, uncontaminated chap, with no background, to deal with these things, but it is not possible in this world. I think you do have to take risks in regard to the security of the country. As I said at the beginning, even if they put you—I won't be personal about it—but let us say put Mr. Stimson or anybody in charge of the innermost secrets of our defense system, there is a risk there. You can't avoid the necessity of balancing to some degree.

So I reemphasize from looking at it, I would think I would come to the conclusion if I were Secretary of War, let us balance all the considerations here and take the calculated risk. It is too bad you have to calculate sometimes. But in the last analysis, you have to calculate what is best for the United States, because there is no Maginot Line in terms—it is just as weak as the Maginot Line in terms of security. . . .

DR. EVANS. You think that there are very few scientists that could do Dr. Oppenheimer's work?

THE WITNESS. That is my impression.

DR. EVANS. That is, you think he knows perhaps more about this, as you mentioned in your vault business, than anybody else in the world?

THE WITNESS. I wouldn't say that; no. But I would certainly put him in the forefront.

DR. EVANS. And you would take a little chance on a man that has great value?

THE WITNESS. Yes, I would; particularly in the light of his other record, at least insofar as I know it. I can't divorce myself from my own impression of Dr. Oppenheimer and what appeals to me as his frankness, integrity, and his scientific background. I would accept a considerable amount of political immaturity, let me put it that way, in return for this rather esoteric, this rather indefinite theoretical thinking that I believe we are going to be dependent on for the next generation.

DR. EVANS. That is, you would look over the political immaturity and possible subversive connections and give the great stress to his scientific information?

THE WITNESS. Provided I saw indications which were satisfactory to me, that he had reformed or matured.

DR. EVANS. I have no more questions.

MR. GRAY. Mr. Garrison?

MR. GARRISON. I would like to put one question, if I may.

MR. GRAY. Yes.

REDIRECT EXAMINATION

By Mr. Garrison: . . .

Q. I would like to put one final question to you. Is it your opinion that in the light of the character, associations, and loyalty of Dr. Oppenheimer as you have known him, that his continued access to restricted data would not endanger the common defense and security?

A. That is my opinion.

MR. GARRISON. That is all.

MR. ROBB. That is all. Thank you, Mr. McCloy.

DAVID TRESSEL GRIGGS: "ZORC are the letters applied by a member of this group to the four people: Z is for Zacharias, O for Oppenheimer, R for Rabi, and C for Charlie Lauritsen"

[Of the scientists who testify against Oppenheimer, David Tressel Griggs has the closest connection to the military. A professor of geophysics at the University of California at Los Angeles, he took a leave of absence to serve as chief scientist of the air force from September 1, 1951, to June 30, 1952. In a discussion with Oppenheimer on May 23, 1952, Griggs said that the General Advisory Committee's 1949 recommendation against developing the H-bomb could have had disastrous consequences: "Oppenheimer asked if I thought he were Pro-Russian or just confused. After a moment I replied frankly that I wish I knew. He then asked if I had 'impugned his loyalty.' I replied that I had. He then said he thought I was paranoid."]

DIRECT EXAMINATION

By Mr. Robb: . . .

Q. May I ask you, sir, was there any particular reason at that time why you paid especial attention to any recommendations or views of Dr. Oppenheimer? . . .

THE WITNESS. It seems to me this question can be answered only in broad context, if you will allow me.

MR. GRAY. Yes; you may answer it any way that seems best to you, Mr. Griggs.

THE WITNESS. It seems obvious to me that what you are asking as I understand it is one of the purposes of these hearings, namely, to investigate loyalty. I want to say, and I can't emphasize too strongly, that Dr. Oppenheimer is the only one of my scientific acquaintances about whom I have ever felt there was a serious question as to their loyalty. The basis for this is not any individual contact that I have had with Dr. Oppenheimer or any detailed knowledge that I have had of his actions. But the basis is other than that and perhaps it is appropriate that I say what it is.

I first warned about this when I joined the Rand project, and was told that Dr. Oppenheimer had been considered during the Los Alamos days as a calculated risk. I heard very little more about this until I came to Washington as chief scientist for the Air Force.

In that capacity I was charged with working directly with General Vandenberg, who was then Chief of Staff of the Air Force, on matters of research and development, and I was charged with giving advice as requested to the Secretary of the Air Force, who was then Mr. Finletter. I worked closely with General Doolittle, who was Special Assistant to the Chief of the Air Force.

Shortly after I came to Washington I was told in a way that showed me it was no loosely thought out—let me correct that statement. I was told in a serious way that Mr. Finletter—or rather, I was told by Mr. Finletter that he had serious question as to the loyalty of Dr. Oppenheimer. I don't know in detail the basis for his fears. I didn't ask. I do know that he had access to the FBI files on Dr. Oppenheimer, at least I think I am correct in making that statement. I had this understanding.

I subsequently was informed from various sources of substantially the information which appeared in General Nichols' letter to Dr. Oppenheimer, which has been published. I feel I have no adequate basis for judging Dr. Oppenheimer's loyalty or disloyalty. Of course, my life would have been much easier had this question not arisen.

However, it was clear to me that this was not an irresponsible charge on the part of Mr. Finletter or on the part of General Vandenberg, and accordingly I had to take it into consideration in all our discussions and actions which had to do with the activities of Dr. Oppenheimer during that year. . . .

Q. Mr. Griggs, did there come a time when a project known as the Lincoln Summer Study was undertaken?

A. Yes.

Q. Can you tell us briefly what that was and when it took place?

A. May I answer a broader question in my own way?

Q. Yes. I am merely trying to bring these matters up and let you tell us about them in your own words.

A. It became apparent to us—by that I mean to Mr. Finletter, Mr. Borden, and Mr. Norton, that there was a pattern of activities all of which involved Dr. Oppenheimer. Of these one was the Vista project—I mean was his activity in the Vista project, and the things I have already talked about. We were told that in the late fall, I believe, of 1951, Oppenheimer and two other colleagues formed an informal committee of three to work for world peace or some such purpose, as they saw it. We were also told that in this effort they considered that many things were more important than the development of the thermonuclear weapon, specifically the air defense of the continental United States, which was the subject of the Lincoln Summer Study. No one could agree more than I that air defense is a vital problem and was at that time and worthy of all the scientific ingenuity and effort that could be put on it. We were, however, disturbed at the way in which this project was started.

It was further told me by people who were approached to join the summer study that in order to achieve world peace—this is a loose account, but I think it preserves the sense—it was necessary not only to strengthen the Air Defense of the continental United States, but also to give up something, and the thing that was recommended that we give up was the Strategic Air Command, or more properly I should say the strategic part of our total air power, which includes more than the Strategic Air Command. The emphasis was toward the Strategic Air Command. . . .

Q. There has been some mention of a group called ZORC. Was there any such group as that that you knew about?

A. ZORC are the letters applied by a member of this group to the four people, Z is for Zacharias, O for Oppenheimer, R for Rabi, and C for Charlie Lauritsen.

Q. Which member of the group applied it?

A. I heard it applied by Dr. Zacharias.

Q. When and under what circumstances?

A. It was in the fall of 1952 at a meeting of the Scientific Advisory Board in Boston—in Cambridge—at a time when Dr. Zacharias was presenting parts of a summary of the Lincoln Summer Study.

Q. In what way did he mention these letters? What were the mechanics of it?

A. The mechanics of it were that he wrote these three letters on the board—

DR. EVANS. Did you say three letters?

THE WITNESS. Four. You said three.

By Mr. Robb:

Q. That was my mistake. Wrote them on what board, a blackboard?

A. Yes.

Q. And explained what?

A. And explained that Z was Zacharias, O was Oppenheimer, R was Rabi, and C was Charlie Lauritsen.

Q. How many people were present?

A. This was a session of the Scientific Advisory Board, and there must have been between 50 and 100 people in the room. . . .

CROSS-EXAMINATION

By Mr. Silverman: . . .

Q. . . . I think you said in your direct testimony, did you not, that such question as you have as to Dr. Oppenheimer's loyalty was not based on any individual contact or detailed knowledge by you of his acts?

A. That is correct.

Q. I think you went further and said you did not feel that you really had an adequate basis for judging his loyalty or disloyalty.

A. That is certainly correct, and I think it is correct that I said it and it is certainly correct that I feel it.

Q. I think you also said that based on hearsay you have been suspicious or troubled about it for some time.

A. Troubled, yes.

Q. Would it be fair to say you have been suspicious of it for some time?

A. The circumstances which I pieced together by hearsay evidence, as I think I testified, were substantially similar to those that were listed among the allegations in General Nichols' letter were sufficient to cause me grave concern.

Q. Weren't you suspicious back at the time when you were first warned about Dr. Oppenheimer's loyalty when you joined the Rand project?

A. This, as I testified this morning, it was said to me that Dr. Oppenheimer during Los Alamos days had been considered a calculated risk. This statement was made to me by a person that I respect and it was not made as an idle statement. I took it seriously.

Q. And thereafter in your contacts with Dr. Oppenheimer you could not help being a little bit on your guard?

A. That is correct.

Q. And perhaps trying a little bit to see what might be beneath the surface of what Dr. Oppenheimer was saying?

A. That is correct. May I amplify this point?

Q. Certainly.

A. As I testified, particularly during my term with the Air Force as chief scientist for the Air Force—I don't want to emphasize this chief scientist business, because it doesn't mean anything, but this is just to identify the time that I am referring to—as I testified, I was on the opposite side of a pretty violent controversy from Dr. Oppenheimer in at least two cases. I was also on the opposite side—I mean on his side about people as to whom I had no question as to loyalty or motives. I have been involved in a great many—not a great many, but a number of pretty strong controversies in the military, and I think it is a fair general observation that when you get involved in a hot enough controversy; it is awfully hard not to question the motives of people who oppose you. This, I am sure, could not but have colored my views on the subject.

The nagging uncertainty in this particular case was the fact that I had heard the loyalty question raised by responsible people in a serious way.

If it ever comes to the day when we can't disagree and disagree violently in public and on national policy, then of course I feel that it will be a calamity for our democracy. I think perhaps I have said enough.

Q. I think since you candidly told us much of the information you have given is based not on your personal knowledge, I would like to review with you the items relating to Dr. Oppenheimer that you have of your own knowledge and see if those are correct. I will just run through them and see if they are correct as to your personal knowledge. . . .

Dr. Oppenheimer's views with respect to the Lincoln summer study, you know only by hearsay?

A. Except as they were expressed during the first 3 days of the study, yes.

Q. In those first 3 days, he didn't say anything about giving up strategic airpower?

A. No.

Q. And you know that Dr. Zacharias—

A. I might point out that after the first session—I think it was the first session—in which Dr. Oppenheimer had taken a fairly active part and he came up to me afterward and said, "Did I do all right?"

Q. And what did you say?

A. I said "Yes," or words to that effect.

Q. Were you just being polite?

A. No.

Q. And you were present when Dr. Zacharias wrote the initials "ZORC" on the blackboard?

A. Yes. . . .

Mr. Gray. When did this meeting take place at which Dr. Zacharias wrote the letters on the board, if you remember?

The Witness. That was at the Scientific Advisory Board meeting in Cambridge in, I believe, September of 1952. It was after the completion of at least the formal phases of the summer study, and it was on the occasion at which Dr. Zacharias was presenting some of the conclusions of the Lincoln summer study to the Scientific Advisory Board of the Air Force. . . .

Mr. Gray. Do you have any questions?

Dr. Evans. No.

Mr. Morgan. No.

Mr. Robb. No.

Mr. Silverman. I am just wondering on this business of Dr. Zacharias writing on the blackboard the initials ZORC.

Luis W. Alvarez: "I realized that the program that we were planning to start was not one that the top man in the scientific department of the AEC wanted to have done"

[Luis W. Alvarez, a professor of physics at the University of California at Berkeley, worked closely with Ernest Lawrence at the radiation laboratory. Lawrence, who could not appear at the hearing because of illness, urged Alvarez not to testify for fear that they would be regarded as part of an anti-Oppenheimer cabal. When Alvarez agreed not to appear, he received a phone call from Lewis Strauss, who "wondered what my excuse was for letting him down. . . . Lewis's emotional intensity increased as he ran out of arguments. As a parting shot he prophesied that if I didn't come to Washington the next day I wouldn't be able to look myself in the mirror for the rest of my life." Alvarez finally decided "that I really would be ashamed to think that I'd been intimidated. So I poured myself a stiff drink, (and) booked a seat on the TWA midnight red-eye flight."]

DIRECT EXAMINATION

By Mr. Robb: . . .

Q. Doctor, directing your attention to September 1949 when the Russians exploded their first atomic bomb, did that cause some concern on your part?

A. Yes; it caused a great deal of concern on my part. I tried to make up my mind what was the right thing to do. I had been spending 4 years doing basic research again. I think of it as sort of being recharged after 5 years of military development work. I had to take awhile to get back into the frame of mind of a practicing physicist. I had been concentrating my attention on that phase of my career and now, suddenly, it appeared that a crisis had arrived and perhaps I should get back into the field of atomic energy.

Q. Why did you think a crisis had arrived?

A. The Russians had exploded an atomic bomb, and I thought that our own program had not been going terribly fast. It certainly had not been going at nearly the rate it had during the war, but this is quite natural.

Q. Did you discuss with any of your colleagues what ought to be done?

A. Yes; I did. I saw Professor Lawrence the next day, and I told him that I thought we should look seriously into the business of constructing the super weapon which had, as far as I knew, been neglected in this 4-year period. I had not followed the situation closely enough to be sure that it had been neglected but that was my impression.

Q. Did you make any inquiry to see whether or not your feeling was correct as to whether it had been neglected?

A. Yes. Professor Lawrence and I got on the phone that afternoon and called Edward Teller at Los Alamos and asked him if we could come down and talk to him in the near future, and, as I remember, within a day or two, we took a plane to Los Alamos where we did talk to Dr. Teller and found out the present rather inadequate status of the super program.

Q. Beginning at about that time and the next few weeks, Doctor, did you keep any notes in the form of a diary as to what your activities were in respect of a program for the development of the super bomb?

A. Yes; I did. . . .

Q. Do you have it with you, Doctor, the original of that diary?

A. Yes, I have my typewritten sheets here. They cover the period of about 3 weeks from the time the Russian bomb was dropped.

Q. Typewritten or longhand?

A. They are in longhand. . . .

Q. I would like to run this through with you and ask you to amplify.

"October 5, 1949. Latimer and I independently thought that the Russians could be working hard on the super and might get there ahead of us. The only thing to do seems to get there first—but hope that it will turn out to be impossible."

Would you explain to us what you meant by that "hope that it will turn out to be impossible."

A. By that I meant that there might be some fundamental reason in the physics of the bomb that would prevent anyone from making it work just in the same sense that people have often said that you cannot make a thermonuclear weapon that will burn up the atmosphere and the ocean. I hoped that some such law would prevail and keep anyone from building it, because then our stockpile of atomic weapons gave us the lead on the Russians.

Q. You mean if it turned out that it would violate some law of nature the Russians could not make it either?

A. That is right, because if they did make it, that would give them a great jump ahead of us and essentially nullify our stockpile of atomic weapons.

DR. EVANS. The laws of thermodynamics might tell you it could not be done?

THE WITNESS. Yes, something of that sort.

By Mr. Robb:

Q. You thought you ought to find out.

A. I said we can't trust this hope, but let us find out. . . .

Q. Did you have any reason to believe at that time that Dr. Oppenheimer would not be ready to go ahead with this program?

A. Of course not. The most enthusiastic person I had ever met on the program of the super weapon was Dr. Oppenheimer. . . .

Q. "October 24, Monday: Made several telephone calls. . . .

"Talked with Teller, who had just met Fermi at airport in Chicago. No reaction from Fermi, as he was tired from his long trip from Italy. Said he felt he could count on Bethe. Felt Oppie was lukewarm to our project and Conant was definitely opposed. Said Los Alamos was trying to set up conference for Nov. 7." . . .

You talked with Teller and so forth. Where did you talk with him?

A. I can't recall.

Q. Was it by phone or in person?

A. I suppose it was by phone, but I really could not be sure. I gather from the entries on this Monday that I was in Berkeley, and I don't recall that Teller came to Berkeley in that period, so I assume it was by phone.

Q. Do you recall whether you knew why he thought he could count on Bethe?

A. I assume that he had had conversations with Bethe and Bethe agreed that the super program should be reactivated. I can't give any definite testimony because he just told me that.

Q. The next item: "Felt Oppie was lukewarm to our project and Conant was definitely opposed."

Does that require any amplification?

A. This is quoting Dr. Teller if I read my notes correctly. I had no conversation with Dr. Oppenheimer on this subject, and I had no reason to feel that he would not be enthusiastic about it. In fact, I assumed he was enthusiastic as were all the other people with whom I talked.

Q. "Said Los Alamos was trying to set up conferences for November 7." Conferences for what?

A. This was the conference that I believe was referred to in one of the first day's notes. Dr. Teller said he thought it would be an excellent idea to bring together all of the men who had thought about problems of the super during the war, together with new theoretical physicists, young ones who had appeared on the scene since the war, and to discuss the present state of the art, to see what new things had come in, just a sort of reorientation conference, I think.

Q. Did that conference come off?

A. That conference as far as I know never did come off. . . .

Q. "October 25, 1949—Tuesday: . . . Talked to Serber about GAC meeting. He volunteered to see Oppie before the meeting. Called Oppie who said he had hoped to be able to talk to him. Therefore Serber is going with us tomorrow and will continue to Princeton and have a day with Oppie, before he leaves for meeting in Washington. . . .

"Chicago meeting—then on to Washington—talked with all GAC and most of AEC Commissioners. Particularly interesting talk with Oppie just after he briefed Bradbury and Norstad at GAC meeting. Pretty foggy thinking."

That is the last entry in your diary?

A. That is right, because after that the project was dead. . . .

Q. Talked to Serber about GAC meeting. Where did that conversation take place?

A. That took place in Berkeley. Could I expand a bit on that?

Q. Would you do that, please sir?

A. Yes. As I said earlier, Dr. Serber was one of the group that had expressed a willingness to work hard on the program of building heavy-water piles. He was to be our chief theoretical adviser, and we were counting on his help.

There is one thing in here which is not written down, and I think I am correct in remembering it this way. I believe I called Dr. Oppenheimer from Berkeley and asked him if I could see him before the General Advisory Commission meeting to talk over our plans. You will note that in this whole diary there is no mention of any talks between me and Dr. Oppenheimer. I was anxious in view of the fact that I had heard that he was lukewarm to the program to have a chance to brief him on the program and if possible to get a little enthusiasm on his part.

As I remember it, Dr. Oppenheimer said he would be very glad to see me in Princeton, and in fact invited me to stay overnight in their guestroom.

Then it turned out that our time in Chicago was limited and I thought I had better stay and talk pile design because I had spoken with Dr. Serber about this meeting with Oppenheimer and Serber said he would be glad to present our case to Dr. Oppenheimer and try to convince him of its worthwhileness. So essentially I deputized Dr. Serber to transmit my point of view to Dr. Oppenheimer. In fact, I was glad to do so, because Dr. Serber and Dr. Oppenheimer are somewhat closer friends than Dr. Oppenheimer and I. They have been closer personally. Dr. Oppenheimer and I were certainly excellent friends at the time and Dr. Serber, I thought, could perhaps do a little better job than I could. I thought and felt strongly that he would present the point of view which was the laboratory point of view at that time, namely, that this was a very worthwhile program and we should get it going.

Q. You had no doubt at all about Dr. Serber's enthusiasm for your program?

A. Absolutely none.

Q. Do you know whether Dr. Serber did go to Princeton to see Dr. Oppenheimer?

A. Yes, he did. . . .

Q. You mention here, "Particularly interesting talk with Oppie just after he briefed Bradbury and Norstad at GAC meeting." Were you at that GAC meeting?

A. No; I had no reason to be at that GAC meeting. That was a closed meeting, if I remember correctly, at which time the Commissioners met with the GAC, and the top military men in the country.

Q. Where were you?

A. I was standing inside the main entrance to the Atomic Energy Commission building and I watched my friends go upstairs, and I saw the famous military men whom I recognized from their pictures follow along. The meeting lasted for some while. I watched the people come back out again and in a few minutes Dr. Oppenheimer came along and invited Dr. Serber and I, who were standing together outside the building, to have lunch with him.

Q. Did you have lunch with him?

A. Yes. We went to a small restaurant in the immediate neighborhood of the Commission building, and that was the first occasion that Dr. Oppenheimer told me of his views on the building of the hydrogen bomb.

Q. What did he tell you?

A. He said that he did not think the United States should build the hydrogen bomb, and the main reason that he gave for this if my memory serves me correctly, and I think it does, was that if we built a hydrogen bomb, then the Russians would build a hydrogen bomb, whereas if we did not build a hydrogen bomb, then the Russians would not build a hydrogen bomb.

I found this such an odd point of view that I don't understand it to this day. I told Dr. Oppenheimer that he might find that a reassuring point of view, but I didn't think that very many people in the country would accept that point of view.

Q. Was Dr. Serber present?

A. Dr. Serber was present and agreed with Dr. Oppenheimer and this surprised me greatly in view of the fact that 2 or 3 days before he had gone to see Dr. Oppenheimer telling me that he would try to convert Dr. Oppenheimer's lukewarmness into some enthusiasm for our project.

Q. What was the impact of all this on you?

A. Well, for the first time I realized that the program that we were planning to start was not one that the top man in the scientific department of the AEC wanted to have done. We thought that we were doing this as a public service. We were interrupting our own work to do this job. We certainly were not going to try to force anybody to take these piles. We had thought all along that everyone would be enthusiastic about having a big source of free neutrons.

Q. Did you stay in Washington until the end of the GAC meeting?

A. I believe I left right away after my conversation with Dr. Oppenheimer. I have no way of refreshing my memory on that. I felt that the program was dead, and that is the reason the diary ends at this point.

Q. Until revived by the Presidential pronouncement in January 1950, was the program dead?

A. Dr. Teller was still working at Los Alamos and as far as I know that was all that was going on in the program.

Q. What did you do?

A. As I remember I went back to doing physics.

Q. Did you reflect on this development which you observed in your conversation with Dr. Oppenheimer?

A. Yes, I did. Of course, I later became aware of the contents of the GAC policy memorandum to the Atomic Energy Commission. I was not allowed to read it because there was no particular reason for me to do so, but I was told that the GAC had said that the United States should not build the hydrogen weapon. I have since heard a great deal of talk about the fact that the GAC was opposing a crash program, but after rereading some of the document last night that is not my impression of what it said.

Q. Which document do you refer to?

A. The GAC policy report. . . .

Q. Now, directing your attention to a time perhaps a couple of months after your return from Washington in 1949, I will ask you if you will recall a conversation with Dr. Vannevar Bush about Dr. Oppenheimer?

A. Yes.

Q. Could you tell us what that was and the circumstances? . . .

What Dr. Bush said to Professor Lawrence and me was that he had been appointed by the President to head an ad hoc committee to assess the evidence for the Russian explosion. The Atomic Energy Commission and the Armed Forces, particularly the Air Force, had collected a good deal of information, all of which tended to indicate that the Russians had exploded a bomb, but before announcing that to the public the President wanted to make sure that the evidence was conclusive. If I remember Dr. Bush correctly, he said that he was made chairman of that. If I can paraphrase Dr. Bush's statement and give them in the first person, they went something like this. He said, "You know, it is a funny thing that I should be made head of such a committee, because I really don't know the technical facts in this field. I am not an atomic physicist, and I am not the one to assess these matters." But, he said, "I think the reason the President chose me is that he does not trust Dr. Oppenheimer and he wants to have someone in whom he has trust as head of this committee."

Dr. Bush then said that the meetings of the committee were very interesting. In fact, he found them humorous in one respect, because he said, "I was ostensibly the chairman of the committee. I called it to order, and as soon as it was called to order, Dr. Oppenheimer took charge as chairman and did most of the questioning." I believe Dr. Bush said that Dr. Oppenheimer wrote the report. This was the first time that I had ever heard anyone in my life say that Dr. Oppenheimer was not to be trusted.

DR. EVANS. Would you make that statement again?

THE WITNESS. This was the first time that anyone had ever said in my presence that Dr. Oppenheimer was not to be trusted. . . .

By Mr. Robb:

Q. Dr. Alvarez, coming now to the winter of 1950, did you serve on a committee called the Long Range Planning Committee?

A. Yes; I did. I did that at the request of Dr. Oppenheimer who called me and said, "We are having a meeting of a committee to try to find out the future of the military applications of atomic energy." He said, "I would like to have you on this committee because I know you represent a point different from mine, and I think it would be healthy to have you on this committee." I felt very happy about this. I thought Dr. Oppenheimer was being very fair in inviting me to join this committee, and I accepted the appointment. . . .

Q. Go ahead, Doctor.

A. There was a good deal of discussion about tactical weapons, small weapons, using small amounts of fissionable materials. There was discussion of the tactical use of these weapons. General Nichols briefed us on the present status of the guided-missiles program, of which he was then Deputy

Director, since there was much interest in the use of atomic warheads on guided missiles. This part of the program I thought was in competent hands so I didn't have much to say one way or the other. I thought Dr. Lauritsen and Oppenheimer handled this part of the program very well, and I had no disagreement with this.

I found, however, that I was in serious disagreement with them on one point and that was that they thought that the hydrogen program was going to interfere seriously with the small-weapons program by taking away manpower at Los Alamos which could otherwise be put on the hydrogen bomb. My view was that the things were not mutually exclusive, if I can use the scientific phraseology. That is, there was no reason to say we have to have hydrogen bombs and not small weapons and vice versa. It seemed to me that there were great resources of scientific manpower in the country and that one could have both of these programs simultaneously. I did not object to the small-weapon program because it would interfere with the hydrogen bomb and I was surprised that they objected to the hydrogen-bomb program because it would interfere with the small-weapons program.

Q. Did Dr. Oppenheimer have anything to say specifically about the hydrogen-bomb program being carried on?

A. I remember one statement that Dr. Oppenheimer made because it shocked me so greatly and I repeated it to several people when I got home. I remember telling Professor Lawrence about it, and I believe I told Dr. Cooksey. Again if I can be excused for paraphrasing and using first person, Dr. Oppenheimer said essentially this: "We all agree that the hydrogen-bomb program should be stopped, but if we were to stop it or to suggest that it be stopped, this would cause so much disruption at Los Alamos and in other laboratories where they are doing instrumentation work that I feel that we should let it go on, and it will die a natural death with the coming tests"—which were the Greenhouse tests—"when those tests fail. At that time will be the natural time to chop the hydrogen-bomb program off."

I assumed I had been put on this committee to present views in favor of the hydrogen bomb because I had been always of that point of view. I didn't object to Dr. Oppenheimer's statement, because he said that he was not planning to stop the program. My feeling at the time was that if the Greenhouse test failed, and then Dr. Oppenheimer or the GAC did something to stop the hydrogen-bomb program, then would be a good time to fight. It seemed to me to be quite useless to express disapproval of this because nothing was being done to stop the program.

However, I found later much to my dismay that my own political naivete in matters of this kind led me astray and I found that the report which I signed, and I am sorry to say I signed, did do the program great harm.

Q. Why?

A. Dr. Teller saw me several months later, and he said, "Luis, how could you have ever signed that report, feeling the way you do about hydrogen bombs?" I said, "Well, I didn't see anything wrong with it. It said the hydrogen-bomb program was an important long-range program. Our particular emphasis was on small weapons, but that is a program which has no standing in the Commission's program now, and I think we should go ahead with it." He said, "You go back and read that report and you will find that that essentially says that the hydrogen-bomb program is interfering with the small-weapons program, and it has caused me no end of trouble at Los Alamos. It is being used against our program. It is slowing it down and it could easily kill it." I have recently reread that report in the last day, and I am also shocked as was Dr. Teller. I can only say in my defense that I have not spent much time on policy reports, staff papers, and things of that sort, and I am not attuned to them and I didn't catch this implication. I should have done so, and I didn't.

Q. Who wrote it?

A. Dr. Oppenheimer wrote it. I think that probably Dr. Lauritsen and Dr. Bacher and I made minor changes in it, but certainly the main draft was written by Dr. Oppenheimer.

[Robb's direct examination concludes at 5:35 P.M., and so a recess is taken, with testimony scheduled to resume the following morning.]

Friday, April 30

[Luis W. Alvarez appears and completes his testimony.]

DIRECT EXAMINATION

By Mr. Robb:

Q. Dr. Alvarez, your diary showed, and you testified that you talked to various individuals about your plan and the plans of others for the development of the thermonuclear weapon in early October 1949; is that right?

A. Yes, sir.

Q. At that time these individuals were enthusiastic for going ahead with it; is that right?

A. That was my very strong impression.

Q. To your knowledge, were those conversations in advance of any talks that these people had with Dr. Oppenheimer?

A. I think that is so, sir. I am sure it is so in the case of Dr. Serber. I am quite sure in the case of Drs. DuBridge and Bacher, and also in the case of Dr. Rabi.

Q. Subsequently these people changed their views; is that right?

A. Quite drastically; yes.

Q. Did you learn at that time whether in the interim they had talked to Dr. Oppenheimer?

A. I am sure that in the interim they talked with Dr. Oppenheimer, because the interim extends until now.

MR. ROBB. That is all I care to ask on direct, Mr. Chairman.

MR. GRAY. Mr. Silverman.

CROSS-EXAMINATION

By Mr. Silverman:

Q. Self evidently these people have talked to a lot of other people?

A. That is absolutely right. . . .

Q. . . . I would like now to turn to the discussions in the panel—I think perhaps you called it the panel on long-range planning, something like that.

A. I believe that was the official name.

Q. I believe you called it that. I am not sure. It may have been referred to at other times as the Military Objectives Committee?

A. Perhaps it was.

Q. In December 1950, you referred to a statement by Dr. Oppenheimer somewhat to the effect that we all agree that the hydrogen-bomb program should be stopped. If we did this and recommended it, it would cause too much disruption at Los Alamos?

A. That is right.

Q. And let it go on and the project would die when the Greenhouse test failed, as Dr. Oppenheimer expected them to. Is that substantially correct?

A. That is substantially the way I remember it, yes.

Q. I would like you to turn to the first part of that statement that we all agree that the hydrogen-bomb program should be stopped. I want to ask you whether it is possible that what Dr. Oppenheimer said was that "We all agree that the hydrogen-bomb program does not look very hopeful now."

A. No, I am quite sure I remember it the other way. It was such a startling statement to me that it is indelibly in my mind. I don't think I could be mistaken on that.

Q. You of course were a representative of the other view?

A. That is right.

Q. And when Dr. Oppenheimer said that "We all agree that the hydrogen-bomb program should be stopped," did you as a member of the panel say, "We don't all agree; I don't."

A. I didn't interrupt him until he finished his statement at the end of which time, as he pointed out, he said he was not going to stop it, and I pointed out since he said he was not going to stop it, there seemed to be no point in arguing about it.

Q. But you did not correct him and say "We do not all agree."

A. No. I am sure from what I have said in this hearing you would know that I did not agree.

Q. It is sometimes necessary on cross-examination to emphasize points.

A. Very well, sir. Had he stopped his statement with that first sentence, I am sure that I would have dissented vigorously.

Q. Was it the fact that everybody there agreed that at that time the hydrogen bomb program did not look very hopeful?

A. I don't know whether everyone did agree on that.

Q. Did you think at that time that the hydrogen bomb program did not look very hopeful?

A. I thought it looked exceedingly hopeful. Again I can only see it through the eyes of people like Edward Teller, who have the technical competence, who know the details of the program. I am not a theoretical physicist. All I can do is base my judgment on people in whom I have great scientific trust.

Q. Wasn't everybody pretty depressed in December 1950?

A. No. I certainly didn't sense that at all, but I was not at Los Alamos. I did not know that things were going very badly. Perhaps they were, I don't know. I was not aware of the fact that people were depressed.

Q. And you had not heard from other people working on the project in December of 1950 that things didn't look so good?

A. I had heard that the requirements for tritium had temporarily taken a turn toward larger quantities being required. But I had seen the requirements go up and down and up and down on many occasions, and this did not disturb me at all. . . .

Q. I think you said that Dr. Oppenheimer indicated that he thought that the Greenhouse tests would fail.

A. Yes.

Q. Just what does that mean?

A. That no thermonuclear reaction would take place in the Greenhouse test explosive device. In order for a thermonuclear reaction to take place, very high temperatures must be reached, as you know. I think that Dr. Oppenheimer felt that those high temperatures would not be reached, if you can permit me to read his mind.

Q. I would rather you tell us what he said.

A. I have already told you what he said.

MR. ROBB. Mr. Chairman, everybody else is reading Dr. Oppenheimer's mind.

MR. GRAY. The Chair will say that there has been a parade of witnesses here who testified on their intimate knowledge of Dr. Oppenheimer, and that they would know exactly what his reaction would be in any particular situation. I do not think this witness should be denied an opportunity to make his own guess about what Dr. Oppenheimer might think.

MR. SILVERMAN. I do not wish to cut a witness off. I would point out between opinion evidence testimony as to a man's character and evidence as to what a man was thinking about a scientific project.

MR. GRAY. I will ask you, Mr. Silverman, if you have not asked witnesses in this proceeding what did Dr. Oppenheimer think about so-and-so.

MR. SILVERMAN. I would certainly not be prepared to say—

MR. GRAY. Would it surprise you to learn that you have asked such a question?

MR. WITNESS. Could I be allowed to say what I was going to say in a different way? I testified that Dr. Oppenheimer made a certain statement, that he thought the thing would fail. There are only two possibilities that the thing should fail, as far as I can see. One is that the device misfired. When the button was pressed, nothing happened. Certainly the atomic bomb primer of the device would work. We have great experience in this line. After that fired, then the temperature of the reactants would rise. If they rose high enough, I doubt if you could find a scientist in the world who would not agree that the thermonuclear reaction would take place. It is taking place in the sun all the time. Therefore, when Dr. Oppenheimer said that the thing would fail, it could mean to me only one thing, namely, that he thought the temperature would not rise high enough. That is why I said I thought I could read his mind.

By Mr. Silverman: . . .

Q. You ultimately signed the report.

A. Yes.

Q. And there is a part of it that you have regretted signing?

A. The thing that I regret is that the report was used to slow down the hydrogen bomb program. The statements having to do with the hydrogen bomb come in the last three paragraphs, save for one rather trivial one.

Q. Did Dr. Oppenheimer use the report to slow down the hydrogen bomb program?

A. I don't know who used the report. I have had Edward Teller tell me, as I said yesterday, that the report was used to slow down the program.

Q. This being a matter where Dr. Oppenheimer personally is very seriously concerned, it becomes a matter of considerable importance as to whether Dr. Oppenheimer used it.

A. Dr. Oppenheimer wrote the report, I am sure. Dr. Oppenheimer ordered the statements presumably in the order of the importance he attached to them, and the super was more or less damned by faint praise. . . .

Q. I think you said Dr. Oppenheimer invited you as the representative of the opposite view.

A. He said as much. As I said, I admired him for doing that.

Q. And you considered yourself the representative of the opposite view?

A. I think that is true, yes.

Q. And that was the opposite view on the hydrogen bomb?

A. That is right. . . .

MR. GRAY. Do you have any questions, Dr. Evans?

DR. EVANS. I have some questions; yes.

Dr. Alvarez, you have been asked a good many questions and been sitting on that chair quite a time, and that main thing that we have gotten out of you is that you have tried to show that Dr. Oppenheimer was opposed to the development of the super weapon; is that true?

THE WITNESS. I believe that has been known for a long time, and I think I just have given some corroborative testimony in this regard.

DR. EVANS. What does this mean in your mind—anything?

THE WITNESS. By itself it means absolutely nothing because I have many other friends in the scientific world who feel precisely this way. The point I was trying to bring out was that every time I have found a person who felt this way, I have seen Dr. Oppenheimer's influence on that person's mind. I don't think there is anything wrong with this. I would certainly try to persuade people of my point of view, and Dr. Oppenheimer is quite free and should try to persuade people of his convictions. I just point out the facts as I see them, that this reaction has always taken place in the people that I know who have been opposed to the bomb.

DR. EVANS. It doesn't mean that he was disloyal?

THE WITNESS. Absolutely not, sir.

DR. EVANS. Might it mean that he had moral scruples about the development of the atomic bomb?

THE WITNESS. I have heard that he has. He has never expressed them to me. I told you the one occasion on which Dr. Oppenheimer expressed to me his reasons for not wanting to build the hydrogen bomb, and it had nothing to do with morals, in the usual sense.

DR. EVANS. You think it might have been peculiar for him to have moral scruples after he had been so active in developing the atomic bomb?

THE WITNESS. I have never had any moral scruples about having worked on the atomic bomb, because I felt that the atomic bomb saved countless lives, both Japanese and American. Had the war gone on for another week, I am sure that the fire raids on the Japanese cities would have killed more people than were killed in the atomic bombs. I am also quite convinced that the atomic bomb stopped the invasion of Japan, and therefore saved well over 100,000 American lives. I believe there are estimates of up to a half million.

DR. EVANS. Don't we always have moral scruples when a new weapon is produced?

THE WITNESS. That is a question I can't answer, sir.

DR. EVANS. After the battle of Hastings, a little before my time—

MR. SILVERMAN. Would you give the time, sir?

DR. EVANS. I cannot give the time, but it was before I was born.

MR. SILVERMAN. That is 1066, sir.

DR. EVANS. There was great talk about ostracizing the long bow, because it was so strong that it could fire an arrow with such force, it occasionally pierced armor and killed a man. They felt they ought to outlaw it.

When the Kentucky rifle came in, it was so deadly that they talked of getting rid of it. When we had poison gas, I made a lot of lectures about it, that it was terrible. So we have had that after every new weapon that has been developed.

THE WITNESS. Yes, I recognize that.

DR. EVANS. This opposition that Dr. Oppenheimer had, might he have been jealous that someone else was becoming prominent in this field, rather than himself?

THE WITNESS. I don't think so; no.

DR. EVANS. You don't think so?

THE WITNESS. No.

DR. EVANS. Do you think that Dr. Oppenheimer had considerable power with men like Conant, Bush, and Groves?

THE WITNESS. I don't think power is the right word. Dr. Oppenheimer is certainly one of the most persuasive men that has ever lived, and he certainly had influence. They respected his opinions and listened to him.

DR. EVANS. Looking by hindsight, do you think he showed good judgment in the fact that he opposed this bomb in the light of present conditions?

THE WITNESS. I think he showed exceedingly poor judgment. I told him so the first time he told me he was opposed to it. I have continued to think so. The thing which I thought at that time was the overpowering reason for building the hydrogen bomb was that if we did not do it, some day we might wake up and read headlines and see pictures of an explosion such as we saw a month or so ago, only this would be done off the coast of Siberia. I felt sure that this would be one of the most disastrous things that could possibly happen to this country. I thought we must not let this happen.

DR. EVANS. His opposition to it, might it mean that he feared the spending of a large sum of money and the using of time on a project that would not work and might thus endanger the security of our country by not going ahead with a project that we knew would work?

THE WITNESS. I think he has expressed an opinion somewhat as you just stated it. . . .

DR. EVANS. Were there a number of other men in the country that could have built the A-bomb?

THE WITNESS. I am sure that there are. I don't want in any way to minimize Dr. Oppenheimer's contribution, because to my way of thinking he did a truly outstanding job at Los Alamos. I think he was one of the greatest directors of a military program that this country has ever seen. I stand in awe of the job he did at Los Alamos. . . .

REDIRECT EXAMINATION

By Mr. Robb: . . .

Q. You testified as others did that Dr. Oppenheimer did a splendid job at Los Alamos. Did it strike you as peculiar that one who had done such a splendid job at Los Alamos could entertain opinions which you considered so wrong in respect of the hydrogen bomb?

A. I was very surprised when I found that he had these opinions, since he had used the super as the primary incentive to get me to join the Manhattan District in the first place. He had spent almost a solid afternoon telling me about the exciting possibilities of the super, and asked me to join and help with the building of such a device. So I was therefore very surprised when I found he had these objections. You will note in my diary that I had no hint of this until essentially the last entry.

Q. To use a homely simile, did it strike you as peculiar that such a wonderful batter as Dr. Oppenheimer should suddenly begin striking out the way he did?

A. It certainly struck me as peculiar.

Q. One further question, Doctor. Have you had any hesitation in answering questions here or in any way restricted your testimony in answer to any question put to you because of the presence here of Dr. Oppenheimer and his counsel?

A. No. I must confess that it is a little hard for personal reasons to say some of the things that I have said, but I have said them anyway.

Lloyd K. Garrison: "The adversary process which we seem to be engaged in should be carried out to the fullest extent"

[Lloyd Garrison now requests permission to see the documentary record regarding the AEC's clearance of Oppenheimer in 1947, particularly any "items of derogatory information." Claiming that this would require the disclosure of confidential FBI reports, Gordon Gray rejects the request.]

Mr. Garrison. . . . If I might just recapitulate for a moment to explain the nature of the request, I previously referred to the fact that back in the middle of February, I asked for the minutes and documents relating to the question of the clearance of Dr. Oppenheimer by the AEC in 1947 . . .

To put it in nontechnical terms, what I would like to ask the board to request of the Commission that we have a statement in as much detail as classification will permit of the items of derogatory information which were contained in the files that went to the members of the Commission. . . .

I don't want to make a great thing out of this. I am not going to argue to this board that the action which the Commission took in 1947 was in any way conclusive or binding upon this board at all. I don't want to make such an argument. I do say it is quite relevant to consider what those five men who knew Dr. Oppenheimer and went through the report thought and believed at that time. . . .

Mr. Gray. I would like to state the impression of the chairman of the board, and be corrected if I am wrong. . . .

Now, with respect to the current request which, if I understand it correctly, is a list of all items of so-called derogatory information about Dr.

Oppenheimer in the hands of this board, again I would have to respond that information which is contained in FBI reports cannot be made available.

I think I shall have to stop my observation at that point. It may be that my interpretation of the procedures under which we operate is faulty, and I would ask counsel for the board if he has anything to add to what I said.

MR. ROBB. I certainly agree that your interpretation is entirely correct, Mr. Chairman. I would add only one observation, which is that so far as we are able to bring it together, all the information and reports which were before the Commission in 1947 are now before this board for its consideration and its evaluation.

Of course, as the chairman has said, the FBI reports under the rules of these hearings may not be made available to counsel for Dr. Oppenheimer or Dr. Oppenheimer.

MR. GRAY. Let me make one other observation. I suppose it would be reasonable for counsel to assume that the board in its effort to get at the truth with respect to any matter of very material consequence has sought to have light thrown on such a matter of material consequence. This, of course, involves, I am sure, the question of anybody's reliance on the good faith of this board. What I am trying to say is that I do not think you are materially disadvantaged by not having the detailed list of information which you have requested.

MR. GARRISON. I would like to make just one observation. I want to make it clear, Mr. Chairman, that so far as the fairness of the members of this board and their desire to do the right thing, I have no doubt whatever. My problem is one of knowing what seems to us to be relevant so that we may comment upon if as one should in presenting Dr. Oppenheimer's case, as well as we can. In a process of this kind I should suppose that the adversary process which we seem to be engaged in should be carried out to the fullest extent that it can be done within the limits of the governmental regulations with respect to the preservation of whatever has to be confidential, that this process will aid rather than to the contrary in the deliberations of the board.

I would like to make one or two things clear in the February discussions and correspondence. The Commission did, indeed, say to Dr. Oppenheimer that he might inspect minutes and reports of the GAC meetings in which he participated, and could also see any documents which he himself signed. What I am talking about here is the action of the Commission in 1947. I am not asking that the FBI reports be disclosed. I appreciate the rule that the reports of the Federal Bureau of Investigation shall not be disclosed to the individual or to his representative. I regretfully have to accept that rule. It does seem to me, however, that, since in the very letter of General Nichols with which we are concerned a very lengthy account is given of numerous derogatory items in the file and disclosure has been made of that, I cannot see how it would violate this rule to have us informed as to the derogatory items which were before the board in 1947. I am not asking for a transcript of the reports or a copy of the reports, but simply for a description of what the board acted on—I mean the Commission acted on.

MR. ROBB. Mr. Chairman, as I interpret Mr. Garrison's last remark, he does not want a copy of the reports or the transcripts of the reports; he merely wants to know their contents, which seems to me to fly right in the face of the rule. I am sorry.

MR. GARRISON. Let me ask this final question: Would it fly in the face of the rule if we were limited merely to being told which of the items now before the board were before the Commission in 1947?

MR. ROBB. I think it would, Mr. Chairman.

MR. GARRISON. I just don't understand that, Mr. Chairman, as to why we can't be told of these items that such-and-such were before the board and such-and-such were not. What disclosure of FBI reports is that any more than this letter itself is a disclosure of FBI reports?

MR. GRAY. I believe that what was before the Commission in 1947, and certainly from the testimony here, cannot be certain, because the recollection of the four former Commissioners who have testified here is uniformly hazy as to what happened. I hope that is not an incorrect statement about their testimony. With respect, in any event, to what was before them at that time we are not certain. I believe what was before them at that time was FBI reports. It seems to me that comes into the rule.

I would make this further observation: That if counsel wishes at some subsequent point in these proceedings to argue the import of the actions of the Commission insofar as they can be reconstructed in 1947, whether February, March, or August, that opportunity will be given. As far as this board is concerned, we must be concerned with everything before us; and what the Commission did in 1947 is, of course, important, but, as you say, not conclusive.

BORIS T. PASH: "Dr. Oppenheimer knew the name of the man, and it was his duty to report it to me"

[The son of a bishop of the Russian Orthodox Greek Church, Boris T. Pash grew up in San Francisco, learned to speak fluent Russian, and entered the U.S. Army's counterintelligence branch during the war. From 1949 to 1952 he worked with the Central Intelligence Agency. At the time he testifies, he is chief of the counterintelligence division in the office of G-2, Headquarters, Sixth Army. When interviewed by Robb and Rolander in March, Pash said that when he read the newspaper accounts of the espionage activities of

Klaus Fuchs, "he felt that he would next be reading about Dr. Oppenheimer's involvement in such activities."]

DIRECT EXAMINATION

By Mr. Robb: . . .

Q. Coming to May 1943, Colonel, I will ask you whether or not at or about that time you began an investigation into certain reported espionage taking place or which had taken place at the Radiation Laboratory in Berkeley?

A. Yes, sir; we did. . . .

Q. At or about that time did you receive certain information from Lt. Lyall Johnson concerning statements made to him by Dr. Oppenheimer?

A. I did. Lyall Johnson reported to me toward the end of August that Dr. Oppenheimer came to him and made some statements which he felt I should know about. My reaction was to request an immediate interview with Dr. Oppenheimer on this matter.

Q. Who was Johnson?

A. Johnson was the intelligence officer for the radiation laboratory.

Q. Do you recall whether or not Johnson gave you any details of that conversation?

A. Johnson told me it concerned a possible espionage effort in connection with the radiation laboratory.

Q. Did you thereafter interview Dr. Oppenheimer?

A. Yes, I interviewed Dr. Oppenheimer on the 26th or 27th of August 1943.

Q. Where did the interview take place, Colonel, and what were the circumstances under which it took place?

A. The interview was conducted on the University of California campus. There was a building in which Lieutenant Johnson had his office. Captain Fidler was a member of the staff. I don't recall his exact capacity at the time. He was in the Army. We used Lieutenant Johnson's office to conduct this interview.

Q. Did you make any arrangements to have it recorded?

A. Yes. We felt that this information was of considerable importance, and we did not want to rely later on on what we may remember, so I made arrangements for an officer in charge of my investigative unit to set up a recording for us.

Q. So far as you know, was that with the knowledge of Dr. Oppenheimer, or was he unaware that it was being recorded?

A. As far as I know, he was unaware.

Q. Subsequent to the interview, were the recordings transcribed?

A. Yes; after hearing what Dr. Oppenheimer had to tell me, I immediately had the recordings transcribed so I could forward them to General Groves' office. I recall we made the first draft off the recordings and we tried to check that as much as we could. Subsequent to that I wanted to hurry this to General Groves, so I recall we started doing a second typing of it, and I stopped the typist and forwarded it by airmail immediately to General Groves' office. . . .

Q. Have you recently refreshed your recollection about this interview by looking over a copy of that transcript?

A. I have.

Q. Do you recall, Colonel, whether or not in that interview Dr. Oppenheimer said anything to you about somebody in the office of the Russian Consul?

A. Of the Soviet Consul, yes.

Q. Is there any question in your mind that was mentioned?

A. No, sir; that was mentioned.

Q. In what connection?

A. Dr. Oppenheimer told me that a man contacted him with the suggestion that technical information can be made available through proper channels to the Soviet Consulate and that there was a man available who was proficient in microfilming, and that there were channels established for the transmission of available information.

Q. Is there any question that Dr. Oppenheimer made that reference to the use of microfilm?

A. No, sir; not in my mind.

Q. Do you recall whether or not Dr. Oppenheimer mentioned to you whether this man who had made the approach had made more than one approach to people on the project?

A. Yes. He indicated three definite approaches that were made.

Q. Is there any question about that in your mind?

A. No, sir.

Q. Did you ask Dr. Oppenheimer who the man was who had made these approaches?

A. Yes, I did. I asked him for the name of the man.

Q. Did he give it to you?

A. No, he did not.

Q. Did he say why he would not give it to you?

A. He stated that this man was a friend of his, he felt that no information was leaking out, and he felt that he did not want to give the man's name under the circumstances since he felt that it wasn't successful in accomplishing his mission.

Q. Were you anxious to know the name?

A. We were. As a matter of fact, I insisted several times and I told Dr. Oppenheimer that without the knowledge of that name our activities were going to be made much more difficult. Since he knew the name of the man, I felt he should furnish it to me. I think we broached that subject through the conversation on several occasions.

Q. Why were you so anxious to know the name?

A. Without the knowledge of the man, our job was extremely difficult. We knew definitely that there were espionage activities conducted in favor of the Soviets in that area. We knew now that there was a new or at least an additional effort being exerted through this man. Our investigative unit was limited in itself, and if we had to start digging to find out who this man is, it would put a tremendous burden on us.

I also felt, if I may say, that Dr. Oppenheimer knew the name of the man, and it was his duty to report it to me. . . .

Q. Dr. Oppenheimer did not give you those names?

A. No; he did not. He told me at the time that two of the men were down at "Y" that we called it, that was Los Alamos, and that one man had either already gone or was to go to site X, which I believe was Oak Ridge.

Q. Did you conduct any investigation as a result of that lead?

A. Yes; we did. That was another tedious project we had. We had to go through files, try to find out who was going to go to site X. We determined, and I took measures to stop—at least I asked General Groves to stop the man's movement to that area.

Q. What man?

A. The third man. I can't recall the name at this time. I am not sure of the name.

Q. But you felt that you had identified somebody who was about to be moved to the site?

A. Yes. As a matter of fact, we did. But at this point I don't remember the man's name.

Q. And you took steps to stop that transfer?

A. Yes. . . . .

Q. Colonel, had you had this information about the approach to Dr. Oppenheimer immediately after it had taken place, would that have made a difference to you in your investigation?

A. It certainly would.

Q. What difference would it have made?

A. Not having the name, I felt at the time, and I think I still feel impeded seriously our investigation.

Q. Why?

A. We had to start an investigation of a factor which was unknown to us. We knew that there was a man, a professor. There were many professors at the University of California. The only thing I knew was that he was not connected with the radiation laboratory, which put it into the University of California, and the staff was tremendous there. . . .

Q. When did you finally learn the name of the unknown professor?

A. The name of the unknown professor was furnished to me by General Groves' office. I can't recall the exact time. I presume it was either the end of September some time—

Q. End of when?

A. September or maybe October. I am not sure of the time.

Q. Let me see if I can refresh your recollection. I will show you a photostat of a teletype addressed to the Area Engineer, University of California, Berkeley, Calif., attention Lt. Lyall Johnson, signed "Nichols," and asked if looking at that you are able now to refresh your recollection about it?

A. Yes; this is the way we received the information.

Q. When was the date?

A. December 13. I must say that I had—there was another somewhat previous—this never reached me.

Q. That never did?

A. No.

Q. How did you get the information?

A. I never got the information—I was gone.

Q. Do you recall that you did receive the information before you went or not?

A. I think I was only informally informed of certain suspicions but I had never received that information.

Q. When did you leave there?

A. About the 26th or 25th of November. It was the end of November. . . .

Q. Colonel, I think I asked you before the noon recess when you first learned the name of Haaken Chevalier, and I believe you said some time in September.

A. Early October or September.

Q. In what connection did that name come to your attention?

A. We were receiving reports of other investigative agencies relating to Communist activities in the area. I don't recall exactly who delivered those reports to us, but they probably came from Washington, from General Grove's office.

Q. What was the purpose of the report about Dr. Chevalier? I don't mean for you to give details.

A. It concerned Communist activities in the area. It concerned contacts with people who were either known or suspected Communists.

Q. I don't want to lead you but I am quite sure you are not very easily led anyway. Was the burden of the report that Dr. Chevalier was in some way connected with Communist activities?

A. That is right.

Q. The identification of Dr. Chevalier as the unknown professor came later?

A. That is right. It didn't come to me then.

Q. It did not come to you?

A. No.

Q. Would you say it came after you left Berkeley?

A. When I returned from a short tour in Europe, after being in the Mediterranean Theater, I was brought up to date on certain things that transpired in my absence.

Q. Is that when you first learned the identity of the unnamed professor?

A. Yes, sir, I believe so.

Q. When did you first begin giving attention and consideration to Dr. Oppenheimer in connection with your investigation of espionage and Communist activities in Berkeley?

A. At the early part of the investigation. It was either late in May or some time early in June.

Mr. Gray. What year?

The Witness. 1943, sir. Excuse me. . . .

Q. On the basis of the information which you had concerning Dr. Oppenheimer, did you consider him to be a security risk?

A. Yes, I would.

Q. Did you then?

A. Yes, I did.

Q. Do you now?

A. Yes, I think I do. I do, yes. . . .

Q. Would you care to elaborate upon your statement that you now consider Dr. Oppenheimer a security risk?

A. As far as I know, Dr. Oppenheimer was affiliated with Communist front activities. I have reason to feel that he was a member of the Communist Party. I have seen no indication which indicates any change from that. I feel that his supposed dropping of the Communist Party activities in the early part of the war need not necessarily express his sincere opinions, since that was done by most all members of the Communist Party. As a result of that, I feel that the opinion I had back in 1943 probably would stand.

Q. You say was done by most all members of the party. Just what do you mean by that?

A. Members of the party who came into the service, members who continued in Government work, disclaimed any affiliation with the party. . . .

CROSS-EXAMINATION

By Mr. Silverman:

Q. Colonel Pash, how often have you met Dr. Oppenheimer?

A. Once, for this interview.

Q. That was that meeting of August 26, 1943?

A. Yes.

Q. And as far as you can recall until today that is the only time you have ever seen him in your life?

A. Physically, yes. . . .

Q. In your one interview with Dr. Oppenheimer, Dr. Oppenheimer did mention the name?

A. Yes.

Q. He volunteered the name?

A. Yes.

Q. At that time—

Mr. Robb. Mr. Chairman, I don't mean to interfere but I think the question whether he volunteered the name is a conclusion. I don't wish to concede—

Mr. Silverman. There have been a fair number of conclusions suggested by you, Mr. Robb.

Mr. Robb. There certainly have.

MR. GRAY. Proceed, Mr. Silverman.

MR. SILVERMAN. Thank you, sir.

By Mr. Silverman:

Q. At the time that Dr. Oppenheimer gave you Mr. Eltenton's name, was Mr. Eltenton already under surveillance by you?

A. We had no connection with Mr. Eltenton. We had his name, but he was not under our surveillance. He was not connected with the radiation laboratory as far as I know.

Q. So that when Dr. Oppenheimer gave you this name, this was an important piece of information for you?

A. No, we had his name, but not in connection with our investigation.

Q. Did you have his name as someone who might be mixed up in an espionage attempt?

A. Yes, as a Communist Party member. We would not have those details as to his activities, because we were not conducting the investigation.

Q. You were conducting an investigation about espionage.

A. Yes, by the limitation agreement we did not investigate people who were not connected with the military or specifically with the radiation laboratory.

Q. So far as you know was there any information—I withdraw that.

You did not have any information that connected Mr. Eltenton with an espionage attempt or approach?

A. We had information which connected him with the contacts of the Soviet contacts, but I personally in my office did not have the details of those contacts.

Q. And did Dr. Oppenheimer say to you that the reason he was not giving you the name of the professor was that he thought the man was innocent?

A. He thought that this was not serious and that he had not achieved anything.

Q. And of course Dr. Oppenheimer was very wrong not to give you that name.

A. Yes.

Q. And I think we would all agree with that. Do you have any information of any leakage of restricted data through Dr. Oppenheimer to any unauthorized person?

MR. ROBB. May I have that read back?

(Question read by the reporter.)

THE WITNESS. No.

By Mr. Silverman:

Q. And Dr. Oppenheimer did tell you that on the one instance when the professor approached him, he refused to have anything to do with it?

A. Yes; he told me that.

Q. And some time in 1943, he did give the professor's name?

A. Yes.

Q. We all agree that Dr. Oppenheimer exercised poor judgment, indeed, and was very wrong not to give you the name of Professor Chevalier. Against that agreement by everyone here, I would like to ask you these questions.

MR. GRAY. Wait a minute. I take it that everyone here includes the members of this board. The hearing is being conducted for the information of the members of this board in the discharge of its functions. I as chairman have been extremely lenient, perhaps unduly so, in allowing counsel to express an opinion. This is not the first time that you have said, Mr. Silverman, that everyone here agrees on something.

I should like to ask you please to refrain from expressions of opinions, and not to try to give a witness an indication that you speak for anybody but yourself, if you are expressing an opinion.

MR. SILVERMAN. Very well, sir. I am sorry.

WILLIAM L. BORDEN: "More probably than not, J. Robert Oppenheimer is an agent of the Soviet Union"

[Robb's last witness is William L. Borden, whose November 7, 1953, letter to the Federal Bureau of Investigation triggered the investigation of Oppenheimer. After graduating from Yale in 1942, Borden served in the air force, returned to Yale for a law degree, and in 1948 became executive director of the Joint Congressional Committee on Atomic Energy. His suspicions about Oppenheimer had been growing ever since November 1950, when he first examined the physicist's AEC security file. In an interview with Robb and Rolander on February 20, 1954, he asserted that Oppenheimer's opposition to the H-bomb could only be explained "on the hypothesis of subversion." For the past year before testifying, the 34-year-old Borden has worked for the atomic power division of Westinghouse Electric Corporation.]

DIRECT EXAMINATION

By Mr. Robb: . . .

Q. Do you have a copy of your letter with you?

A. I have one in front of me.

Q. Would you be good enough to read it?

A. This letter is dated November 7, 1953.

Q. While our friends are looking at that, I might ask you whether you know Dr. Oppenheimer personally?

A. I have met him on a few occasions.

MR. ROBB. May we proceed, Mr. Chairman?

MR. SILVERMAN. One moment, please.

MR. GRAY. I would like to ask the counsel what the purpose of delay is. He is simply going to read this.

MR. SILVERMAN. Mr. Chairman, I can hardly conceive that a letter, with due respect to Mr. Borden, by a gentleman stating what he adds the evidence up to can be enormously helpful to the board which has itself heard the evidence. There are statements in this letter, at least one that I see, which I don't think anybody would be very happy to have go into this record, and under those circumstances, I would like to look at it a minute longer. There may be serious question whether anybody will be helped by having this letter in the record.

MR. GRAY. I think you are now raising a question that counsel cannot determine, Mr. Silverman.

MR. SILVERMAN. Of course not, sir.

MR. GRAY. If you have any argument about it, I shall be glad to have it. If you wish to protest the reading of the letter into the record, you are certainly at liberty to do so. I take it, however, that it is evident that Mr. Borden is before the committee, he states that this letter is his own letter, he wrote it without consultation with the Commission, that it represents the views he held in November 1953, it represents the views he holds today, he is the individual concerned, he is being confronted by Dr. Oppenheimer and Oppenheimer's counsel and will be available for cross-examination. In view of the fact that being here as he is under subpoena, which has been made clear, presumably this being his opinion, this is what he would testify to. I simply don't see the objection to reading the letter. If I am wrong about that, I should be glad to hear it.

MR. SILVERMAN. Mr. Chairman, much of the material in this letter, or some of the material in this letter, at least, is matter that has already been before the board.

MR. GRAY. Mr. Silverman, you are not suggesting that we should not hear from any witnesses who will testify to the same matters previous witnesses have testified to?

MR. SILVERMAN. Let me say it this way. The thing that struck my eye at once is subdivision (e) on page 2. That troubles me going into the record. If you think it will advance things to have it in, all right.

MR. GRAY. I would like to take a moment to consider that objection.

MR. GARRISON. Mr. Chairman, the third paragraph on page 4, and some comparable material brings in accusations here that have not before been made in this record or even indicted in the Commission's letter.

MR. GRAY. You are referring to what?

MR. GARRISON. To the third paragraph on page 4, and to the first clause on page 4, and also the last clause on page 3.

MR. GRAY. Mr. Garrison, is there any question in your mind that if this is the view of the witness, he would not so testify?

MR. GARRISON. I have no question about that.

MR. GRAY. I am puzzled by the objection to his reading the letter he wrote in November 1953, which he states now represents his present views as distinguished from giving his present views at this time. I am just honestly not clear as to what the objection is.

MR. GARRISON. It is simply my feeling, Mr. Chairman, that if these represent his present views, and the Commission's counsel has brought him here to testify to this board about accusations which are not in the Commission's letter and are not even suggested in them, and have never before been suggested in these proceedings, we now have a new case which it seems to me either does not belong here or should be included in the Commission's letter, either in the first instance or by amendment.

MR. GRAY. I think now you are making a point that the board should examine . . . that was certainly not clear to me from anything Mr. Silverman said earlier.

I would therefore ask everyone to retire from the room except the board and counsel for the board.

(All persons with the exception of the board and counsel for the Board left the hearing room, and after a brief time reentered the room.)

MR. GRAY. In response to the objection raised by counsel for Dr. Oppenheimer, I would have this to say on behalf of the board:

No. 1, the material which the witness was about to read constitutes testimony by the witness, and does not become a part of the letter of notification from the General Manager of the Commission to Dr. Oppenheimer. I would remind counsel that under the regulations pursuant to which this proceeding is conducted the requirements are that this Board makes specific findings with respect to the items in the letter of notification.

I should also remind counsel that much of the testimony here given has not necessarily reflected either items in the letter of the General Manager of the Commission to Dr. Oppenheimer, or Dr. Oppenheimer's reply to that letter. With the exception of the personal items referred to on page 2, and I will have something to say to the witness about that, the material as I understand it specifically referred to by Mr. Garrison is stated as a conclusion of the author of the letter. Again I take it that the witness would be permitted to present his conclusion about matters which are before this board. Witnesses have done so with constancy throughout this proceeding. Therefore, after consultation with the members of the board, the witness will be allowed to read this letter, and all concerned will understand that this is a part of his testimony which is not necessarily accepted by the Commission, does not become a part of the Commission's letter of notification, nor are the conclusions drawn in the testimony necessarily to be considered accepted by the board. It is the conclusion of the witness, one of many whom we have had before the board, with respect to matters concerned in this proceeding. . . .

I would say to counsel that it is not my understanding from conversations with the board that testimony of this witness is in any way going to broaden the inquiry of the board.

Thomas A. Morgan, a member of the Personnel Security Board. Courtesy of Hagley Museum and Library.

MR. GARRISON. How can it avoid it, sir? Supposing you should believe the witness? Here is a witness produced by counsel engaged by the Commission and delegated with the responsibility by this board of calling such witnesses he wishes, and he brings a witness in to make this kind of an accusation not dreamed of in this proceeding up to this point, and not mentioned in the letter. I think if anything could be more of a surprise and more calling for time, if this is to be the subject matter of the inquiry, I don't know what it is.

MR. GRAY. I should like to ask, Mr. Garrison, whether you knew of the existence of this letter?

MR. GARRISON. I had heard rumors that Mr. Borden had written a letter; yes, sir. I had no notion that this kind of material was in it.

MR. GRAY. This is a conclusion of a witness that you are speaking to now.

MR. GARRISON. Yes; but I take it you are going to permit the witness to adduce his evidence upon these topics. Otherwise, there is no point of his reading the letter unless he is going to testify about it.

I would suggest, Mr. Chairman—I don't want to delay the proceeding—

MR. GRAY. The board is very much concerned with protecting the interests of the individual concerned, the Government and the general public. So that I do not consider this discussion a matter of delay.

MR. ROBB. Mr. Chairman, might I suggest one thing? I assume that in the event the witness should be asked whether or not upon the basis of the evidence he has considered that he considers Dr. Oppenheimer a security risk, and he should say that he did, and should then be asked to give his reasons, he might very well give the reasons that he set forth in this letter under conclusions. I can't see much difference. I think it would not be contended the scope of the inquiry is thereby broadened or would be thereby broadened.

MR. GARRISON. Mr. Robb is making a point of form and not of substance, Mr. Chairman. We are here put on notice in advance—this is the only way in which it happens to come up—that this witness proposes to make accusations of a new character not touched upon in the letter, and not suggested before in these proceedings by anybody, even by the most vigorous critics of Dr. Oppenheimer.

MR. ROBB. Mr. Chairman, might I say one thing for the record? The witness wrote this letter on his own initiative and his own responsibility, setting out certain matters of evidence, I think all of which, if not all, certainly most all of which, are mentioned in the letter from General Nichols to Dr. Oppenheimer. This letter was to Mr. Hoover. The letter is a part of the files before the board. It is, I think, an important letter. It seemed to the Commission, it seemed to us, that under those circumstances it was only fair to Dr. Oppenheimer and his counsel that this witness should be presented here, confronted by Dr. Oppenheimer, and his counsel, subjected to cross-examination on the matters set out in this letter.

The conclusions drawn by this witness in his letter are not allegations in the letter from General Nichols to Dr. Oppenheimer. They will not be allegations in any possible amendment of that letter. The conclusions are the conclusions of the witness alone. They are conclusions which he has drawn from the evidence just as other witnesses on behalf of Dr. Oppenheimer have drawn the conclusions that Dr. Oppenheimer is not a security risk, but on the contrary is a man of great honesty, integrity, and patriotism.

I assume that if the witness having written this letter had concluded from the evidence set out by him that Dr. Oppenheimer was not a security risk, that he was a splendid American, a man of honor, that Mr. Garrison would have no objection to reading those conclusions. It seems to me it cuts both ways, Mr. Chairman.

MR. GARRISON. May I ask how long the Commission has had this letter in its file?

MR. ROBB. I don't know, Mr. Garrison. Some time, of course.

MR. GARRISON. Did it have it prior to the letter of December 23, 1953?

MR. ROBB. Mr. Garrison, I don't think I should be subjected to cross-examination by you, but I can say to you that I am sure Mr. Hoover did not wait 8 months to send it over to the Commission.

MR. GARRISON. Mr. Chairman, at the bottom of page 3, it says, "From such evidence considered in detail the following conclusions are justified." You can call them conclusions or allegations; it is all the same thing.

MR. GRAY. This is simply the testimony of a witness.

MR. GARRISON. This is the testimony of a witness produced by the Commission's counsel to whom this task has been delegated, on his own responsibility bringing in here to make accusations of the kind that I don't think belong here.

MR. GRAY. I will state to counsel for Dr. Oppenheimer that copies of this letter have been in the possession of the board along with all other material and have been read by members of this board. Mr. Borden's conclusions are, therefore, known to the members of this board. The board has certainly made no suggestion to the Commission and the general manager of the Commission has not otherwise taken the initiative to broaden the inquiry to include these stated conclusions of the witness. If you prefer not to have Dr. Oppenheimer confronted by a witness and cross-examined by his counsel with respect to material which you know is in the possession of the board, of course that would be your decision in what you consider to be the best protection of the interests of Dr. Oppenheimer.

I gather that is what you are saying, because you have been informed by the chairman that a copy of this letter is in the possession of the members of the board. That, again, if I need to repeat this, does not in any way indicate that it is anything more than one part of material consisting of a record which is to be thousands of pages long, and various other data voluminous in nature which are before this board. You may not assume that any of the conclusions of any of the witnesses may necessarily be those of the board. As far as this board is concerned—I hope I may speak for my colleagues—I do not think we will insist on either direct or cross-examination of this witness. The conclusion which we had reached in the period during which you were excused from the room was that we would proceed. However, I shall be glad to consult further with the members of the board to determine whether we shall proceed with the introduction of this letter.

I take it that counsel would not object to direct examination of this witness? You are not objecting to the witness?

MR. GARRISON. No.

MR. GRAY. Mr. Morgan has just observed to me that he felt that it was the fairest thing to Dr. Oppenheimer to give him and his counsel the opportunity to examine the witness with respect to this letter which was in the possession of the board. He doesn't insist that we proceed. I have not yet consulted Dr. Evans.

DR. EVANS. That is all right with me.

MR. GARRISON. Mr. Chairman, it is needless to say that we would much rather have an opportunity to cross-examine if the board considers that this topic is properly a part of the case. If the board considers that it is, then let us proceed with it. I trust that in view of the circumstances if it be your decision to proceed, that to the extent that we need time here to prepare on this new kind of an allegation, that we may have it.

MR. GRAY. Yes.

(Discussion off the record.)

MR. GARRISON. Mr. Chairman, with respect to the objection previously raised by Mr. Silverman, we withdraw that objection and prefer that the letter in its entirety be read, if we are to go ahead with it.

MR. GRAY. All right, sir.

THE WITNESS. This letter is dated November 7, 1943. A copy went to the Joint Committee on Atomic Energy. The original went to Mr. J. Edgar Hoover, Director, Federal Bureau of Investigation, Washington, D.C.:

"Dear Mr. Hoover: This letter concerns J. Robert Oppenheimer.

"As you know, he has for some years enjoyed access to various critical activities of the National Security Council, the Department of State, the Department of Defense, the Army, Navy, and Air Force, the Research and Development Board, the Atomic Energy Commission, the Central Intelligence Agency, the National Security Resources Board, and the National Science Foundation. His access covers most new weapons being developed by the Armed Forces, war plans at least in comprehensive outline, complete details as to atomic and hydrogen weapons and stockpile data, the evidence on which some of the principal CIA intelligence estimates is based, United States participation in the United Nations and NATO and many other areas of high security sensitivity.

"Because the scope of his access may well be unique, because he has had custody of an immense collection of classified papers—"

DR. EVANS. Documents. You said papers.

THE WITNESS. That is right. Perhaps I should state that the copy I have before me is one that I typed myself, and it is possible that it does not conform.

"Because the scope of his access may well be unique, because he has had

custody of an immense collection of classified papers covering military, intelligence, and diplomatic as well as atomic-energy matters, and because he
also possesses a scientific background enabling him to grasp the significance of classified data of a technical nature, it seems reasonable to estimate
that he is and for some years has been in a position to compromise more
vital and detailed information affecting the national defense and security
than any other individual in the United States.

"While J. Robert Oppenheimer has not made major contributions to the
advancement of science, he holds a respected professional standing among
the second rank of American physicists. In terms of his mastery of Government affairs, his close liaison with ranking officials, and his ability to influence high-level thinking, he surely stands in the first rank, not merely
among scientists but among all those who have shaped postwar decisions in
the military, atomic energy, intelligence, and diplomatic fields. As chairman or as an official or unofficial member of more than 35 important Government committees, panels, study groups, and projects, he has oriented or
dominated key policies involving every principal United States security department and agency except the FBI.

"The purpose of this letter is to state my own exhaustively considered
opinion, based upon years of study, of the available classified evidence, that
more probably than not J. Robert Oppenheimer is an agent of the Soviet
Union.

"This opinion considers the following factors, among others:

"(a) He was contributing substantial monthly sums to the Communist
Party;

"(b) His ties with communism had survived the Nazi-Soviet Pact and the
Soviet attack upon Finland;

"(c) His wife and younger brother were Communists;

"(d) He had no close friends except Communists;

"(e) He had at least one Communist mistress;

"(f) He belonged only to Communist organizations, apart from professional affiliations;

"(g) The people whom he recruited into the early wartime Berkeley
atomic project were exclusively Communists;

"(h) He had been instrumental in securing recruits for the Communist
Party; and

"(i) He was in frequent contact with Soviet espionage agents.

"2. The evidence indicating that—

"(a) In May 1942, he either stopped contributing funds to the Communist Party or else made his contributions through a new channel not yet discovered;

"(b) In April 1942 his name was formally submitted for security clearance;

"(c) He himself was aware at the time that his name had been so submitted; and

"(d) He thereafter repeatedly gave false information to General Groves, the Manhattan District, and the FBI concerning the 1939–April 1942 period.

"3. The evidence indicating that—

"(a) He was responsible for employing a number of Communists, some of them nontechnical, at wartime Los Alamos;

"(b) He selected one such individual to write the official Los Alamos history;

"(c) He was a vigorous supporter of the H-bomb program until August 6, 1945 (Hiroshima), on which day he personally urged each senior individual working in this field to desist; and

"(d) He was an enthusiastic sponsor of the A-bomb program until the war ended, when he immediately and outspokenly advocated that the Los Alamos Laboratory be disbanded.

"4. The evidence indicating that:

"(a) He was remarkably instrumental in influencing the military authorities and the Atomic Energy Commission essentially to suspend H-bomb development from mid-1946 through January 31, 1950;

"(b) He has worked tirelessly, from January 31, 1950, onward, to retard the United States H-bomb program;

"(c) He has used his potent influence against every postwar effort to expand capacity for producing A-bomb material;

"(d) He has used his potent influence against every postwar effort directed at obtaining larger supplies of uranium raw material; and

"(e) He has used his potent influence against every major postwar effort toward atomic power development, including the nuclear-powered submarine and aircraft programs as well as industrial power projects."

From such evidence, considered in detail, the following conclusions are justified:

"1. Between 1929 and mid-1942, more probably than not, J. Robert Oppenheimer was a sufficiently hardened Communist that he either volunteered espionage information to the Soviets or complied with a request for such information. (This includes the possibility that when he singled out the weapons aspect of atomic development as his personal specialty, he was acting under Soviet instructions.)

"2. More probably than not, he has since been functioning as an espionage agent; and

"3. More probably than not, he has since acted under a Soviet directive in influencing United States military, atomic energy, intelligence, and diplomatic policy.

"It is to be noted that these conclusions correlate with information furnished by Klaus Fuchs, indicating that the Soviets had acquired an agent in Berkeley who informed them about electromagnetic separation research during 1942 or earlier.

"Needless to say, I appreciate the probabilities identifiable from existing evidence might, with review of future acquired evidence, be reduced to possibilities; or they might also be increased to certainties. The central problem is not whether J. Robert Oppenheimer was ever a Communist; for the existing evidence makes abundantly clear that he was. Even an Atomic Energy Commission analysis prepared in early 1947 reflects this conclusion, although some of the most significant derogatory data had yet to become available. The central problem is assessing the degree of likelihood that he in fact did what a Communist in his circumstances, at Berkeley, would logically have done during the crucial 1939–42 period—that is, whether he became an actual espionage and policy instrument of the Soviets. Thus, as to this central problem, my opinion is that, more probably than not, the worst is in fact the truth.

"I am profoundly aware of the grave nature of these comments. The matter is detestable to me. Having lived with the Oppenheimer case for years, having studied and restudied all data concerning him that your agency made available to the Atomic Energy Commission through May 1953, having endeavored to factor in a mass of additional data assembled from numerous other sources, and looking back upon the case from a perspective in private life, I feel a duty simply to state to the responsible head of the security agency most concerned the conclusions which I have painfully crystalized and which I believe any fairminded man thoroughly familiar with the evidence must also be driven to accept.

"The writing of this letter, to me a solemn step, is exclusively on my own personal initiative and responsibility.

"Very truly yours,

"(Signed)   William L. Borden,
"(Typed)   William L. Borden."

MR. ROLANDER. Mr. Chairman, I had copies of this letter made, and Mr. Borden read from the copies, and I think there is one error in the copy that he read. That begins where the letter says, "This opinion considers the following factors among others: (1) The evidence indicating that as of April of 1942" and then it proceeds.

MR. SILVERMAN. Indicating that as of what date?

MR. ROLANDER. "This opinion considers the following factors, among others: "1. The evidence indicating that as of April 1942 (*a*)."

MR. GRAY. Now, I should like to make a statement with respect to this letter which I am authorized to make by the two other members of the board which I think may ease Mr. Garrison's problem as he has seen it in this discussion.

I would say to you that the board has no evidence before it that Dr. Oppenheimer volunteered espionage information to the Soviets or complied with a request for such information; that he has been functioning as an espionage agent or that he has since acted under Soviet directive, with one qualification as to that latter point, which I am sure will not surprise you. That is, there has been testimony by various witnesses as to whether members of the Communist Party, as a matter of policy at the time of the war years or entering into Government or military service, complied with policy or policy directions in that regard. With respect to that qualification, which I believe appears already in the record, and which is certainly no surprise to Dr. Oppenheimer and his counsel, I repeat that the members of the board feel that they have no evidence before them with respect to these matters which I have just recited.

I repeat, therefore, that there are now before the board in the nature of conclusions of the witness, stated to be his own conclusions on the basis of other material which is set forth in some detail, and I believe practically all of which has been referred to without making a judgment whether it has been established or not.

MR. ROBB. May I proceed?

MR. GRAY. Yes.

By Mr. Robb:

Q. Mr. Borden, may I ask you, sir, why you waited until you left the joint committee to write that letter?

A. Mr. Robb, this case has concerned me over a period of years. My concern has increased as time passed. Several actions were taken with respect to it while I was working for the joint committee. It has consisted in the preparation of 400 questions raised on the case. This was the final work that I performed before leaving the committee. I felt at that time that I had not previously fully measured up to my duty on this matter. As of the time I left, the preparation of those questions constituted for me the discharge of the duty. However, no position was taken in the formulation of those questions, or at least if there was a position, it was implicit only.

After I left, I took a month off and this matter pressed on my mind. The feeling grew upon me that I had not fully discharged what was required of me in view of the fact that I had not taken a position.

Accordingly, by approximately mid-October, I had crystalized my thinking to the point where I felt that this step was necessary. There is a letter which I have written to the joint committee on this subject, if you wish me to refer to it, or to read it to you.

Q. Is there anything, Mr. Borden, that you can now add to what you have set out in this letter as your conclusions?

A. I have no desire to add anything.

Q. I am not asking you that, sir. Is there anything that you feel that is appropriate for you to tell this board in addition to what you have set out in that letter?

A. I feel, Mr. Robb, that it is my obvious duty to answer any questions that are asked me. If I were to volunteer information, I think it is obvious that I could talk over a long period of time.

Q. I am not asking you to volunteer, but what I want to know is, Does that letter fully state your conclusions?

A. This letter reflects my conclusions as of now.

Q. Does it fully reflect your conclusions?

A. Yes.

Q. So there is nothing that you feel you should add to it?

A. That is correct. Perhaps I misunderstood you.

Q. Let me see whether or not you feel any hesitation about answering any questions that either have been or may be put to you here, because of the presence of Dr. Oppenheimer and his counsel.

A. I do not.

Q. The answer is no?

A. The answer is no.

MR. ROBB. I think that is all I care to ask. You may cross-examine.

MR. GRAY. We will now take a recess until Monday at 2 o'clock for many reasons. One is commitments identified with this enterprise as to schedule. Second, I think it is useful if time is required for Mr. Garrison. I would hope that my statement that I made to the board takes care of most of the difficulties that we discussed.

MR. GARRISON. Is it to be understood that the witness will be back here on Monday?

MR. GRAY. The witness is under subpoena, and he is not happy to be here in the first place. It is understood that he will be.

Monday, May 3

[When the hearing recessed on Friday, Oppenheimer's lawyers were divided over whether to cross-examine William L. Borden. In view of Gordon Gray's assertions that Borden's testimony was not going "to broaden the inquiry of the board," and that "the board has no evidence before it that Dr. Oppenheimer volunteered espionage information to the Soviets," the defense team decided over the weekend not to cross-examine him. In view of the flimsy nature of many of Borden's allegations, this was surely a mistake. An FBI internal memorandum, unknown of course to Garrison, conceded: "Borden's letter contains his own assumptions and conclusions. He admits that the material, at least in part, is only a possibility. Many of Borden's statements are distorted and restated in his own words in order to make them appear more forceful than the true facts indicate." As the hearing enters its final week, Garrison briefly explains the reasons for the decision.]

MR. GRAY. Mr. Garrison.

MR. GARRISON. Mr. Chairman, I would like to make a short statement, sir.

Over the weekend we have examined Mr. Borden's letter to Mr. Hoover of November 7, 1953, which he read into the record at the last session. Mr.

Borden in his brief testimony stated that the letter constituted his conclusions, and that he had nothing to add. It is quite clear that the letter consists not of evidence, but of Mr. Borden's opinions arrived at from studying FBI reports and other unspecified data. These opinions relate essentially to the items contained in General Nichols' letter to Dr. Oppenheimer of December 23, 1953, which have been canvassed in the testimony, and the documents before this board. It is apparent that except for Mr. Borden's conclusions about espionage, for which there is no evidence, and as to which the chairman has assured us there is no evidence before the board, Mr. Borden's opinions represent his interpretation of evidentiary matters which this board has been hearing about for the past 3 weeks from persons who actually participated in the particular events which have been the subject matter of this investigation.

In view of these considerations, it has seemed to us that if we were now to ask Mr. Borden to develop further his opinions and conclusions, we would merely be inviting argument about the interpretation of evidence.

While the board has been lenient in permitting argument by witnesses, it hardly seems to us that we would be justified in provoking or inviting opinions and argument which could run the gamut of all the evidence before the board.

For these reasons it has seemed to us appropriate to respond to Mr. Borden's letter in our rebuttal and summation as we expect to do. Consequently, we shall dispense with cross-examination unless the board should wish to ask Mr. Borden questions, in which event we would like to reserve the right to do ours when the board is through.

MR. GRAY. Of course, it is the right of Dr. Oppenheimer and counsel to decline to cross-examine any witness before this board. Obviously there is nothing in our procedure which requires cross-examination.

Mr. Garrison has stated that this letter constitutes conclusions of the witness which, I think he has stated, was the case on direct examination. I think, however, it appropriate that the record reflect the fact which would be very obvious to anyone who reads it, that there has been a great deal of testimony here of conclusions with respect to these matters which were contained in General Nichols' letter to Dr. Oppenheimer, and witnesses called by Dr. Oppenheimer, and his counsel, have repeatedly stated that they had certain conclusions with respect to these matters which related to Dr. Oppenheimer's loyalty, character, and associations.

I think the present witness has not sought to state anything other than these are his own conclusions.

MR. GARRISON. That is right, Mr. Chairman. I did not mean to suggest that other witnesses have not stated their conclusions and opinions. Of course, they have. I meant merely to say that those conclusions were derived from testimony of their own with respect to matters in which they had participated either with Dr. Oppenheimer or in other connections from which they derived their conclusions.

J. Robert Oppenheimer: "I wish I could explain to you better why I falsified and fabricated"

[After the board accepts a "stipulated table of corrections" to the transcribed versions of Oppenheimer's tape-recorded interviews with Boris T. Pash, on August 26, 1943, and John Lansdale, on September 12, 1943, Gordon Gray notifies Garrison that the board will feel free to consider matters that have been raised in the testimony even if they were not included in the AEC's original letter to Oppenheimer; Garrison replies that "we certainly raise no question of the broadening of the Commission's letter in order to avoid surprise." Then Oppenheimer is recalled to face questions from Gray, Ward Evans, and Roger Robb.]

EXAMINATION

By Mr. Gray:

Q. Dr. Oppenheimer, I think it is probably my duty to remind you that you are still under oath in this proceeding.

A. Thank you.

Q. I have some questions I would like to ask you, and possibly some other members of the board will.

    I want now to go back to the so-called Chevalier incident.

A. Right.

Q. I should like to give you something of a summary of what I believe to have been your testimony before the board. If it is not an accurate summary in your opinion, or your counsel thinks it is not an accurate summary, I would like to know about it. But on the basis of a summary, then, of your testimony, I should like to ask some questions.

    The summary would be this: You said that Chevalier was your friend in whom you had confidence, and that you were convinced that his remarks about passing information to the Russians were innocent. For these reasons, you testified, it did not occur to you for a long time that you should report this incident to the security officers, and when you did tell them about it, you declined to name Chevalier, because you were convinced that he was innocent, and in effect wanted to protect him from the harassment of an investigation because of your belief in his innocence.

    You testified on the other hand that the story of the Chevalier incident which you told to Colonel Pash in August 1943, and reaffirmed to Colonel Lansdale in September 1943, was false in certain material respects. Let me repeat, you testified here that that story was false in material respects. I believe you testified that this story was a cock and bull story, and that the whole thing was a pure fabrication except for the name Eltenton, and that this fabrication was in some very considerable circumstantial detail, and your testimony here as to your explanation for this fabrication was that you were an idiot, and that you were reluctant to mention Chevalier and no doubt somewhat reluctant to mention yourself.

However, I believe that your testimony indicated that you agreed that if the story you told Pash had been true, it showed that Chevalier was deeply involved, that it was not just a casual conversation, that it would not under those circumstances just have been an innocent and meaningless contact, and that it was a criminal conspiracy.

In short, with respect to that portion of your testimony I believe you led the board to believe that you thought that if your story to Colonel Pash had been true it looked like a very unsavory situation to say the very best about it.

Now, here is my question: If Chevalier was your friend and you believed him to be innocent and wanted to protect him, then why did you tell a complicated false story that on the face of it would show that the individual was not innocent, but on the contrary, was rather deeply involved with several people in what might have been a criminal espionage conspiracy?

Or to put the question in another way, I ask you whether it is not a fair inference from your testimony that your story to Pash and Lansdale as far as it went was a true story, and that the fabrication may have been with respect to the current version.

A. Let me take the second part of your question first.

Q. Yes.

A. The story I told to Pash was not a true story. There were not three or more people involved on the project. There was one person involved. That was me. I was at Los Alamos. There was no one else at Los Alamos involved. There was no one in Berkeley involved. When I heard the microfilm or what the hell, it didn't sound to me as though this were reporting anything that Chevalier had said, or at that time the unknown professor had said. I am certain that was not mentioned. I testified that the Soviet consulate had not been mentioned by Chevalier. That is the very best of my recollection. It is conceivable that I knew of Eltenton's connection with the consulate, but I believe I can do no more than say the story told in circumstantial detail, and which was elicited from me in greater and greater detail during this was a false story. It is not easy to say that.

Now, when you ask for a more persuasive argument as to why I did this than that I was an idiot, I am going to have more trouble being understandable.

I think I was impelled by 2 or 3 concerns at that time. One was the feeling that I must get across the fact that if there was, as Lansdale indicated, trouble at the Radiation Laboratory, Eltenton was the guy that might very well be involved and it was serious. Whether I embroidered the story in order to underline that seriousness or whether I embroidered it to make it more tolerable that I would not tell the simple facts, namely, Chevalier had talked to me about it, I don't know. There was no other people involved, the conversation with Chevalier was brief, it was in the nature of things not utterly casual, but I think the tone of it and his own sense of not wishing to have anything to do with it, I have correctly communicated.

I think I need to say that it was essential that I tell this story, that I should have told it at once and I should have told it completely accurately, but that it was a matter of conflict for me and I found myself, I believe, trying to give a tip to the intelligence people without realizing that when you give a tip you must tell the whole story. When I was asked to elaborate, I started off on a false pattern.

I may add 1 or 2 things. Chevalier was a friend of mine.

DR. EVANS. Did you say is a friend.

THE WITNESS. He was a friend of mine.

DR. EVANS. Today?

THE WITNESS. He was then. We may talk later of our present relations. He was then a friend of mine. As far as I know he had no close relations with anyone else on the project. The notion that he would go to a number of project people to talk to them instead of coming to me and talking it over as we did would have made no sense whatever. He was an unlikely and absurd intermediary for such a task. I think there are circumstances which indicate that there was no—that there would not have been such a conspiracy—but I am in any case solemnly testifying that there was no such conspiracy in what I knew, and what I know of this matter. I wish I could explain to you better why I falsified and fabricated.

By Mr. Gray:

Q. Of course, the point I am trying to make with you, and that is the reason for the question I asked, is the inference to be drawn from your motive at the time, as I think you have testified, was the protection of an innocent person, because the story you told was certainly not calculated to lead to the conclusion of innocence on Chevalier's part. These inferences necessarily present themselves.

Let me ask this: First, you heard Colonel Pash testify that as a result of the interview with him in which you indicated that there were three other people involved, he and his associates actually held up orders with respect to an individual who was to transfer to Oak Ridge, I think. Were you aware of that at the time?

A. I was not, not until Friday.

Q. I think a few moments ago, you questioned whether you had discussed microfilm in this interview with Colonel Pash.

A. Then I didn't make myself clear. I asserted that I had not discussed it with Chevalier or Chevalier with me. When I mentioned to Colonel Pash, it came in the form of microfilm or whatever the hell, that was the phrase, which is not very precise. May I add a point, Mr. Chairman?

MR. GARRISON. Just a minute. You are clear he means the phrase in the recording as it was played?

MR. GRAY. Yes, I understand.

THE WITNESS. May I add a point. When I did identify Chevalier, which was to General Groves, I told him of course that there were no three people, that this had occurred in our house, that this was me. So that when I made this damaging story, it was clearly with the intention of not revealing who was the intermediary.

By Mr. Gray:

Q. Again with respect to Chevalier, can you recall any efforts you have ever made in his behalf with respect to passport difficulties or problems that he may have had? I think you testified about one.

A. Yes. I remember that at the time when his wife had divorced him and he was determined to go to France, I recommended counsel to him to obtain an American passport. He had also a French passport. Without discussing it with me, nor I believe with anyone else, while the negotiations or the effort to secure an American passport were in process, he did leave on his French passport.

Q. Is it clear to you that in your visit in the late fall of 1953 to Paris, you did not in any way get involved in Dr. Chevalier's passport problems as of the present time?

A. I don't believe I became involved in them. I am not even sure he discussed them with me.

Q. You say he did discuss them with you?

A. I am not even sure he discussed them with me. I am sure he discussed one point with me at length, which was his continued employment at UNESCO.

Q. You don't remember discussing with him the best possible way to get information on his part about a passport, or the way to obtain a passport?

A. That could well have happened and I would have referred him to the embassy.

Q. Did you in fact do so?

A. If I were sure I would tell you.

Q. I am putting some of the same questions to you now, Dr. Oppenheimer, that Mr. Robb put earlier.

A. Right.

Q. You had luncheon I believe with Mr. Wymans of the embassy?

A. That is right.

Q. I believe you testified on the question of Mr. Robb you did not discuss Mr. Chevalier's passport problem with Mr. Wymans?

A. No, I saw Mr. Wymans long before I saw Mr. Chevalier; not long before, but well a week before.

Q. Have you been in communication with Chevalier since the time you had luncheon with Mr. Wymans?

A. Yes; I saw Chevalier after my lunch with Wymans, but not the other way around.

Q. Have you been in communication with Chevalier since the evening you spent with him?

A. The next day we drove out to visit Malraux.

Q. Yes; you testified about that. Have you been in communication with him since that time?

A. No. Well, we had a card from him, just for my birthday.

DR. EVANS. When did you get that card?

THE WITNESS. Around my birthday, which was during these hearings. I don't recall this. I could have advised Chevalier to consult Wymans with regard to his passport.

By Mr. Gray:

Q. I am sure that you could have, because I believe it to be true that he did, and specifically stated that it was at your suggestion that he do so. I want again to ask you whether you had conversations with anybody else other than Chevalier about his passport problem while you were in Paris in the late fall? I think I am asking you, is it clear to you that you did not?

A. It is quite clear to me. If—I believe I saw no one at the Embassy after seeing Chevalier or no one connected with the Embassy.

Q. Do you have any guess or knowledge as to whether Chevalier today is active in Communist Party affairs?

A. I have a strong, strong guess that he is not. I have no knowledge. His new wife is an extremely sensible, wholly un-Communist girl. The other person we saw together was a man who has become a violent anti-Communist and is now apolitical. I don't have knowledge.

Q. The record shows, I believe, Dr. Oppenheimer, that you continued probably until sometime in 1942 to make financial contributions which went to Communist causes, with money passing to different people, but among others, Folkoff was one who was known to you to be a Communist Party officer.

A. That is right.

Q. Did you discuss these contributions with Mrs. Oppenheimer? Was she aware that you were making these contributions?

A. I would assume that we discussed everything in our life at that time.

Q. Did she make any contributions on her own account?

A. I have no knowledge of that.

Q. I see.

A. I am sure that everything was quite open between us. She has told me that she may have given Steve Nelson some money. She remembers that not as a contribution for a cause, but as something she was giving Nelson for his own use. But I have no recollection of it.

Q. If you made contributions as late as 1942, and this fact were known to Mrs. Oppenheimer, it was certainly clear to her at that time, or should have been clear to her at that time, that these funds were going to Communist Party causes because of her previous membership and presumably full awareness of the methods of operation.

A. I hate to say so, but I think as to this you will have to ask her. My recollection of her Communist Party experience was a very limited one—very hard work with the steel union and mimeographing and things like that—and I doubt whether she was at any time what you would call an expert on how Communists dealt with things.

Q. I don't think I have heard suggested at any time that Mrs. Oppenheimer was politically naive. I don't believe that you have made that suggestion, although there has not been much testimony about her, I might say that anything I have read or heard in or about these proceedings would indicate nothing other than a pretty full knowledge of what she was about. I agree with you, however, that some of these questions should be put to her.

I want to go back now, Dr. Oppenheimer, to a portion of your testimony which related to this matter of ceasing political activity by those who came into the active service on the project. I believe you testified that as to some of these individuals, whose names I don't recall at the moment, you told them that they would have to cease their political activities, and you testified that by that you meant making speeches, et cetera.

Now, do you today take the view that ceasing political activity, whatever is encompassed in that phrase, is an adequate safeguard even though you think you know the individual and trust his innocence and loyalty completely?

A. Today? No. Well, I think there is nothing better to go on than the judgment of a man, but I am not suggesting that it should not be supplemented by whatever evidence is available as to what the man is up to.

Q. Let me put a hypothetical question to you.

A. Perhaps I did not understand you.

Q. Suppose you today had a friend in whom you had the highest degree of confidence as to his loyalty to this country and his discretion and his character; assume further that you could make the judgment to your own satisfaction that this man would never yield in the matter of protecting the security interests of this country? Incidentally, you happen to have reason [to believe] that he was a member of the Communist Party. I am asking whether again you would say, well, it depends on the individual.

A. Let me first point out an implausibility in the hypothetical question. I would not today suppose that a man who is a member of the Communist Party, was now or recently a member of the Communist Party, whatever his other merits, could put the interests of the United States above those of a foreign power. But if we can relax it a little bit and say that I know a man who once was a member or who I had reason to think was once a member of the Communist Party, and whom I knew well and trusted, and of whom there was question of his employment on serious secret work, I would think it would not be up to me to determine whether his disengagement from the Communist Party was genuine. I would think that at this time investigation would be called for. But I could have a very strong conviction as to whether that disengagement had in fact occurred and was real or whether the man was fooling me.

I would like that conviction to be supported by other evidence. It should be. In other words, I would not act today as I did in 1943 for a whole lot of reasons.

Q. What would you consider to be adequate in the way of an act of disengagement? What kind of thing?

A. A man's acts, his speech, his values, the way he thinks, the way he talks, and the fact of his disengagement. The fact that there are no longer any threads binding him to an organization or connecting him with an organization. These would be some of the things. And no doubt his candor.

Q. Would you expand on this candor point a little bit because I am wondering whether you are saying that his own statement about disengagement is to be made a primary factor in a determination.

A. That certainly does depend on the man. His statement that there was something to disengage from is something I should think would be relevant. . . .

Q. As long as your memory serves, did you . . . think we should have a policy, whether publicly announced or not, which would lead us to suffer atomic attack upon our cities before we would make a similar attack upon Soviet cities?

A. I think the question of our own cities, Mr. Gray, never came into this report, or at least was not the prominent thing. The prominent problem—

Q. I didn't ask about the report, then. I asked in your best recollection was this a view you entertained.

A. That we would welcome an attack on our own cities?

Q. No; I don't think that is an accurate restatement of my question. I said that we would suffer an attack upon our cities with the use of atomic weapons before we would ever make a strategic strike against the U.S.S.R.

A. Oh, lord, no. I mean the very first thing we would do against the U.S.S.R. is to go after the strategic air bases and to the extent you can the atomic bases of the U.S.S.R. You would do everything to reduce their power to impose an effective strategic attack upon us.

Q. Which might include attacks on cities and industrial concentrations.

A. It might, although clearly they are not the forward component of the Strategic Air Command.

Q. Perhaps we are tangled up with the question of strategic?

A. I have always been clear that the thing that you do without fail and with certainty is to attack every air base that has planes on it or may have planes on it the first thing. I believe our report said that.

Q. I will try again. Did you have at that time the view that we should not use the atomic weapons against any militarily promising target which might include cities in the U.S.S.R. until after such weapons had been used against such targets in this country?

A. I think I have never been entirely clear on that. This seemed to me one of the most difficult questions before us. I am sure that I have always felt that it should be a question that we were capable of answering affirmatively and capable of thinking about at the time.

Q. This is not clear in your mind as to what our position should be, you say. Have you ever thought about it in terms of a public announcement as to policy in that regard?

A. This has always struck me as very dangerous.

Q. Then you did not advocate a public announcement?

A. You mean have I publicly advocated it?

Q. No. I mean did you feel that the United States should make a public announcement about its policy, whatever it might be, with regard to the use of atomic weapons against the Soviet Union against whatever targets might present themselves?

A. In the 9 years we have been talking about these things, I have said almost everything on almost every side of every question. I take it you are asking whether in some official document I unequivocally recommended that we make a public pronouncement of our policy with regard to this, and to that my best and fairly certain answer is "No."

Q. I really asked you what your own personal view was.

A. I think that we had better not make public announcements about what we are going to do, if and when. But I do think we need to know more about it and think more about it than we had some years ago. . . .

Q. I have asked you a lot of questions about how the crash program, as the issue, came before the General Advisory Committee in the meeting in October 1949. Perhaps I asked you some questions about that.

A. I think you did.

Q. But in any event, has the testimony, all that you have heard in the last weeks, made it clearer to you how this came as the alternative, crash program or not?

A. I am a little clearer. I think the greatest clarification came from Dr. Alvarez' testimony. It is clearer to me now than it has been before that in the meeting with the Commission, the Commission probably through its chairman— told us what was on their minds. It is clear to me that the Commission was being beseiged by requests to authorize this, to proceed with that, all on the ground that these were the proper ways to expedite the thermonuclear program, and all on the ground that the thermonuclear program was the thing to do. It is clear to me that the Commission asked for our views on this.

Q. Looking back on it, do you feel that the GAC in consistency and with technical integrity could have recommended something short of the crash program, but something at the same time that was more active and productive than the alternate program?

A. Indeed I do. Indeed I do. We could have very well written the report to the following effect, that the present state of the program is such and such as we see it. This we did do. That in order to get on with it, this and this and this and this would need to be done. This we did do. We could have said that the present state of fog about this is such that we don't really know just what the problem is that is to be decided. Let us get to work and remove as much of this fog as fast as possible.

We could further have said the decision as to whether this is the important, the most important, an important, an undesirable or disastrous course involves lots of considerations of which we are dimly aware in the military and political sphere, and we hope that these will be taken into account when the decision is made. We could have written such a report.

I think apart from what personal things, feelings, still of the people involved, the best explanation of why we wrote the kind of report we did was that we said what we thought, rather than pointing out that there were other people who could be asked to evaluate (*a*) because we thought, and (*b*) because the pressure, the threat of public discussion, and the feel of the time was such that we thought our stating our own case, which was a negative case, was a good way, and perhaps the only way to insure mature deliberation on the basic problem, should we or shouldn't we.

Q. And your position as reflected in the report under no circumstances should we?

A. I think that is not quite right. I think the report itself limits itself to saying that we are reluctant, we don't think we should make a crash program, we are agreed on that, and that the statement in the majority annex that it would be better if these weapons were never brought into being was a wish, but it was not a statement that there were no circumstances under which we would also have to bring them into being.

Q. Wouldn't you say that the impression that the majority annex was calculated to give was that those who signed it were opposed to anything that would lead to the development of the hydrogen bomb?

A. That is right, under the then existing circumstances.

Q. So that really the majority in effect would not have been sympathetic with any acceleration of the program which would lead to the development of the bomb?

A. Of course. That does not mean that we would not have been sympathetic to studies and clarification. This was a question of whether you were going to set out to make it, test it, and have it.

May I make one other comment? This was not advice to Los Alamos as to what it should or should not study. This was not advice to the Commission as to what it should or should not build. Some such advice we gave in that report. This was an earnest, if not very profound, statement of what the men on that committee thought about the desirability of making a superbomb.

Q. And they felt that it was undesirable?

A. We did.

Q. If the Commission had taken their advice, or if the Government ultimately had taken the advice of the General Advisory Committee, we would not now have it.

A. I am not certain of that, but it is possible.

Q. Your advice, it seems to me, has said, and as I interpreted it, the majority annex was that we should never have it. I would guess if that advice had been taken literally the Commission would have—

A. The majority annex I still think never said that we should not have it. I think it said that it would be better if such weapons never existed.

Q. I think this is an important point, and I would like to hold on that.

A. All right. But could we have the context which I also have forgotten?

Q. Yes. I will try not to take it out of context.

MR. ROBB. Here is the majority annex.

MR. GARRISON. Mr. Chairman, would it not be helpful if Dr. Oppenheimer could look at the report which he has not seen for some time?

THE WITNESS. I saw it the other day.

MR. GRAY. I will show it to him again. I want to pick out the portions that I think are pertinent here, and let him make any observations about context. The security officer cautioned me that I am really getting on difficult ground.

May I interline this?

MR. ROLANDER. Yes.

THE WITNESS. Does the majority annex contain information which should not be on this record?

MR. GRAY. I do not know.

(Mr. Rolander handed copy of report to Dr. Oppenheimer.)

THE WITNESS. I would like to quote the entire paragraph, if that is permissible. I see something—well, I don't know.

MR. GRAY. I see no reason why the whole paragraph should not be quoted.

MR. ROLANDER. It is all right.

THE WITNESS. This is the fourth paragraph of a six paragraph annex:

"We believe a super bomb should never be produced. Mankind would be far better off not to have a demonstration of the feasibility of such a weapon until the present climate of world opinion changes."

That is that paragraph in its entirety.

By Mr. Gray:

Q. That language is pretty clear, isn't it, that "We believe a super bomb should never be produced"?

A. Sure it is.

Q. So that there was not any question that the six people of the majority were saying that we should not take steps to develop and produce.

A. Let me indicate to you—

MR. GARRISON. Mr. Chairman, could he read it once more, because it is the first we heard it.

THE WITNESS. This is one paragraph. The document is full of the word "mankind" and this paragraph reads:

"We believe a super bomb should never be produced. Mankind would be far better off not to have a demonstration of the feasibility of such a weapon until the present climate of world opinion changes."

Let me indicate—

By Mr. Gray:

Q. The question I would ask which would be related to this paragraph is—I am not attacking the motivation of those who held that belief, I am simply saying that the belief is clearly stated there, that the super bomb should never be produced.

A. That a super bomb should never be produced. But look at what that means. If we had had indication that we could not prevent the enemy from doing it, then it was clear that a super bomb would be produced. Then our arguments would be clearly of no avail. This was an exhortation—I will not comment on its wisdom or its folly—to the Government of the United States to seek to prevent the production of super bombs by anyone.

Q. Again, without reference to its wisdom or its folly, is it unreasonable to think that the Commission, reading this report or hearing it made, whichever form it took, would believe that the majority of the General Advisory Committee recommended that the Government not proceed with steps which would lead to the production of a super bomb?

A. That is completely reasonable. We did discuss this point with the Commission on two subsequent occasions. On one occasion we made it clear that nothing in what we had said was meant to obtain, should it be clear or should it be reasonably probable that the enemy was on this trail.

In another, we made it clear that there was a sharp distinction between theoretical study and experiment and invention and production and development on the other hand. So that the Commission, I think, had a little more than this very bald statement to go on. . . .

Q. . . . It would appear that the majority of the members of the GAC at that time felt unqualifiedly that they opposed not only the production, but the development.

A. Right.

Q. So that my question to you is, in this proceeding there has been a lot of testimony that the GAC was opposed to a particular crash program. Isn't it clear that it was not only the crash program that the majority of the GAC found themselves in opposition to, but they were just opposed to a program at all which had to do with thermonuclear weapons?

A. I think it is very clear. May I qualify this?

Q. Yes, you may.

A. I think many things could have qualified our unqualified view. I have mentioned two of them. I will repeat them. One is indications of what the enemy was up to. One of them is a program technically very different from the one that we had before us. One of them a serious and persuasive conclusion that the political effort to which we referred to in our annexes could not be successful.

Q. Now, following the Government's decision in January 1950, would it be unfair to describe your attitude toward the program as one of passive resistance?

A. Yes.

Q. That would be unfair?

A. I think so.

MR. GARRISON. Unfair, Mr. Chairman?

MR. GRAY. He said unfair to so describe it.

By Mr. Gray:

Q. Would it be unfair to describe it as active support?

A. Active could mean a great many things. I was not active as I was during the war. I think it would be fairer to describe it as active support as an adviser to the Commission, active support in my job on the General Advisory Committee. Not active support in the sense that I rolled up my sleeves and went to work and not active support in the sense that I assumed or could assume the job of attracting to the work the people who would have come to a job in response to a man's saying, "I am going to do this; will you help me."

Q. You testified that you did not seek to dissuade anyone from working on the project.

A. Right.

Q. There have been a good many others who have given similar testimony. It also, however, has been testified that there would have been those who would have worked on the project had you encouraged them to do so.

A. There has been testimony that there were people who believed this.

Q. Yes. Do you believe that?

A. I think it possible. Let me illustrate. In the summer of 1952, there was this Lincoln summer study which had to do with continental defense. On a few limited aspects of that I know something. On most I am an ignoramus. I think it was Zacharias that testified that the reason they wanted me associated with it was that that would draw people into it. The fact that I was interested in it would encourage others. In that sense I think that if I had gone out to Los Alamos even if I had done nothing but twiddled my thumbs, if it had been known that I had gone out to promote the super, it might have had an affirmative effect on other people's actions. I don't believe that you can well inspire enthusiasm and recruit people unless you are doing something about it yourself.

Q. Furthermore, it was fairly well known in the community—that is, the community of physicists and people who would work on this—that you had not been in favor of this program prior to the Government's decision. That probably was a factor?

A. I would think inevitably so.

Q. Do you think that it is possible that some of those individuals who were at Princeton whose names were suggested for the project might have gone had they thought you were enthusiastic for the program?

A. I don't believe this was the issue. For one thing, I know that I said to all of them that it was a very interesting program and that they should find out about it. For another—I am talking about a group of people that has been testified to, but as to whom I don't know who they were, I don't know what these names are—but the issue has usually been, should a man give up his basic research in science in favor of applied work, and I believe it was on that ground and on the personality ground as to whether they did or did not want to work with Dr. Teller, and whether they did or did not want to go to Los Alamos, the decisions would have been made. I don't think my lack of enthusiasm—I don't believe I would have manifested any, nor do I believe it would have been either persuasive or decisive. This is in that period after we were going ahead.

Q. Do you remember at approximately what date it was that you offered to resign as chairman of the General Advisory Committee?

A. Yes, approximately. It was when Mr. Dean had taken office, the first time I saw him. That would have been perhaps late summer of 1950. I believe I testified that at the time of the President's decision Dr. Conant told me he had recently talked with the Secretary of State, that the Secretary of State felt that it would be contrary to the national interest if either he or I at that time resigned from the General Advisory Committee; that this would promote a debate on a matter which was settled. The question was how soon after that could this be done.

I talked to Mr. Dean, not primarily about quitting the Advisory Committee, but about quitting the chairmanship about which by then I felt not too comfortable. That would have been August, September of 1950.

MR. GRAY. I think I have no more questions. Dr. Evans.

DR. EVANS. Dr. Oppenheimer, you said you had received a birthday card from Chevalier?

THE WITNESS. Yes.

DR. EVANS. He is now in France, is that it?

THE WITNESS. Yes.

DR. EVANS. Is he teaching or writing?

THE WITNESS. I remember very much what he is doing because he discussed this with us. He is translating, and part of his job is translating for UNESCO, or was. I don't know that it still is. . . .

By Mr. Robb:

Q. Doctor, what was the address on that card from Dr. Chevalier? Was it addressed to you at Princeton or here?

A. I think it was addressed to Princeton and forwarded here. I don't know.

Q. Was there any note with the card?

A. I think there was.

Q. Do you recall what it said?

A. No; I can find this. It is back—

Q. Do you receive a card from him every year at your birthday?

A. No; this was my 50th birthday.

Q. Do you know how he knew that?

A. No.

Q. Do you recall what the note said?

A. Not very much.

Q. Any?

A. It didn't say very much, and I don't recall it. It was written by his wife and it said greetings from our Butte.

Q. Our what?

A. Our Butte. They live on a hill.

Q. Doctor, you testified you didn't feel too comfortable as chairman of GAC in 1950; is that right?

A. Yes.

Q. Why not?

A. Because on a very major point of policy I had expressed myself, had become identified with a view which was not now national policy. I thought that there could be strong arguments for having as chairman of that committee someone who had from the beginning been enthusiastic and affirmative.

Q. Did you feel that others of the scientific community might well feel that you still were not enthusiastic?

A. This is not a consideration that crossed my mind at that time. I think I had more in mind that when on an important thing a man is overruled, his word is not as useful as it was before.

Q. Do you now feel that others in the scientific community might then have believed that you still were not very enthusiastic about the thermonuclear?

A. I know that now.

Q. Do you now feel that your lack of enthusiasm which might have been communicated to other scientists might have discouraged them from throwing themselves into the program?

A. I think this point has been discussed a great deal. I don't have substantive knowledge about it. I think that the critical, technical views which the General Advisory Committee expressed from time to time had a needling effect on the progress at Los Alamos which probably had something to do with the emergence of the brilliant inventions.

Q. To get back to the question, Doctor, would you mind answering that question?

A. Could you say it again?

MR. ROBB. Would you read it?

(Question read by the reporter.)

THE WITNESS. I suppose so.

By Mr. Robb: . . .

Q. Was there in the draft of the report which you prepared or your visit to Pasadena in the fall of 1951 any suggestion that the United States should announce that no strategic air attack would be directed against Russia unless such an attack were first started by Russia, either against the European Zone of Interior or against our cities or against our European allies?

A. I have testified on this as fully as I could in response to the chairman's questions.

Q. I want to have it specific, if I may, Doctor—a specific response to that particular question.

MR. GARRISON. Mr. Chairman, is Mr. Robb reading from the record?

MR. ROBB. No, sir, I am not. I don't have it. This is a draft, and we can't find this draft.

THE WITNESS. I can tell you where you can find it.

By Mr. Robb:

Q. Before you do that, would you mind answering the question?

A. I would mind answering it, because I have been over this ground as carefully as I know how. When you say "suggest," I don't know whether you mean recommendation or consideration.

Q. Was there any language in the report to that effect?

A. To what effect; that this might be the state of affairs?

Q. That this might be a good idea.

MR. GARRISON. What might be a good idea? I am lost.

By Mr. Robb:

Q. Was there any language in the draft to the effect that it would be a good idea if the United States should announce that no atomic attack would be directed against Russia unless such an attack was first started by Russia either against our Zone of Interior or against our European allies?

A. To the very best of my recollection, we said we may be faced with a situation in which this occurs.

Q. We may be faced with a situation in which that was desirable; is that right?

A. Yes; in which it is wise, or in which it is done.

Q. Was there any language in the final draft or the final report which said that?

A. In the final draft of the final report it said that in the consideration of the use of our strategic airpower, one of the factors should be the deterrent value—I have not got the words—the deterrent value of this strategic air in the protection of European cities.

Q. Do you consider that to be different from the language we have talked about before?

A. It is manifestly different language.

Q. Yes. And don't you think the difference is important?

A. It was very important to our readers. . . .

Q. Doctor, you testified that Mrs. Oppenheimer has told you that she may have given some money to Steve Nelson; is that correct?

A. Yes.

Q. Did she tell you how much?

A. No.

Q. Did you ask her?

A. Yes.

Q. What did she say?

A. She said she didn't remember. Not that she had told me that she had given, but that she may have given.

Q. Did you ever give Nelson any money?

A. I don't believe so. . . .

Q. You mentioned having seen Miss Tatlock on various occasions. Were any of those occasions meetings of Communist groups?

A. No.

Q. Or left-wing groups?

A. If you are willing to include Spanish bazaars. I never saw her at a political meeting.

Q. Did you ever see her at a meeting where a Communist talk was given?

A. I certainly don't remember.

MR. GARRISON. What kind of a talk?

MR. ROBB. Communist.

MR. GARRISON. A Communist talk?

MR. ROSS. Yes.

THE WITNESS. We went together to some CIO affair, but I don't remember who talked.

MR. GRAY. Could this have been the FAECT?

THE WITNESS. No, it wasn't. It was in San Francisco. I don't know what it was.

By Mr. Robb:

Q. Did you ever go with her to any meeting of any kind at which literature was passed out?

A. The only meeting at which literature was passed out that I recollect is the one at my brother's house, which I described.

Q. Was Miss Tatlock there?

A. No.

Q. What kind of literature was that, Communist literature that was passed out?

A. I think so; yes.

Q. At that meeting were any pledges of contributions made by any of the people present?

A. I am not certain. My impression is that it was some kind of a dues gathering.

Q. I believe you testified to that.

A. I am not certain. . . .

Q. Doctor, is it your testimony that you told a false story to Colonel Pash so as to stimulate him to investigate Eltenton?

A. That appears not to have been necessary.

Q. Was that your testimony?

A. No, it is not. I testified that I had great difficulty explaining why I told him a false story, but that I believed that I had two things in mind. One was to make it clear that there was something serious, or rather I thought there might be something serious, and the other was not to tell the truth.

Q. Did you have any reason to believe that Colonel Pash would not be active in investigating the story you told?

Mr. Garrison. Mr. Chairman, isn't this covering ground that has already been gone over this afternoon with you, and already over again in cross-examination? I mean do we have to go on and on with this?

Mr. Gray. I think that clearly this is one of the important things in the Commission's letter. I think I will ask Mr. Robb to proceed unless he feels he is simply covering ground that has already been covered.

Mr. Garrison. I think he ought to try as much as possible not to put words in the witness' mouth.

Mr. Robb. I am cross-examining him.

By Mr. Robb:

Q. I asked you whether you had any reason to believe that Colonel Pash would not be active in investigating your story?

A. I had no reason to believe anything. I had never met Colonel Pash before.

Q. Are you really serious, as you stated to the Chair, that you told Colonel Pash for the purpose of stimulating him?

A. I have been very serious in all my testimony and certainly not less in this very bizarre incident.

Q. You would agree that testimony is somewhat bizarre, wouldn't you?

A. That is not what I said.

Mr. Garrison. Mr. Chairman, he is arguing with the witness.

Mr. Robb. No; I am asking.

Mr. Garrison. You are asking, wouldn't you agree, and this and that, which seems to me to be argument. I let it go if the chairman thinks not. But it seems to me to be an attempt to make him say what does not come from him in his own natural way.

Mr. Robb. The word "bizarre" was his, not mine.

The Witness. I said the incident was bizarre. . . .

Tuesday, May 4

Katherine Oppenheimer: **"I left the Communist Party. I did not leave my past, the friendships, just like that"**

[Garrison recalls Vannevar Bush in order to rebut Luis Alvarez's assertion that Bush had told him that President Harry Truman did not trust Oppenheimer. Bush declares, "I am quite sure I didn't say to him that the President had doubts about Dr. Oppenheimer simply because it was not true." Then Katherine Oppenheimer is recalled, with most of the questions coming, once again, from Gordon Gray and Ward Evans.]

EXAMINATION

By Mr. Gray:

Q. We have asked you to come before the board again for some further questions. . . .

I want to refer now to the contributions that Dr. Oppenheimer was making through Isaac Folkoff and possibly others as late as sometime in 1942. Were you familiar with the fact that these contributions were being made at the time?

A. I knew that Robert from time to time gave money; yes.

Q. Do you remember whether he gave money on any regular or periodic basis?

A. Do you mean regular, or do you mean periodic?

Q. I really mean regular.

A. I think he did not.

Q. Were you aware that this money was going into Communist Party channels?

A. Through Communist Party channels?

Q. Yes.

A. Yes.

Q. You had yourself broken with the Communist Party as early as 1937, I believe?

A. 1936 I stopped having anything to do with the Communist Party.

Q. Would it be fair to say that Dr. Oppenheimer's contributions in the years as late as possibly 1942 meant that he had not stopped having anything to do with the Communist Party? I don't insist that you answer that yes or no. You can answer that any way you wish.

A. I know that. Thank you. I don't think that the question is properly phrased.

Q. Do you understand what I am trying to get at?

A. Yes; I do.

Q. Why don't you answer it that way?

A. The reason I didn't like the phrase "stopped having anything to do with the Communist Party" because I don't think that Robert ever did—

DR. EVANS. What was that?

THE WITNESS. It is because I don't think Robert ever had anything to do with the Communist Party as such. I know he gave money for Spanish refugees; I know he gave it through the Communist Party.

By Mr. Gray:

Q. When he gave money to Isaac Folkoff, for example, this was not necessarily for Spanish refugees, was it?

A. I think so.

Q. As late as 1942?

A. I don't think it was that late. I know that is some place in the record.

Q. I may be in error. My recollection is that Dr. Oppenheimer testified that these contributions were as late as 1942. Am I wrong about that?

A. Mr. Gray, Robert and I don't agree about everything. He sometimes remembers something different than the way I remember it.

Q. What you are saying is that you don't recall that the contributions were as late as 1942?

A. That is right.

Q. Are you prepared to say here now that they were not as late as 1942?

A. I am prepared to say that I do not think that they were that late.

Q. But you do think it is possible that they could have been?

A. I think it is possible.

Q. I mean, it is possible, if you don't have a very clear recollection—

MR. SILVERMAN. Would it be helpful for me to state my recollection of the evidence on this point, or would you rather not, sir?

MR. GRAY. No, I would prefer to proceed. What I am trying to get at, Mrs. Oppenheimer, is at what point would you say Dr. Oppenheimer's associations or relationships with people in the Communist Party ceased?

THE WITNESS. I do not know, Mr. Gray. I know that we still have a friend of whom it has been said that he is a Communist.

MR. ROBB. I beg your pardon?

THE WITNESS. I said I know we still have a friend of whom it has been said that he is a Communist.

MR. GRAY. You refer to Dr. Chevalier?

THE WITNESS. Yes.

MR. GRAY. I really was not attempting to bring him into the discussion at this point. I believe the import of the testimony you gave the other day was that at one time you felt that the Communist Party in this country was of an indigenous character and was not controlled or directed by international communism.

THE WITNESS. That is right.

MR. GRAY. I think also that you testified that knowing today what you do, you would think it would be a mistake to be identified—

THE WITNESS. That is right.

MR. GRAY. Now, I am trying to get at the point of by what mechanics one who has been associated becomes clearly disassociated.

THE WITNESS. I think that varies from person to person, Mr. Gray. Some people do the bump, like that, and even write an article about it. Other people do it quite slowly. I left the Communist Party. I did not leave my past, the friendships, just like that. Some continued for a while. I saw Communists after I left the Communist Party. I think that I did not achieve complete clarity about it until quite a lot later.

MR. GRAY. About when would that be, do you suppose?

THE WITNESS. I find that very hard to say, but I have been thinking about it. I would roughly date a lot of it around Pearl Harbor.

MR. ROBB. Around what, Mrs. Oppenheimer?

THE WITNESS. Pearl Harbor. I mean as sort of an end point. There were other things that happened much earlier that made me feel that the Communist Party was being quite wrong.

MR. GRAY. Would you attempt to date Dr. Oppenheimer's conclusion to that effect?

THE WITNESS. Yes.

MR. GRAY. About when would that be?

THE WITNESS. I thought you said to that effect, meaning Pearl Harbor.

MR. GRAY. No. I mean by that the conclusion that the Communist Party was quite wrong. At what time would you guess that he came to the same conclusion with clarity?

THE WITNESS. I think earlier than I.

MR. GRAY. Earlier than you?

THE WITNESS. Yes.

MR. GRAY. Which would have been earlier than December 1941?

THE WITNESS. Yes. . . .

DR. EVANS. Mrs. Oppenheimer, there has been a lot of talk here about the Communists and fellow travelers. Could you tell me so that you and I can understand the difference between a Communist and a fellow traveler?

THE WITNESS. To me, a Communist is a member of the Communist Party who does more or less precisely what he is told.

DR. EVANS. He does what?

THE WITNESS. Rather precisely what he is told to do by the Communist Party.

I think a fellow traveler could be described as someone to whom some of the aims of the Communist Party were sympathetic and in this way he knew Communists. For instance, let us take the classic example that is bandied about all the time nowadays; that is, the Spanish War. Many people were on the side of the Republicans during the Spanish War. So were the Communists. I think the people who were not Communists and were on the side are now always known as fellow travelers.

DR. EVANS. Did you ever try to get your husband to join the party?

THE WITNESS. No.

DR. EVANS. You never did?

THE WITNESS. I was not a Communist then.

DR. EVANS. How is that?

THE WITNESS. I was not a Communist then. I would not have dreamed of trying to get anybody to be a member of the Communist Party.

Dr. Evans. Do you think you have been completely disillusioned now or are you still fuzzy?

The Witness. No, I have been disillusioned for a long time. . . .

By Mr. Robb:

Q. Mrs. Oppenheimer, did you used to read the People's Daily World?

A. I have seen it, yes.

Q. That is the west coast Communist newspaper?

A. That is right.

Q. Did you see it around your house in Berkeley?

A. I think it got delivered to our house on Shasta Road.

Q. On where?

A. On Shasta Road.

Q. Who subscribed to it, you or Dr. Oppenheimer?

A. I do not know. I did not subscribe to it. Robert says he did. I sort of doubt it. The reason I have for that is that I know we often sent the Daily Worker to people that we tried to get interested in the Communist Party without their having subscribed to it. So I do not know whether or not Robert subscribed to it. I know it was delivered to the house.

Q. You say "we"; do you mean the Communists? Do you mean when you were a Communist?

A. Yes, that is what I mean. . . .

Q. You mentioned that you still had a friend who people say was a Communist. Was that Dr. Chevalier you had in mind?

A. Yes.

Q. You heard it said that he still is a Communist?

A. No, I have heard it said he was.

Q. Did you know anything about his activities in Communist causes?

A. I think he went to Spanish relief parties. I know he had this party at his house at which Schneiderman spoke.

Q. Had you finished your answer?

A. I am trying to think if I knew anything else about him. I think I know no other facts in that direction.

Q. Did you ever see his name in the Daily Worker or the Daily People's World as having endorsed the so-called purge trials in Russia?

A. No.

Q. You saw Dr. Chevalier in France last fall?

A. That is right, in December.

Q. In Paris?

A. In Paris.

Q. How long were you in Paris on that occasion?

A. Well, let's see. We went over—I think we spent 2 days and then went up to Copenhagen and came back, and I think we spent something like a week again. It may have been 5 days or it may have been a little longer than a week; I do not remember.

Q. Was it on the first 2 days that you saw Dr. Chevalier?

A. No.

Q. You mean after you came back from Copenhagen you saw him?

A. I think so, yes.

Q. Do you recall how you happened to get in touch with him?

A. Yes, I do.

Q. Would you tell us that?

A. I called his wife and said we would like to see them. She said that Haakon was in Italy, but she thought he would be back and she would let us know.

Q. Do you remember how you happened to have her telephone number?

A. It was in the book. I think it was in the book. I think I looked it up. On the other hand, I may have had a note from Haakon in my purse with the telephone number on it, which I would have taken along because if we went to Paris we wanted to see them.

Q. Do you recall how you happened to know they were in Paris at all?

A. Yes. I think Haakon wrote us.

Q. How long before you went there?

A. I think he has written us probably 3 or 4 times in the last few years.

Q. I suppose he expressed a hope that if you came there you would look him up?

A. Certainly. . . .

Q. I believe you had lunch with the Chevaliers or dinner.

A. Dinner. We had dinner at their house.

Q. And then did you take them to lunch or something?

A. Oh, yes, no.

Q. Did they take you to lunch?

A. No. Haakon called for us and we went out to see Malraux.

Q. Do you remember any discussion about Dr. Chevalier's passport difficulties?

A. I do not remember it but it has been recalled to me since.

Q. How was it recalled to you?

A. I think Robert mentioned it to me.

Q. Would you tell us what he had to say about it?

A. He said that he had been asked whether Haakon had spoken to him about it and he did not remember it.

Q. Did Dr. Oppenheimer tell you pretty generally what he had been asked about matters of which you had knowledge?

A. Yes. . . .

By Mr. Silverman: . . .

Q. Did you, in fact, attempt to dissuade your husband from making contributions or having associations with Communist Party people?

A. I think not.

[Jerrold Zacharias is recalled by Garrison to challenge David Tressel Griggs's assertion that he chalked "ZORC" on the blackboard at a meeting of the Scientific Advisory Committee in 1952. The first time he came across the phrase, he insists, was in the *Fortune* magazine article of May 1953, and he considered it a "journalistic trick." Zacharias also asserts that Griggs attempted to "sabotage" the Lincoln summer study by using "obstructive tactics." Reading portions of Griggs's testimony before the board, he continues, "my blood begins to boil a bit." Then, Albert Gordon Hill, a professor of physics at MIT and director of the Lincoln Laboratory, is sworn in and confirms Zacharias's recollection: "All the soul and memory searching I can do, I first saw it in an issue of *Fortune* that came out just about a year ago." Hill claims Zacharias did not write "ZORC" on the blackboard, as Griggs alleged: "I cannot believe that, because it would have been a cute trick in a very public and formal meeting, and I know Zacharias well enough to know that I would have been quite angry with him had he done it. I am convinced he did not do it." The hearing adjourns after Garrison explains that he has not reached a final decision "as to whether to ask Dr. Oppenheimer to make a rebuttal or not," and promises to let the board know within a few hours.]

Wednesday, May 5

J. ROBERT OPPENHEIMER: **"I felt, perhaps quite strongly, that having played an active part in promoting a revolution in warfare, I needed to be as responsible as I could with regard to what came of this revolution"**

[Finally deciding to call Oppenheimer in rebuttal, his lawyers provide him with an opportunity to clarify certain matters. But Roger Robb has another surprise in store: two letters—never before seen by the defense, one only recently declassified and the other being declassified on the spot—that Oppenheimer wrote in September and October 1944, to his friend and fellow physicist, Richard C. Tolman, in which he appears to argue in favor of developing thermonuclear weapons. For one of the few times during the hearing, Oppenheimer's resentment, as well as his lawyers', at the procedural unfairness come to the surface.]

DIRECT EXAMINATION

By Mr. Silverman:

Q. Dr. Oppenheimer, Dr. Alvarez testified that when he came to Los Alamos there was a hydrogen liquefaction plant there. Will you tell us what that was used for?

A. Yes. It was actually one of the first structures erected at Los Alamos, and reflected the opinion, which turned out to be erroneous, that going from the fission weapon to the fusion weapon would not be too tough a step.

Its initial purpose was to make studies of the thermodynamics, and steresis phenomena in the liquefaction of hydrogen isotopes. This work was also conducted by a subcontractor at the University of Ohio.

About halfway through the war, a number of points arose which changed the program. One I think Dr. Teller referred to. He discovered in the work we had earlier done we had left out something very important and very serious, which proved that the ideas we had had about how to make this machine would not work in the form we then had. The pressure on the whole laboratory to get the fission job done and the difficulties of that job both increased. The cryogenic facility actually played a small part in our researches for the fission job but I do not propose to describe it. I think it is classified. . . .

I believe that very little was done with the cryogenic facility in the last year before the war ended.

I may, if this is still responsive to your question, describe what else was going on at Los Alamos during the war related to the thermonuclear program.

Q. I wish you would, yes.

A. As nearly as I can recollect, there were two groups in addition to the cryogenic group concerned. One was Dr. Teller's group which toward the end of the war was in the part of the laboratory that Fermi as associate director ran. It was called the advanced development division, and several young people under Teller were figuring and calculating on aspects of the thermonuclear program. There was another group in which there were three members of the British mission, and a number of Americans who were measuring the reactivity of the materials which seemed to us relevant to a hydrogen bomb, and who actually completed some measurements on this before the war was over. I think this is about the whole story.

Q. As a matter of characterization, would you say that at Los Alamos during the war years the laboratory was actively working on the development of the thermonuclear bomb?

A. We planned to be, but we were in fact not.

Q. And why not?

A. I have outlined the two major reasons. First, we didn't know how to do it, and second, we were busy with other things.

Q. At the end of the war, was there any expression to you of Government policy with respect to going ahead with the thermonuclear weapon?

A. I think I have already testified, but I am willing to repeat. After the Trinity
test, the Alamagordo test, but before Hiroshima, I went to Chicago to consult General Groves largely about the major mechanics of the overseas mission, and how we would meet our time schedules. In the course of that, I
put up to General Groves—I think I had already put in writing an account of
the problem—the fact that we had not moved forward, and perhaps had
moved somewhat backward on the thermonuclear program, and was this
something that he wanted the laboratory to take hold of. This was while the
war was still on. He was fairly clear in saying no. I believe—I will not speculate as to his reasons for that, but it was clear to me. . . .

Groves said that in the present state of the world, the work on weapons
must continue, but that this did not include, he thought, the super. That
was about all. These were not formal expressions of opinion; they were
from my boss to me in a most informal way at a time when I was preparing
not to retain active responsibility.

By Mr. Silverman:

Q. Dr. Teller testified about a board of four people at the end of the war, or
near the end of the war, who he understood decided that the thermonuclear
program should not be pushed. Can you cast some light on that?

A. I think I can. I think I know what Dr. Teller was talking about.

There was a panel of four people. Their names were Arthur Compton,
Ernest Lawrence, Enrico Fermi and me, Robert Oppenheimer. We had been
asked to advise on the use of the bombs, on the general nature of the future
atomic energy program, but we were asked specifically through Mr. Harrison, on behalf of the Secretary of War, to prepare as detailed an account as
we could of everything we knew that could be done or needed doing in the
field of atomic energy.

This was not just military things. It involved the use of isotopes and the
power problem and the military problems. As a part of this report, we discussed improvements in atomic weapons and in the carrier problem. As a
part of this report, we discussed the thermonuclear bomb, the super, as it
was called. That was all we had in mind then. I believe that section was
written by Fermi. I believe that Dr. Teller correctly testified that his own
view on what the problem was, was attached as a slightly dissenting or even
strongly dissenting view to our account.

We wrote an account which was not a recommendation of policy at all, as
I remember, but was an analysis of where we thought the matter stood. I
think General Nichols' letter to me quotes from it, and says this program did
not appear on theoretical grounds as certain then as the fission-weapon program had at some earlier stage. This was a rather long and circumstantial

account of what we knew about it. It was not intended and was not a statement of what should be done. It was an assessment of the technical state of the problem.

This board had no authority to decide, it was not called on to recommend a decision, it did not decide nor recommend a decision. It described. I think Dr. Teller was a little mistaken about what our function was. . . .

Q. Dr. Alvarez testified that at a meeting of the Military Objectives Panel in about December 1950, you said something to the effect that "We all agree that the hydrogen bomb program should be stopped, but to do so will disrupt the people at Los Alamos and other laboratories, so let us wait for the Greenhouse tests, and when those fail that will be the time to stop the program." Can you cast any light on that?

A. I am clear as to what my views were, and therefore fairly clear as to what I would have said, which resembles to some extent what Dr. Alvarez recounted. I did not think the Greenhouse test would fail. It was well conceived technically, and there was no ground for such an opinion. * * * I could not have said that I expected it to fail, because I didn't think it would, and I could not have said that I expected it to fail, because this sort of statement about a test is something none of us ever made. The reason for making the test was that we wanted to find out.

What I did believe, and for the wisdom of this view I am not making an argument, was that the real difficulties with the super program, as it then appeared, were not going to be tested by this Greenhouse test; that the test was not relevant to the principal question of feasibility. I am fairly sure that in the course of discussions at the panel, we would have commented on this.

On the question of where the super program stood, on the relevance of that to the Greenhouse test, of the doubts that I felt as to whether this part of the Greenhouse test was a sensible thing technically to do, I would have said that to stop this part of the Greenhouse test, even though it made no technical sense, would be disruptive and destructive of all parts of the Los Alamos program.

I think that is the true story of what I would have said at this panel meeting and Dr. Alvarez' recollection is in some respects mistaken.

Q. What were your views as to the feasibility of the Super at that time?

MR. ROBB. What time are we talking about?

MR. SILVERMAN. This is December 1950, at the time of the military objectives panel.

THE WITNESS. On the basis of then existing ideas it was highly improbable that this could be made; that we needed new ideas if there was to be real hope of success.

May I add one comment? In actual fact this component of the Greenhouse test had a beneficial effect on the program. This was in part because the confirmation of rather elaborate theoretical prediction encouraged everybody to feel that they understood and when they then made very ambitious inventions, the fact that they had been right in the past gave confidence to their being right in the future.

It may also to a smaller extent have provided technical information that was useful. Certainly its psychological effect was all positive. It would have been a great mistake to stop that test.

By Mr. Silverman:

Q. And you thought so at the time and said so?

A. But not for the right reasons.

Q. There have been discussions on your views on continental defense and tactical and strategic use of weapons and so on. Perhaps if we could do this very briefly, could you give very briefly your views on continental defense?

A. As of when?

Q. As of now, if you like. As of the last year or two.

A. If the board is not saturated with this, I will say a couple of sentences.

Q. As of the time of the Lincoln study.

A. The immediate view after the war was that defense against atomic weapons was going to be a very tough thing. The attrition rates of the Second World War, though high, were wholly inadequate to this new offensive power.

Q. By the attrition rates, you mean the number of attacking airplanes you could shoot down and kill?

A. Precisely. In the spring of 1952, the official views of what we could do were extremely depressing, * * * and there were methods of attack which appeared to be quite open to the enemy where it was doubtful that we would either detect or intercept any substantial fraction of the aircraft at all.

I knew that on some aspects of the defense problem, valuable work was in progress at Lincoln and elsewhere. I knew something of the Charles study. * * * My view is that this is by no means a happy situation, and I know of no reason to think that it ever will be a happy situation, but that the steps that are now being taken and others that will come along as technology develops are immensely worth taking if they only save some American lives, if they only preserve some American cities, and if they only create in the planning of the enemy some doubt as to the effectiveness of their strikes. I don't know whether this answers the question.

Q. I think that answers the question.

A. I have never gone along with the 90 to 95 percent school. I hope they are right, but I have never believed them.

Q. The 90 to 95 percent school is the school—

A. That thinks you can eliminate practically all of the enemy attack.

Q. What did you conceive to be the relation between continental defense and strategic airpower?

A. First, strategic airpower is one of the most important ingredients of continental defense. Both with the battle of Europe and with the intercontinental battle clearly the best place to destroy aircraft is on the ground on enemy fields, and that is a job for strategic airpower.

Second, at least the warning elements and many of the defensive elements of continental defense are obviously needed to protect the bases, the aircraft, which take part in the strategic air campaign. This is the two-way relation which I think has been testified to by others. This has always been my understanding.

Q. It has been suggested that perhaps you had more interest in the tactical than the strategic use of atomic weapons. Could you comment on that?

A. It has been talked about a great deal. When the war ended, the United States had a weapon which revolutionized strategic air warfare. It got improved a little. The Air Force went hard to work to make best possible use of it. * * * Even during World War II we had a request through General Groves from the Army as to whether we could develop something that would be useful in the event of an invasion of Japan to help the troops that would be faced with an entrenched and determined enemy. The bomb that was developed and embellished in the years 1945 to 1948, and the aircraft that go with it, the whole weapons system, can of course be used on any target, but it is a very inappropriate one for a combat theater. Therefore, there was a problem of developing the weapon, the weapon system, the tactics to give a new capability which would be as appropriate as possible under fire, and in the combat theater. This is not because it is more important. Nothing could be more important than the armament that we had, and which is now to be extended, perhaps to some extent superseded, by thermonuclear weapons. It was simply another job which needed doing, and which is not competitive, ought not to be competitive any more than continental defense is, which is another part of the defense of the country and of the free world. That job was slow in accomplishment. It is accomplished now, or largely accomplished now.

MR. SILVERMAN. I have no further questions of Dr. Oppenheimer.

MR. GRAY. I wonder if you have any, Mr. Robb?

MR. ROBB. I have a few; yes, sir.

CROSS-EXAMINATION

By Mr. Robb:

Q. Doctor, I want to show you a carbon copy of a letter dated September 20, 1944, addressed to Dr. R. C. Tolman, 2101 Constitution Avenue, Washington, D.C., bearing the typewritten signature, "J. R. Oppenheimer," and ask you if you wrote that.

MR. SILVERMAN. May I look at it?

MR. ROBB. I am sorry, it is declassified with certain deletions which have just been circled here.

THE WITNESS. I am sure I wrote it. Would you give me the courtesy of letting me read it?

By Mr. Robb:

Q. You mean read it aloud?

A. No.

Q. Sure, that is why I showed it to you.

A. I remember the circumstances.

Q. Have you read it now?

A. Yes.

Q. Including the portions that were circled?

A. Right; which I think they are relevant to the sense of the whole letter.

Q. Doctor, do you think if we read this into the record that you can paraphrase those portions in some innocuous way?

A. Let us see how it goes.

Q. It doesn't seem to be very much, and we did that once before.

MR. ROBB. Mr. Chairman, might I ask to have this read by Mr. Rolander? When you get to the portions that are deleted—

MR. SILVERMAN. I really find this a very disturbing procedure.

MR. GRAY. All right, you can state your concern.

MR. SILVERMAN. My concern is that here on what I hope is the last day of the hearing we are suddenly faced with a letter which I have not seen, which I know nothing about, and which is going to be read into the record, and I haven't the vaguest idea of what it is about.

THE WITNESS. It is from my file.

MR. SILVERMAN. There are lots of things in the file.

MR. ROBB. Mr. Chairman, Dr. Oppenheimer testified, as I understand his testimony, to certain opinions which were expressed to him, and I think by him in the period 1944–45, about the thermonuclear.

THE WITNESS. No.

MR. ROBB. I think there were certain discussions he had with Groves and others.

THE WITNESS. In 1945?

MR. ROBB. In 1945; yes.

I think the letter pertains to that general subject. I think the board ought to have the letters before the board.

MR. GRAY. There seems to be no question about this is a letter written by Dr. Oppenheimer. I believe he has identified it.

I repeat, Mr. Silverman, what I have said many times, and what I hope has been demonstrated by the conduct of this proceeding, that if you are taken by surprise by anything that happens in this procedure, we will give you an opportunity to meet a difficulty arising.

MR. SILVERMAN. At this moment I haven't any idea that whether I am going to be taken by surprise. I do think it would have been a very easy matter to give us a paraphrased copy of this letter in advance.

MR. ROBB. Mr. Chairman, until Dr. Oppenheimer testified about this this morning, we had no idea that this letter would become relevant at this particular time. If Mr. Silverman does not want Dr. Oppenheimer to have a chance to comment on the letter, that is all right with me.

MR. SILVERMAN. I really think that is not the question at all. The real question that I suggest is that it would have been a very easy thing to let us have some intimation of what this is about, instead of having it just flounder here—I don't know whether we are caught by surprise or not. I don't know what we are talking about.

MR. ROBB. You know, Mr. Chairman, it seems to me that Mr. Silverman is most anxious to be outraged. I don't know why.

MR. SILVERMAN. Mr. Chairman, is that remark to remain on the record?

MR. GRAY. I know we have had frequent exchanges between counsel which are on the record.

MR. SILVERMAN. The suggestion that I am anxious to be outraged suggests that I am putting on some kind of an act—

MR. ROBB. Mr. Chairman, there is some suggestion that I have done something improper in anticipating what Dr. Oppenheimer is going to testify.

MR. SILVERMAN. I frankly am about documents being produced that we have not seen and being produced at the last minute. This is an inquiry and not a trial, and it would not happen at a trial. I still don't know what is in this document. For all I know it is a very helpful document.

MR. GRAY. It may well be. The Chairman of the board makes this statement, that while this is an inquiry and not a trial, there are involved in this proceeding counsel who have not always agreed. I think I can speak for my colleagues on the board when I say that this board takes cognizance of this fact, and the fact that observations of counsel appear on the record do not in any way indicate agreement or disagreement on the part of this board with observations by counsel. As far as producing the testimony here has been concerned, there has been the greatest amount of latitude afforded both to Dr. Oppenheimer and his counsel and to Mr. Robb throughout. I must say that I don't think frankly that the observations of counsel on either side are matters which will be of too much interest and concern to this board. I suggest that you proceed, Mr. Robb.

MR. ROBB. Would you go ahead and read it?

MR. ROLANDER. I will hand Dr. Oppenheimer a copy of this letter.

THE WITNESS. Is this an unexpurgated copy?

MR. ROLANDER. It has the portions that are classified circled. The letter is dated September 20, 1944, addressed to Dr. R. C. Tolman, 2101 Constitution Ave., Washington, D.C.:

"Dear Richard. The accompanying letter makes some suggestions about procedure in the matter of site Y recommendations for postwar work. As you will recognize, the problem of making sensible recommendations is complicated by the fact that we do not know how far this project will get during its present life. It seems a reasonable assumption that we will succeed in making some rather crude forms of the gadget per se, but that the whole complex of problems associated with the super will probably not be pushed by us beyond rather elementary scientific considerations.

"I should like, therefore, to put in writing at an early date the recommendation that the subject of initiating violent thermonuclear reactions be pursued with vigor and diligence, and promptly. In this connection I should like to point out that gadgets of reasonable efficiency and suitable design can almost certainly induct significance thermonuclear reactions in deuterium even under conditions where these reactions are not self-sustaining"—

Then there is a portion that has been deleted.

By Mr. Robb:

Q. Can you paraphrase that for us, doctor?

A. Yes. It is a part of the program of site Y to explore this possibility.

MR. ROLANDER. Continuing, "It is not at all clear whether we shall actually make this development during the present project, but it is of great importance that such"—and then there is a blank.

THE WITNESS. I think that can just be left out.

MR. ROLANDER. —"Such blank gadgets form an experimentally possible transition from a simple gadget to the super and thus open the possibility of a not purely theoretical approach to the latter.

"In this connection also I should like to remind you of Rabi's proposal for initiating thermonuclear reactions"—and then blanks.

"At the present time site Y does not contemplate undertaking this, but I believe that with a somewhat longer time scale than our present one, this line of investigation might prove profitable.

"In general, not only for the scientific but for the political evaluation of the possibilities of our project, the critical, prompt, and effective exploration of the extent to which energy can be released by thermonuclear reactions is clearly of profound importance. Several members of this laboratory, notably Teller, Bethe, von Neumann, Rabi, and Fermi have expressed great interest in the problems outlined above and I believe that it would be profitable to have a rather detailed discussion of the present technical status— which I know to be confused—which should be made available to the committee before it draws up its final recommendations.

"Sincerely yours,

"J. R. Oppenheimer."

By Mr. Robb:

Q. Doctor, before we go into any discussion, I will show you a carbon copy of another letter dated October 4, 1944, addressed to Dr. R. C. Tolman, 2101 Constitution Avenue, Washington, D.C., bearing the typewritten signature, "J. R. Oppenheimer," and ask you if you will read that and tell us if you wrote it.

MR. SILVERMAN. Is this a continuation of the same correspondence, Mr. Robb?

MR. ROBB. Yes; I think so. I am trying to get this unclassified so I can hand you a copy of it, Mr. Silverman.

MR. MARKS. When was this document unclassified that you are about to hand to us?

MR. SILVERMAN. It is being declassified now. . . .

By Mr. Robb:

Q. Doctor, who was Dr. Tolman?

A. He was a very close and dear friend of mine. He had been Vice Chairman of the National Defense Research Committee. When I assumed the responsibility for Los Alamos I introduced him or saw that he was introduced to General Groves. General Groves asked him to be one of his two scientific consultants. He was a member, possibly secretary, of the Committee of Review, which visited Los Alamos in the spring of 1943, and pointed out some things that we needed to do if we were to be a successful laboratory. He was a frequent and helpful visitor to Los Alamos throughout the war. He was at one time, and I would assume at the time these letters were addressed to him, a member of a committee, possibly chairman of a committee appointed by General Groves which was a precursor to the scientific panel to the interim committee in trying to sketch out for the benefit of the Government what the postwar problems in atomic energy might be. These included military and nonmilitary problems.

I think that these letters were addressed to him in that capacity.

Q. And site Y was what?

A. Los Alamos. . . .

Q. At the time you wrote these letters, you were in favor of going ahead with a program for the development of a thermonuclear weapon, weren't you?

A. The letters speak for themselves. I believe they speak exactly what I meant.

Q. Did you mean that?

A. I meant these letters.

Q. Did you mean that you were in favor of going ahead with the thermonuclear?

A. I would like to read the phrases.

Q. What I am getting at, Doctor, laying aside the technical language, wasn't that the ordinary meaning of that you said, that you though you ought to get busy on the thermonuclear?

A. Among other things.

Q. Yes.

A. With the exploration of the thermonuclear.

Q. Did there come a time when you changed that view in subsequent years?

A. Manifestly by October 29, 1949, I was saying very different things.

Q. Yes. Doctor, something was said about the liquid hydrogen plant at Los Alamos. That was constructed for the purpose of working on a fusion weapon, wasn't it, or hydrogen weapon?

A. For preliminary research on ingredients that we thought would be essential in a hydrogen weapon.

Q. Yes. In the matter of reactors, there are various kinds of reactors, aren't there?

A. Indeed there are.

Q. Those built for commercial purposes, those built for research purposes, and those built for production of weapons purposes, isn't that right?

A. I have yet to see one built for commercial purposes but I hope I some day will.

Q. I am asking for information.

A. There are, as I testified, reactors for the development of reactors, reactors for production, reactors for research, and reactors that serve more than one purpose.

Q. You were asked about how many reactors were built during your tenure as chairman of the GAC and I think you said nine, was it?

A. No. I think you asked me during the entire period how many were started, and I think I said about a dozen and a half. Mr. Silverman asked me up to the first of 1950 how many were started, and I said perhaps eight.

Q. Were those eight built for research or production?

A. This is better found in the reports of the Commission. I believe that 3 or 4 were reactor development reactors, namely, to improve the art of reactor development. A couple, 2 or 3 were for supplementary production, and 2 or 3 were for research.

Q. Was any of them a so-called heavy-water reactor?

A. No. I am not quite sure there was not a research reactor at the Argonne, but there was no production reactor involving heavy water.

Q. You spoke of the long range detection matter and the three methods which we speak of rather cryptically. Is it true, Doctor, that it was the opinion of certain qualified people that the one method which you supported might not detect a Russian explosion if it occurred under certain circumstances?

A. We argued about that, and I advocated that opinion.

Q. That it might not?

A. That the Russians might hide an explosion, that this was unlikely, but that they might do it if we relied only on this one method.

Q. In other words, the other methods were necessary to make sure that you could detect the explosion?

A. That's right. May I add that I know of no instance in which the method I advocated has not detected the explosion and in which the others have. . . .

Q. Doctor, you have spoken somewhat of strategic and tactical airpower and strategic and tactical uses of weapons and all that; you of course don't conceive yourself to be an expert in war, do you, or military matters?

A. Of course not. I pray that there are experts in war.

Q. Have you from time to time, however, expressed rather strong views one way or the other in the field of military strategy and tactics?

A. I am sure that I have. I don't know what specific views or instances you are referring to, but I am sure the answer to your question is "Yes."

Q. I am not referring to any for the moment.

A. I am sure the answer to your question is "Yes."

Q. Doctor, I am a little curious and I wish you would tell us why you felt it was your function as a scientist to express views on military strategy and tactics.

A. I felt, perhaps quite strongly, that having played an active part in promoting a revolution in warfare, I needed to be as responsible as I could with regard to what came of this revolution.

Q. To draw a parallel, Doctor, of course you recall that Ericsson designed the first ironclad warship.

A. I don't. I am reminded of it.

Q. Beg pardon?

A. I am reminded of it.

Q. Do you think that would qualify him to plan naval strategy merely because he built the *Monitor*?

MR. SILVERMAN. Aren't we really getting into argument?

THE WITNESS. I don't think that I ever planned military—

MR. GRAY. Wait just a minute. Are you objecting?

MR. SILVERMAN. Yes, I think this is argument.

MR. GRAY. Argument?

MR. SILVERMAN. Yes, of course.

MR. GRAY. It seems to me that this board has listened for weeks to witnesses who have probed into Dr. Oppenheimer's mind, have said what we would do under circumstances, have stated with certainty what he would, what his opinions are, witnesses who disagreed on this, and I think that counsel has not failed to ask almost any question of any witness that has appeared here. I can't think of questions that could be remotely related to Dr. Oppenheimer that have not been asked.

My ruling is that Mr. Robb will proceed with his question.

THE WITNESS. Now I have forgotten the question.

MR. ROBB. Perhaps we better have it read back.

(Question read by the reporter.)

THE WITNESS. Merely because he built the *Monitor* would not qualify him to plan naval strategy.

By Mr. Robb:

Q. Doctor, do you think now that perhaps you went beyond the scope of your proper function as a scientist in undertaking to counsel in matters of military strategy and tactics?

A. I am quite prepared to believe that I did, but when we are talking about my counseling on military strategy and tactics, I really think I need to know whom I was counseling and in what terms. I am sure that there will be instances in which I did go beyond, but I do not wish to give the impression that I was making war plans or trying to set up military planning, nor that this practice was a very general one.

MR. GRAY. I think the witness is entitled to know whether Mr. Robb has in mind committees, panels, and other bodies on which Dr. Oppenheimer served or something else.

MR. ROBB. I was merely trying to explore in general Dr. Oppenheimer's philosophy in respect of this matter. That is what I had in mind. I was not pinpointing on any particular thing, Doctor, and I wanted to get your views on it as to proper function.

THE WITNESS. I served on a great many mixed bodies. This controversial Vista project was not a civilian project. There were a great many military consultants. I learned a great deal from them. The formulation of the views or Vista depend to a very large extent on discussions, day-to-day discussions with working soldiers and staff officers. The committees in the Pentagon on which I sat were usually predominantly committees of military men. I also sat on some bodies where there were no military men. I would have thought that in an undertaking like Vista the joint intelligence, in which I played an extremely small part, of a lot of bright technical and academic people—not all scientists—and of a lot of excellent staff officers and military officers was precisely what gave value to the project.

By Mr. Robb:

Q. Doctor, you stated in response to a question by Mr. Silverman that among other things the job of the strategic airpower was to destroy enemy aircraft on the fields. Do you recall that?

A. Yes.

Q. Do you confine the job of strategic airpower to that, or would you also include the destruction of enemy cities and centers of manufacture?

A. The Strategic Air Command has not only very secret but extremely secret war plans which define its job.

Q. I am asking you for your views on its job.

A. You mean what it should do?

Q. Yes, sir.

A. I think that it should be prepared to do a great variety of things, and that we should maintain at all times full freedom to decide whether in the actual crisis we are involved in, this or that should be done. It must obviously be capable of destroying everything on enemy territory.

Q. Do you think that it should do that in the event of an attack on this country by Russia?

A. I do.

MR. ROBB. That is all. Thank you. . . .

REDIRECT EXAMINATION

By Mr. Silverman:

Q. Do you think that a scientist can properly do his job of advising the military on the potential of newly developed weapons without having some idea of the use that they are to be put to, and some idea of the tactical and strategic use?

A. It depends. I believe we developed the atomic bomb without any idea at all of military problems. The people who developed radar needed to know precisely, or to have a very good idea of what the actual military campaign and needs were. Certainly you do a much better job if you have a feeling for what the military are up against. In peacetime it is not always clear, even to the military, what they will be up against.

Q. You were shown two letters by Mr. Robb, one dated September 20, 1944, I think, and the other October 4, 1944. Do those letters in any way modify the testimony you gave on direct examination as to the scale and intensity of the thermonuclear effort at Los Alamos?

A. Oh, no.

MR. SILVERMAN. That is all.

MR. GRAY. May I have that read back?

(Question and answer read by the reporter.)

THE WITNESS. May I amplify? I testified what I could recollect, and I think it is complete, of what was going on at Los Alamos during my period there in the thermonuclear program. I was asked whether these letters caused me to have a different view of what was going on there and I said they did not.

MR. GRAY. I understand, thank you.

Mr. Robb, do you have any questions?

MR. ROBB. I have nothing further.

THE WITNESS. May I make a comment. I don't care whether it is on the record or off.

MR. GRAY. Yes.

THE WITNESS. I am grateful to, and I hope properly appreciative of the patience and consideration that the board has shown me during this part of the proceedings.

MR. GRAY. Thank you very much, Dr. Oppenheimer.

Thursday, May 6

LLOYD K. GARRISON: "His life has been an open book"

[The hearing is called to order at 9:30 A.M. By 10:00, after a few loose ends are tied up, Lloyd K. Garrison begins his summation. Speaking without a prepared text, only occasionally referring to notes, and inviting questions from the board, he spends three hours summarizing the case for reinstating Oppenheimer's security clearance.]

SUMMATION

MR. GARRISON. Mr. Chairman and members of the board, I would like to thank you again for waiting over until this morning to give me a little more time to prepare what I might say to you. I want to thank each of you also for your great patience and courtesy and consideration which you have extended us all through these weeks that we have been together.

I think I should take judicial notice of the fact that unless Dr. Evans has some possible question, that I understand that you did not seek the positions which you are here occupying, and I appreciate the fact that you are rendering a great public service in a difficult and arduous undertaking.

As we approach the end of this period in which we have been together, my mind goes back to a time before the hearings began when the Commission told me that you were going to meet together in Washington for a week before the hearings began here to study the FBI files with the aid of such staff as might be provided. I remember a kind of sinking feeling that I had at that point—the thought of a week's immersion in FBI files which we would never have the privilege of seeing, and of coming to the hearings with that intense background of study of the derogatory information.

I suggested two things to the Commission. One, that I might be permitted to meet with you and participate with you during the week in discussions of the case without, as I knew would have to be the case, actual access to the FBI documents themselves, but at least informally participating with you in discussions about what the files contained.

This the Commission said was quite impractical because of the confidential nature of the material, and I then suggested that I meet with you at your very first session in Washington to give you very informally a little picture of the case as we saw it, so that you might at least have that picture as you went about your task, and also that we might have a chance to explore together the procedures which would be followed in the hearings. That request likewise was not found acceptable.

It was explained to me that the practice in these proceedings was that the board would conduct the inquiry itself and would determine itself whether or not to call witnesses and so forth, and it was therefore necessary for the board to have a thorough mastery of the file ahead of time.

We came together then as strangers at the start of the formal hearings and we found ourselves rather unexpectedly in a proceeding which seemed to us to be adversary in nature. I have previously made some comments upon this procedure. I don't want to repeat them here. I do want to say in all sincerity that I recognize and appreciate very much the fairness which the members of the board have displayed in the conduct of these hearings, and the sincere and intense effort which I know you have been making and will make to come to a just understanding of the issues. . . .

Now, I think that the basic question—the question which you have to decide—can be boiled down to a very short form. Dr. Oppenheimer's position is that of a consultant. He is to give advice when his advice is sought. This is up to the Atomic Energy Commission as to when and where and under what circumstances they shall seek his advice. That, of course, is not a question that this board is concerned with. The basic question is whether in the handling of restricted data he is to be trusted. That, it seems to me, is what confronts this board, that bare, blunt question.

In trying to reach your determination, you have some guides, some things that you are to take into consideration. The statute speaks of character, associations, and loyalty. Certainly loyalty is the paramount consideration. If a man is loyal, if in his heart he loves his country and would not knowingly

J. Robert Oppenheimer, 1954. AIP Emilio Segrè Visual Archives.

or willingly do anything to injure its security, then associations and character become relatively unimportant, it would seem to me.

I suppose one can imagine a case of a loyal citizen whose associations were so intensely concentrated in Communist Party circles—it is hard for me to suppose this of a loyal citizen, but I suppose one might reach a case where the associations were so intense and so pervasive—that it would create some risk of a chance word or something doing some harm, a slip, and so forth.

In the case of character, I suppose that a loyal citizen could still endanger the national security in the handling of restricted data if he were addicted to drunkenness or to the use of drugs, if he were a pervert. These conditions, we of course don't have here. . . .

So I say to you, Mr. Chairman and members of the board, that in the Commission's own view of the matter it is the man himself that is to be considered, commonsense to be exercised in judging the evidence, and that it is appropriate to consider in the final reckoning the fact that our long-range success in the field of atomic energy depends in large part on our ability to attract into the program men of character and vision with a wide variety of talents and viewpoints. . . .

So I think we come down in the end, Mr. Chairman, to the basic acid question before the board, whether in the overall judgment of you three men, after considering and weighing all the evidence, that Dr. Oppenheimer's continued right of access to restricted data in connection with his employment as a consultant would endanger the national security and the common defense, or be clearly inconsistent with the national security.

It would seem to me that in approaching that acid question the most impelling single fact that has been established here is that for more than a decade, Dr. Oppenheimer has created and has shared secrets of the atomic energy program and has held them inviolable. Not a suggestion of any improper use by him of the restricted data which has been his in the performance of his distinguished and very remarkable public service.

Now, at this moment of time, after more than a decade of service of this character, to question his safety in the possession of restricted data seems to me a rather appalling matter.

I would like to tell you what this case seems to me to look like in short compass. I wish we could dispose of it out of hand on the basis of the fact that I have just mentioned to you, that for more than a decade Dr. Oppenheimer has been trusted, and that he has not failed that trust. That in my judgment is the most persuasive evidence that you could possibly have. But I know that you will have to go into the testimony and the evidence, the matters in the file before you, and I would like to sum up, if I may, what it looks like to me to be like.

Here is a man, beginning in 1943—beginning in 1942, actually—taken suddenly out of the academic world in which up to that time he had lived, and suddenly in 1943 put in charge by General Groves of the vast and complex undertaking of the establishment and operation of the laboratory at Los Alamos, a man who suddenly finds himself in administrative charge of the scientific direction of some 4,000 people in a self-contained community in a desert. He performs by common consent an extraordinary service for his country, both administratively and militarily. After the war he hopes to go back to his academic work, back to physics, but the Government keeps calling upon him almost continuously for service. Secretary Stimson puts him on his Interim Committee on Atomic Energy, the Secretary of State puts him on the consultant group in connection with the program for the control of atomic energy before the U.N., he writes a memorandum to Mr. Lilienthal within a month of his appointment which contains the essence of the plan which the United States is to adopt, a plan which would have called for the breaking down of the Iron Curtain, and which was to prove extremely distasteful to the Russians. He serves Mr. Baruch at the United Nations and after Mr. Baruch retires, he served General Osborne, and General Osborne has told us here of his firmness and his realism and his grasp of the problems of the conflict and the difficulties of dealing with the Russians.

He makes speeches and he writes articles setting forth the American program and the essence of it, and supporting it. Some of those you have heard before you.

The President appoints him to the General Advisory Committee in January of 1947, and then he is elected chairman by his fellow members, and he serves on that for 6 years. He helps to put Los Alamos back on its feet. He has earlier supported the May-Johnson bill as a means of insuring that this work at Los Alamos or the work on atomic weapons wherever it be conducted can go forward.

He backs in his official work every move calculated to expand the facilities of the Commission, to enlarge raw material sources, to develop the atomic weapons for long-range detection, so that we may find out what the Russians are doing, if and when they achieve the atomic bomb.

After Korea when we are in the midst of an actual shooting war with a military establishment then found to be very depleted, he interests himself in the development of atomic weapons for the battlefield in connection not merely with our problems of intervention in situations like Korea, but more importantly for the defense of Europe against totalitarian aggression.

Finally, he interests himself in continental defense as a means of helping to preserve the home base from which both strategically and tactically any war must be fought. In these and in other ways through half a dozen other committees he gives something like half his time to the United States Government as a private citizen.

Now he is here in this room and the Government is asking the question, is he fit to be trusted. . . .

It seems to me that in the face of all of the long catalog of efforts of Dr. Oppenheimer since 1945, let alone at Los Alamos, but since 1945, to strengthen our defenses, to build up Los Alamos, to expand the weapons program, to make us strong in atomic energy, and strong in weapons and strong in defense, it is fantastic to suppose that in the face of all those efforts he should be harboring a motive to destroy his own country in favor of Russia. Just the mere proposition is unthinkable on its face. . . .

Now, this whole Chevalier incident has, I am convinced, assumed undue importance, and must be judged in perspective. It has been so extensively analyzed here in cross-examination, in the reading of transcripts of interviews of 11 years ago, the hearing of a recording, Colonel Pash's presence here, it is almost as if this whole Chevalier case brought into this room here at 16th and Constitution Avenue in 1954 had happened yesterday in the setting of today, and that we are judging a man for something that has happened almost in our presence.

I get that illusion of a foreshortening of time here which to me is a grisly matter and very, very misleading. This happened in 1943. It happened in a wholly different atmosphere from that of today. Russia was our so-called gallant ally. The whole attitude toward Russia, toward persons who were sympathetic with Russia, everything was different from what obtains today. I think you must beware above everything of judging by today's standards things that happened in a different time and era. . . .

I could go on and I think I won't. You will read the record, and I know that you will take these judgments deeply seriously. You had 3½ weeks now with the gentleman on the sofa. You have learned a lot about him. There is a lot about him, too, that you haven't learned, that you don't know. You have not lived any life with him. You have not worked with him. You have not formed those intangible judgments that men form of one another through intimate association, and you can't. It is impossible for you to do so. And I think that you should take most earnestly to heart the judgment of those who have.

Here he is now with his life in one sense in your hands, and you are asked to say whether if he continues to have access to restricted data he may injure the United States of America, and make improper use of that. For over a decade that he has had this position of sharing in the atomic energy information, never a suggestion of an improper use of data. His life has been an open book. General Wilson, one of his critics, on the H-bomb end of things, testified—I have forgotten the exact words, but we probably have it around here—that if anybody had demonstrated his loyalty by affirmative action, it is Dr. Oppenheimer, and this affirmative action runs all through his record. . . .

There is more than Dr. Oppenheimer on trial in this room. I use the word "trial" advisedly. The Government of the United States is here on trial also. Our whole security process is on trial here, and is in your keeping as is his life—the two things together. There is an anxiety abroad in the country, and I think I am at liberty to say this to you, because after all, we are all Americans, we are all citizens, and we are all interested here in doing what is in the public interest, and what is best for our country. There is an anxiety abroad that these security procedures will be applied artificially, rigidly, like some monolithic kind of a machine that will result in the destruction of men of great gifts and of great usefulness to the country by the application of rigid and mechanical tests. America must not devour her own children, Mr. Chairman and members of this board. If we are to be strong, powerful, electric, and vital, we must not devour the best and the most gifted of our citizens in some mechanical application of security procedures and mechanisms.

You have in Dr. Oppenheimer an extraordinary individual, a very complicated man, a man that takes a great deal of knowing, a gifted man beyond what nature can ordinarily do more than once in a very great while. Like all gifted men, unique, sole, not conventional, not quite like anybody else that ever was or ever will be. Does this mean that you should apply different standards to him than you would to somebody like me or somebody else that is just ordinary? No, I say not. I say that there must not be favoritism in this business. You must hew to the line and do your duty without favor, without discrimination, if you want to use those words.

But this is the point that if you are to judge the whole man as the Commission itself in its regulations and its decisions really lays upon you the task of doing, you have then a difficult, complicated man, a gifted man to deal with and in judging him, you have to exercise the greatest effort of comprehension. Some men are awfully simple and their acts are simple. That doesn't mean that the standards are any different for them. The standards should be the same. But this man bears the closest kind of examination of what he really is, and what he stands for, and what he means to the country. It is that effort of comprehension of him that I urge upon you.

I am confident, as I said, that when you have done all this, you will answer the blunt and ugly question whether he is fit to be trusted with restricted data, in the affirmative. I believe, members of the board, that in doing so you will most deeply serve the interests of the United States of America, which all of us love and want to protect and further. That I am sure of, and I am sure that is where the upshot of this case must be.

Thank you very much.

MR. GRAY. Thank you Mr. Garrison. . . .

MR. GARRISON. Mr. Chairman, may I thank you again for having borne so patiently with me and for the great consideration you have shown to us throughout the proceedings.

MR. GRAY. Thank you.

MR. GARRISON. Mr. Morgan and Dr. Evans, the same.

DR. EVANS. Thank you.

MR. MORGAN. Thank you.

MR. GRAY. We now conclude this phase of the proceedings. I think that I have already indicated to Dr. Oppenheimer that if we require anything further, he will be notified.

We are now in recess.

THE DECISION

The Personnel Security Board Reports, May 27

GORDON GRAY AND THOMAS A. MORGAN: "We have . . . been unable to arrive at the conclusion that it would be clearly consistent with the security interests of the United States to reinstate Dr. Oppenheimer's clearance"

[When the hearing ended, the three members of the Personnel Security Board left for their respective homes for a much-needed rest. They returned to Washington on May 17 and ten days later presented their findings. All of them agreed that Oppenheimer was a loyal citizen, but Gordon Gray and Thomas A. Morgan nevertheless maintained that he was a security risk. In private correspondence, Gray was even less sympathetic to Oppenheimer than he was in the majority report. Asserting that he and Morgan had shown "restraint and compassion," Gray admitted that he would more accurately have conveyed his feelings about Oppenheimer's reliability if he had used a double negative: that is, rather than making the positive assertion that he was loyal, the majority should have said that they could not conclude that he was not loyal. The historian Barton Bernstein has examined this gap "between the muddled but occasionally generous written opinion and the far more harsh private judgment reached by the majority."]

Mr. K. D. Nichols,
General Manager, U.S. Atomic Energy Commission,
1901 Constitution Avenue NW., Washington 25, D.C.
Dear Mr. Nichols:

On December 23, 1953, Dr. J. Robert Oppenheimer was notified by letter that his security clearance had been suspended. He was furnished a list of items of derogatory information and was advised of his rights to a hearing under AEC procedures. On March 4, 1954, Dr. Oppenheimer requested that he be afforded a hearing. A hearing has been conducted by the Board appointed by you for this purpose, and we submit our findings and recommendation.

Dr. Ward V. Evans dissents from the recommendation of the majority of the Board, and his minority report is attached. He specifically subscribes to the "Findings" of the majority of the Board, and to a portion of the material entitled "Significance of the Findings."

INTRODUCTION

It must be understood that in our world in which the survival of free institutions and of individual rights is at stake, every person must in his own way be a guardian of the national security. It also must be clear that, in the exercise of this stewardship, individuals and institutions must protect, preserve, and defend those human values for which we exist as a nation, as a government, and as a way of life.

The hard requirements of security, and the assertion of freedoms, together thrust upon us a dilemma, not easily resolved. In the present international situation, our security measures exist, in the ultimate analysis, to protect our free institutions and traditions against repressive totalitarianism and its inevitable denial of human values. Thoughtful Americans find themselves uneasy, however, about those policies which must be adopted and those actions which must be taken in the interests of national security, and which at the same time pose a threat to our ideals. This Board has been conscious of these conflicts, presenting as they do some of the grave problems of our times, and has sought to consider them in an atmosphere of decency and safety.

We share the hope that some day we may return to happier times when our free institutions are not threatened and a peaceful and just world order is not such a compelling principal preoccupation. Then security will cease to be a central issue; man's conduct as a citizen will be measured only in the terms of the requirements of our national society; there will be no undue restraints upon freedom of mind and action; and loyalty and security as concepts will cease to have restrictive implications.

This state of affairs seems not to be a matter of early hope. As we meet the present peril, and seek to overcome it, we must realize that at no time can the interests of the protection of all our people be less than paramount to all other considerations. Indeed, action which in some cases may seem to be a denial of the freedoms which our security barriers are erected to protect, may rather be a fulfillment of these freedoms. For, if in our zeal to protect our institutions against our measures to secure them, we lay them open to destruction, we will have lost them all, and will have gained only the empty satisfaction of a meaningless exercise.

We are acutely aware that in a very real sense this case puts the security system of the United States on trial, both as to procedures and as to substance. This notion has been strongly urged upon us by those who recommended clearance for Dr. J. Robert Oppenheimer, and no doubt a similar view is taken by those who feel he should not be cleared.

If we understand the two points of view, they may be stated as follows: There are those who apprehend that our program for security at this point in history consists of an uneasy mixture of fear, prejudice, and arbitrary judgments. They feel that reason and fairness and justice have abdicated and their places have been taken by hysteria and repression. They, thus, believe that security procedures are necessarily without probity and that national sanity and balance can be served only by a finding in favor of the individual concerned. On the other hand, there is a strong belief that in recent times our government has been less than unyielding toward the problem of communism, and that loose and pliable attitudes regarding loyalty and security have prevailed to the danger of our society and its institutions. Thus, they feel that this proceeding presents the unrelinquishable opportunity for a demonstration against communism, almost regardless of the facts developed about the conduct and sympathies of Dr. Oppenheimer.

We find ourselves in agreement with much that underlies both points of view. We believe that the people of our country can be reassured by this proceeding that it is possible to conduct an investigation in calmness, in fairness, in disregard of public clamor and private pressures, and with dignity. We believe that it has been demonstrated that the Government can search its own soul and the soul of an individual whose relationship to his Government is in question with full protection of the rights and interests of both. We believe that loyalty and security can be examined within the frameworks of the traditional and inviolable principles of American justice.

The Board approached its task in the spirit of inquiry, not that of a trial. The Board worked long and arduously. It has heard 40 witnesses including Dr. J. Robert Oppenheimer and compiled over 3,000 pages of testimony in addition to having read the same amount of file material.

Dr. Oppenheimer has been represented by counsel, usually four in number, at all times in the course of the proceedings. He has confronted every witness appearing before the Board, with the privilege of cross-examination. He is familiar with the contents of every relevant document, which was made available to the Board, except those which under governmental necessity cannot be disclosed, such as reports of the Federal Bureau of Investigation. He has, in his own words, received patient and courteous consideration at the hands of the Board. The Board has, in the words of his chief counsel, displayed fairness in the conduct of the hearings. And, finally, perhaps it should be said that the investigation has been conducted under the auspices of the responsible agency which has the obligation of decision.

As it considered substance, the Board has allowed sympathetic consideration for the individual to go hand in hand with an understanding of the necessities for a clear, realistic, and rugged attitude toward subversion, possible subversion, or indeed broader implications of security.

It was with all these considerations in mind that we approached our task. . . .

FINDINGS

Significance of the findings of the Board

The facts referred to in General Nichols' letter fall clearly into two major areas of concern. The first of these, which is represented by items 1 through

23, involves primarily Dr. Oppenheimer's Communist connections in the earlier years and continued associations arising out of those connections.

The second major area of concern is related to Dr. Oppenheimer's attitudes and activities with respect to the development of the hydrogen bomb.

The Board has found the allegations in the first part of the Commission letter to be substantially true, and attaches the following significance to the findings: There remains little doubt that, from late 1936 or early 1937 to probably April 1942, Dr. Oppenheimer was deeply involved with many people who were active Communists. The record would suggest that the involvement was something more than an intellectual and sympathetic interest in the professed aims of the Communist Party. Although Communist functionaries during this period considered Dr. Oppenheimer to be a Communist, there is no evidence that he was a member of the party in the strict sense of the word.

Using Dr. Oppenheimer's own characterization of his status during that period, he seems to have been an active fellow-traveler. According to him, his sympathies with the Communists seem to have begun to taper off somewhat after 1939, and very much more so after 1942. However, it is not unreasonable to conclude from material presented to this Board that Dr. Oppenheimer's activities ceased as of about the time he executed his Personnel Security Questionnaire in April 1942. He seems to have had the view at that time and subsequently that current involvement with Communist activities was incompatible with service to the Government. However, it also would appear that he felt that former Communist Party membership was of little consequence if the individual concerned was personally trustworthy.

Dr. Oppenheimer's sympathetic interests seemed to have continued beyond 1942 in a diluted and diminishing state until 1946, at which time we find the first affirmative action on his part which would indicate complete rejection. In October 1946, he tendered his resignation from the Independent Citizens Committee of the Arts, Sciences, and Professions, Inc., and he now says it was at this time that he finally realized that he could not collaborate with the Communists, whatever their aims and professed interests. We would prefer to have found an affirmative action at an earlier date.

The Board takes a most serious view of these earlier involvements. Had they occurred in very recent years, we would have found them to be controlling and, in any event, they must be taken into account in evaluating subsequent conduct and attitudes.

The facts before us establish a pattern of conduct falling within the following Personnel Security Clearance criteria: Category A, including instances in which there are grounds sufficient to establish a reasonable belief that an individual or his spouse has (1) Committed or attempted to commit or aided or abetted another who committed or attempted to commit any act of sabotage, espionage, treason, or sedition. (2) Establish an association with espionage agents of a foreign nation * * * (3) Held membership or joined any organization which had been declared by the Attorney General to be * * * Communist, subversive * * * These criteria under the AEC procedures establish a presumption of security risk.

The Board believes, however, that there is no indication of disloyalty on the part of Dr. Oppenheimer by reason of any present Communist affiliation, despite Dr. Oppenheimer's poor judgment in continuing some of his past associations into the present. Furthermore, the Board had before it eloquent and convincing testimony of Dr. Oppenheimer's deep devotion to his country in recent years and a multitude of evidence with respect to active service in all sorts of governmental undertakings to which he was repeatedly called as a participant and as a consultant.

We feel that Dr. Oppenheimer is convinced that the earlier involvements were serious errors and today would consider them an indication of disloyalty. The conclusion of this Board is that Dr. Oppenheimer is a loyal citizen.

With respect to the second portion of General Nichols' letter, the Board believes that Dr. Oppenheimer's opposition to the hydrogen bomb and his related conduct in the postwar period until April 1951, involved no lack of loyalty to the United States or attachment to the Soviet Union. The Board was impressed by the fact that even those who were critical of Dr. Oppenheimer's judgment and activities or lack of activities, without exception, testified to their belief in his loyalty.

The Board concludes that any possible implications to the contrary which might have been read into the second part of General Nichols' letter are not supported by any material which the Board has seen.

The Board wishes to make clear that in attempting to arrive at its findings and their significance with respect to the hydrogen bomb, it has in no way sought to appraise the technical judgments of those who were concerned with the program.

We cannot dismiss the matter of Dr. Oppenheimer's relationship to the development of the hydrogen bomb simply with the finding that his conduct was not motivated by disloyalty, because it is our conclusion that, whatever the motivation, the security interests of the United States were affected.

We believe that, had Dr. Oppenheimer given his enthusiastic support to the program, a concerted effort would have been initiated at an earlier date.

Following the President's decision, he did not show the enthusiastic support for the program which might have been expected of the chief atomic adviser to the Government under the circumstances. Indeed, a failure to communicate an abandonment of his earlier position undoubtedly had an effect upon other scientists. It is our feeling that Dr. Oppenheimer's influence in the atomic scientific circles with respect to the hydrogen bomb was far greater than he would have led this Board to believe in his testimony before the Board. The Board has reluctantly concluded that Dr. Oppenheimer's candor left much to be desired in his discussions with the Board of his attitude and position in the entire chronology of the hydrogen-bomb problem.

We must make it clear that we do not question Dr. Oppenheimer's right to the opinions he held with respect to the development of this weapon. They were shared by other competent and devoted individuals, both in and out of Government. We are willing to assume that they were motivated by deep moral conviction. We are concerned, however, that he may have departed his role as scientific adviser to exercise highly persuasive influence in matters in which his convictions were not necessarily a reflection of technical judgment, and also not necessarily related to the protection of the strongest offensive military interests of the country.

In the course of the proceedings, there developed other facts which raised questions of such serious import as to give us concern about whether the retention of Dr. Oppenheimer's services would be clearly consistent with the security interests of the United States.

It must be said that Dr. Oppenheimer seems to have had a high degree of discretion reflecting an unusual ability to keep to himself vital secrets. However, we do find suggestions of a tendency to be coerced, or at least influenced in conduct over a period of years.

By his own testimony, Dr. Oppenheimer was led to protest the induction into military service of Giovanni Rossi Lomanitz in 1943 by the outraged intercession of Dr. Condon. It is to be remembered that, at this time Dr. Oppenheimer knew of Lomanitz's connections and of his indiscretions. In 1949, Dr. Oppenheimer appeared in executive session before the House Un-American Activities Committee, and at that time was asked about his friend, Dr. Bernard Peters. Dr. Oppenheimer confirmed the substance of an interview with the security officer which took place during the war years and in which he had characterized Dr. Peters as a dangerous Red and former Communist. This testimony soon appeared in the Rochester, N.Y., newspapers. At this time, Dr. Peters was on the staff of the University of Rochester. Dr. Oppenheimer, as a result of protestations by Dr. Condon, by Dr. Peters himself, and by other scientists, then wrote a letter for publication to the Rochester newspaper, which, in effect, repudiated his testimony given in secret session. His testimony before this Board indicated that he failed to appreciate the great impropriety of making statements of one character in a secret session and of a different character for publication, and that he believed that the important thing was to protect Dr. Peters' professional status. In that episode, Dr. Condon's letter, which has appeared in the press, contained a severe attack on Dr. Oppenheimer. Nevertheless, he now testifies that he is prepared to support Dr. Condon in the loyalty investigation of the latter. . . .

Whether the incidents referred to clearly indicate a susceptibility to influence or coercion within the meaning of the criteria or whether they simply reflect very bad judgment, they clearly raise the question of Dr. Oppenheimer's understanding, acceptance, and enthusiastic support of the security system. Beginning with the Chevalier incident, he has repeatedly exercised an arrogance of his own judgment with respect to the loyalty and reliability of other citizens to an extent which has frustrated and at times impeded the workings of the system. In an interview with agents of the FBI in 1946, which in good part concerned itself with questions about Chevalier, when asked about a meeting which Dr. Oppenheimer had attended, at which Communists and Communist sympathizers were in attendance, he declined to discuss it on the ground that it was irrelevant, although the meeting itself was held in Chevalier's home. In a subsequent interview, he declined to discuss people he had known to be Communists.

Indeed, in the course of this proceeding, Dr. Oppenheimer recalled pertinent details with respect to Communist meetings and with respect to individuals with Communist connections, which he had never previously disclosed in the many interviews with Government authorities, in spite of the fact that he had been interviewed regarding such matters.

In 1946 or 1947, he assisted David Bohm in getting a position at Princeton and at least on a casual basis, continued his associations with Bohm after he had reason to know of Bohm's security status. He testified that today he would give Bohm a letter of recommendation as a physicist, and, although not asked whether he would also raise questions about Bohm's security status, he in no way indicated that this was a matter of serious import to him.

While his meeting with Lomanitz and Bohm immediately prior to their appearance before the House Un-American Activities Committee in 1949, at which time both pleaded the fifth amendment, may have been a casual one as he testified, he nevertheless discussed with them their testimony before that committee.

Moreover, his current associations with Dr. Chevalier, as discussed in detail in item No. 23, are, we believe, of a high degree of significance. It is not important to determine that Dr. Oppenheimer discussed with Chevalier matters of concern to the security of the United States. What is important is that Chevalier's Communist background and activities were known to Dr. Oppenheimer. While he says he believes Chevalier is not now a Communist, his association with him, on what could not be considered a casual basis, is not the kind of thing that our security system permits on the part of one who customarily has access to information of the highest classification.

Loyalty to one's friends is one of the noblest of qualities. Being loyal to one's friends above reasonable obligations to the country and to the security system, however, is not clearly consistent with the interests of security.

We are aware that in these instances Dr. Oppenheimer may have been sincere in his interpretation that the security interests of the country were not disserved; we must, however, take a most serious view of this kind of continuing judgment.

We are constrained to make a final comment about General Nichols' letter. Unfortunately, in the press accounts in which the letter was printed in full, item No. 24, which consisted of 1 paragraph, was broken down into 4 paragraphs. Many thoughtful people, as a result, felt that the implication of one or more of these paragraphs as they appeared in the press standing alone was that the letter sought to initiate proceedings which would impugn a man on the ground of his holding and forcefully expressing strong opinions. It is regrettable that the language of the letter or the way in which it publicly appeared might have given any credence to such an interpretation. In any event, the Board wishes strongly to record its profound and positive view that no man should be tried for the expression of his opinions.

RECOMMENDATION

In arriving at our recommendation we have sought to address ourselves to the whole question before us and not to consider the problem as a fragmented one either in terms of specific criteria or in terms of any period in Dr. Oppenheimer's life, or to consider loyalty, character, and associations separately.

However, of course, the most serious finding which this Board could make as a result of these proceedings would be that of disloyalty on the part of Dr. Oppenheimer to his country. For that reason, we have given particular attention to the question of his loyalty, and we have come to a clear conclusion, which should be reassuring to the people of this country, that he is a loyal citizen. If this were the only consideration, therefore, we would recommend that the reinstatement of his clearance would not be a danger to the common defense and security.

We have, however, been unable to arrive at the conclusion that it would be clearly consistent with the security interests of the United States to reinstate Dr. Oppenheimer's clearance and, therefore, do not so recommend.

The following considerations have been controlling in leading us to our conclusion:

1. We find that Dr. Oppenheimer's continuing conduct and associations have reflected a serious disregard for the requirements of the security system.

2. We have found a susceptibility to influence which could have serious implications for the security interests of the country.

3. We find his conduct in the hydrogen-bomb program sufficiently disturbing as to raise a doubt as to whether his future participation, if characterized by the same attitudes in a Government program relating to the national defense, would be clearly consistent with the best interests of security.

4. We have regretfully concluded that Dr. Oppenheimer has been less than candid in several instances in his testimony before this Board.

Respectfully submitted.

Gordon Gray, *Chairman.*
Thomas A. Morgan.

WARD V. EVANS: "Our failure to clear Dr. Oppenheimer will be a black mark on the escutcheon of our country"

[Ironically, Ward V. Evans, the lone dissenter, had seemed throughout the course of the hearing to be the member of the board who was most hostile to Oppenheimer. When he returned to Washington from Chicago, however, Evans surprised Gray and Morgan by arguing in behalf of reinstating Oppenheimer's clearance, leading them, Robb, and Rolander to conclude, according to the FBI, that "someone had 'gotten to' him." The first draft of Evans's opinion was so poorly written that Gray feared it would embarrass the board, and so he asked Roger Robb to help rewrite it. That might account for its failure to address some of the more important arguments advanced by the majority.]

Ward V. Evans, a member of the Personnel Security Board. Courtesy Northwestern University Archives.

MINORITY REPORT OF DR. WARD V. EVANS

I have reached the conclusion that Dr. J. Robert Oppenheimer's clearance should be reinstated and am submitting a minority report in accordance with AEC procedure. . . .

I am in perfect agreement with the majority report of its "findings" with respect to the allegations in Mr. Nichols' letter . . .

The derogatory information in this letter consisting of 24 items has all been substantiated except for one item. This refers to a Communist meeting held in Dr. Oppenheimer's home, which he is supposed to have attended.

On the basis of this finding, the Board would have to say that Dr. Oppenheimer should not be cleared.

But this is not all.

Most of this derogatory information was in the hands of the Commission when Dr. Oppenheimer was cleared in 1947. They apparently were aware of his associations and his left-wing policies; yet they cleared him. They took a chance on him because of his special talents and he continued to do a good job. Now when the job is done, we are asked to investigate him for practically the same derogatory information. He did his job in a thorough and painstaking manner. There is not the slightest vestige of information before this Board that would indicate that Dr. Oppenheimer is not a loyal citizen of his country. He hates Russia. He had communistic friends, it is true. He still has some. However, the evidence indicates that he has fewer of them than he had in 1947. He is not as naive as he was then. He has more judgment; no one on the Board doubts his loyalty—even the witnesses adverse to him admit that—and he is certainly less of a security risk than he was in 1947, when he was cleared. To deny him clearance now for what he was cleared for in 1947, when we must know he is less of a security risk now than he was then, seems to be hardly the procedure to be adopted in a free country.

We don't have to go out of our way and invent something to prove that the principle of "double jeopardy" does not apply here. This is not our function, and it is not our function to rewrite any clearance rules. The fact remains he is being investigated twice for the same things. Furthermore, we don't have to dig deeply to find other ways that he may be a security risk outside of loyalty, character, and association. He is loyal, we agree on that. There is, in my estimation, nothing wrong with his character. During the early years of his life, Dr. Oppenheimer devoted himself to study and did not vote or become interested in political matters until he was almost 30. Then, in his ignorance, he embraced many subversive organizations.

His judgment was bad in some cases, and most excellent in others but, in my estimation, it is better now than it was in 1947 and to damn him now and ruin his career and his service, I cannot do it.

His statements in cross examination show him to be still naive, but extremely honest and such statements work to his benefit in my estimation. All people are somewhat of a security risk. I don't think we have to go out of our way to point out how this man might be a security risk.

Dr. Oppenheimer in one place in his testimony said that he had told "a tissue of lies." What he had said was not a tissue of lies; there was one lie. He said on one occasion that he had not heard from Dr. Seaborg, when in fact he had a letter from Dr. Seaborg. In my opinion he had forgotten about the letter or he would never have made this statement for he would have known that the Government had the letter. I do not consider that he lied in this case. He stated that he would have recommended David Bohm as a physicist to Brazil, if asked. I think I would have recommended Bohm as a physicist. Dr. Oppenheimer was not asked if he would have added that Bohm was a Communist. In recent years he went to see Chevalier in Paris. I don't like this, but I cannot condemn him on this ground. I don't like his about face in the matter of Dr. Peters, but I don't think it subversive or disloyal.

He did not hinder the development of the H-bomb and there is absolutely nothing in the testimony to show that he did.

First he was in favor of it in 1944. There is no indication that this opinion changed until 1945. After 1945 he did not favor it for some years perhaps on moral, political or technical grounds. Only time will prove whether he was wrong on the moral and political grounds. After the Presidential directive of January 31, 1950, he worked on this project. If his opposition to the H-bomb caused any people not to work on it, it was because of his intellectual prominence and influence over scientific people and not because of any subversive tendencies.

I personally think that our failure to clear Dr. Oppenheimer will be a black mark on the escutcheon of our country. His witnesses are a considerable segment of the scientific backbone of our Nation and they endorse him. I am worried about the effect an improper decision may have on the scientific development in our country. Nuclear physics is new in our country. Most of our authorities in this field came from overseas. They are with us now. Dr. Oppenheimer got most of his education abroad. We have taken hold of this new development in a very great way. There is no predicting where and how far it may go and what its future potentialities may be. I would very much regret any action to retard or hinder this new scientific development.

I would like to add that this opinion was written before the Bulletin of the Atomic Scientists came out with its statement concerning the Oppenheimer case.

This is my opinion as a citizen of a free country.

I suggest that Dr. Oppenheimer's clearance be restored.

Ward V. Evans.

Lloyd K. Garrison's Reply to Kenneth D. Nichols, June 1

LLOYD K. GARRISON: "How can this be?"

[Under normal circumstances, decisions regarding security clearance rested with the AEC's general manager, Kenneth D. Nichols. But on May 18, the commissioners voted 3-2 to make the final determination in the Oppenheimer case themselves. On May 28, Nichols forwarded the Personnel Security Board's report to Oppenheimer, informing him of his right to request a review by the board and giving him twenty days in which to file a written brief. Otherwise, Nichols said, he would submit his own recommendation to the AEC. Fearing that further review would involve an unacceptable delay (or might render the case moot since Oppenheimer's consultant's contract would expire on June 30), Garrison, Oppenheimer, and Marks decided to dispense with an appeal to the board and to place the case squarely before the commissioners. Garrison's request to present oral arguments to the commissioners, however, was turned down; only a written brief could be filed. His letter to Nichols, Garrison recalled, presented "the major arguments which we were later to incorporate into the brief." The letter received the backing of eighty-year-old John W. Davis, one of the most prominent attorneys in the nation, who had been the Democratic candidate for president in 1924, and who would have represented Oppenheimer at the hearing if the AEC had been willing to hold it in New York City rather than in Washington, D.C.]

Dear General Nichols:

Dr. Oppenheimer has received your letter of May 28, 1954, in which you enclosed a copy of the "Findings and Recommendation of the Personnel Security Board" dated May 27. In this document the Board unanimously found that Dr. Oppenheimer was a loyal citizen, but by a 2 to 1 vote, Dr. Ward V. Evans dissenting, recommended that Dr. Oppenheimer's clearance should not be reinstated. Dr. Oppenheimer has asked me to send you this reply on his behalf. . . .

To begin with, the majority's conclusion not to recommend the reinstatement of Dr. Oppenheimer's clearance stands in such stark contrast with the Board's findings regarding Dr. Oppenheimer's loyalty and discretion as to raise doubts about the process of reasoning by which the conclusion was arrived at. All members of the Board agreed:

(1) That the Nation owed scientists "a great debt of gratitude for loyal and

magnificent service" and that "This is particularly true with respect to Dr. Oppenheimer."

(2) That "we have before us much responsible and positive evidence of the loyalty and love of country of the individual concerned," and "eloquent and convincing testimony of Dr. Oppenheimer's deep devotion to his country in recent years and a multitude of evidence with respect to active service in all sorts of governmental undertakings to which he was repeatedly called as a participant and as a consultant."

(3) That "even those who were critical of Dr. Oppenheimer's judgment and activities or lack of activities, without exception, testified to their belief in his loyalty."

(4) That "we have given particular attention to the question of his loyalty, and we have come to a clear conclusion, which should be reassuring to the people of this country, that he is a loyal citizen. If this were the only consideration, therefore, we would recommend that the reinstatement of his clearance would not be a danger to the common defense and security."

(5) That "It must be said that Dr. Oppenheimer seems to have had a high degree of discretion reflecting an unusual ability to keep to himself vital secrets."

In spite of these findings of loyalty and of discretion in the handling of classified data, the majority of the Board reached the conclusion that Dr. Oppenheimer's clearance should not be reinstated. How can this be? The majority advanced four considerations as controlling in leading them to their conclusion.

The first two—an alleged "serious disregard for the requirements of the security system," and an alleged "susceptibility to influence"—rest upon an appraisal of the evidence which we do not think is justified by the record. Taking sharp issue, as we do, with the majority's treatment of the incidents cited in support of these two considerations, we cannot undertake here to review the detailed evidence, but propose to do so in the brief. . . .

The third and fourth considerations advanced by the majority for concluding that Dr. Oppenheimer was a "security risk" warrant more extended comment here.

The third item—Dr. Oppenheimer's "conduct in the hydrogen bomb program," characterized as "disturbing"—and the fourth—alleged "lack of candor" in several instances in his testimony—require discussion, because they involve questions of policy and procedure which we wish particularly to draw to the Commission's attention in a preliminary way.

In the case of the third consideration—Dr. Oppenheimer's so-called disturbing conduct in the hydrogen bomb program—the Board's unanimous findings of fact again stand in stark contrast with the conclusion of the majority. Thus the Board unanimously found:

(1) That Dr. Oppenheimer's opposition to the H-bomb program "involved no lack of loyalty to the United States or attachment to the Soviet Union."

(2) That his opinions regarding the development of the H-bomb "were shared by other competent and devoted individuals, both in and out of Government."

(3) That it could be assumed that these opinions "were motivated by deep moral conviction."

(4) That after the national policy to proceed with the development of the H-bomb had been determined in January 1950, he "did not oppose the project in a positive or open manner, nor did he decline to cooperate in the project."

(5) That the allegations that he urged other scientists not to work on the hydrogen bomb program were unfounded.

(6) That he did not, as alleged, distribute copies of the General Advisory Report to key personnel with a view to turning them against the project, but that on the contrary this distribution was made at the Commission's own direction.

In short, all the basic allegations set forth in General Nichols' letter to Dr. Oppenheimer on December 23, 1953, regarding any improper action by him in the H-bomb problem were disproved.

In the face of these unanimous findings, the majority then conclude that "the security interests of the United States were affected" by Dr. Oppenheimer's attitude toward the hydrogen bomb program. Why? Because, according to the majority of the Board:

"We believe that, had Dr. Oppenheimer given his enthusiastic support to the program, a concerted effort would have been initiated at an earlier date.

"Following the President's decision, he did not show the enthusiastic support for the program which might have been expected of the chief atomic adviser to the Government under the circumstances. Indeed, a failure to communicate an abandonment of his earlier position undoubtedly had an effect upon other scientists."

Without taking into account the factual evidence, which in our opinion should have led the Board to an opposite conclusion, we submit that the injection into a security case of a scientist's alleged lack of enthusiasm for a particular program is fraught with grave consequences to this country. How can a scientist risk advising the Government if he is told that at some later day a security board may weigh in the balance the degree of his enthusiasm for some official program? Or that he may be held accountable for a failure to communicate to the scientific community his full acceptance of such a program? . . .

As to the majority's comments about Dr. Oppenheimer's alleged lack of "candor" in "several instances in his testimony," we shall ask the Commission to take special note of the observations in Dr. Evans' minority opinion that while Dr. Oppenheimer's "statements in cross-examination show him to be still naive," they also show him to be "extremely honest and such statements work to his benefit in my estimation" and that while "his judgment was bad in some cases" it was "most excellent in others but it is better now than it was in 1947," when the Atomic Energy Commission unanimously cleared him. . . . .

We wish to make two more observations of a general character.

First, we trust that the Commission in weighing the evidence, including the instances of alleged lack of candor, will take into account certain procedural difficulties which beset the presentation of Dr. Oppenheimer's case. Weeks before the hearing commenced we asked you and the Commission's general counsel for much information which we thought relevant to our case but which was denied us—documents and minutes concerning Dr. Oppenheimer's 1947 clearance and a variety of other material. Much of this information did come out in the hearings but usually only in the course of cross-examination when calculated to cause the maximum surprise and confusion and too late to assist us in the orderly presentation of our case. Some of the information which was denied to us before the hearing was declassified at the moment of cross-examination or shortly before and was made available to us only during cross-examination or after.

It is true that Dr. Oppenheimer was accorded the privilege of reexamining, prior to the hearings, reports and other material in the preparation of which he had participated. But he was not given access to the broad range of material actually used and disclosed for the first time at the hearings by the Commission's special counsel who had been retained for the case. And of course Dr. Oppenheimer was not given access to the various documents which, according to the Board's report "under governmental necessity cannot be disclosed, such as reports of the Federal Bureau of Investigation."

The voluminous nature of this undisclosed material appears from the Board's report. It notes that in our hearings the Board heard 40 witnesses and compiled over 3,000 pages of testimony; and we then learn from the report that "in addition" the Board has "read the same amount of file material." We can only speculate as to the contents of this "file material." We cannot avoid the further speculation as to how much of this material might have been disclosed to Dr. Oppenheimer in the interests of justice without any real injury to the security interests of the Government if established rules of exclusion, which the Board felt bound to apply and we to accept, had not stood in the way.

Having in mind the difficulties and handicaps which have been recounted above, we urge upon the Commission as strongly as possible the following:

(1) That in weighing the testimony, and particularly those portions where documents were produced on cross-examination in the manner described above, the Commission should constantly bear in mind how, under such circumstances, the natural fallibility of memory may easily be mistaken for disingenuousness;

(2) That in the consideration of documentary material not disclosed to Dr. Oppenheimer, the Commission should be ever conscious of the unreliability of ex parte reports which have never been seen by Dr. Oppenheimer or his counsel or tested by cross-examination; and

(3) That if in the course of the Commission's deliberations the Commission should conclude that any hitherto undisclosed documents upon which it intends to rely may be disclosed to us without injury to what may be thought to be overriding interests of the National Government, they should be so disclosed before any final decision is made.

Our final observation has to do with the general structure of the Board's report, and with what has been omitted from it which we feel the Commission should put in the forefront of its consideration if it is to view this case in anything like the true perspective of history—a history through which Dr. Oppenheimer has lived and which in part he has helped to create.

The Board's opinion, as required by the AEC Procedures, makes specific findings on each allegation of "derogatory information" contained in your letter of December 23, 1953. These findings, which are placed at the beginning of the report, are not thereafter, except in Dr. Evans' dissenting opinion, considered in the context of Dr. Oppenheimer's life as a whole. Dr. Oppenheimer's letter to you of March 4, 1954, in answer to yours of December 23, 1953, stated at the outset that "the items of so-called 'derogatory information' set forth in your letter cannot fairly be understood except in the context of my life and work."

In his letter Dr. Oppenheimer tried to describe the derogatory information about him in that context. There is, in fact, little in the Board's findings that did not appear from what Dr. Oppenheimer volunteered about himself in his original letter to you. Over and above that, he gave a picture of his life and times without which the items of derogatory information cannot fairly be understood—a picture to which many witnesses added who had known him intimately and had worked side by side with him in the positions of high responsibility which the Government, first in war and then in peace and then in the cold war, successively devolved upon him. This picture, which is glimpsed in Dr. Evans' vivid opinion, does not appear at all in the main body of the report, nor is any mention made of the many witnesses who testified at his behest. . . .

The witnesses included 10 former and present members of the General Advisory Committee, and 5 former Atomic Energy Commissioners. . . .

Because we believe that the "man himself" can only be understood, and therefore fairly judged, by the closest attention to the testimony of those who have known him and worked intimately with him, as well as to his own testimony, we are particularly hopeful that the Commission will permit us to file a brief and to be heard.

In closing this letter we wish to record our appreciation of the patience and consideration accorded to Dr. Oppenheimer and his counsel by Mr. Gray, Mr. Morgan and Dr. Evans throughout the nearly 4 weeks of hearings, and our recognition of the sacrifices which they made in the public interest in assuming the long and arduous task assigned to them.

Mr. John W. Davis has authorized me to say that he joins in this letter and will join in the brief.

Very truly yours,

Lloyd K. Garrison.

Kenneth D. Nichols's Recommendations to the AEC, June 12

KENNETH D. NICHOLS: **"I have given consideration to the nature of the cold war . . . and the horrible prospects of hydrogen bomb warfare if all-out war should be forced upon us"**

[Kenneth D. Nichols, the general manager of the AEC, had written the original letter informing Oppenheimer of the charges against him, and now he would recommend a course of action to the commissioners. A graduate of West Point, Nichols had obtained a doctorate in hydraulic engineering at the State University of Iowa, and returned to teach at the military academy. During the war he served as district engineer for the Manhattan Project. Although stationed at Oak Ridge, Tennessee, he reported to General Groves and became acquainted with Oppenheimer. He later became a consultant to the Joint Committee on Atomic Energy, and, in 1953, general manager. On June 3, he informed Garrison that the AEC would accept a written brief, but it "does not feel that it can accede to your suggestion that there be oral argument as well." Garrison assumed that Nichols would simply forward the Personnel Security Board's findings to the AEC, along with a recommendation. But that is not what happened.

Instead, on June 12, Nichols submitted a confidential report that radically altered the grounds for denying Oppenheimer's clearance. Nichols omitted all the allegations concerning the hydrogen bomb, but now introduced the question of "veracity," raising issues that had neither been included in his original "indictment" nor discussed by the Gray panel. To Nichols, Oppenheimer's continued friendship with Haakon Chevalier was particularly ominous. "The non-charitable view is this," he told the commissioners in a briefing, "why would Oppenheimer of his own initiative come here to Washington . . . to get a briefing on weapons, go out to Los Alamos on a briefing of weapons, just prior to going to Paris to see Chevalier?" Oppenheimer's attorneys had no opportunity to read Nichols's letter, much less respond to the new charges, before the AEC rendered its decision.]

United States Atomic Energy Commission,
Washington 25, D.C., June 12, 1954
Memorandum for: Mr. Strauss, Dr. Smyth, Mr. Murray, Mr. Zuckert, Mr. Campbell.
Subject: Dr. J. Robert Oppenheimer. . . .

FACTORS CONSIDERED

In making my findings and determination I have considered the question whether a security risk is involved in continued clearance of Dr. Oppenheimer I have taken into account his contributions to the United States atomic energy program and in addition I have, in accordance with AEC procedures, considered the effect which denial of security clearance would have upon the program. . . .

SECURITY FINDINGS

I have reviewed the entire record of the case, including the files, the transcript of the hearing, the findings and recommendation of the Personnel Security Board, and the briefs filed by Dr. Oppenheimer's attorneys on May 17, 1954, and June 7, 1954, and have reached the conclusion that to reinstate the security clearance of Dr. Oppenheimer would not be clearly consistent with the interests of national security and would endanger the common defense and security.

I concur with the findings and recommendation of the majority of the Personnel Security Board and submit them in support of this memorandum. In addition, I refer in particular to the following considerations:

1. *Dr. Oppenheimer's Communist activities.*—The record contains no direct evidence that Dr. Oppenheimer gave secrets to a foreign nation or that he is disloyal to the United States. However, the record does contain substantial evidence of Dr. Oppenheimer's association with Communists, Communist functionaries, and Communists who did engage in espionage. He was not a mere "parlor pink" or student of communism as a result of immaturity and intellectual curiosity, but was deeply and consciously involved with hardened and militant Communists at a time when he was a man of mature judgment.

His relations with these hardened Communists were such that they considered him to be one of their number. He admits that he was a fellow traveler, and that he made substantial cash contributions direct to the Communist Party over a period of 4 years ending in 1942. The record indicates that Dr. Oppenheimer was a Communist in every respect except for the fact that he did not carry a party card.

These facts raise serious questions as to Dr. Oppenheimer's eligibility for clearance reinstatement.

It is suggested that Dr. Oppenheimer has admitted many of the facts concerning his past association with Communists and the Communist Party. Whether this be true or not, it appears to me that Dr. Oppenheimer's admissions in too many cases have followed, rather than preceded, investigation which developed the facts. It appears that he is not inclined to disclose the facts spontaneously, but merely to confirm those already known. I find no great virtue in such a plea of guilt; certainly it does not cause me to dismiss Dr. Oppenheimer's past associations as matters of no consequence simply on the ground that he has admitted them.

2. *The Chevalier incident.*—Dr. Oppenheimer's involvement in the

Chevalier incident, and his subsequent conduct with respect to it, raise grave questions of security import.

If in 1943, as he now claims to have done, he knowingly and willfully made false statements to Colonel Pash, a Federal officer, Dr. Oppenheimer violated what was then section 80, title 18, of the United States Code [18 U.S. Code, sec. 80, provides in pertinent part: "Whoever * * * shall knowingly or willfully falsify or conceal or cover up by any trick, scheme, or device a material fact, or make or cause to be made any false or fraudulent statement or representations * * * in any matter within the jurisdiction or agency of the United States * * * shall be fined not more than $10,000 or imprisoned not more than 10 years, or both."] in other words if his present story is true then he admits he committed a felony in 1943. On the other hand, as Dr. Oppenheimer admitted on cross-examination, if the story Dr. Oppenheimer told Colonel Pash was true, it not only showed that Chevalier was involved in a criminal espionage conspiracy, but also reflected seriously on Dr. Oppenheimer himself.

After reviewing both the 16-page transcript (as accepted by the Board) of the interview between Dr. Oppenheimer and Colonel Pash on August 26, 1943, and recent testimony before the Board, it is difficult to conclude that the detailed and circumstantial account given by Dr. Oppenheimer to Colonel Pash was false and that the story now told by Dr. Oppenheimer is an honest one. Dr. Oppenheimer's story in 1943 was most damaging to Chevalier. If Chevalier was Dr. Oppenheimer's friend and Dr. Oppenheimer, as he now says, believed Chevalier to be innocent and wanted to protect him, why then would he tell such a complicated false story to Colonel Pash? This story showed that Chevalier was not innocent, but on the contrary was deeply involved in an espionage conspiracy. By the same token, why would Dr. Oppenheimer tell a false story to Colonel Pash which showed that he himself was not blameless? Is it reasonable to believe a man will deliberately tell a lie that seriously reflects upon himself and his friend, when he knows that the truth will show them both to be innocent?

It is important to remember also that Dr. Oppenheimer did not give his present version of the story until 1946, shortly after he had learned from Chevalier what Chevalier himself had told the FBI about the incident in question. After learning of this from Chevalier, Dr. Oppenheimer changed his story to conform to that given to the FBI by Chevalier.

From all of these facts and circumstances, it is a fair inference that Dr. Oppenheimer's story to Colonel Pash and other Manhattan District officials was substantially true and that his later statement on the subject to the FBI, and his recent testimony before the Personnel Security Board, were false. . . .

In my opinion, Dr. Oppenheimer's behavior in connection with the Chevalier incident shows that he is not reliable or trustworthy; his own testimony shows that he was guilty of deliberate misrepresentations and falsifications either in his interview with Colonel Pash or in his testimony before the Board; and such misrepresentations and falsifications constituted ["]criminal, . . . dishonest . . . conduct.["]

Further, the significance of the Chevalier incident combined with Dr. Oppenheimer's conflicting testimony from 1943 to 1954 in regard to it were not, of course, available in whole to General Groves in 1943, nor was the complete record on the Chevalier incident considered by the Atomic Energy Commission in 1947. Consideration of the complete record plus a cross-examination of Dr. Oppenheimer under oath were not accomplished by anyone prior to the personnel Security Board hearing in 1954.

3. *Dr. Oppenheimer's veracity.*—A review of the record reveals other instances which raise a question as to the credibility of Dr. Oppenheimer in his appearance before the Personnel Security Board and as to his character and veracity in general.

(*a*) The record suggests a lack of frankness on the part of Dr. Oppenheimer in his interviews with the FBI. It appears that during this hearing he recollected details concerning Communist meetings in the San Francisco area which he did not report in previous interviews with the FBI.

(*b*) Dr. Oppenheimer told the FBI in 1950 that he did not know that Joseph Weinberg was a Communist until it became a matter of public knowledge. When confronted with the transcript of his interview with Colonel Lansdale on September 12, 1943, he admitted that he had learned prior to that date that Weinberg was a Communist.

(*c*) It is clear from the record that Dr. Oppenheimer was a great deal more active in urging the deferment of Rossi Lomanitz and his retention on the atom bomb project than he said he was in his answer to my letter of December 23, 1953. Furthermore, Dr. Oppenheimer testified that if he had known that Lomanitz was a Communist he would not have written the letter to Colonel Lansdale of the Manhattan District on October 19, 1943, supporting Lomanitz' services for the project. However, the record reflects that Dr. Oppenheimer told Colonel Lansdale of the Manhattan District on September 12, 1943, that he had learned that Lomanitz was a Communist.

(*d*) Dr. Oppenheimer admitted in his testimony before the Board that in 1949 he wrote a letter to a newspaper which might have misled the public concerning his testimony before the House Un-American Activities Committee on Dr. Bernard Peters. He testified that an earlier article in the newspaper which summarized his testimony was accurate, yet the effect of his published letter was to repudiate the earlier article.

(*e*) Dr. Oppenheimer in his answer to my letter of December 23, 1953, and in his testimony before the Board with respect to the H-bomb program undertook to give the impression that in 1949 he and the GAC merely opposed a so-called "crash" program. It is quite clear from the record, however, that the position of the majority of the GAC, including Dr. Oppenheimer, was that a thermonuclear weapon should never be produced, and that the United States should make an unqualified commitment to this effect. In discussing the building of neutron-producing reactors, a majority of the GAC, including Dr. Oppenheimer, expressed the opinion that "the super program itself should not be undertaken and that the Commission and its contractors understand that construction of neutron-producing reactors is not intended as a step in the super program." The testimony of Dr. Oppenheimer viewed in light of the actual record certainly furnished adequate basis for the majority of the Board not believing that Dr. Oppenheimer was entirely candid with them on this point.

(f) Dr. Oppenheimer testified before the Board that the GAC was unanimous in its basic position on the H-bomb. He specifically said that Dr. Seaborg had not expressed his views and that there was no communication with him. It should be noted that the statement that "there was no communication with him" was volunteered by Dr. Oppenheimer in his testimony on cross-examination before the Board. However, Dr. Oppenheimer received a letter from Dr. Seaborg, expressing his views, prior to the October 29, 1949, GAC meeting.

4. *Dr. Oppenheimer's continued associations after World War II.*—Dr. Oppenheimer has continued associations which raise a serious question as to his eligibility for clearance. He has associated with Chevalier on a rather intimate basis as recently as December 1953, and at that time lent his name to Chevalier's dealings with the United States Embassy in Paris on a problem which, according to Dr. Oppenheimer, involved Chevalier's clearance. Since the end of World War II he has been in touch with Bernard Peters, Rossi Lomanitz, and David Bohm under circumstances which, to say the least, are disturbing.

5. *Obstruction and disregard of security.*—Dr. Oppenheimer's actions have shown a consistent disregard of a reasonable security system. In addition to the Chevalier incident, he has refused to answer questions put to him by security officers concerning his relationships and knowledge of particular individuals whom he knew to be Communists; and he has repeatedly exercised an arrogance of his own judgment with respect to the loyalty and reliability of his associates and his own conduct which is wholly inconsistent with the obligations necessarily imposed by an adequate security system on those who occupy high positions of trust and responsibility in the Government.

FINDING OF SECURITY RISK IS NOT BASED ON
DR. OPPENHEIMER'S OPINIONS

Upon the foregoing considerations relating to the character and associations of Dr. Oppenheimer, I find that he is a security risk. In making this finding I wish to comment on the item of derogatory information contained in my letter of December 23, 1953, which relates to the hydrogen bomb . . .

It should be emphasized that at no time has there been any intention on my part or the Board's to draw in question any honest opinion expressed by Dr. Oppenheimer. Technical opinions have no security implications unless they are reflections of sinister motives. However, in view of Dr. Oppenheimer's record coupled with the preceding allegation concerning him, it was necessary to submit this matter for the consideration of the Personnel Security Board in order that the good faith of his technical opinions might be determined. The Board found that, following the President's decision, Dr. Oppenheimer did not show the enthusiastic support for the program which might have been expected of the chief atomic adviser to the Government under the circumstances; that, had he given his enthusiastic support to the program, a concerted effort would have been initiated at an earlier date, and that, whatever the motivation, the security interests of the United States were affected. In reviewing the record I find that the evidence establishes no sinister motives on the part of Dr. Oppenheimer in his attitude on the hydrogen bomb, either before or after the President's decision. I have considered the testimony and the record on this subject only as evidence bearing upon Dr. Oppenheimer's veracity. In this context I find that such evidence is disturbing. . . .

CONCLUSION

I have conscientiously weighed the record of Dr. Oppenheimer's whole life, his past contributions, and his potential future contributions to the Nation against the security risk that is involved in his continued clearance. In addition, I have given consideration to the nature of the cold war in which we are engaged with communism and Communist Russia and the horrible prospects of hydrogen bomb warfare if all-out war should be forced upon us. From these things a need results to eliminate from classified work any individuals who might endanger the common defense or security or whose retention is not clearly consistent with the interests of national security.

Dr. Oppenheimer's clearance should not be reinstated.

K. D. Nichols,
General Manager

Publishing the Transcript, June 13–15

On June 1, Lloyd K. Garrison had released to the press the texts of the Personnel Security Board's majority and dissenting reports, and his letter to Kenneth D. Nichols defending Oppenheimer. Garrison's associate Allen Ecker had provided reporters with a covering memorandum that highlighted the Board's comments that were most favorable to Oppenheimer. All of this infuriated AEC chairman Lewis L. Strauss who thought that Oppenheimer and his attorneys were maneuvering to swing public opinion to their side. He also imagined that Oppenheimer might selectively release those portions of the actual transcript of the hearing that made him look good. But Strauss knew from FBI reports that Oppenheimer's attorneys feared that publication of the entire transcript, not just selective portions, would damage their case. So Strauss wanted very much to find some way to publish the full transcript. The stumbling block was that Gordon Gray had promised all the witnesses that their testimony, in accordance with AEC regulations, would be kept strictly confidential.

There then ensued a most remarkable series of events. On Friday, June 11, AEC commissioner Eugene M. Zuckert left Washington for his home in Stamford, Connecticut. He had with him a staff document, 241 pages in length, that summarized the most important events in the case and included pertinent excerpts from the testimony. He thought he placed the document in his briefcase when he got off the train, but on Saturday morning, when he looked for it, he realized he had left it by mistake under his seat. He immediately informed the AEC of what had happened, and the FBI began a search for the missing document. Fearing the worst, the commissioners convened for an emergency meeting on Saturday night, June 12. Strauss argued that the integrity of the hearing had been compromised, that selected portions might appear in the press, and that the AEC should make it public as quickly as possible. Two of the commissioners, however, opposed immediate action on the grounds that the witnesses had been promised confidentiality.

The commissioners adjourned at midnight, and forty-five minutes later the FBI learned from its office in Boston that the document had been safely recov-

President Eisenhower and Lewis L. Strauss, March 1954. National Park Service, courtesy Dwight D. Eisenhower Library.

ered. The New York, New Haven, and Hartford train on which Zuckert was traveling had continued on to Boston, where, at 6:00 A.M. on Saturday morning, an attendant had found the package and turned it into the lost-and-found office. There it remained until midnight, when various urgent, not to say frenzied, inquiries, finally turned it up. The folder, marked confidential, was held for the arrival of an AEC official who flew to Boston on Sunday, June 13, and carried it safely back to Washington.

So on Monday, June 14, when the commissioners again met to discuss publication, there was exactly no risk that any portion of the transcript had fallen into unauthorized hands. But they nevertheless voted four to one in favor of publication. Only Henry De Wolf Smyth opposed publishing the testimony. The others accepted Strauss's argument that releasing it would set the record straight and correct the distorted picture Oppenheimer's lawyers had created when they gave out the Personnel Security Board's verdict and their own reply. Nichols, Mitchell, and Rolander then spent most of Monday and Tuesday on the telephone, notifying as many witnesses as they could reach that the transcript was about to be released.

Meanwhile, the Government Printing Office struggled to get the text of the transcript—comprising three thousand typewritten pages or three-quarters of a million words—into print. By 6:00 P.M. on Tuesday, June 15, the book was ready, and it was made available to the press, to be released to the public at noon on Wednesday.

Decision and Opinions of the AEC, June 29

LEWIS L. STRAUSS: "We find Dr. Oppenheimer is not entitled to the continued confidence of the Government . . . because of the proof of fundamental defects in his 'character'"

[Lewis L. Strauss began his career in public life in 1917, when, at the age of 21, he became an assistant to U.S. food administrator Herbert Hoover. Afterward, he joined Kuhn, Loeb & Co., an international banking firm, and during World War II he worked for the navy's Bureau of Ordinance. In 1954, Strauss was serving his second term on the Atomic Energy Commission. First appointed by Harry S. Truman in 1946, he served until 1950; he was made chairman by Dwight D. Eisenhower in 1953. From the beginning, Strauss worried about what he regarded as lax security procedures, and in 1949 he strongly advocated the development of thermonuclear weapons. His majority opinion, which two other commissioners signed, is noteworthy not only for what it says but also for what it fails to say: unlike both Gordon Gray and Kenneth D. Nichols, Strauss barely mentions Oppenheimer's many years of valuable service to his country. The historians Richard G. Hewlett and Jack M. Holl have concluded: "The Commission's decision read like a judgment in a criminal case demanding punishment for misconduct in the past rather than a security evaluation predicting Oppenheimer's future behavior, based upon all relevant data."]

The Atomic Energy Commission announced today that it had reached a decision in the matter of Dr. J. Robert Oppenheimer.

The Commission by a vote of 4 to 1 decided that Dr. Oppenheimer should be denied access to restricted data. Commissioners Strauss, Murray, Zuckert, and Campbell voted to deny clearance for access to restricted data, and Commissioner Smyth voted to reinstate clearance for access to restricted data. Messrs. Strauss, Zuckert, and Campbell signed the majority opinion; Mr. Murray concurred with the majority decision in a separate opinion. Dr. Smyth supported his conclusion in a minority opinion.

Certain members of the Commission issued additional statements in support of their conclusions. These opinions and statements are attached.

United States Atomic Energy Commission,
Washington 25, D.C., June 29, 1954.

The issue before the Commission is whether the security of the United States warrants Dr. J. Robert Oppenheimer's continued access to restricted data of the Atomic Energy Commission. The data to which Dr. Oppenheimer has had until recently full access include some of the most vital secrets in the possession of the United States.

Having carefully studied the pertinent documents—the transcript of the hearings before the Personnel Security Board (Gray Board), the findings and recommendation of the Board, the briefs of Dr. Oppenheimer's counsel, and the findings and recommendation of the General Manager—we have concluded that Dr. Oppenheimer's clearance for access to restricted data should not be reinstated.

The Atomic Energy Act of 1946 lays upon the Commissioners the duty to reach a determination as to "the character, associations, and loyalty" of the individuals engaged in the work of the Commission. Thus, disloyalty would be one basis for disqualification, but it is only one. Substantial defects of character and imprudent and dangerous associations, particularly with known subversives who place the interests of foreign powers above those of the United States, are also reasons for disqualification.

On the basis of the record before the Commission, comprising the transcript of the hearing before the Gray Board as well as reports of Military Intelligence and the Federal Bureau of Investigation, we find Dr. Oppenheimer is not entitled to the continued confidence of the Government and of this Commission because of the proof of fundamental defects in his "character."

In respect to the criterion of "associations," we find that his associations with persons known to him to be Communists have extended far beyond the tolerable limits of prudence and self-restraint which are to be expected of one holding the high positions that the Government has continuously entrusted to him since 1942. These associations have lasted too long to be justified as merely the intermittent and accidental revival of earlier friendships.

Neither in the deliberations by the full Commission nor in the review of the Gray Board was importance attached to the opinions of Dr. Oppenheimer as they bore upon the 1949 debate within the Government on the question of whether the United States should proceed with the thermonuclear weapon program. In this debate, Dr. Oppenheimer was, of course, entitled to his opinion.

The fundamental issues here are apart from and beyond this episode. . . .

In weighing the matter at issue, we have taken into account Dr. Oppenheimer's past contributions to the atomic energy program. At the same time, we have been mindful of the fact that the positions of high trust and responsibility which Dr. Oppenheimer has occupied carried with them a commensurately high obligation of unequivocal character and conduct on his part. A Government official having access to the most sensitive areas of restricted data and to the innermost details of national war plans and weapons must measure up to exemplary standards of reliability, self-discipline, and trustworthiness. Dr. Oppenheimer has fallen far short of acceptable standards.

The record shows that Dr. Oppenheimer has consistently placed himself outside the rules which govern others. He has falsified in matters wherein he was charged with grave responsibilities in the national interest. In his associations he has repeatedly exhibited a willful disregard of the normal and proper obligations of security.

As to "character"

(1) Dr. Oppenheimer has now admitted under oath that while in charge of the Los Alamos Laboratory and working on the most secret weapon development for the Government, he told Colonel Pash a fabrication of lies. Colonel Pash was an officer of Military Intelligence charged with the duty of protecting the atomic-weapons project against spies. Dr. Oppenheimer told Colonel Pash in circumstantial detail of an attempt by a Soviet agent to obtain from him information about the work on the atom bomb. This was the Haakon Chevalier incident. In the hearings recently concluded, Dr. Oppenheimer under oath swears that the story he told Colonel Pash was a "whole fabrication and tissue of lies."

It is not clear today whether the account Dr. Oppenheimer gave to Colonel Pash in 1943 concerning the Chevalier incident or the story he told the Gray Board last month is the true version.

If Dr. Oppenheimer lied in 1943, as he now says he did, he committed the crime of knowingly making false and material statements to a Federal officer. If he lied to the Board, he committed perjury in 1954.

(2) Dr. Oppenheimer testified to the Gray Board that if he had known Giovanni Rossi Lomanitz was an active Communist or that Lomanitz had disclosed information about the atomic project to an unauthorized person, he would not have written to Colonel Lansdale of the Manhattan District the letter of October 19, 1943, in which Dr. Oppenheimer supported the desire of Lomanitz to return to the atomic project.

The record shows, however, that on August 26, 1943, Dr. Oppenheimer told Colonel Pash that he (Oppenheimer) knew that Lomanitz had revealed information about the project. Furthermore, on September 12, 1943, Dr. Oppenheimer told Colonel Lansdale that he (Oppenheimer) had previously learned for a fact that Lomanitz was a Communist Party member.

(3) In 1943, Dr. Oppenheimer indicated to Colonel Lansdale that he did not know Rudy Lambert, a Communist Party functionary. In fact, Dr. Oppenheimer asked Colonel Lansdale what Lambert looked like. Now, however, Dr. Oppenheimer under oath has admitted that he knew and had seen Lambert at least half a dozen times prior to 1943; he supplied a detailed description of Lambert; he said that once or twice he had lunch with Lambert and Isaac Folkoff, another Communist Party functionary, to discuss his (Oppenheimer's) contributions to the Communist Party; and that he knew at the time that Lambert was an official in the Communist Party.

(4) In 1949, Dr. Oppenheimer testified before a closed session of the House Un-American Activities Committee about the Communist Party membership and activities of Dr. Bernard Peters. A summary of Dr. Oppenheimer's testimony subsequently appeared in a newspaper, the Rochester Times Union. Dr. Oppenheimer then wrote a letter to that newspaper. The effect of that letter was to contradict the testimony he had given a congressional committee.

(5) In connection with the meeting of the General Advisory Committee on October 29, 1949, at which the thermonuclear weapon program was considered, Dr. Oppenheimer testified before the Gray Board that the General Advisory Committee was "surprisingly unanimous" in its recommendation that the United States ought not to take the initiative at that time in a thermonuclear program. Now, however, under cross-examination, Dr. Oppenheimer testifies that he did not know how Dr. Seaborg (1 of the 9 members of Dr. Oppenheimer's committee) then felt about the program because Dr. Seaborg "was in Sweden, and there was no communication with him." On being confronted with a letter from Dr. Seaborg to him dated October 14, 1949—a letter which had been in Dr. Oppenheimer's files—Dr. Oppenheimer admitted having received the letter prior to the General Advisory Committee meeting in 1949. In that letter Dr. Seaborg said: "Although I deplore the prospects of our country putting a tremendous effort into this, I must confess that I have been unable to come to the conclusion that we should not." Yet Dr. Seaborg's view was not mentioned in Dr. Oppenheimer's report for the General Advisory

Committee to the Commission in October 1949. In fact the existence of this letter remained unknown to the Commission until it was disclosed during the hearings.

(6) In 1950, Dr. Oppenheimer told an agent of the Federal Bureau of Investigation that he had not known Joseph Weinberg to be a member of the Communist Party until that fact become public knowledge. Yet on September 12, 1943, Dr. Oppenheimer told Colonel Lansdale that Weinberg was a Communist Party member.

The catalog does not end with these six examples. The work of Military Intelligence, the Federal Bureau of Investigation, and the Atomic Energy Commission—all, at one time or another have felt the effect of his falsehoods, evasions, and misrepresentations.

Dr. Oppenheimer's persistent and willful disregard for the obligations of security is evidenced by his obstruction of inquiries by security officials. In the Chevalier incident, Dr. Oppenheimer was questioned in 1943 by Colonel Pash, Colonel Lansdale, and General Groves about the attempt to obtain information from him on the atomic bomb project in the interest of the Soviet Government. He had waited 8 months before mentioning the occurrence to the proper authorities. Thereafter for almost 4 months Dr. Oppenheimer refused to name the individual who had approached him. Under oath he now admits that his refusal to name the individual impeded the Government's investigation of espionage. The record shows other instances where Dr. Oppenheimer has refused to answer inquiries of Federal officials on security matters or has been deliberately misleading.

As to "associations"

"Associations" is a factor which, under the law, must be considered by the Commission. Dr. Oppenheimer's close association with Communists is another part of the pattern of his disregard of the obligations of security.

Dr. Oppenheimer, under oath, admitted to the Gray Board that from 1937 to at least 1942 he made regular and substantial contributions in cash to the Communist Party. He has admitted that he was a "fellow traveler" at least until 1942. He admits that he attended small evening meetings at private homes at which most, if not all, of the others present were Communist Party members. He was in contact with officials of the Communist Party, some of whom had been engaged in espionage. His activities were of such a nature that these Communists looked upon him as one of their number.

However, Dr. Oppenheimer's early Communist associations are not in themselves a controlling reason for our decision.

They take on importance in the context of his persistent and continuing association with Communists, including his admitted meetings with Haakon Chevalier in Paris as recently as last December—the same individual who had been intermediary for the Soviet Consulate in 1943.

On February 25, 1950, Dr. Oppenheimer wrote a letter to Chevalier attempting "to clear the record with regard to your alleged involvement in the atom business." Chevalier used this letter in connection with his application to the State Department for a United States passport. Later that year Chevalier came and stayed with Dr. Oppenheimer for several days at the latter's home. In December 1953, Dr. Oppenheimer visited with Chevalier privately on two occasions in Paris, and lent his name to Chevalier's dealings with the United States Embassy in Paris on a problem which, according to Dr. Oppenheimer, involved Chevalier's clearance. Dr. Oppenheimer admitted that today he has only a "strong guess" that Chevalier is not active in Communist Party affairs.

These episodes separately and together present a serious picture. It is clear that for one who has had access for so long to the most vital defense secrets of the Government and who would retain such access if his clearance were continued, Dr. Oppenheimer has defaulted not once but many times upon the obligations that should and must be willingly borne by citizens in the national service.

Concern for the defense and security of the United States requires that Dr. Oppenheimer's clearance should not be reinstated.

Dr. J. Robert Oppenheimer is hereby denied access to restricted data.

> Lewis L. Strauss, *Chairman.*
> Eugene M. Zuckert, *Commissioner.*
> Joseph Campbell, *Commissioner.*

Eugene M. Zuckert: "This matter certainly reflects the difficult times in which we live"

[The only lawyer on the AEC, Eugene M. Zuckert was a graduate of Yale (1933) and Yale Law School (1937) who worked for the Securities and Exchange Commission from 1937 to 1940. A Democrat, he had been serving as assistant secretary of the air force since 1947 when, in 1952, President Truman appointed him to the AEC (with his term to expire on June 30, 1954). Although he joined Strauss's opinion, Zuckert here expresses a very different rationale for denying Oppenheimer's clearance.]

In subscribing to the majority decision and the substance of the Commission opinion, I have considered the evidence as a whole and no single factor as decisive. For example, Dr. Oppenheimer's early Communist associations by themselves would not have led me to my conclusion. The more recent connections, such as those with Lomanitz and Bohm, would not have been decisive. The serious 1943 incident involving Chevalier would not have been conclusive, although most disturbing and certainly aggravated by the continuation of the relationship between Chevalier and Dr. Oppenheimer. Individual instances of lack of veracity, conscious disregard of security considerations, and obstruction of proper security inquiries would not have been decisive.

But when I see such a combination of seriously disturbing actions and events as are present in this case, then I believe the risk to security passes acceptable bounds. All these actions and events and the relation between them make no other conclusion possible, in my opinion, than to deny clearance to Dr. Oppenheimer.

There follow some additional observations of my own which I believe are pertinent in the consideration of this case and the problems underlying it.

It is a source of real sadness to me that my last act as a public official should be participation in the determination of this matter, involving as it does, an individual who has made a substantial contribution to the United States. This matter certainly reflects the difficult times in which we live. . . .

One of the difficulties in the development of a healthy security system is the achievement of public understanding of the phrase "security risk." It has unfortunately acquired in many minds the connotation of active disloyalty. As a result, it is not realized that the determination of "security risk" must be applied to individuals where the circumstances may be considerably less derogatory than disloyalty. In the case of Dr. Oppenheimer, the evidence which convinced me that his employment was not warranted on security grounds did not justify an accusation of disloyalty.

The "security risk" concept has evolved in recent years as a part of our search for a security system which will add to the protection of the country. In that quest, certain limited guidelines have emerged. With respect to eligibility of people for sensitive positions in our Government we have said, in effect, that there must be a convincing showing that their employment in such positions will not constitute a risk to our security. Except in the clearest of cases, such as present Communist membership, for example, the determination may not be an easy one. In many cases, like the one before us, a complex qualitative determination is required. One inherent difficulty is that every human being is to some degree a security risk. So long as there are normal human feelings like pain, or emotions like love of family, everyone is to some degree vulnerable to influence, and thus a potential risk in some degree to our security.

Under our security system it is our duty to determine how much of a risk is involved in respect to any particular individual and then to determine whether that risk is worth taking in view of what is at stake and the job to be done. It is not possible, except in obvious cases, to determine in what precise manner our security might be endangered. The determination is rather an evaluation of the factors which tend to increase the chance that security might be endangered. Our experience has convinced us that certain types of association and defects of character can materially increase the risk to security.

Those factors—many of which are set forth in the majority opinion—are present in Dr. Oppenheimer's case to such an extent that I agree he is a security risk. . . .

There is one final comment which I should add. My decision in this matter was influenced neither by the actions nor by the attitudes of Dr. Oppenheimer concerning the development of thermonuclear weapons. Nor did I consider material any advice given by Dr. Oppenheimer in his capacity as a top level consultant on national security affairs.

In my judgment, it was proper to include Dr. Oppenheimer's activities regarding the thermonuclear program as part of the derogatory allegations that initiated these proceedings. Allegations had been made that Dr. Oppenheimer was improperly motivated.

The Gray Board, although doubting the complete veracity of Dr. Oppenheimer's explanations, found that these most serious allegations were not substantiated. I have carefully reviewed the evidence and concur in the finding.

JOSEPH CAMPBELL: "The General Manager has arrived at the only possible conclusion available to a reasonable and prudent man"

[When Dwight D. Eisenhower became president of Columbia University in 1948, he met Joseph Campbell, the university's treasurer and vice president of business affairs. In 1953, after his election, Eisenhower appointed Campbell, a Republican, to the AEC. Like Zuckert, he also signed Strauss's opinion but offers an additional explanation for his vote.]

. . . On June 28, 1954, the question of the clearance of Dr. Oppenheimer was presented to the Commission and by a vote of 4 to 1 it was decided that clearance should be denied him. . . .

My vote was to sustain the recommendations of the Gray Board and the General Manager . . .

I have carefully studied the recommendations of the General Manager and have concluded that from the presentation of the testimony before the Personnel Security Board and the information made available to the parties in the proceedings from the investigative files, the General Manager has arrived at the only possible conclusion available to a reasonable and prudent man.

The finding, by the General Manager, that the services of Dr. Oppenheimer are not indispensable to the atomic energy program, is compelling. . . .

I conclude, therefore, that serious charges were brought against Dr. Oppenheimer; that he was afforded every opportunity to refute them; that a board was appointed, composed of men of the highest honor and integrity, and that in their majority opinion Dr. Oppenheimer did not refute the serious charges which faced him; that the record was reviewed by the General Manager, keenly aware of his serious responsibility in this matter, and that he concurred, and even strengthened the findings of the Personnel Security Board.

If the security system of the United States Government is to be successfully operated, the recommendations of personnel security boards must be honored in the absence of compelling circumstances. If the General Manager of the

Atomic Energy Commission is to function properly, his decisions must be up-
held unless there can be shown new evidence, violations of procedures, or
other substantial reasons why they should be reversed.

Therefore, I voted to reaffirm the majority recommendation of the Personnel
Security Board and to uphold the decision of the General Manager. Clearance
should be denied to Dr. Oppenheimer.

Thomas E. Murray: "Dr. Oppenheimer failed the test. . . . He was disloyal"

[By training, Thomas E. Murray was a mechanical engineer. He got his start
working for his father whose company designed electric power plants. When
his father died in 1929, he inherited an estate worth $10 million, and he
eventually held two hundred patents in electrical and welding fields. A
Democrat and a leading Roman Catholic layman, Murray was appointed to
the AEC by President Truman in 1950. Alone among those who passed judgment on Oppenheimer, Murray finds him to be "disloyal," although that
finding derives from a definition of the word that clearly reveals the cold war
context in which the case is being decided.]

I concur in the conclusion of the majority of the Commission that Dr. J.
Robert Oppenheimer's access to restricted data should be denied. However, I
have reached this conclusion by my own reasoning which does not coincide
with the majority of the Commission. Therefore, I submit my separate opinion. . . .

The American citizen recognizes that his Government, for all its imperfec-
tions, is a government under law, of law, by law; therefore he is loyal to it.
Furthermore, he recognizes that his Government, because it is lawful, has the
right and the responsibility to protect itself against the action of those who
would subvert it. The cooperative effort of the citizen with the rightful action
of American Government in its discharge of this primary responsibility also
belongs to the very substance of American loyalty. This is the crucial principle in the present case.

This general definition of loyalty assumes a sharper meaning within the
special conditions of the present crisis. The premise of the concrete, contemporary definition of loyalty is the fact of the Communist conspiracy. Revolu-
tionary communism has emerged as a world power seeking domination of all
mankind. It attacks the whole idea of a social order based upon freedom and
justice in the sense in which the liberal tradition of the West has understood
these ideas. Moreover, it operates with a new technique of aggression; it has
elaborated a new formula for power. It uses all the methods proper to conspiracy, the methods of infiltration and intrigue, of deceit and duplicity, of false-

hood and connivance. These are the chosen methods whereby it steadily seeks to undermine, from within, the lawful governments and communities of the free world.

The fact of the Communist conspiracy has put to American Government and to the American people a special problem. It is the problem of protecting the national security, internal and external, against the insidious attack of its Communist enemy. On the domestic front this problem has been met by the erection of a system of laws and Executive orders designed to protect the lawful Government of the United States against the hidden machinery of subversion.

The American citizen in private life, the man who is not engaged in governmental service, is not bound by the requirements of the security system. However, those American citizens who have the privilege of participating in the operations of Government, especially in sensitive agencies, are necessarily subject to this special system of law. Consequently, their faithfulness to the lawful Government of the United States, that is to say their loyalty, must be judged by the standard of their obedience to security regulations. Dr. Oppenheimer was subject to the security system which applies to those engaged in the atomic energy program. The measure of his obedience to the requirements of this system is the decisive measure of his loyalty to his lawful Government. No lesser test will settle the question of his loyalty. . . .

When all these distinctions and qualifications have been made, the fact remains that the existence of the security regulations which surround the atomic-energy program puts to those who participate in the program a stern test of loyalty.

Dr. Oppenheimer failed the test. The record of his actions reveals a frequent and deliberate disregard of those security regulations which restrict a man's associations. He was engaged in a highly delicate area of security; within this area he occupied a most sensitive position. The requirement that a man in this position should relinquish the right to the complete freedom of association that would be his in other circumstances is altogether a reasonable and necessary requirement. The exact observance of this requirement is in all cases essential to the integrity of the security system. It was particularly essential in the case of Dr. Oppenheimer.

It will not do to plead that Dr. Oppenheimer revealed no secrets to the Communists and fellow travelers with whom he chose to associate. What is incompatible with obedience to the laws of security is the associations themselves, however innocent in fact. Dr. Oppenheimer was not faithful to the restrictions on the associations of those who come under the security regulations.

There is a further consideration, not unrelated to the foregoing. Those who stand within the security system are not free to refuse their cooperation with the workings of the system, much less to confuse or obstruct them, especially by falsifications and fabrications. It is their duty, at times an unpleasant duty, to cooperate with the governmental officials who are charged with the enforcement of security regulations. This cooperation should be active and hon-

est. If this manner of cooperation is not forthcoming, the security system itself, and therefore the interests of the United States which it protects, inevitably suffer. The record proves Dr. Oppenheimer to have been seriously de-
ficient in his cooperation with the workings of the security system. This
defect too is a defect of loyalty to the lawful government in its reasonable efforts to preserve itself in its constitutional existence. No matter how high a
man stands in the service of his country he still stands under the law. To permit a man in a position of the highest trust to set himself above any of the laws
of security would be to invite the destruction of the whole security system.

In conclusion, the principle that has already been stated must be recalled
for the sake of emphasis. In proportion as a man is charged with more and
more critical responsibilities, the more urgent becomes the need for that full
and exact fidelity to the special demands of security laws which in this over-
shadowed day goes by the name of loyalty. So too does the need for cooperation with responsible security officers.

Dr. Oppenheimer occupied a position of paramount importance; his relation to the security interests of the United States was the most intimate possible one. It was reasonable to expect that he would manifest the measure of
cooperation appropriate to his responsibilities. He did not do so. It was reasonable to expect that he would be particularly scrupulous in his fidelity to
security regulations. These regulations are the special test of the loyalty of the
American citizen who serves his Government in the sensitive area of the
Atomic Energy program. Dr. Oppenheimer did not meet this decisive test. He
was disloyal.

I conclude that Dr. Oppenheimer's access to restricted data should be denied.

HENRY DE WOLF SMYTH: "There is no indication in the entire record that Dr. Oppenheimer has ever divulged any secret information"

[The only scientist on the AEC, Henry De Wolf Smyth held a doctorate in
physics from both Princeton (1921) and Cambridge (1923). He had spent his
entire academic career at Princeton, serving as chairman of the physics department from 1935 to 1950, and naturally got to know Oppenheimer. A
consultant to the Office of Scientific Research and Development during the
war, Smyth was appointed to the AEC in 1949. On Monday morning, June
28, the AEC voted 4-1 not to renew Oppenheimer's clearance; Smyth, however, did not receive written copies of the other commissioners' opinions
until that evening, leaving him less than twelve hours in which to compose
his dissent. He worked on it with two friends, telling them, "You know, it's
funny I should be going to all this work for Oppenheimer. I don't even like

the guy very much." The decisions were released at 4:00 P.M. on June 29, thirty-two hours before Oppenheimer's consultant's contract expired.]

I dissent from the action of the Atomic Energy Commission in the matter of Dr. J. Robert Oppenheimer. I agree with the "clear conclusion" of the Gray Board that he is completely loyal and I do not believe he is a security risk. It is my opinion that his clearance for access to restricted data should be restored.

In a case such as this, the Commission is required to look into the future. It must determine whether Dr. Oppenheimer's continued employment by the Government of the United States is in the interests of the people of the United States. This prediction must balance his potential contribution to the positive strength of the country against the possible danger that he may weaken the country by allowing important secrets to reach our enemies.

Since Dr. Oppenheimer is one of the most knowledgeable and lucid physicists we have, his services could be of great value to the country in the future. Therefore, the only question being determined by the Atomic Energy Commission is whether there is a possibility that Dr. Oppenheimer will intentionally or unintentionally reveal secret information to persons who should not have it. To me, this is what is meant within our security system by the term security risk. Character and associations are important only insofar as they bear on the possibility that secret information will be improperly revealed.

In my opinion the most important evidence in this regard is the fact that there is no indication in the entire record that Dr. Oppenheimer has ever divulged any secret information. The past 15 years of his life have been investigated and reinvestigated. For much of the last 11 years he has been under actual surveillance, his movements watched, his conversations noted, his mail and telephone calls checked. This professional review of his actions has been supplemented by enthusiastic amateur help from powerful personal enemies.

After reviewing the massive dossier and after hearing some forty witnesses, the Gray Board reported on May 27, 1954, that Dr. Oppenheimer "seems to have had a high degree of discretion reflecting an unusual ability to keep to himself vital secrets." My own careful reading of the complete dossier and of the testimony leads me to agree with the Gray Board on this point. I am confident that Dr. Oppenheimer will continue to keep to himself all the secrets with which he is entrusted.

The most important allegations of the General Manager's letter of December 23 related to Dr. Oppenheimer's conduct in the so-called H-bomb program. I am not surprised to find that the evidence does not support these allegations in any way. The history of Dr. Oppenheimer's contributions to the development of nuclear weapons stands untarnished.

It is clear that Dr. Oppenheimer's past associations and activities are not newly discovered in any substantial sense. They have been known for years to responsible authorities who have never been persuaded that they rendered Dr.

Henry De Wolf Smyth, 1957. Orren Jack Turner, courtesy AIP Emilio Segrè Visual Archives.

Oppenheimer unfit for public service. Many of the country's outstanding men have expressed their faith in his integrity.

In spite of all this, the majority of the Commission now concludes that Dr. Oppenheimer is a security risk. I cannot accept this conclusion or the fear behind it. In my opinion the conclusion cannot be supported by a fair evaluation of the evidence.

Those who do not accept this view cull from the record of Dr. Oppenheimer's active life over the past 15 years incidents which they construe as "proof of fundamental defects in his character" and as alarming associations. I shall summarize the evidence on these incidents in order that their proper significance may be seen. . . .

The Chevalier incident involved temporary concealment of an espionage attempt and admitted lying, and is inexcusable. But that was 11 years ago; there is no subsequent act even faintly similar; Dr. Oppenheimer has repeatedly expressed his shame and regret and has stated flatly that he would never again so act. My conclusion is that of Mr. Hartley Rowe, who testified, "I think a man of Dr. Oppenheimer's character is not going to make the same mistake twice."

Dr. Oppenheimer states that he still considers Chevalier his friend, although he sees him rarely. In 1950 just before Chevalier left this country to take up residence in France, he visited Dr. Oppenheimer for 2 days in Princeton; in December 1953, Dr. Oppenheimer visited with the Chevaliers in Paris at their invitation. These isolated visits may have been unwise, but there is no evidence that they had any security significance. . . .

Associations.—It is stated that a persistent and continuing association with Communists and fellow travelers is part of a pattern in Dr. Oppenheimer's actions which indicates a disregard of the obligations of security. On examination, the record shows that, since the war, beyond the two visits with the Chevaliers, Dr. Oppenheimer's associations with such persons have been limited and infrequent. He sees his brother, Frank Oppenheimer (an admitted former Communist who left the party in 1941) not "much more than once a year" and then only for "an evening together." By chance, while returning from the barber, he ran into Lomanitz and Bohm on the streets of Princeton in May 1949. Dr. Peters called on him once to discuss testimony given by Dr. Oppenheimer before the House Committee on Un-American Activities. He has seen Bohm and 1 or 2 other former students at meetings of professional groups. I find nothing in the foregoing to substantiate the charge that Dr. Oppenheimer has had a "persistent and continuing" association with subversive individuals. These are nothing more than occasional incidents in a complex life, and they were not sought by Dr. Oppenheimer.

Significance has been read into these occasional encounters in the light of Dr. Oppenheimer's activities prior to 1943.

The Gray Board found that he was an active fellow traveler, but that there was no evidence that he was a member of the party in the strict sense of the word. Dr. Oppenheimer's consistent testimony, and the burden of the evidence, shows that his financial contributions in the 1930's and early 1940's were directed to specific causes such as the Spanish Loyalists, even though they may have gone through individual Communists.

The Communists with whom he was deeply involved were all related to him by personal ties: his brother and sister-in-law, his wife (who had left the party before their marriage), and his former fiancée, Jean Tatlock. Finally, while there are self-serving claims by Communists on record as to Dr. Oppenheimer's adherence to the party, none of these is attributed to Communists who actually knew him, and Steve Nelson (who did know him) described him in a statement to another Communist as not a Marxist. The evidence supports Dr. Oppenheimer's consistent denial that he was ever a Communist.

Dr. Oppenheimer has been repeatedly interrogated from 1943 on concerning his associations and activities. Beyond the one admitted falsehood told in the Chevalier incident, the voluminous record shows a few contradictions between statements purportedly made in 1943 and subsequent recollections during interrogations in 1950 and 1954. The charges of falsehood concerning Weinberg and Lambert relate to such contradictions, and are dependent on a garbled transcript. In my opinion, these contradictions have been given undue significance. . . .

The instances that I have described constitute the whole of the evidence extracted from a lengthy record to support the severe conclusions of the majority that Dr. Oppenheimer has "given proof of fundamental defects in his character" and of "persistent continuing associations." Any implication that these are illustrations only and that further substantial evidence exists in the investigative files to support these charges is unfounded.

With the single exception of the Chevalier incident, the evidence relied upon is thin, whether individual instances are considered separately or in combination. All added together, with the Chevalier incident included, the evidence is singularly unimpressive when viewed in the perspective of the 15 years of active life from which it is drawn. Few men could survive such a period of investigation and interrogation without having many of their actions misinterpreted or misunderstood.

To be effective a security system must be realistic. In the words of the Atomic Energy Commission security criteria:

"The facts of each case must be carefully weighed and determination made in the light of all the information presented, whether favorable or unfavorable. The judgment of responsible persons as to the integrity of the individuals should be considered. The decision as to security clearance is an overall, commonsense judgment, made after consideration of all the relevant information as to whether or not there is risk that the granting of security clearance would endanger the common defense or security."

Application of this standard of overall commonsense judgment to the whole record destroys any pattern of suspicious conduct or catalog of falsehoods and evasions, and leaves a picture of Dr. Oppenheimer as an able, imaginative human being with normal human weaknesses and failings. In my opinion the conclusion drawn by the majority from the evidence is so extreme as to endanger the security system.

If one starts with the assumption that Dr. Oppenheimer is disloyal, the incidents which I have recounted may arouse suspicion. However, if the entire record is read objectively, Dr. Oppenheimer's loyalty and trustworthiness emerge clearly and the various disturbing incidents are shown in their proper light as understandable and unimportant.

The "Chevalier incident" remains reprehensible; but in fairness and on all of the evidence, this one admitted and regretted mistake made many years ago does not predominate in my overall judgment of Dr. Oppenheimer's character and reliability. Unless one confuses a manner of expression with candor, or errors in recollection with lack of veracity, Dr. Oppenheimer's testimony before the Gray Board has the ring of honesty. I urge thoughtful citizens to examine this testimony for themselves, and not be content with summaries or with extracts quoted out of context.

With respect to the alleged disregard of the security system, I would suggest that the system itself is nothing to worship. It is a necessary means to an end. Its sole purpose, apart from the prevention of sabotage, is to protect secrets. If a man protects the secrets he has in his hands and his head, he has shown essential regard for the security system.

In addition, cooperation with security officials in their legitimate activities is to be expected of private citizens and Government employees. The security system has, however, neither the responsibility nor the right to dictate every detail of a man's life. I frankly do not understand the charge made by the majority that Dr. Oppenheimer has shown a persistent and willful disregard for the obligations of security, and that therefore he should be declared a security risk. No gymnastics of rationalization allow me to accept this argument. If in any recent instances, Dr. Oppenheimer has misunderstood his obligation to security, the error is occasion for reproof but not for a finding that he should be debarred from serving his country. Such a finding extends the concept of "security risk" beyond its legitimate justification and constitutes a dangerous precedent.

In these times, failure to employ a man of great talents may impair the strength and power of this country. Yet I would accept this loss if I doubted the loyalty of Dr. Oppenheimer or his ability to hold his tongue. I have no such doubts.

I conclude that Dr. Oppenheimer's employment "will not endanger the common defense and security" and will be "clearly consistent with the interests of the national security." I prefer the positive statement that Dr. Oppenheimer's further employment will continue to strengthen the United States.

I therefore have voted to reinstate Dr. Oppenheimer's clearance.

Henry D. Smyth, *Commissioner.*

CONCLUSION: "AN ABUSE OF THE POWER OF THE STATE"

Even as the AEC was reaching its decision, Oppenheimer had resumed his duties at the Institute for Advanced Study. Lewis L. Strauss, who was coincidentally a member of the Institute's governing board, attempted to oust Oppenheimer as director, but the effort failed and his appointment was renewed in October 1954.

He issued no statement regarding the AEC decision, other than to comment that Henry De Wolf Smyth's minority opinion was "fair and considered, made with full knowledge of the facts, [and] says what needs to be said."[1] Privately, he was more forthright. He told Joseph Alsop that the Personnel Security Board's findings were an "outrage" and that the entire proceeding represented "an abuse of the power of the state."[2] When a friend later suggested that the hearings had been like a dry crucifixion, Oppenheimer replied, "You know, it wasn't so very dry. I can still feel the warm blood on my hands."[3] His public silence reflected, in part, his fear that scientists "were thinking of quitting government projects." The message he wanted to convey was: "The country needs its scientists. Don't resign or quit or fuss."[4]

A scientists' boycott of nuclear weapons programs to protest the AEC decision never materialized. But a protest of sorts did occur over a related issue and it elicited a revealing response from Oppenheimer. In the fall of 1954, the physics department at the University of Washington invited Oppenheimer to deliver a week-long series of lectures as a Walker-Ames visiting professor. But

1. Bernstein, "In the Matter," 249.
2. Ibid., 249.
3. John Mason Brown, cited in Peter Goodchild, *J. Robert Oppenheimer: Shatterer of Worlds* (Boston, 1981), 270.
4. Bernstein, "In the Matter," 249.

the university's president, Henry Schmitz, vetoed the appointment on the grounds that it would not be in the best interests of the institution. In February 1955, when the news broke, many faculty members protested as did scholars around the country. A number of prominent scientists who were planning to visit the university to give lectures or take part in symposia—including Victor Weisskopf, a physicist at MIT, and several biochemists and physiologists—announced they would boycott the university. Oppenheimer, contacted by a reporter for the Seattle *Post-Intelligencer*, was asked: "Do you think it right that these scientists [boycotters] embarrass the University?" He described his response in a letter to a friend in the physics department: "I replied: the University has embarrassed itself."[5]

The same could surely have been said of the United States. It took too many years, but eventually the government recognized the wrong it had done to a patriotic citizen and tried to right it. In 1961, John F. Kennedy became president and brought to Washington as advisers a number of Oppenheimer's admirers, including McGeorge Bundy (who assuredly was unaware he had turned up in an FBI report only seven years earlier). The new chairman of the AEC was Oppenheimer's friend, the physicist Glenn T. Seaborg. At a White House dinner in 1962, he asked Oppenheimer if he would submit to another security hearing in order to clear his name. "Not on your life," he allegedly replied.[6] But in April 1963, the Kennedy administration announced that Oppenheimer would receive the AEC's annual award given in memory of Enrico Fermi. President Lyndon B. Johnson presented the plaque to him in December 1963, along with a check for $50,000.

It took longer for the FBI to make amends. The agency maintained a file on Oppenheimer, although it naturally grew thinner as the years passed, until his death on February 18, 1967, from throat cancer. One of the last items in the file is the obituary notice in the *New York Times*. Ironically, however, the FBI was to become involved in a posthumous effort to defend the scientist's reputation. In April 1994, exactly forty years to the month after the AEC hearing had been held, new allegations surfaced, this time to the effect that J. Robert Oppenheimer—and not only Oppenheimer, but also Enrico Fermi and Leo Szilard—had actually helped pass atomic secrets to the Soviet Union during World War II.

Time Magazine published the allegations in "The Oppenheimer Files," a nine-page excerpt from the book *Special Tasks*, the memoirs of Pavel Sudoplatov, as recorded by Jerrold L. and Leona P. Schecter. A self-styled "Soviet spymaster," the 87-year-old Sudoplatov had been deputy chief of foreign intelligence for the KGB during World War II. His book claimed that "the most vital information for developing the first Soviet atomic bomb came from scientists designing the American atomic bomb at Los Alamos, New Mexico—

5. Oppenheimer to E. Uehling, March 24, 1955, University of Washington physics department MSS, Box 5 (University of Washington).

6. Goodchild, *J. Robert Oppenheimer*, 275.

Robert Oppenheimer, Enrico Fermi, and Leo Szilard."⁷ Sudoplatov, however, provided not a shred of evidence to support his assertion. Among the many who claimed that the charge was groundless was FBI director Louis J. Freeh. Writing to Les Aspin, the chairman of the president's Foreign Intelligence Advisory Board, Freeh said: "The FBI has classified information available that argues against the conclusions reached by the author of 'Special Tasks.' The FBI, therefore, considers such allegations to be unfounded."⁸

Early in July 1954, just a few days after the AEC announced its verdict, J. Robert Oppenheimer was interviewed by a reporter who asked whether he thought he resembled a character in a Greek tragedy. In some plays, Oppenheimer replied enigmatically, "a sense of the drama comes from the chorus."⁹ He might rather have cited the lines of Xerxes, who had also sought to control the forces of nature, if less dramatically than the "father of the atomic bomb," by building a bridge of ships across the Hellespont. Xerxes paid a high price: the loss of the Persian army at Salamis. Yet Oppenheimer, who paid a different kind of price, could still have reflected with Aeschylus's tragic hero: "Dismay, and rout, and ruin, ills that wait / On man's afflicted fortune, sink us down."

7. Pavel Sudoplatov et al., *Special Tasks: The Memoirs of an Unwanted Witness, a Soviet Spymaster* (Boston, 1994), 172.
8. The *New York Times*, May 3, 1995.
9. Stern, *Oppenheimer Case*, 426.

SUGGESTED READING

Bernstein, Barton J. "Four Physicists and the Bomb: The Early Years, 1945–1950." *Historical Studies in the Physical Sciences* 18 (1988): 231–62.

———. "In the Matter of J. Robert Oppenheimer." *Historical Studies in the Physical Sciences* 12 (1982): 195–252.

———. "The Oppenheimer Conspiracy." *Discover* (March 1985): 22–32.

———. "The Oppenheimer Loyalty-Security Case Reconsidered," *Stanford Law Review* 42 (1990): 1383–1484.

Chevalier, Haakon. *Oppenheimer: The Story of a Friendship.* New York, 1965.

Davis, Nuel Pharr. *Lawrence and Oppenheimer.* New York, 1968.

Dyson, Freeman. *Disturbing the Universe.* New York, 1979.

———. *Weapons and Hope.* New York, 1984.

Goodchild, Peter. *J. Robert Oppenheimer: Shatterer of Worlds.* Boston, 1981.

Herken, Gregg. *Counsels of War.* New York, 1985.

———. *The Winning Weapon: The Atomic Bomb in the Cold War, 1945–50.* Princeton, 1980.

Hewlett, Richard G. and Oscar E. Anderson. *The New World, 1939–1947: A History of the United States Atomic Energy Commission.* University Park, Pa., 1962.

Hewlett, Richard G. and Francis Duncan. *Atomic Shield, 1947–1952: A History of the United States Atomic Energy Commission.* University Park, Pa., 1969.

Hewlett, Richard G. and Jack M. Holl. *Atoms for Peace and War, 1953–1961: Eisenhower and the Atomic Energy Commission.* Berkeley, 1989.

Hijiya, James A. "The *Gita* of J. Robert Oppenheimer." *Proceedings of the American Philosophical Society* 144 (June 2000): 123–67.

Holloway, David. *Stalin and the Bomb: The Soviet Union and Atomic Energy, 1939–1956.* New Haven, 1994.

Holloway, Rachel L. *In the Matter of J. Robert Oppenheimer: Politics, Rhetoric, and Self-defense.* Westport, Conn., 1993.

Kevles, Daniel J. *The Physicists: The History of a Scientific Community in Modern America.* Cambridge, Mass., 1995.

Kunetka, James W. *Oppenheimer: The Years of Risk.* Englewood Cliffs, N.J., 1982.

Major, John. *The Oppenheimer Hearing.* New York, 1971.

Rhodes, Richard. *Dark Sun: The Making of the Hydrogen Bomb.* New York, 1995.

——. *The Making of the Atomic Bomb.* New York, 1986.

Schweber, S. S. *In the Shadow of the Bomb: Bethe, Oppenheimer, and the Moral Responsibility of the Scientist.* Princeton, 2000.

Sherwin, Martin J. *A World Destroyed: The Atomic Bomb and the Grand Alliance.* New York, 1975 (rev. ed., 1987).

Smith, Alice Kimball and Charles Weiner, eds. *Robert Oppenheimer: Letters and Recollections.* Cambridge, Mass., 1980.

Stern, Philip M. *The Oppenheimer Case: Security on Trial.* New York, 1969.

Strout, S. Cushing. "The Oppenheimer Case: Melodrama, Tragedy, and Irony." *The Virginia Quarterly Review* 40 (1964): 268–80.

——. "Telling the Oppenheimer Story: From the AEC to the BBC." *The Yale Review* 73 (1983): 122–30.

Wang, Jessica. *American Science in an Age of Anxiety: Scientists, Anticommunism, and the Cold War.* Chapel Hill, 1999.

York, Herbert F. *The Advisors: Oppenheimer, Teller, and the Superbomb.* Stanford, 1989.

INDEX